WOMEN UNLIMITED
THE DIRECTORY FOR LIFE

DEDICATED TO NELSON 'BEAR' WAKEFIELD
THE LITTLE PRINCE

PENGUIN BOOKS

Published by the Penguin Group
Penguin Books Ltd, 27 Wrights Lane, London W 8 5 T Z , England
Penguin Books USA Inc., 375 Hudson Street, New York, New York 10014, USA
Penguin Books Australia Ltd, Ringwood, Victoria, Australia
Penguin Books Canada Ltd, 10 Alcorn Avenue, Toronto, Ontario, Canada M V 4 3 B 2
Penguin Books (N Z) Ltd, 182 – 190 Wairau Road, Auckland 10, New Zealand

Penguin Books Ltd, Registered Offices: Harmondsworth, Middlesex, England

First published 1997

Copyright © Women Unlimited, 1997

The moral right of the authors has been asserted

Disclaimer/waiver
The contents of this book are intended as a general guide and not as a substitute for professional advice based on the detailed facts and circumstances of any particular situation, which is beyond the scope of this book.

Nothing in this book is to be construed as giving professional or legal advice of any sort. Readers should not rely on this book when considering specific action but should seek professional advice. Any opinions given in this book are those of the authors, except where expressly indicated otherwise.

C☺NTENTS

Introduction 4

List of Topics 7

WORK 21

TECHNOLOGY 45

MONEY 65

CARS 105

LAW 133

POLITICS 153

SEX, DRUGS (& ROCK 'N' ROLL) 167

RELATIONSHIPS 197

HEALTH 207

BEAUTY 233

HOME 253

BABIES 285

FAMILY 311

DEATH 331

The Directory 335

W**∞**MEN UNLIMITED

Melanie Agace: designer, teacher at the Royal College of Art. Formerly worked for The Prince of Wales, designer at 'Makona', a Hungarian architectural practice in Budapest and Art direction in pop videos, commercials and films.

Amanda Burgess: film financier, formerly head of media banking at Berliner Bank, involved with projects such as *The Crying Game, Cliffhanger*, etc. Now independent consultant to the industry. Other interests include floristry and impending motherhood.

Charlotte Skene Catling: trained as an architect. Has worked in architecture in Berlin, and as an illustrator in New York and London. Currently completing a book on architectural notation.

Suzi Godson: graphic designer. Established 'Design 4' in 1996 which now has an international client base in film, fashion, art and media. Mother of Scarlet, Ruby and Amber.

Marysia Woroniecka: executive producer for a Web design consultancy, 'The primary group,' specializing in the creation and development of online programming solutions for clients in the fashion, beauty, photography and media industries. Now based in New York.

W😍MEN UNLIMITED
THE DIRECTORY FOR LIFE

What is it?
The Directory for Life is a resource of simple, accessible facts and guidelines on everyday issues. It's the first place to look whether you're trying to avoid being overcharged by a builder, need to negotiate an overdraft or simply want a 'high tech' moisturizer. Although it's been written, researched and designed by women, the subjects and issues affect everyone – both male and female.

Why?
Today, more than ever before, we're bombarded with information. But most sources are either very specialized, incomprehensible, or just dull. Subjects such as finance, the law and technology may seem daunting, but you really don't have to be an expert to grasp the basics. This book is a central source giving you short cuts to a multitude of subjects. Without telling you what to do, it will help you to handle situations with more confidence.

Why and how did we write it?
We were tired of finding ourselves in situations where we were ill-informed or unprepared. The final trigger was 'another intimidating garage bill'. When we met, we realized we had all been through a catalogue of similar experiences which left us feeling inadequate and fustrated. We decided to do something about it.

We have mixed experience, in banking, building, writing, design, technology, teaching, parenthood. We formed a group (Women Unlimited) and after two years of hell, headaches and hysteria, we finally produced this book. But in the process, we discovered that many of the subjects which we viewed as monotonous or impenetrable, didn't need to be.

How to use it
Start with the List of Topics on pages 7 – 20. Subjects are cross-referenced when they appear in more than one chapter. In the Directory at the back, you will find contact numbers for organizations, helplines, net addresses and further reading or source material. Use the book to help deal with existing situations, but even better, go through the subjects you know nothing about and you'll be ready for anything.

We have included a feed-back page at the end of the book and welcome comments and suggestions for future editions. This is just the beginning . . .

ACKN☺WLEDGEMENTS

This book is dedicated to Ben, Jeremy, Malcolm and Jon, who have been waiting for it to be over, and to Scarlet, Ruby and Amber, who saw a lot of their father. Our biggest thank you must go to Monica Schmoller for her unstinting patience, enthusiasm and help beyond the call of duty in pulling this whole project into shape. Enormous thanks also to Penelope Dunn and to Helen Fraser, Anya Waddington, Mark Handsley and all the team at Penguin for their help and commitment to what often seemed like an impossible endeavour.

We would particularly like to thank all those who have contributed material to the Directory, and especially: Diane Skene Catling; Jennifer Nadel; Jackie Hurt; Jane Withers; Sarah Walter; Sally Mackereth; Samantha Penwaiden; Myer Taub; Charlie Polizzi; Miera Bedi; Nigel Coates; Ben Evans; Tanya Thompson; Patrick Russel; Elisa Johnson; Dr Paul Nordstrom August; Wyn Davies; Charlotte Philips; Jenny Cook; Rachel Fenlon; Jill Kitto; Judy Richardson; Jane Stone; Neil Herbert; Jeremy Agace and David Wickes.

Inspirations: Diana, Princess of Wales. Madonna. Anita Roddick. The Spice Girls. k d lang. Courtney Love. Helen Sharman. Helen Mirren. Margaret Thatcher. Glenda Jackson. Claire Short. Penelope Leach. Katherine Hamnett. Zaha Hadid. Rachel Whiteread. Helen Chadwick. Jane Brown. Delia Smith. Oprah Winfrey. Roseanna Barr. Sally Gunnell. Michelle de Bruin. Germaine Greer. E. Annie Proulx.

And those who have contributed their time and support in reading, checking and criticizing (constructively!) our efforts: Judy Klienman for the kick start. Judy Allen. Jonathan Atkins. Ann Burgess. Jon Burgess. Tessa Blackstone. Gillian Duffield. Andrew Fenlon. Julia Sleaford. Scott Lowe. Zoe Willis. Sally Wood. Elaine Jones. Andrea Chappell. Dylan Jones. Solange Azagury Partridge and Murray – the funniest man alive. Eve McSweeny. Rachel Weisz. Rose Garnett. Yvonne Roberts. Alex de Rijke. Briony Fletcher. Dr Jeanie Spears. William Seighart and Mary Ann Seighart for words of wisdom in the early days. Rita Clifton. Nadia Nicholas. Jay Pondjones for introducing us to Mother. UCH Neonatal Unit, who cared for Ruby and Amber. Simon Prosser for his endless encouragment. Charlotte Horton. Mark Hix for catering. Heather Byars. Gay Haines. CIA Media's Marco Rimini. Barry from SVP Services. S. Khawaje. Underworld, Tricky, Radiohead, 24-hour petrol stations and Apple Macintosh.

We have been amazed at how forthcoming people and organizations were in helping us put the Directory together and are very grateful for their patience. A special thanks to: Fiona Price at Fiona Price and Partners; Bernadette Vallely; Mary Mitchel from the Financial Forum for Women; Working Mothers Association; City Women's Network; British Association of Women Entrepreneurs; Business and Professional Women UK; Fawcett Society; Sue Robinson from the Retail Motor Industry Federation; Shelly Maxwell from the RAC Press Office; Rebecca Rees from the AA; Kevin Thomas from the Driving Standards Agency; Relate; Bliss; Women's Health Resource Centre; Brook Advisory Service; Which?; Consumer Association; CAB; Directory Enquires and Yellow Pages; Rupert Winlaw, press officer of the Law Society; Roger Ede, Secretary to the Criminal Law Committee; Department of Education and Employment; New Ways to Work; Cyberia Café; Association of British Insurers; Transport 2000; Natural Death Centre; Women's Aid Helpline; Salvo; National Women's Commission; Women's Computer Centre.

Finally a big thank you to all our friends for tolerating our strange and obsessive behaviour over the past two years: Tara; Camilla Nickerson; Neville Wakefield; Jack Wilson; Jenny Cook; Harriet Logan; Henry Bourne; Danny Klienman; Lucy and Harry Enfield; Cathy Kasterine; Mathew Eckersley; Jenny Romyn; Caroline Wood; Jamie Agace; Mark Mills; Gus Mills; Lil Heyman Eddy and Lisa Villiers; Rebecca du Pont; Joseph Bennet; Belinda Allen; Paul and Denise Benny; Sean Mathias; Tom Croft, Dorothy Berwin; Laura Bickford; Ian Softly and Sarah Curtis; James Roeber; Marc Quinn; Georgie Byng; Danny Moynihan; Katrina Boorman; Jay Joplin and Sam Taylor Wood; Louisa Young; Nick and Ellen South; Rohan Daft; Joe Corre; Serena Rees and new born; Richard Strange; Tina Blakeney; the mad Nicholsons; Desmond Skene Catling; Mandana, Andrew, Richard and everyone else at Andrew Edmunds; Harriet Stewart + 1; Julian Vogul; Paula Harrison; Mandy Lane; Jim and Max Gottlieb; Kim Lavery; Alice Rawsthorne; Joe Donnelly; Miranda McMinn; the Tweddell family and T.

LIST OF TOPICS

WORK

STARTING OUT 22

What do you want to do? 22

Evaluate your skills 22

Career counselling 22

Women in business 23

A–Z OF CAREER OPTIONS 23

FINDING A JOB 24

Where to look 25

In your neighbourhood 25

Agencies 25

Agency fees 25

Exceptions 25

Headhunters 26

Other options 26

Working in the EU 26

Some sources 26

Deciphering job ads 26

TRAINING AND RESKILLING 26

Training 26

Your options 27

Access courses 27

University degrees 27

NVQs and GNVQs 27

BTECs 27

City and Guilds 27

Royal Society of Arts 27

Training and Enterprise Councils (TECs) 27

Practical details 28

Returning to work 28

Funding 28

Studying in the EU 28

PREPARATION 30

Writing a CV 30

Interviews 30

Confidence 31

At the interview 31

Assessment centres 32

Psychological testing 32

Medical examination 32

NEW WAYS TO WORK 32

Part-time work 32

Other options 33

Flexitime 33

Job sharing 33

Term-time working 33

Career-break schemes 33

Sabbaticals 33

Working from home 33

Tips 33

Costs 33

EMPLOYMENT ISSUES 34

Employment contracts 34

Duties as an employee 35

Overtime 35

Hours/holidays 35

Safety at work 35

Injury in the workplace 36

Maternity rights 36

LOSING YOUR JOB 36

Wrongful dismissal 36

Unfair dismissal 36

Industrial tribunals 37

Fair dismissal 37

Giving proper notice 37

PROBLEMS AT WORK 38

Personal crisis 38

Sexual harassment 38

What is it? 38

Action to take 38

Further problems 38

Sex discrimination – the Law 40

Racial discrimination 40

Negotiating redundancy payoffs 40

You and your boss 40

VDUs and RSI 40

STARTING A BUSINESS   41

Initial considerations   41

The business plan   41

Legal issues   42

Things to consider   42

Company names   42

Licences   42

Trademarks, copyright and patents   42

Trading laws   42

Financial implications   42

Essential points   42

Management   44

TECHNOLOGY

PCS AND MACS   46

Getting technical   46

Mac v. IBM   46

Computer basics   47

Buying a PC   48

A typical ad   48

Buyer's tips   48

Support   48

Laptops/notebooks   49

Buying laptops/ notebooks   49

CD-ROM   50

Buying into CD-ROM   50

Buying printers   50

THE NET   50

The Internet   50

Net history   51

World Wide Web (WWW)   51

Web pages   51

Browsers   51

Pros and cons   51

Creating a website   52

To get on the Net   52

Modems   52

Internet Service Providers   52

Online Service Providers   54

Newsgroups   54

e-mail   54

Internet Relay Chat   55

Avatars   55

Virtual Reality Modelling Language   55

Internet phone   55

Viruses   55

Netnasty   56

CYBER HEALTH   56

Telematics/audio visual connections   56

GADGETS   56

Mobile phones   56

The package   58

The phone itself   58

Types of network   58

Before signing up   58

Insuring your mobile   59

Pagers   59

Contracts   59

Aesthetics   59

Pager v. mobile   60

Likely users   60

Electronic organizers   60

Palmtop computing   60

Before buying   60

FAX   60

Fax facts   61

A–Z OF CYBERSPEAK   61

MONEY

BUDGETS   66

BANKS/BUILDING SOCIETIES   66

Opening an account   67

Bank services   68

Cheque book   68

Standing orders   68

Direct debits   68

Other services   68

Tips	68
PLASTIC	**69**
Credit cards	69
Chargecards	69
Storecards	70
Charity or affinity cards	70
Tips	70
Credit reference agencies	70
ADVICE ON FINANCE	**72**
Financial advisers	72
Other financial advice	73
Payment of advisers	73
Taking the advice	73
Tips	73
Complaints	74
SAVINGS AND INVESTMENTS	**74**
Strategy	74
Risks	74
Schemes	75
Bank and building society accounts	75
TESSAs	75
National Savings	75
Unit Trusts	76
Investment Trusts	76
Personal Equity Plans (PEPs)	76

Monitoring	77
LOANS/BORROWING	**78**
Loans and overdrafts	78
Interest-free loans	78
Hire purchase (HP)	79
Pawnbrokers	79
Interest rates	79
Credit agreements	79
Repayment and debt	79
MORTGAGE	**80**
Endowment mortgages	80
Repayment mortgages	81
Pension mortgages	81
Interest rates and special deals	81
Variable-rate mortgages	81
Fixed-rate mortgages	81
Mortgage statements	81
Additional extras	82
Loan to valuation fee	82
Stamp duty	82
Legal costs	82
Estate agent's fee	82
Renting your property	83
Tips	83
PENSIONS	**83**
The state pension	84
The basic state pension	84
SERPS	84

Tips	85
Company pensions	85
Final salary schemes	85
Money purchase schemes	86
Comparison	86
Tips	86
Personal pension plans	87
Tips	87
Additional voluntary contributions (AVCs)	87
Changing jobs	88
TAX	**88**
What counts as income?	89
Tax allowances	89
Tax relief	89
Tax codes	89
Self-assessment	90
Tips	90
Capital gains tax	90
Inheritance tax (IHT)	91
INSURANCE	**91**
Life assurance	92
Term assurance	92
Whole life assurance	92
Occupational/medical history	92
Building insurance	93
Contents insurance	93

Keeping costs down 94

Claiming 94

When you make a claim 94

Loss adjusters 95

How to complain 95

Pet insurance 95

Wedding insurance 95

School fees 96

HEALTH INSURANCE 96

Private medical insurance 96

General tips 97

Permanent health insurance 98

Critical illness policies 98

Alternative health insurance 98

General tips 99

MATERNITY FINANCE 99

Maternity benefits 100

Taking a longer break 100

Returning to work 100

BENEFITS 101

Types of benefit 101

Claiming benefits 101

The self-employed 102

The Child Support Agency (CSA) 102

WILLS 102

Executors/ administrators 103

Probate 103

Who should write your will? 103

Living wills 104

Legal Aid 104

CARS

LEARNING TO DRIVE 106

Provisional driving licences 106

Driving lessons 106

Study the Highway Code 106

Tips for the test 106

Applying for the test 106

Advanced motorist test 106

TAX, MOT ETC. . . 107

Road tax 107

MOT certificate 107

Registration document/log book 107

Insurance 107

CAR CARE 107

Basic checks 107

Basic upkeep 108

MOT tests 108

Servicing 108

GARAGES 108

Shop around 108

Finding the right garage 109

Dealing with garages 109

Tips before you pay 109

If there is a problem 110

The Law 110

BREAKDOWN TIPS 110

Keep in your car 111

Things you should know 111

Changing a flat tyre 111

Flat battery 111

Damp distributor 112

Overheating engine 112

If a fuse blows 112

Motorway breakdown 112

CAR SAFETY & THE LAW 112

Accidents 112

Tips in an accident 113

Driving offences 114

Motoring Law 114

Car protection 114

Extra safety features 114

KIDS IN CARS 114

Tips for child car seats 114

Seats: what to look for 114

CAR SECURITY 116

How to stay secure 116

Car security equipment	116	Selling privately	125	**LAW**	
Safety while driving	116	Classified ads	126	**THE LEGAL SYSTEM**	134
BUYING A USED CAR	117	Auctions	126	Reforms to the law	134
Choosing a car	117	Computer bureau	126	Who's who?	134
Phone tips	117	Car marts	126	Solicitors	134
Buying from dealers	118	Owners' clubs	126	Contentious work	134
Buying privately	118	What is your car worth?	126	Non-contentious work	134
Car auctions	118	Things to do	126	Barristers	134
Checking the car	118	Handling private buyers	128	Judges	136
Bodywork	119	Paperwork and legal obligations	128	Magistrates	136
Interior	119			**GETTING LEGAL ADVICE**	136
Under the bonnet	119	**CAR INSURANCE**	128		
Test driving	120	Premium payments	128	Accident line	136
The negotiation	120	Voluntary excess payments	129	Citizens' Advice Bureaux	138
BUYING A NEW CAR	120			Law centres	138
Tips for choosing	120	No claims discount	129	Legal advice centres	138
Terminology	122	Car groups	129	Legal Aid	138
Where to buy a new car	122	Security	129	Conditional fees	138
Franchised dealers	122	Levels of insurance	129	Lawyers for business	138
Car brokers	122	Other insurance	130	Trade unions	138
New car negotiations	122	Cutting costs	130	**FINDING A LAWYER**	139
Buying a foreign car	122	How to buy insurance	130	Choosing a lawyer	139
Watch out for . . .	123	Brokers	130	Guides and directories	139
CAR FINANCE	123	By telephone	130	Costs	139
Useful terms to know	123	Classic car insurance	130	Representing yourself	140
Where to go for finance	123	Questions to ask	130	In court	140
General tips on finance	125	Accidents and claims	130	Complaining about solicitors' fees	140
SELLING A CAR	125	**BIKES**	132		
Selling to a dealer	125	Choosing a bike	132	Avoiding overcharging	141

Are you being over-charged?	**141**	Services	**147**			

Are you being over-charged? **141**

Remuneration **141**

'Taxation' **142**

Negligence **142**

CONSUMER LAW **142**

Learn how to complain **143**

Contracts **143**

Consumer protection **143**

Credit reference agencies **143**

Implied terms **144**

Criminal sanctions **144**

The small print **144**

Discrimination **144**

Obligations of the seller **144**

If you are the seller **144**

Obligations of the buyer **146**

Accepting goods **146**

Stolen goods **146**

Signing **146**

Entire contract clause **146**

Buying in your home **146**

Ordering by phone **146**

Postal selling **146**

Selling by telephone **147**

Pyramid selling **147**

Guarantees **147**

Hire purchase **147**

Services **147**

Charges for services **148**

Forgotten goods **148**

Hiring **148**

Injury or death **148**

SMALL CLAIMS **148**

Small claims court **149**

Letter before action **149**

Check the details **149**

Summonses **149**

Prepare your case **149**

The hearing **149**

The outcome **150**

Enforcing your claim **150**

CRIMINAL LAW **150**

Stopped and questioned **150**

Stopped and searched **150**

Searched in public **150**

Arrest **151**

Your rights **151**

The criminal law **151**

Crime **151**

Compensation **152**

Making a claim **152**

The size of the award **152**

POLITICS

GOVERNMENT **154**

The House of Commons **154**

The House of Lords **154**

Whips **154**

From Bill to Act **154**

Labour Party **155**

Conservative Party **155**

Liberal Democrats **155**

How to vote **156**

What MPs do? **156**

MPs' work **156**

PR **157**

WOMEN AND WESTMINSTER **157**

Voting trends **157**

Women's priorities **157**

The 300 Group **158**

Emily's List UK **158**

EUROPE **158**

The Maastricht Treaty **158**

The Social Chapter **158**

The ECU **158**

The European superstate **158**

GETTING INVOLVED **160**

Standing as an MP **160**

Standing as an MEP **160**

Standing as a councillor **160**

HOW TO INFLUENCE GOVERNMENT   160

What can you do?   160

Pressure groups   160

Influencing policy   161

Local government   161

Local government ombudsman   161

Using the courts   162

Professional lobbyists   162

HOW TO CAMPAIGN   162

Beginning a campaign   162

Preventative action   164

Support for campaigns   164

Demonstration/rally   164

Tips for effective letters   165

Handling the media   165

Tips for public speaking   165

Fund-raising   165

Research   165

Sources of information   166

SEX, DRUGS (& ROCK 'N' ROLL)

SEX   168

Know your body   168

The clitoris   168

Anatomy of the G-spot   168

What's in a name?   168

Preparations for sex   168

Giving and receiving pleasure   169

Stimulating the clitoris   170

How to do it yourself   170

Cunnilingus   171

Signs of arousal   171

The female orgasm   172

The G-spot again   172

The combined orgasm   174

Men   174

Points about the penis   174

Stimulating the penis   174

Tips for fellatio   176

Controlling ejaculation   176

The prostate gland   176

External stimulation of the prostate   176

Stimulation of prostate   177

Combined male orgasm   178

Anal sex for a woman   178

Intercourse   178

Sex in a relationship   179

Sex in pregnancy   179

Sex for older women   179

ALTERNATIVE SEXUALITY   180

Homosexuals   180

Lesbians   180

Bisexuality   180

Transgendered   180

Transvestism   180

Transsexuals   182

Coming out   182

Being told   182

CONTRACEPTION   182

Abortion   183

Three legal methods   183

HIV AND AIDS   183

Can be transmitted by   183

Can't be transmitted by   183

'Methods of contraception'   184

Safe sex   186

Aids tests   186

SEXUALLY TRANSMITTED DISEASES   186

Treatments   186

ALCOHOL   186

Facts   186

Hangovers   187

Symptoms   187

Cause   187

Prevention   187

Head from hell For breakfast   187

'STD chart'   188

ADDICTIONS   190

Most commonly used / addictive substances   190

Alcohol	190	What to do	195	**ABUSIVE RELATIONSHIPS**	203
Amphetamines	190	If you contact the police	195	The Law	203
Amyl nitrates	190	The legal process	195	How to leave	203
Anabolic steroids	190	Court	196	**DIVORCE**	203
Cannabis	190	Trauma	196	Key statistics	203
Cocaine/crack	191			Irretrievable breakdown	203
Downers	191			The cost	204
Ecstasy/E	191	**RELATIONSHIPS**		Procedure	204
LSD	191	**DATING**	198	Children	204
Magic mushrooms	191	The Internet	198	**SEPARATION**	206
Opiates	192	Dating agencies	198	Informal separation	206
Solvents and gases	192	Advertising	198	Formal separation	206
Tobacco	192	Safety tips	198	By magistrate's court order	206
Emergencies	192	**TIPS FOR RELATIONSHIPS**	198	Judicial separation	206
Detecting drug abuse	192				
Getting help	192	**MARRIAGE**	199		
Drugs and the Law	192	Plans	199		
SMOKING AND HOW TO STOP	193	Checklist	200	**HEALTH**	
		How	200	**DIET**	208
What happens	193	Civil marriages	200	Dieting	208
How to quit	193	Legal formalities	200	Tips	208
SELF-DEFENCE	193	Licensed venues	200	**FOOD**	209
On the street	193	Religious ceremony	200	Shopping list	209
At home	194	Out of this country	200	Tips for healthy eating	210
Telephone nuisance	194	Legal issues	202	Basic de-tox	210
Defending yourself	194	Legal implications	202	Food supplements	210
The legal situation	194	Marriage contracts	202	Vitamins	210
Sensitive body parts	194	Things to include	202	Minerals	211
RAPE	194	Tax and finance	202	Amino acids	211

What to take and when 211

'Supplements chart' 212

Allergies/cravings 213

Know your food 213

Labelling 213

Additives 213

EATING DISORDERS 213

Anorexia nervosa 214

Bulimia 214

Compulsive eating 214

EXERCISE 214

Tips 214

How fit are you? 215

Two types of exercise 215

Aerobic 215

Anaerobic 215

How much? 215

**A–Z OF EXERCISE
OPTIONS** 215

Personal trainers 218

WOMEN'S HEALTH 218

General guide-lines 218

Women and cancer 219

Breast cancer 220

Examination, screening
and treatment 220

Cervical cancer 220

Ovarian cancer 222

Uterine cancer 222

Other diseases of the
reproductive organs 223

Endometriosis 223

Treatment 223

Osteoporosis 223

Who's at risk? 223

Treatment 223

Ovarian cysts 223

Treatment 224

Pelvic inflammatory
disease (PID) 224

Treatment 224

Fibroids of the uterus 224

Treatment 224

Menstruation 224

Absent periods 224

Painful periods 225

PMS 225

Menopause 225

NHS 226

General practitioners 226

Changing your doctor 226

Referral to hospital 226

Medical negligence 226

Medical Law 226

In a case of negligence 227

**STRESS, ANXIETY AND
DEPRESSION** 227

Causes 227

Symptoms 227

Depression 227

Causes 228

Symptoms 228

Other forms of
depression 228

Manic depression 228

Seasonal affective
disorder (SAD) 228

Options for treatment 228

Doctor/GP 228

Self-help 228

Counselling 229

Psychiatry 229

Psychoanalysis 229

Psychotherapy 230

Specialized areas 230

Coping with a
depressive 230

Terminology 230

**ALTERNATIVE
TREATMENTS** 231

Finding a practitioner 231

Practitioners – the Law 231

Options 231

BEAUTY

SKIN 234

Tips for healthy skin 234

Caring for your skin 234

Toners and astringents 234

Moisturizers 234

Exfoliants/skin scrubs 235

Acne 235

Cellulite 235

What contributes to
cellulite? 235

How to treat it 235

**BEAUTY PRODUCTS
DEMYSTIFIED** 236

Beauty without cruelty 236

Things to consider 236

Terminology 236

MAKE-UP 238

Foundation 238

Concealer 238

Powder 240

Eyes 240

Eye make-up 240

Eyelashes 240

Eyebrows 240

Blusher 241

Lipstick, liners 241

Faking it 242

Skin colour correctors 242

Camouflage 242

NATURAL BEAUTY 243

Scrubs 243

Exfoliants and toners 243

Moisturizers and masks 243

HAIR HEALTH 244

Tips for healthy hair 244

Dealing with dandruff 244

Dying hair – options 244

Heading for change 244

HAIR REMOVAL 244

Bleaching 244

Low tech solutions 245

Shaving 245

Waxing 245

Sugaring 245

Hair removal cream 245

Permanent solutions 245

TATTOOS/BODY PIERCING 245

TEETH 246

Cosmetic dentistry 246

**MAKE THE MOST OF
YOURSELF** 247

Style 247

How to take advantage 247

Lingerie 247

Dressing 10lb slimmer 248

Shopping 248

Second-hand shopping 248

Sales/sample shopping 248

TRAVEL 249

Tips for flying 249

Dealing with jet lag 249

COSMETIC SURGERY 249

'Cosmetic surgery' 250

Surgery options 252

Key questions 252

Other options 252

Methods 252

HOME

RENTING/LETTING 254

Renting 254

Finding a property 254

Contracts 254

Breach of obligation 254

Housing associations 255

Local authority 255

Temporary housing 255

Rights as a sitting
tenant 255

Letting 255

Things to consider 256

Tenancy agreements 256

Assured shorthold
tenancy 256

Assured tenancies 256

Implied covenant 256

Right to buy 257

BUYING A HOME 257

Your requirements 257

Lease or freehold?	258	Household removal	263	**ELECTRICS**	270
Leasehold	258	Storage	264	The electricity market	270
Freehold	258	**DESIGN YOUR HOME**	264	The basics	270
Finding a home	258	What do you want?	264	Jargon	271
Your options	258	Space and light	264	Electrical outlets	271
DIY survey	259	Tips for lighting	264	Electrostress	271
Things to consider	259	Manipulating space	265	'How electricity is distributed in a house'	271
The buying process	260	Paint	265		
Financing	260	Natural paints	265	Planning your system	272
Cost assessment	260	Tips for storage	265	Basic maintenance	272
Solicitor/conveyancer	260	Useful sources	266	Replacing a fuse	272
Making an offer	260	Property value	266	Wiring a plug	272
The right survey	261	**BUILDING WORK**	266	Lights	272
Valuation	261	Planning permission	266	**PLUMBING**	273
Home buyer's survey and valuation (HBSV)	261	Planners	266	The basics	273
		What you need permission for	266	'How plumbing works'	273
Building survey	261			Hot water	274
Finding a surveyor	261	Building regulations	266	Maintenance tips	274
Failed surveys	261	Grants	267	Leaky taps	274
If things go wrong	261	Architects/building surveyors	267	Dirty/discoloured water	274
Post-completion duties	262			Loose loo lever	274
SELLING A HOME	262	Choosing one	267	Air locks	274
Preparing	262	Fees	267	Blocked sink waste trap	274
How	262	Surveyors	268	Blocked lavatory	274
Estate agents	262	Choosing tradespeople	268	Water quality	275
DIY selling	262	Quotes	268	**HEATING**	275
Tips for negotiation	262	Tips for contracts	268	The market place	275
Legal procedure	263	Greener materials	270	'Wet' heating systems	275
MOVING	263	Taking legal action	270	'Dry' warm-air systems	276

Other heating systems	276	Tips	282	Artificial insemination by husband (AIH)	288
Jargon	276	Insurance	283	Surrogacy	288
Maintenance	276	Telephone helplines	283	Age of recipient	288
Bleeding a radiator	276	An unsatisfactory job	283	Who is eligible?	288
Fuels for central heating	276	The Law	283	The Law	288
Energy efficiency	276	**HOME SECURITY**	283		
Saving energy	277	How burglars break in	283	The legal rights of the unborn child	288
Solar power	277	Protection	284	**MISCARRIAGE**	289
MAINTENANCE	277	Preventative measures	284	Key points	289
Cleaning tips	277	Locks, alarms, timers	284	What is miscarriage?	289
Guide to stain removal	278			Remembering your baby	290
Laundry tips	278	**BABIES**		Trying again	290
Back of the packet	278	**GETTING PREGNANT**	286	**PREGNANCY**	290
Allergies in the home	279	Top tips	286	The developing baby	290
Recycling	279	Conception	286	At 12 weeks	290
Tips	280	When is the best time?	286	At 19 weeks	290
APPLIANCES	280	Best position?	286	At 28 weeks	290
Guarantees/warranties	280	How will you know?	286	By 35 weeks	290
Get the best deal	280	Symptoms of early pregnancy	286	Discomforts	290
Calling out engineers	280			Diet	291
Renting	280	Testing	286	Tests during pregnancy	291
Breakdowns	281	**ASSISTED CONCEPTION**	287	'Other pregnancy tests'	292
TRADESPEOPLE	281	Conception	287	**BIRTH**	293
Damp	281	Treatments for women	287	Top tips	293
Common problems	281	Hormone treatment	287	Pre-birth shopping list	293
Tips	281	In vitro fertilization (IVF)	288	Who's who?	293
Subsidence	282	Egg donation	288	Where and how?	293
Rot	282	Donor insemination	288	Home delivery	293
Finding a tradesperson	282				

Hospital delivery	293	Cot death prevention guide-lines	300	Disability – key points	306
Options	294			**ADOPTION AND FOSTERING**	306
Packing for hospital	294	Crying/sleeping	300		
Pain relief	294	Teething	300	Requirements	307
		Colic	302	Inter-country adoption	307
Stages of labour/ birth	296	Useful remedies for newborns	302	Tracing a parent	307
Birth	296			Fostering	307
Birthing partners	296	**ILL BABIES**	302	**GETTING HELP**	308
Episiotomy	296	General illness	302	Where to look	308
Induction	297	Often serious	303	Childcare options	308
Forceps	297	Emergency	303	Playgroups	308
		Resuscitation	303	Childminders	308
Ventouse (vacuum extraction)	297	Fit or convulsion	303	Crèche/workplace nursery	308
Caesarean	297	Burn or scald	303		
Breech	297	Accidents	303	Live-in nanny	308
After the birth	297	Signs of meningitis	303	Live-out nanny	309
		THE LAW	303	Au pairs	309
POSTNATAL DEPRESSION	297	Rights of mothers	304	Things to consider	309
		Rights of children	304	Jargon	309
Treatment	298			Telephone questions	310
BABY CARE	298	Parental Responsibility forms	304	Interview questions	310
Key points	298			Observations during the interview	310
Feeding a new baby	298	DNA testing	304		
Breast-feeding facts	298	**IMMUNIZATION**	304	If it isn't working	310
Bottle-feeding facts	298	The vaccines	305		
Weaning	299	**MULTIPLE BIRTHS**	305		
Hygiene and bathing	299	**SPECIAL CARE**	305	**FAMILY**	
Warmth	299	A neonatal unit	305		
Bedtime tips	299	The facts	306	'The Cradle to the Club'	310–20
Cot death	300	What can you do?	306	**HEALTH**	321

Medical emergency	**321**	
Breathing	**321**	
Choking: unconscious	**321**	
Choking: conscious	**321**	
Severe bleeding	**321**	
Signs of meningitis	**322**	
Viral/bacterial infection?	**322**	

SCHOOL **323**

Pre-school children	**323**
Nurseries	**323**
Primary/secondary school	**323**
Finding the right school	**324**
The right to appeal	**324**
Allocation of places	**324**
The National Curriculum	**324**
Types of school	**324**
Direct grant	**325**
Grant-maintained	**325**
Public	**325**
School rules	**325**

Sex education	**325**
School uniforms	**325**
Religion	**325**
Discipline	**325**
Exclusion	**325**
Suspension	**325**
Expulsion	**325**
School attendance and truancy	**326**
Learning at home	**326**

CHILD ABUSE **327**

Behavioural indications	**327**
Sexual abuse	**327**
Peer group abuse	**327**
Who to contact	**328**
What will happen	**328**
Children in care	**328**
Suspected of abuse	**328**

ALTERNATIVE FAMILY STRUCTURES **330**

Single-parent statistics	**330**
Living together	**330**
Step-families	**330**
Gay parenting	**330**

DEATH

BASICS **332**

If someone dies at home	**332**
Unexpected death	**332**
If death occurs abroad	**332**
Donating to science	**332**
Inquests	**332**
Registering a death	**333**
Tell the registrar	**333**
The registrar will give you	**333**
Responsibility	**333**
Grief	**333**
Losing a child	**333**

FUNERALS **334**

Cremation	**334**
Cemeteries/churchyards	**334**
At home	**334**
Deep freeze	**334**

WORK

The biggest barriers we still face are sexual segregation, unequal pay – and no minimum wage. There is often also the problem of the 'second shift' – returning home from 'paid work' and being expected to do all the 'unpaid work' of running a home. Finally, once we have a job, it's difficult to take time off to go to interviews; we feel that we can't afford to retrain and don't want to risk leaving to gamble on getting something better. Women who take a break to have children may feel out of touch and going back into the job market can seem as intimidating as starting out for the first time. This cycle of insecurity leaves thousands of people out of work or trapped in jobs they hate.

But there are solutions, and generally if you love what you do, you will be more successful. Most of us vastly underestimate our capabilities. There are now women in every field of employment. The number of self employed women has doubled in the past decade, and women start 40% of all new British businesses. We are beginning to create a new, flexible employment model – something taken for granted in many European countries – to replace the traditional job structure.

This chapter will help you if you are trying to find a job, keep a job, change direction, retrain and update your skills, return to work after a break, or set up on your own.

STARTING OUT

Confidence is the biggest issue. To reach for what you want, you have to believe that you're up to it. Confidence isn't a gift that some have and others haven't; it's a combination of attitude and behaviour which can be learned.

WHAT DO YOU WANT TO DO?

First you have to work out what it is you really want. Draw up a list of your goals and priorities. Identify the career best suited to your aptitudes, interests, personality and values. Some people take a long time to decide what they really want to do, and it's not unusual to start to plan a career relatively late in life, maybe after having children. Graduates may have a clear picture of what they want, but some find that their degree isn't relevant to the career they wish to pursue. If you are a school leaver, ask yourself what you really enjoyed most at school and see how it can be turned into a career.

EVALUATE YOUR SKILLS

What are your strengths and weaknesses? What is your education and work experience to date? What do you like to do with your time? Are any of these equitable as skills? Do you enjoy driving? Taxi driving is very compatible with parenting. Are you a good organizer? Running the parents' association is valid experience. Your personal experience of life can add up to some very important transferable work skills, so analyse your achievements to date very carefully.

Ask yourself:
• What have I done, what were the responsibilities and achievements?
• What do I enjoy?
• Education/training?
• Employment?
• Interests/activities?

• Volunteer Work?
• What do I want from the job?
• Salary: what are the minimum and maximum you could manage with. Work out your existing financial commitments.
• Job location: are you prepared to travel far?
• Consider the transport facilities available to you.
• Job prospects: do you want a job that has further career development implications for you?
• How much pressure can you cope with?

CAREER COUNSELLING

Defining what you want to do can be the hardest part. Career counselling can help open up your options.

• Your local authority has a Careers Service which offers career guidance and has a library of information. Make an appointment which will include assessing the opportunities available to you, assessing your own potential and making a plan of action. The extent of the service will depend on the local authority.
• A good starting point is your local Training and Enterprise Council (TEC). There are approximately 82 nationwide and they provide advice on training, contacts for work experience and courses for running your own business.
• The Careers Research and Advisory Centre is a registered charity and an independent agency which promotes career development through conferences, publications and consultancy. Contact them for more information.
• Private career counselling services: before committing yourself tell them your needs, ask them exactly what they can do for you and how much it will cost. Shop around because fees vary. Choose one that's approved by the Institute of Career Guidance.
• The Career Development Centre for Women (CDC4W) offers career and planning advice. There is a charge for an interview. Contact them for more information.
• The respective professional bodies may have further information about the careers open to you in the **A–Z of Career Options.**
• If you are a student, your university/college will have a career guidance department which will offer comprehensive advice for your future.

- Contact the Careers, Occupations and Information Centre for a list of books of different careers.

WOMEN IN BUSINESS

The difficulties for women are pervasive: the absence of proper childcare provision, inflexible structures for careers and work, indirect and direct discrimination. Women's full-time wages are between 12 and 45% less than those of men. Once they have had their children, women have the potential to work a further 25–35 years although 90% of women who leave work for domestic reasons return to a lower-paid, lower-responsibility job with fewer career possibilities. Women still shoulder most of the responsibility for looking after children and the home; as a result nearly half of all women in employment work part time leaving them fewer rights and opportunities and less stability. 77% of working women are concentrated in four types of occupation: catering, cleaning, professional services and clerical jobs. Approximately 3% of company directors are women and even the most successful women only earn about 75% of the income enjoyed by their male counterparts.

A–Z OF CAREER OPTIONS

This lists the initial point of contact. To find out more about academic qualifications see addresses in the Directory.

- **Accountant:** Chartered Association of Certified Accountants or the Association of Cost and Management Accountants
- **Actor:** British Actors Equity Association or the National Council for Drama Training
- **Acupuncturist:** British Acupuncture Council
- **Advertising:** Advertising Association or the Institute of Practitioners in Advertising
- **Anthropologist:** Royal Anthropological Institute of Britain and Ireland
- **Archaeologist:** Council for British Archaeology and Institute of Archaeology
- **Architect:** Architects Registration Council of the United Kingdom or the Royal Institute of British Architects
- **Artist:** ADAR (Art and Design Admissions Registry)
- **Barrister:** Council of Legal Education, Faculty of Advocates, General Council of the Bar
- **Broadcasting:** journalist, reporter, programme assistant, producer's assistant, studio manager, director, producer, film editor, make-up, costume designer, dresser, camera operator, sound operator, secretaries, etc.: BBC Corporate Recruitment Service, personnel department at ITV, Skillset at Channel 4
- **Building:** Construction Industry Training Board and the Women's London Manual Trades
- **Catering and accommodation management:** Hospitality Training Foundation, Hotel and Catering Training Company, Hotel and Catering International Management Association
- **Chemist:** Royal Society of Chemistry
- **Chiropractor:** British Chiropractic Association
- **Civil Service:** Graduate and Schools Liaison Branch
- **Commerce:** The Management Information Centre/Institution of Industrial Managers
- **Company secretary:** The Institute of Chartered Secretaries and Administrators
- **Computing:** British Computer Society, Association of Computer Professionals, Women's Computer Centre
- **Conservation:** English Nature, National Trust, Natural Environmental Research Council, Museum Association, United Kingdom Institute for the Conservation of Historic and Artistic Works
- **Dancing:** Royal Academy of Dancing, Council for Dance Education and Training
- **Dentist:** General Dental Council
- **Design:** Design Council
- **Detective:** Association of British Investigators
- **Dietitian:** British Dietetic Association
- **Economist:** Institute of Economic Affairs
- **Electrician:** Institute of Electrical Engineers
- **Engineer:** Civil Engineering Careers Service, Engineering Council

- **Estate agent:** The National Association of Estate Agents
- **Fashion:** CAPITB Group (Clothing and Allied Products Industry Training Board)
- **Film production:** Skillset, British Film Institute, Broadcasting, Entertainment, Cinematography and Theatre Union, Movie Producers Alliance (MPA)
- **Florist:** Floristry Training Council
- **Food science and technology:** Food and Drink Industry Training Organization
- **Forensic scientist:** Forensic Science Society
- **Garage work:** Retail Motor Industry Federation
- **Gardener:** Royal Horticultural Society
- **Hairdresser:** Hairdressing Training Board, National Hairdressers Federation
- **Health service:** NHS Training Division, Institute of Health Services Management
- **Homoeopathy:** British School of Homoeopathy, Society of Homoeopaths
- **Hotel work:** see catering
- **Information technology:** British Computer Society Institute for the Management of Information Systems
- **Insurance:** Chartered Insurance Institute, Insurance Industry Training Council
- **Interior designer:** IDDA (Interior Decorators and Designers Association)
- **Jeweller:** National Association of Goldsmiths
- **Journalist:** Chartered Institute of Journalists, National Council for the Training of Journalists
- **Landscape architect:** The Landscape Institute
- **Local government:** Local Government Opportunities
- **Management consultant:** Institute of Management Consultants
- **Marine biologist:** Institute of Biology, Plymouth Marine Laboratory
- **Marketing:** Chartered Institute of Marketing, Market Research Society
- **Medicine:** British Medical Association, Royal College of Nursing
- **Musician:** Incorporated Society of Musicians, Musicians Union
- **Optician:** British College of Optometrists
- **Pharmacist:** Association of the British Pharmaceutical Industry, National Pharmaceutical Association
- **Photographer:** British Institute of Professional Photography, Association of Fashion, Advertising and Editorial Photographers
- **Physiotherapist:** Chartered Society of Physiotherapy
- **Plumber:** Construction Industry Training Board, Institute of Plumbing
- **Police:** your local police station, Police Recruiting Department
- **Psychologist:** British Psychological Society
- **Public relations:** Institute of Public Relations
- **Publishing:** Publishers Association, Women in Publishing, Publishing Qualifications Board
- **Secretary:** Institute of Qualified Private Secretaries
- **Social work:** CCETSW (Central Council for Education and Training for Social Workers)
- **Solicitor:** Careers office of the Law Society
- **Sports:** Institute of Professional Sport, Sports Council
- **Stockbroker:** Securities Institute
- **Surveyor:** Royal Institution of Chartered Surveyors
- **Teacher:** Teacher Training Agency, Advisory Service on Entry to Teaching
- **Translator:** Institute of Linguists, Translators Association
- **Travel Agent:** ABTA, Institute of Travel and Tourism
- **Vet:** British Veterinary Association
- **Writer:** Society of Authors, Institute of Scientific and Technical Communicators
- **Youth and community work:** National Youth Agency
- **Zoologist:** Institute of Biology

The *Kogan Page* career books are extremely good guides to individual career alternatives and are available in most bookshops, or ring their inquiry line.

FINDING A JOB

Job hunting can be a painful process and may involve feelings of rejection and frustration. Job hunting can seem like a career in itself. Try contacting the firms direct to see if they have vacancies.

WHERE TO LOOK
- **The national press:** different days specialize in particular careers:

- **Daily Express**
  Tuesday – Education
  Thursday – General Employment

- **Daily Mail**
  Thursday – General Employment

- **Daily Mirror**
  Thursday – General Employment

- **Daily Telegraph**
  Thursday – General Employment

- **Financial Times**
  Monday – Accountancy
  Wednesday – Finance, Banking
  Thursday – Accountancy

- **Guardian**
  Monday – Creative Media
  Tuesday – Education
  Wednesday – Public Sector
  Thursday – IT
  Friday – General Employment

- **Independent**
  Monday – Media and Sales
  Tuesday – IT
  Wednesday – Legal and Finance
  Thursday – Education/Graduate Appointments

- **The Times**
  Tuesday – Legal
  Wednesday – Marketing and Secretarial
  Thursday – Executive Appointments
  Friday – Education

- **Daily Record/Herald/Evening Times**
  Have general job advertising all week

- **Local press:** useful if you want to move and work in a particular area. Get a listing of all the local newspapers from the *BRAD directory* (British rates and data) available from most local libraries.

- **Free magazines:** usually published by the local council.
- **The ethnic community press:** *Caribbean Times*, the *Voice* and the *Asian Times* all advertise posts with an emphasis on equal opportunity policies.
- **Specialized press:** the professions have their own journals. The *BRAD directory* lists over 3,000 journals. Look them up in your local library or contact the professional bodies to find out about their journals.

IN YOUR NEIGHBOURHOOD
- Local job centres: for manual, secretarial, clerical, domestic and sales jobs. New jobs offered daily. If you sign on, there are people in the dole office who can assess your skills and help get you back to work.
- Local library: there is often a noticeboard advertising jobs.

AGENCIES
Private recruitment agencies/consultants: these assess your skills and try and place you in a job. There are 15,000 nationwide and most are listed in the *CEPEC Recruitment Guide* – contact CEPEC for a copy. They tend to specialize in particular professions, and if they find you a job it is up to you to obtain all the necessary information about the job and salary directly from the employer.

AGENCY FEES
- The agency takes you on its books: when you are successfully placed in a job your new employer pays the agency a commission.
- It is a criminal offence for an employment agency to charge you commission.

Exceptions
- The modelling and entertainment industries where there is an agency/client relationship. When the model/entertainer is charged commission, the employer must not be.
- Au pairs looking for work abroad may be charged once a family is found for them, though it is much more usual for the family to pay the agency fee.
- The agency can charge you for courses they run, if they are looking for a job for you.
- Temps can be employed directly by the agency in

which case the agency is responsible for wages, holiday and sick pay.

HEADHUNTERS

These are agencies that search for people with specific talents and offer them jobs on behalf of employers. If you have good qualifications, are successful in your field or have special skills, find the appropriate agencies through CEPEC and send them your CV asking them to put you on file.

OTHER OPTIONS

Using the Internet: hundreds of recruitment firms use the Net to advertise vacancies. Approximately 76% of UK Internet users are aged between 18 and 44, which is the ideal demographic profile of job seekers. Here are a few of the successful UK firms on the Web:

- **Reed Personnel Services:**
  http://www.reed.co.uk
- **Careers Services Unit:**
  http://www.unimelb.edu.au/ExtRels//
  CCU/index.html
- **Unixis Solutions:**
  http://demon.co.ukunixix/database.html
- **PeopleBank:**
  http://www.peoplebank.com/emphwip.html
- **CareerNet:**
  http://www.bankone.com/careernet/html
- **Guardian:** http://recruitment.guardian.uk
- **Teletext:** information on job vacancies is broadcast through ITV/Channel 4 teletext service.
- **Top jobs on the Net:** http://www.topjobs.net
- **Price Jamieson:**
  http://www.pricejam.com/noframe/grad.html

WORKING IN THE EU

As a member of the EU you have a right to live and work within the EU without a work permit, although you may need other documentation. Check that your qualifications are recognized by the country with the Public Enquiry Office at Department of Employment and Education in London. For more information contact the Overseas Placing Unit of the Employment Service in Sheffield. They also produce various publications about working abroad.

Some sources
- **Employment agencies:** a list of agencies dealing with work in the EU can be obtained from the Federation of Recruitment and Employment Services in London.
- **Special journals:** *Overseas Jobs Express,* the *European* and the *Guardian* on Tuesdays.
- The Central Bureau for Educational Visits and Exchanges at the British Council in London has various publications available as well as advice.
- The Commission for the European Communities has extensive information on working in the EU. They have a library that is open to the public.
- Vacation work publications offer a wide range of books on working abroad.

DECIPHERING JOB ADS

Ads are often open to interpretation because they are designed to give a feel for the job. Advertising is expensive so information is kept brief. Here are some tips in evaluating whether the ad is relevant to your experience.
- Read between the lines: if they ask for a qualification but instead you have relevant experience, go ahead and apply.
- Companies don't always know what they want. It's up to you to show your suitability in your application.
- If you're not clear about the job being offered, call up the company and ask personnel for more information.
- If you know you don't have the right qualifications yet, but you like the sound of the company, apply anyway and ask them to put your CV on file in case a job does comes up that you might be eligible for.

TRAINING
AND RESKILLING

TRAINING

Unless you are lucky enough to have a very clear vocation, it may take a long time to decide what you are really good at and make a career out of it – macramé or belly dancing? The most obvious way to prepare for training is to get the relevant GCSEs and A-levels and go on to college; however it's not the only way. If you are interested in a particular career, approach the related professional body (see **A–Z of Career Options**) about the necessary qualifications, relevant courses or appropriate experience that will help you get a foot in the door.

If you are thinking of setting up your own business you should do a business/management course and produce detailed business plans and market surveys before trying to raise finance. You might also want to work for one of your competitors and make your mistakes on their payroll.

Women who take time out to have children often find that when they want to return to work they need to brush up old skills or learn new ones before they can get back into the job marketplace. Getting to grips with new computer programs, finding relevant weekend workshops or going back to college full time will put you on a more equal footing with other candidates. Start by reading *Second Chance: a National Guide to Adult Education and Training Opportunities and Occupations* in your local library.

YOUR OPTIONS

• **Access courses:** designed to give people without any qualifications a route into a university and provide a recognized alternative to A-levels.
• **University degrees:** you don't have to have A-levels and GCSEs to go to university. Some degree and postgraduate courses have flexible arrangements for adults wanting to do part-time courses. Read the *UCAS Handbook* published by the Universities and Colleges Admissions Service (UCAS). ECCTIS is a computerized service listing all the courses available in higher and further education, available at most libraries and career services. The Lucy Cavendish College in Cambridge is exclusively for women over the age of 25 and you don't need A-level qualifications to get in.
• **NVQs and GNVQs:** General National Vocational Qualifications (GNVQs) are courses which give background knowledge to a range of careers.

National Vocational Qualifications (NVQs – SVQs in Scotland) are relevant to specific careers. There are five levels of ability, no time limit for completion and no previous skills required. Contact the National Council for Vocational Qualifications and in Scotland the Scottish Qualifications Authority for more information.
• **BTECs:** the Business and Technology Education Council offers recognized qualifications in a wide range of subjects. BTEC courses can be taken in colleges of further/higher education, approved training colleges, companies and schools. There are two types of qualification: certificates and diplomas. Contact BTEC for more information.
• **City and Guilds:** awards qualifications in over 400 different subjects. The courses are run in colleges of further education, adult education institutes and training centres with no real entry requirements or time limits to complete. Contact City and Guilds for more information.
• **Royal Society of Arts:** offers a wide range of qualifications in office skills open to anyone. Contact the RSA Customer Information Bureau for more information.
• **Training and Enterprise Councils (TECs):** there are 79 independent companies supporting the central Government strategy for raising local skills. TECs run all kinds of schemes, apprenticeships, youth training, training for work and business and enterprise services. Contact the TEC National Council for more information.
• **Correspondence courses:** the National Extension College and the Open University (Britain's largest institution of higher education) offer a vast range of courses at degree and postgraduate level. The Open Business School offers short courses covering international marketing,management, accounting, starting your own business etc. The Open College of the Arts (affiliated to the Open University) provides training in the arts but without a recognized qualification at the end. No qualifications are needed to start any of these courses. Most courses include studying at home in your own time, through a programme of specially prepared material. Fees range from £70 to £500. Ensure that the courses are accredited by the Open and Distant Learning Quality Council.

- Adult education centres offer day and evening classes of every kind and may serve as a useful introduction into a new area of work. In London look in *Floodlight* available from newsagents.

PRACTICAL DETAILS

In order to make sure that a course is right check:
- how long it lasts
- is it full or part time; what are the hours?
- what entry qualifications are needed?
- fees and any extra expenses, equipment etc.
- are there any grants available?
- how is the course assessed?
- is special supervision available if required?
- are there any course/industry connections for job introductions?
- is there a crèche?

RETURNING TO WORK

Women with children can have problems in finding courses or jobs that they can combine with family life. The Women's Returners' Network is a charity advising women on how to return to work. Courses are available to help confidence building, job-hunting skills, finding work placements, voluntary nurseries or crèches (see **Getting Help** in **Babies**). Read the *Women's Returners' Network's Directory of Training* (£13.95) which covers all kinds of courses available in your area.

FUNDING

The cost of education and training is high combined with the practical difficulties of child-care. A certain amount of public funding does exist and employers also invest money in training. Check the full costs of a course before committing yourself.
- If your course is funded by the local Training and Enterprise Council you may be eligible for a training allowance.
- If you are a returner or single parent on benefit you may be eligible for Government-funded training for work. A good all-round guide is the *Unemployment and Training Rights Handbook* by Dann Fin from your local library or TEC.
- If you can't get a grant you can apply for a career development loan to cover up to 80% of your course fees, and in some cases childminding fees will also be assessed. Contact your local TEC for details or call Career Development Loans which sends out information on behalf of a couple of banks on special loans for training.
- If you are working whilst taking an NVQ you may be able to get some income tax relief: get the leaflet *Tax Relief for Vocational Training IR 119* from your local tax office.
- Your local Education Guidance Service for adults or job centre will have more information on funding.
- Local Education Authorities manage two types of grants: mandatory and discretionary. Mandatory grants are available for students taking full-time courses such as degree courses, diplomas, BTEC. Discretionary grants are available for Access courses, A-levels, full-time GCSEs.
- The National Union of Students will be able to give advice on student loans.
- Contact the Educational Grants Advisory Service for information on grants available for people who are not eligible for statutory funding.
- The Department of Education and Employment publishes *Student Grants and Loans.*

- **Sponsorship:** there are many publications available listing firms willing to sponsor students and training. Try
- *Sponsorship for Students,*
  published by Biblios
- *Directory of Grant Making Trusts*
  published by the Charities Aid Foundation
- *Educational Grants Directory*
  published by the Directory of Social Change.
  These are expensive books to buy so check in your local library first.

STUDYING IN THE EU

The Treaty of Rome allows every EU citizen to work in any EU member state. Some educational qualifications are recognized across Europe like NVQs/SVQs. For more information contact the Qualifications Public Enquiry Point at the Department of Education in London. The Education and Employment Dispatches Department publishes *The European Choice: a Guide to Opportunities for Higher Education in Europe* (quote FHE3503). It's free. If you want to

study in the EU the British Council has information on exchanges and courses available.

PREPARA-TION

WRITING A CV

Your curriculum vitae or CV is a vital document in helping you get a job. It will tell your potential employer all the information s/he needs to be able to invite you for an interview and should therefore present you to your best advantage. You never get a second chance to make a first impression so make sure you get it right first time.

- Wherever possible your CV should be typed in a professional format. It is worth paying to get it done by a trained typist if you can't do it yourself. You will also be able to have a number of original copies done at the same time. Go to a computer bureau or local library that has computer facilities.
- Create your own headed white or cream A4 paper and make sure your spelling and grammar are correct.
- It should be as concise as possible and preferably only one side.
- After your name, address, nationality and date of birth you should list your main and most relevant qualifications (no need to go back to Grade 1 ballet!). Then state your work experience starting with the most recent and, if relevant, include any promotions, prizes or awards.
- Add any pertinent additional information at the end, e.g. interests, clean driving-licence.
- You should use clear and concise language with headings setting out 'blocks' of facts. Yours will not be the only CV received so you need to create an immediate impression.
- Use your CV to say as much about yourself as you can without going over the top. You need to provide the reader with sufficient information to catch her/his interest but not so much that all their questions are already answered.
- Make sure your CV lists the skills most appropriate for the job you are applying for.
- Never lie and never try to hide the facts as they will probably be discovered eventually.
- Always be prepared to back up what you say in your CV, i.e. be prepared to speak in French at an interview if you have said that you are fluent (if you only have school book French you could blow your chances even if you are a suitable candidate in every other way).
- If you have been made redundant it usually reflects more on the company than it does on you.
- Do not be afraid to include details of unpaid work under 'work history' or 'voluntary work'.
- Make sure you keep your CV up-to-date at all times.
- Always keep spare copies for future use.
Information on writing CVs can be found at your local library or careers office.

INTERVIEWS

Everyone hates interviews but unfortunately we all have to face them at some time or another. Whether you are returning to work, looking for part-time work or becoming the next prime minister, the principles of being interviewed are much the same and the secret to success is good preparation.

Prior to your interview

- Set your objective and be realistic about what you can achieve: you are not going to get a job offer from your first meeting with a member of the personnel department.
- Find out as much information as you can about the company and the job in question.
- Know how to get there and how long it will take you. Always plan to arrive early and leave extra time for public transport delays or parking problems.
- Take any relevant paperwork, a copy of your CV and the letter you have received inviting you for interview. Don't weigh yourself down with unnecessary baggage: only take the essentials – hairbrush, make-up etc.
- Be confident of all the details on the job specification and on your CV.

- Prepare answers to the main questions you might expect and anything your CV might throw up.
- Make sure you have eaten before the interview: there is nothing more off-putting than a rumbling tummy!
- Wear clothes you are comfortable in – dark colours and classic shapes are a safe bet. Get a good haircut, do your roots and make sure your shoes are clean.
- Try and relax! Remember, they want to see you.

CONFIDENCE

- Be positive about your own abilities.
- Know how to talk about any weakness or failure in a positive light, i.e. be prepared to explain how you overcame any difficulty and what you have learned from any negative experience.
- Be prepared to explain any gaps in your CV or work history. Be honest, do not deny that you have been made redundant.
- You may be dealing with a highly trained and organized interviewer or someone with very little experience of interview techniques who won't necessarily give you the opportunity to make the best of yourself. An experienced interviewer will use open questions which will allow you to expand on the subject, whereas less experienced people may ask questions that only require a yes or no answer. Recognizing the difference in the two styles will allow you to tailor your responses.
- Don't be afraid to show that you have a sense of humour.

AT THE INTERVIEW

- Body language: greet your interviewer with a firm handshake. Try and look relaxed when you sit down and sit well into the chair, not perched on the edge. Do not fold your arms or cross your legs unless at the ankles, i.e. don't adopt a defensive position.
- Do not smoke or accept a cup of tea or coffee: cups and saucers are hard to balance if you are concentrating on speaking and particularly if you are perched on the edge of the chair!
- Maintain eye contact with your interviewer as this gives the impression of confidence. If you find this hard to do, look at their ear instead – they will get the same impression.

Your interviewer will want to know:
Can you do the job?
Will you do the job?
Will you fit in?

- Listen to the questions and make sure you answer what was asked and not what you wanted to be asked.
- Only give additional information if you consider it relevant. Don't waffle.
- Do not answer a question until you have put your brain in gear: there is nothing wrong with pausing before you answer a question.
- Be prepared to talk about your interests, personality and family, your ambitions and motivation and why you applied to this particular company.
- A favoured question is to ask about your weaknesses or faults: it is better to make one up and have an answer ready than to say that you do not have any – nobody's perfect!
- Don't give monosyllabic answers, do not argue and clarify anything that you do not understand before answering.
- Don't talk too much or too quickly.
- Don't leave the interview without finding out what will happen next, who you will have to see, when you will be contacted, etc. Reaffirm your interest in the position and say what a pleasure it has been to see him or her.
- Don't commit yourself to pay and terms during an interview. Allow yourself time to look through contracts at home. Work out what you need and what they can afford before you start the discussion and only negotiate with the person who is actually able to make the decisions.

ASSESSMENT CENTRES

These are used to gain greater knowledge about candidates and may provide information which will be more relevant to the everyday working environment in the position they are applying for.
Assessment centres may include

- Group activities to assess how individuals respond to group and/or problem solving situations.
- Social activities such as dinners to see how individuals conduct themselves and interact with each other.
- One-to-one or panel interviews with senior line managers.

PSYCHOLOGICAL TESTING

- Psychological questionnaires fall into two areas: personality and ability.
- It is unwise to try and fake answers to a personality test because these are easily detected.
- There is no real preparation you can do for personality tests but there is for ability or IQ tests.
- You can sharpen your skills by doing crosswords and number puzzles and it might be worth borrowing some IQ books from the library.
- Practice will not make you any cleverer but will ensure that you reach your full potential.

MEDICAL EXAMINATION

Some companies will insist on a medical before hiring you. If you use recreational drugs it is worth knowing that cocaine and cannabis can be detected in your bloodstream up to four weeks after use.

NEW WAYS TO WORK

Currently 14% of families in Britain are single-parent households and over half of mothers go out to work. The rigid structure of full-time working is hard to balance with the demands of the home and family. Most European countries provide childcare and parental leave schemes to enable mothers to work full time, but Britain is slow to follow. More mothers now work than stay at home and flexible working arrangements need to become more available.

PART-TIME WORK

24% of employment is part time in Britain. Part-timers are mostly confined to low pay, low status and job insecurity. If you work 16 hours or more a week you have most employment rights and if you remain with the company for more than two years you earn the right to redundancy pay. If you work for less than eight hours a week, you essentially have no rights at all. All part-time workers now get maternity leave and pay. It can be hard to find out who offers flexible working. New Ways to Work is an organization advising on more flexible ways of working. They run workshops for employers: contact them for more information, advice and a list of specialist publications. It has a list of employment agencies that specialize in finding jobs for part-timers. Another useful book to read is *New Work Options* by Christine Ingham, published by Thorsons.

OTHER OPTIONS

- **Flexitime:** employees are paid for an allotted number of hours per week, spread as they choose.
- **Job sharing:** an arrangement whereby two people share one full-time job between them. They share the work, pay, holidays and benefits. The advantages are that you can retain your position on the career ladder, complement each other's skills and do a high-level job on a part-time basis. The disadvantages are that you tend to work more hours than you are paid for and you may be treated as a part-timer. Read *Job Sharing: a Practical Guide* by Pam Walton available from New Ways to Work.
- **Term-time working:** school holidays can be a headache for working women and take up to 14 weeks a year. Is there a way you could be given unpaid time off during school holidays? Play schemes are available in some schools for kids whose mums are working during the holidays. See **Getting Help** in **Babies** chapter.
- **Career-break schemes:** the employer allows a planned time away from work with a guaranteed job at the end of the break.
- **Sabbaticals:** some employers allow selected employees to take an extended period of leave. This can be used for career development, i.e. retraining, or a well-earned break. These are fairly rare in Britain and are usually given to employees who have been in the same company for a long time.

If you would like to change the way you work:
- Research the issue thoroughly and the particular type of flexible work arrangements you prefer.
- Obtain examples of good practice if possible.

- Put a strong case together setting out exactly how it would work.
- Make a clear list of benefits to the employer as well as highlighting how potential problems will be dealt with.
- Try out the idea on friends and colleagues first.

WORKING FROM HOME

Five million people in Britain are self-employed with the vast majority working from home. They are the fastest growing sector of the economy. High redundancies, the growth of the Internet and better technology are all helping to add to the numbers. People are drawn to the idea of flexible working routines and self-reliance. The obvious disadvantages are loneliness, domestic interruptions, lack of feedback from a superior and the need to be constantly motivated.

TIPS

- Check the deeds of your property or your lease to make sure that it is within your rights to work from home in an official capacity. If it is prohibited you might need to negotiate a change in your deeds or lease, obtain planning permission for a change of property usage or consider buying the freehold, see the **Right to buy** section in the **Home** chapter.
- You may need to get extra householder's insurance to cover all your equipment. Tolson Messenger have published a small guide called *A Brief Guide to Home Business Insurance*. Call them up for a free copy. Some specialist insurance brokers offer packages for homeworkers, including Tolson Messenger, London & Edinburgh and Michael Pavey insurance brokers. Banks also can offer special home insurance packages.
- A fact sheet on starting an office from home is available from Home Run, a company that specializes in giving information to those just starting out in business from home. Send an SAE.

COSTS

The costs of setting up a home office are often underestimated.
- Dedicate a telephone line and an answering machine to your work. Look for the most competitive business rates offered, check on cable lines

as opposed to standard telephone services (see **Telephone services** in **Technology** chapter).

- Buy only essential computer software, don't go overboard for your needs. Work out your exact software requirements, spreadsheet programs, database facilities, etc. (see **PCs and Macs** in **Technology** chapter).
- Investigate leasing your equipment because technology changes so quickly and it may affect your tax situation.
- Buy a proper chair with back support.
- You may need to install blinds: if your computer is in front of a window you can damage your eyesight.
- You may need to build or buy a desk: your eye should be level with your computer screen and your elbow at a downward slant to the keyboard.

EMPLOY-MENT ISSUES

Everyone suffers a crisis, personal or work related, at some time. It's not unusual. Here are some tips on how to work your way through it, minimizing the disruption to your work and life in general.

EMPLOYMENT CONTRACTS

These are extremely important documents, and will inevitably be referred to should there be any problems in the employer/employee relationship. If you have worked for 13 weeks (the hours worked are irrelevant), your employer is required by law to provide a written statement called 'written particulars' (usually a summary of the intent of the pending contract) of the terms of employment. If any changes are made to the terms, the employee must be told within one month of the change being made and the employee must have easy access to any details.

The written particulars may lead to a contract (or you may get a contract immediately).

The contract should include and consider

- parties to the contract (i.e. you and your employer)
- when the contract begins and ends
- your rights and when you become entitled to them
- job title
- job requirements
- who you report to
- the hours
- the place of work
- the wages: how much and when
- holiday pay and holiday entitlement

Have information on the following

- trade union arrangements
- overtime: is it expected? Is it compulsory? Will you be paid more for it?
- promotion: what are the opportunities?
- is there any training provided?
- social welfare facilities
- health and safety rules
- work rules, disciplinary codes
- job flexibility: will you be expected to change your duties?
- job mobility: if the employer needs you to work elsewhere, will you be expected to move?
- restrictive covenants: are there any clauses that could limit you in choosing a job should you leave the firm in the future, i.e. confidentiality clauses or geographic restriction linked to a 'conflict of interests'?
- sick pay
- pension rights
- date temporary employment is to end (if applicable)
- details of any collective agreements
Check the job description in the contract; if it is very precise you may be able to refuse certain duties.

If there is no written agreement, you still have some protection under implied terms. These are basic requirements which may not be written in a contract but which both you and your employer are automatically expected by law to observe.

DUTIES AS AN EMPLOYEE

The employee must carry out the work to a 'reasonable standard' for which s/he is employed, and not act against the employer's interests, which obviously includes helping a competitor. Unless you are asked to do something illegal, or 'unreasonable' (and the definition of unreasonable can be problematic), you are duty bound to carry it out. You are also restricted from disclosing confidential information relating to your employer. Having left your job, you can use general information and skills acquired during your work, but not confidential information. Obviously some jobs involve the employee being party to more confidential information than others, and in these instances there may be an enforceable clause written into the contract.

OVERTIME

You must work for the number of hours stated in your contract. Always work out the overtime hours and terms within the contract.

HOURS AND HOLIDAYS

EU restrictions may lead to change, but at present there are no rules that govern working hours other than the hours stated in the contract. This includes hours spent working, the length of time you can work without a break, overtime, shift work. Every worker residing in the EU shall have the right to annual paid leave and a weekly rest period at some point in the future. The amount varies according to custom within the industry you are working in.

SAFETY AT WORK

Your employer is legally obliged to make the workplace as safe as possible under the Health and Safety at Work Act 1974. To this end, they must ensure that your workmates are competent, that the system of working is safe, that the equipment and plant are properly serviced and in a safe condition for work. Should a failure to meet these requirements result in harm coming to you as an employee, and you can prove that the employer has acted negligently, you can sue for damages. However, if you have been partly responsible for the accident, your claim will be

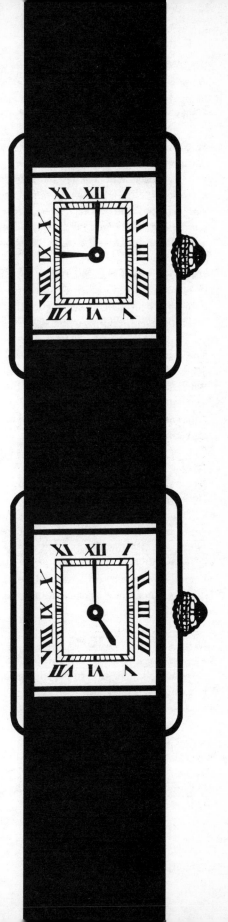

reduced accordingly. Motor accidents are the cause of many claims: if you are injured while being driven by a workmate in the 'course of your employment', your employer is liable.

Safe working conditions are governed by detailed statutory requirements concerning design, layout and the provision of facilities and equipment. The Factories Act covers a whole range of different working conditions, from dry cleaners to power plants. For full details contact the local health and safety inspector (they're in the phone book).

INJURY IN THE WORKPLACE
- It is important not to accept any financial compensation before seeking both legal and medical advice: your injury may be worse than you originally thought.
- The accident should be reported to the employer immediately and entered in the firm's accident book.
- Witnesses are important: take all relevant names and get written statements. Photograph defective equipment and try to prevent it from being repaired until your lawyer is satisfied.
- Get legal advice: contact a representative from your trade union.
- If necessary, see your doctor and make sure notes are kept.
- Find out whether others have had similar accidents or complained about the equipment and get statements in writing.
- Claim the welfare benefits you are entitled to.
- Keep records of any expenses incurred as a result of your injury, and calculate the loss of earnings for you and your family.

MATERNITY RIGHTS
All pregnant employees are entitled to:
- reasonable time off to keep appointments regarding their pregnancy
- a period of 14 weeks' statutory maternity leave, regardless of length of service but you have to give notice that you are pregnant
- benefit from the normal terms of contract
- return to the job
- statutory maternity pay. See **Maternity and Finance** in **Money** chapter.

LOSING YOUR JOB

If you feel that you have been wrongfully dismissed, there are two ways of handling it, depending on the circumstances. At present, cases of 'wrongful dismissal' are tried in the civil courts, while 'unfair dismissals' are dealt with at industrial tribunals. If you have been in continuous employment for longer than two years, you can request a written statement outlining the reasons for your dismissal. This cannot be refused, and must be supplied within 14 days of the request. Employers are not obliged to provide you with a reference, but if they do, it cannot be malicious otherwise they will be liable under ordinary laws of defamation.

WRONGFUL DISMISSAL
(proper notice not given)
- there must have been a breach of contract
- you have six years from the 'breach' within which to claim
- it is within the Legal Aid system
- the loser is liable to pay the winner's costs

UNFAIR DISMISSAL
(sacked unreasonably)
- there does not have to have been a breach of contract
- employee must apply within three months
- there is a continuous service requirement (you must have been working for two years full time or five years part time) except where the claim is related to sex or race discrimination, trade union activities (including non-membership)
- there is currently a maximum award of £11,300, plus a basic award
- the employer can be ordered to reinstate the employee

- cases are not within the Legal Aid system
- the union you are a member of can help provide representation

INDUSTRIAL TRIBUNALS

(employment disputes)

Trade unions, redundancy payment claims, unfair dismissal and discrimination in the workplace are the main areas covered by the law as far as work is concerned. The aim is to promote good industrial relations, but the rights of the British employee are weak compared with those of many European countries. Recently, European law has had an enormous impact on the way in which employees are treated here. Many of the recent Acts of Parliament relating to work have been the direct result of pressure from the EU. Industrial tribunals are the way most problems relating to work are resolved. Over half the cases heard concern unfair dismissal. The incorporation of new and more complicated legislation has led to long waits for a system that is becoming increasingly overloaded. It is best to know your rights before you begin. By law, employers have general duties to all employees which need not be written into your contract but are still enforceable. They include:

- **Treatment of the employee:** you must not be treated unreasonably, humiliated, or singled out and persecuted.
- **The payment of the employee:** you must be paid for any work you have done according to the terms of the contract.
- **Concern for your general health and safety:** if more than five people are employed, a safety policy must be issued by the employer.
- **Equality in the workplace:** you cannot be discriminated against on racial or sexual grounds.

You can get an application form, 'Form ITI', for an industrial tribunal from any job centre or employment office.

The basic rules:
- It is not necessary to be represented by a lawyer: a trade union official, friend or associate can act on your behalf.
- Each party must cover their own legal costs. The loser does not pay the winner's costs; costs are rarely awarded in industrial tribunals. (This is ostensibly to discourage the use of lawyers. However, employers usually have legal representation, while employees don't which can put them at a real disadvantage.)
- The claim cannot be financed by Legal Aid, regardless of the employee's circumstances. Under the 'green form scheme' it may be possible to get help and advice on preparing for the case and filling in the forms.
- There are fewer formalities than in an ordinary court, which means that you may be able to include hearsay and written statements in your evidence.
- There are strict time limits attached: three months for unfair dismissal cases and six months for redundancy claims.

FAIR DISMISSAL

The grounds on which employers can defend themselves include:

- the employee's inability to do the job and poor conduct. Note: even if you have been fairly dismissed, you are still entitled to notice. Check *Discipline at Work*, a booklet available from the Arbitration and Conciliatory Service (ACAS).
- In cases of 'gross misconduct' (where the employee has consciously breached a term in the contract, has acted dishonestly or accessed unauthorized information), the employee may be liable for 'summary dismissal', 'sacking on-the-spot', which takes immediate effect.

GIVING PROPER NOTICE

Unless otherwise stated in your contract, the amount of notice your employer is required to give will depend on how long you have been employed. Theoretically, if you fail to give your employer sufficient notice, they are entitled to sue you, though in practice this only happens in exceptional circumstances.

Under the Employment Protection Act 1978, the statutory minimums are:

- If you have been working for less than a month you don't need to give any notice.
- If you have been working for between one month and two years you can give one week's notice, however most companies expect you to give one

month's notice and this may be in your contract.
- If you have worked for a company for longer than two years, you must give one week's notice for every year worked.

PROBLEMS AT WORK

PERSONAL CRISIS
- Take immediate action and tell your boss. It's important to explain before your work starts to suffer and you are hauled up in front of them. You'll need to convince them that your problem won't become their problem. Discuss a plan of action, days off, assistance with your workload.
- Avoid telling everyone at work and public displays of emotion: it's important you keep boundaries between your personal life and the office.
- Prioritize your work, keep focused by making a hit list of tasks and forcing yourself to stick to them to keep a routine going in your life.
- Organize yourself, starting with your desk, files, returning phone calls promptly: all these things will increase your confidence and feeling of control over the situation.
- Under stress (emotional or work), it is very common to make mistakes, so be thorough: check and check over again the work that you do.
- If panic sets in take five minutes out and practise some calming breathing techniques.

SEXUAL HARASSMENT
Sexual harassment can be one of the most upsetting and humiliating experiences a person can suffer. It can affect your confidence as well as your physical and mental health.

WHAT IS IT?
There is no clear definition of sexual harassment but it is essentially unacceptable behaviour which is based on your sex, which is unreasonable, unwelcome and offensive.

Examples include
- unwelcome sexual attention
suggestions that sexual favours may further your career
- insults or ridicule of a sexual nature
- lewd, suggestive or over-familiar behaviour
- display or circulation of sexually suggestive material
Unwanted sexual attention is sexual harassment if it continues after you make it clear that you find it unacceptable. However, one incident can be enough to constitute sexual harassment if it is sufficiently serious.

ACTION TO TAKE
- Firstly make it clear to the person who is harassing you that their behaviour is unwelcome and you want it to stop. Ask a friend or colleague to be present as a witness. This may be enough to stop it. Write a letter if you can't face them and keep a copy.
- If it continues, talk to your manager.
- Where possible consult your personnel officer. They will advise you what to do next. This might be to make a formal complaint.
- If it is your manager who is harassing you, talk to someone higher up. If this is not possible seek help from a Citizens' Advice Bureau or from the Equal Opportunities Commission.
- Keep a record of all incidents, dates, correspondence and reactions to your complaint.
- Tell your colleagues in the office. It might seem embarrassing but you may find that you are not the only one.
- If it is putting you under stress go and see a doctor or counsellor.
- Follow up the complaint, ask how it is going to be investigated and ask to be kept informed of events.
- Contact Women Against Sexual Harassment which is an advisory and support network for people who are going through it.

FURTHER PROBLEMS
- If the sexual harassment stops and you are satisfied with the outcome you don't need to do anything else.
- If the harasser begins a campaign against you by passing work to others or ignoring you, etc. then report this as well.

- If the harassment doesn't stop and your report has been ignored, seek advice from outside on how to take it to the industrial tribunal.
- If your employer decides that your complaint is well founded but takes no action, you may have an additional claim against them, either of victimization or sex discrimination. Seek advice.

SEX DISCRIMINATION – THE LAW

Sexual harassment at work may be unlawful sex discrimination. It may be possible to bring a complaint to an industrial tribunal under the Sex Discrimination Act 1975. The complaint must be brought within three months of the incident.

Unfair dismissal: if a person is dismissed because they object to conduct they find unacceptable, they can complain that the dismissal is unfair under the Employment Protection Act 1978.

They can also complain that their dismissal is unfair if their employer has failed to investigate an allegation of serious sexual harassment.

RACIAL DISCRIMINATION

There are as many as 130,000 racially motivated incidents a year. When people are treated less favourably than others because of their race it is direct discrimination. Indirect discrimination is less obvious although it often acts as a bar against people from certain racial groups getting certain jobs in the first place. If you are coloured or from an ethnic minority, you may experience harassment that is both sexual and racial. If so, you may have claims under the Sex Discrimination Act and the Race Relations Act 1976. Seek advice from the Equal Opportunities Commission and the Commission for Racial Equality. Read the leaflet *Advice and Assistance* from the Commission for Racial Equality for more detailed information.

NEGOTIATING REDUNDANCY PAYOFFS

Men are twice as likely as women to be made redundant.
- Understand the strength of your negotiating position. Employers are prepared to pay more if you go quietly: they will try to avoid fighting an industrial tribunal case if at all possible.
- Make sure you receive accrued holiday entitlement.

- Negotiate over benefits such as company cars and health benefits: it is often very cheap for the employer to maintain these payments for a while.
- Discuss the moral obligations, such as your length of service.
- Ensure that your package is structured tax efficiently; ask the company's tax adviser about the situation.
- Insist on a good reference even if you leave on bad terms.

YOU AND YOUR BOSS

Most of us will have to deal with a tyrannical boss at some time.
- Understand what your boss wants from you, find out what pressures they are under.
- Make friends with the boss's secretary who might be able to tell you what the stress points are.
- If you have made a mistake, accept responsibility for it in a discussion with your boss. If you are not in the wrong, show your boss evidence or insist that they talk you through the whole situation.
- If the situation persists and attempts to talk through it with your boss have failed, inform a more senior staff member that you are having problems.

VISUAL DISPLAY UNITS (VDUS) AND REPETITIVE STRAIN INJURY (RSI)

New laws have emerged to reflect the different ways in which people work today. In Britain, over seven million people work on computers and most are aware of the specific discomfort associated with them. The Display Screen Equipment Regulations outline the legal duties of employers to protect their employees who are 'habitual users'. If an employer is in breach of the regulations, employees will be able to claim compensation for any resulting 'injury' such as RSI.

Employers must ensure that
- screens are free of glare and do not flicker
- the brightness and contrast are adjustable
- free eye tests are available, and free glasses supplied to those needing them for VDU use
- there are regular breaks from the screen or changes of activity
- there is adequate lighting and ventilation in the workplace

• suitable office furniture is supplied (e.g. desks must be the right height and have non-reflective surfaces)

STARTING A BUSINESS

96% of all firms in the UK can be categorized as 'small businesses'. There is lots of free help and advice available through high street banks, the Department of Trade and Industry (DTI) and your local Enterprise Agencies if you are considering going it alone. Read *Starting and Running Your Own Business* by Dennis Millar. Starting up your own business is a major commitment and not to be entered into lightly.

INITIAL CONSIDERATIONS
• Should you start a business from scratch, buy an existing going concern or even take out a franchise?
• Why do you want to run your own business? Be sure of your own motives.
• Are you up to it physically, mentally and financially?
• What effect could it have on your family or personal circumstances, e.g. if you were working from home?
• What risks are you prepared to take – what if it all went wrong? How could you reduce those risks?
• Look at similar businesses and see where their strengths and weaknesses lie and why they succeeded or failed.
• Is there a ready market for your product?
• Get an accountant.
• Do you have a good management team?
• Who is your competition? What will make you different?
• Who will be your customers?
• How will you determine your prices?
• How and who will market and promote your product?
• Who would you have to rely on: suppliers etc?
• Can you rely on them? What if you were let down?
• What sort of professional advice would you need?
• Write your own mission statement, i.e. the ratio-nale for you setting up your own business, the focus for what you intend to do and what you want to achieve.

BUSINESS PLAN
Your business plan is the backbone of your business. You will need to show it to anyone you want to involve in establishing the business and raising finance so it should be a clear and concise document setting out the following:
• Details of the business and the business aims for the initial 12 to 36 months at least.
• Details of your product and its marketplace.
• Finance is the most important part of the plan. You should give details of moneys already in the company and financial requirements you will have (if any!) for the period covered in the business plan. State why you need the funds, how they will be used and how you intend to pay them back.
• Budgets and cashflow forecasts: it is difficult to budget when you start up a new business as all your forecasts are made on the basis of assumptions. For this reason you should be realistic and as conservative as possible. Try and build in some reserves as a cushion in case the worst happens; however you must be able to explain the logic behind your figures.
• Your budgets will include both fixed costs, i.e. ones that will not change such as rent, insurance, salaries, etc., and variable costs, i.e. ones that are directly linked to producing your goods or services and that will change from month to month. You should make sure you are aware which is which and be able to explain why, when and how you expect your variable costs to change.
• Once you have prepared a budget you will be able to draw up a cashflow indicating what your income and expenditure will be on a monthly basis and when and how much the company is likely to need by way of additional finance. Again this should be realistic and should build in a time lag for receiving income due.
• Information on the key personnel involved.
• Details of your premises and any assets owned by the company (particularly if they could be used for security when trying to raise finance).
• Most banks are eager to attract small business

accounts and provide information packs with specimen budget and cashflow schedules and advice on how to draw up business plans. It is worth booking an appointment with a small business adviser to obtain basic help and advice before you embark on your business plan.

LEGAL ISSUES

Before you start trading there are a number of legal issues to consider. What form should your business take?

- **Sole trader:** this is the simplest form, operating under your own name or 'trading as . . . ' If you use a name other than your own and ownership of the business is not immediately apparent, you must display your name on all letterheads, invoices and receipts and at all places where your business is conducted. As a sole trader you are personally liable for all debts and have no limited liability.
- **Partnership:** the same legal rules apply to a partnership as to a sole trader, the main difference being that there can be 2–20 partners in a partnership. You may find you are liable for the debts of the other partners if they disappear, so it's strongly advisable to have a proper partnership document drawn up. This should set out the details of how partners are to be paid, whether decisions are to be made jointly or separately and what happens if a partner leaves.
- **Limited company:** the main difference between a partnership and a limited company is limited liability. The directors of a company are not personally liable for the company's debts (with the exception of National Insurance contributions). The main issues with a limited liability company are: choosing an acceptable name that is not already registered at Companies House and defining the purpose of the company and its internal procedures.

THINGS TO CONSIDER

- **Company names:** there are restrictions on the use of certain words such as 'Royal' or 'International'. Check with Companies House or the Business Names Registration.
- **Licences:** some companies need special licences to trade, e.g. children's nurseries, cafés/restaurants,

travel agents; check with your solicitor.
- **Trademarks, copyright and patents:** these all act to give your product or service extra protection and prevent your ideas, designs or inventions (intellectual property) being exploited by your competitors. You should seek initial advice from your solicitor as to what you need to protect and then apply to the Patent Office or the Copyright or Trademark Registry.
- **Trading laws:** check with your solicitor which, if any, trading laws apply to your goods or services. There are three laws that affect almost all small businesses:

1 Goods must live up to their description or the claims you make for them. If goods are faulty the customer is entitled to a full or partial refund. It is illegal to state that you have a 'No refund' policy.
2 Goods must meet certain safety standards.
3 Business premises: make sure you are legally allowed to run a business from the chosen premises and that you are complying with the terms of the lease, mortgage or any relevant by-laws. You may need separate planning permission if you are using your home as your business premises and you should make sure that your insurance company is also aware of the position.

FINANCIAL IMPLICATIONS

You will clearly have to keep good financial records of your business activities but these are also a legal requirement to support your payments and claims for VAT, tax and National Insurance. If you are a limited company you are legally required to submit your annual report and accounts to Companies House.

If you intend to store data electronically, e.g. on a personal computer, you will be required to register your business under the Data Protection Act 1984 which sets down a number of rules for the use of computers in business.

ESSENTIAL POINTS

1 Check out the local authority business rates.
2 Tax is payable on profits and income in the form of income tax for a sole trader or partnership and corporation tax for a limited liability company. Tax

liabilities can be reduced if you offset business expenses against gross profit.

3 VAT: if your turnover will be over the annual limit set by the Government you must register for VAT. In certain other circumstances it will be worth you registering if your turnover is below this threshold: if you are a net payer of VAT, i.e. you pay more than you receive, as you should be able to reclaim the difference. VAT returns have to be prepared on a quarterly basis. If in doubt as to whether to register you should read the official guide from the Customs and Excise office or ask your accountant.

4 If you are to employ people on a regular basis you will be required to give them a written statement of their terms of employment and you will also be responsible for paying their income tax and National Insurance contributions. You should keep your local tax office advised of the financial payments made to each employee and your local Contributions Agency will be able to advise you on what amounts of NI should be paid by you as the employer based on the sums you pay your employees.

5 Financial accounts have to be prepared on an annual basis. You should seek advice on business accounting before preparing your accounts. If you are a limited company with a turnover over a certain size you will be required to get your accounts independently audited by professional accountants.

6 Most importantly, when you set up your own business you should review your personal finances. Check that you have adequate provision for your pension, life assurance and health insurance. See the appropriate sections in the **Money** chapter.

Also make sure that the Inland Revenue and the DSS are informed about your business.

MANAGEMENT

- Keep all your records up to date and monitor your cash inflow and outflow very carefully.
- Regularly measure your performance against your business plan and keep any relevant parties informed of any variances.
- Make sure you have good professional advisers and use them sensibly.
- Do not run before you can walk; build up your business on a steady basis that you can maintain. Don't expand too quickly.

TECHNO-LOGY

Some people have integrated 'technology' so smoothly into their lives that their 'gadgets' become almost an extension of their limbs. For others, the word alone can inspire instant panic. Those who discover how much life can be improved with a basic grasp of technology often undergo a strange transformation akin to religious conversion. On the other hand, an excessive dependence can lead to a social life limited to 'virtual friends' and a severe case of 'Carpal Tunnel Syndrome'.

Though we may not 'feel' technologically advanced, most of the things we do are influenced by technology, sometimes without our being aware. There are computer chips in virtually every technical instrument we touch – from the telephone and TV remote control to the microwave and cashpoint. Women, who are generally more wary of 'high technology' than men, have emerged, ironically, as being particularly adept. Our instinctive lateral thinking is perfectly attuned to 'computer logic'.

This chapter guides you through the general computing systems currently available, the Internet and web-sites, cyber health, mobile phones, faxes and gadgets. Through the A–Z of Cyberspeak you can impress (or irritate) your friends with the vocabulary of a 'super dweeb'.

PCS AND MACS

The computer, screen, keyboard and mouse are now as familiar as the microwave. Receiving e-mail and surfing the Net are a part of daily life in most offices and a growing number of homes around the country. Computers have revolutionized the way we work and computer communications are the main reason why more and more people can and do work from home.

The latest and possibly most significant development is the arrival of the Internet which has millions of users worldwide. With such vast amounts of information at our fingertips, the big question must be, what the hell are we going to do with it all?

GETTING TECHNICAL

Before deciding to enrich your lifestyle with any new chip-based equipment, identify your needs – not just in terms of what type of model you need, but whether you need it at all. The computer manufacturers rely on someone buying the latest up-to-date thing – it doesn't have to be you. However, hardware manufacturers have found that the business market is saturated and they are now targeting the domestic market and radically simplifying the PC. They want to make it as standard a household appliance as your vacuum cleaner. They have already developed prototype PCs which can be built into your TV set and are net linked to different software packages. As soon as they can get the production costs down you can kiss your old-fashioned Teletext goodbye.

What the hell is a bit, byte, RAM, ROM, CPU, VDU or Jpeg and is it contagious? There is currently a huge drive for computer literacy in schools and there is no shortage of expensive conferences and courses around.

MAC V. IBM

Although 'Personal Computer' (PC) actually refers to the desktop technology pioneered and licensed by IBM, it was in fact Apple who produced the first really personal computer. Their Graphical User Interface (GUI) was much simpler to use than the text-based operating system needed for IBMs (MS-DOS: Microsoft Disk Operating System) and 'user friendly' was what was needed for computers to break through to the masses. But Macs (as Apple Macintosh computers came to be known) didn't develop the same kind of market share as MS-DOS systems and, since they didn't license their technology to manufacturers who could bang out cheaper versions (clones), they were always considerably more expensive. IBM on the other hand licensed their operating system to other companies who created computers that could support the same software as each other. By not licensing their system Apple remained elitist but it quickly became apparent that it wasn't the computer that was important but the software. Because millions of people had bought Compaq, Brother, Olivetti, ICL/Fujitsu, Packard Bell or Escom machines, companies like Microsoft were able to make zillions of dollars selling them software that they had developed for the IBM operating system. As a result, almost 90% of computer users have IBM type hardware.

From now on we shall refer to PCs (i.e. IBM compatible) and Macs.

If you are working in a way that requires word-processing, spreadsheet, accountancy or Internet software then a suitably powered PC will be all you require. These machines are designed for work like this and the introduction of Microsoft Windows which copies the user friendliness of the Mac has made it even easier.

The Internet is following suit and with systems like 'Java' and 'VRML' (Virtual Reality Modelling Language) readily available for MS-DOS, online designers are already switching over. However Apple have a remarkably loyal following especially in the visual arts. This may be because in the design business, many of the people who output designers' work are kitted with Apple technology. Until this end of the business changes, most artists and designers will probably continue to buy Macintosh products.

COMPUTER BASICS

- All computers need to run an Operating System: the software that allows you to use the hardware, e.g. Windows 95 or Mac OS 7 and UNIX. All come with some basic versions of the most commonly used software – like word-processing, drawing, fax and scheduling, but you'll have to acquire full versions of the software that you need in order to be fully operational.
- Bytes, megabytes and gigabytes: byte is the unit which is used to measure the capacity for storage and operational power of your computer. One megabyte is approximately one million bytes, and one gigabyte or gig approximately one thousand million bytes.
- All computers have a Hard Drive. Hard drive is 'storage' capacity. This is where software – and all that's created with the software (i.e. files containing letters, designs, proposals etc.) – is stored. A new computer with the latest software usually has a 1-gigabyte hard drive. If you find you are running out of space you can connect an external hard drive which allows you to back up or store your information on disk.
- It is very important to *back up* all your work on the computer as sometimes things can go wrong and you can lose work. *Back up* means copying it onto disks and storing them.
- All computers use Random Access Memory (RAM): RAM size is 'doing' capacity. It is also measured in megabytes (MB) and is sometimes referred to simply as memory. The more of this you have, the more your computer can do at the same time. The minimum currently needed to run Windows 95 or Mac OS 7+ is about 8 MBs but you should try and get 16 MBs or more.
- All computers use processors to run. The most powerful processor in common use for Windows is Intel's Pentium Pro. Intel are not the only processor manufacturers although they and

Microsoft have successfully given this impression. Others such as AMD and CYRIX are as good and sometimes cheaper.

- All computers depend not only on chips for their power but also on the clock speed of their processor. This is measured in megahertz (MHz). PCs available right now have anything from 90–200+ MHz processors – and they're getting faster all the time.
- You can find out more in the *Idiot's Guide to Computers* by Angus Kennedy.

BUYING A PC

The cyber world moves fast so ALWAYS check magazines like *Computer Shopper* or *Mac User* for the latest models, prices and new developments in technology. Also use any pre-sales support offered by retailers and manufacturers. It is also possible to rent computers from some rental shops, Radio Rentals for example: look in your local telephone directory for your nearest shop. The advantages are that you can upgrade the equipment and may get some service support. If you can afford it, you might want to speak to a computer consultant.

A TYPICAL AD

When you're scanning computer ads you might find something like the following:

Multimedia (including CD-ROM, Sound Card, Video Card, speakers). Desktop System with SVGA 15 inch Monitor. Pentium. Processor speed: 120 MHz with 8 MB RAM upgradable to 40 MB. 1.2 gig hard drive. 28.8Kbps internal modem.

Use the **A–Z of Cyberspeak** at the end of this chapter to decipher it until you are more familiar with the lingo. Then decide what you need.

BUYER'S TIPS

You need to know a little bit to arm yourself against salespeople on commission.

- Get as much RAM and processor speed (MHz) as you possibly can for your money. The larger the memory, the more you pay but the higher the performance.

- Hard drive space is the cheapest of all hardware components, it's getting cheaper all the time and can be upgraded.
- The processor regulates the speed at which your PC deals with information, among other things. It will be important for playing any of the high-powered games on the market or graphics applications. The higher the figures given, the faster a computer will work. Discuss the range at length with the salesperson.
- Go for software first. Keep in mind what you want to do with it, then choose your PC. For example if you intend to use your computer for word-processing, retrieving and sending e-mail and basic accountancy, then you do NOT need to spend a fortune on a top-of-the-line multimedia set up. However if you want to do all those things, your 12-year-old son wants to play computer games and your daughter is a budding graphic designer, you might want to take this into account.
- Don't buy software or hardware without support, see below.
- Lots of systems come with 'bundles' of software included in the price. Make sure you actually want or need this before being taken in by the 'great value' sales pitch.
- *Which? Computer* magazine recommends waiting for software or PCs that have been on the market for at least six months and have had any problems ironed out.
- Remember, the price you see is not the price you pay. Once you start investing in support fees, insurance, extra software, ink cartridges, magazines, floppy disks for back-up copies, 'How To' books etc., you've doubled the ticket. Ask about the potential costs of these: they do vary from computer to computer.
- Try to choose equipment you can upgrade or exchange when you feel it's obsolete (usually within three years), including upgrading memory, processor and the monitor.
- Your system should also have technical support and a telephone service. Check whether there's a charge for this.

SUPPORT

Unlike the US, the UK doesn't have computer

helplines where the price of the call covers the charge. Your manufacturer should offer you at least a year of post-sales support with a helpline number, for free or very little. Alternatively you can take out a contract with a local call-out service, or get on the Net: newsgroups particularly are mines of computer information. In the beginning you will be surprised at how much you can sort out by reading the manuals and the more experienced you get, the less intimidating it all is.

LAPTOPS/NOTEBOOKS

As handy as an attaché case, the laptop – and its smaller cousin, the notebook – are becoming as powerful as desktop PCs and if you can afford it this is the way to go. They make your personal and professional life truly portable. Their 'liquid crystal display' screens are better for your eyes and built in fax/modem links mean you are never out of touch. Laptops are about a third more expensive than same spec desktop versions.

BUYING LAPTOPS/NOTEBOOKS

- Apple PowerBooks are the fashionable choice and are reasonably priced but there are many IBM ones available also.
- Be wary of buying a laptop from a lesser known company as the components are not as interchangeable as they are for desktop models, and repairs may be tricky.
- The same rules apply for RAM, chip, processor speed and hard drive space as for desktops (see above).
- Don't forget to check out the life and weight of batteries: a major consideration.

- The real difference – and the major influence on cost – is the quality of the screen. The important considerations are size, clarity, precision and how distorting the effects of angle seem to be. The bigger, clearer and less prone to distortion the laptop, the greater the price tag, although flat screen technology is advancing rapidly and prices are coming down.
- If you're intending to use your laptop at home as well as on the move it is worth investing in a docking station which allows you to connect up to a full size keyboard, monitor and mouse.

CD-ROM

ROM stands for Read Only Memory: this is a disk of stored information that you cannot write onto. However there are now relatively inexpensive CD writers (approx £500) which would be worth investing in if you are a photographer and want to distribute your portfolio to a large number of people. What's revolutionary about them is how much information they store (the equivalent of 350 600 MB floppy disks); the diversity of what can be stored (anything from a complete set of encyclopaedias to books); and the quality with which stored graphics can be delivered.

BUYING INTO CD-ROM

- The CDs are expensive and often gimmicky, rather than important or educational. Read as many magazine reviews as you can before splashing out.
- To access a CD-ROM you need a CD-ROM drive. You can buy them separately, as a feature external to a PC, but the likelihood is that if you're buying a PC now it will automatically come with a built-in CD-ROM drive.
- If you do decide to buy an external drive, remember that apart from the drive itself you will also need speakers, sufficient processor speed (around 120 MHz), 40cm screen, sound card, video card and at least 8MB of RAM.
- Your CD-ROM drive will also play your favourite music CDs while you work.

BUYING A PRINTER

The chances are the PC you buy will have a natural printer choice as partner, though this is not always the case. The same rules apply to buying printers as they do to computers: research your actual and projected needs. There are many different kinds and qualities: colour, laser, bubble jet, ink jet, and some have the added value of being portable or can double up as fax machine's copiers and even scanners. You can get colour printers at very reasonable rates now but the inks are expensive and don't last long.

THE NET

William Gibson coined the term cyberspace in his science-fiction fantasy novel, *Neuromancer* (1984). In the novel it refers to a near-future computer network where users mentally travel through matrices of data. The images cyberspace: it is the combination of interlocking electronic technology working globally to enable the transmission, storage and retrieval of information. It is a communications facility that passes through space and time – accessed at the touch of a button. It is a giant open phone call.

THE INTERNET

The Internet is currently the fastest growing media. Provided you have the technology, the Internet (or Net) can offer you access to information about anything from anywhere. Essentially it is made up of hundreds of small networks of computers which are connected by the international phone system and other dedicated links. To connect to the Net you need a modem (approx. £100 for the fastest 33.6 Kbps) and a subscription to one of the main servers or providers. You can buy these over the phone (approx. £130 per annum plus the cost of the calls): find servers' ads in the back of computer mags and ring around for subscription prices and level of support. The server will provide you with basic software which you install on your computer and use to log on or access the Net. When you are logged on you are essentially making a phone call but despite the fact that you are getting information from Japan you will only be paying local call rates. In the US local calls are free, watch out for offers from telecom providers.

Eventually it will affect every aspect of our lives. It is changing the very nature of computing as we speak and before long it's probable that everyday gadgets around the home or in the car will be linked by microcomputers that communicate with each other via the Net. Think of the Net as the early stages of telephones, television, radio and film rolled into one. Read the *Rough Guide to the Internet and the World Wide Web* and *Wired* magazine.

NET HISTORY

The Net's inception at the end of the 60s was fuelled by Cold War paranoia. The US military, frightened that their communications system could be wiped out by one nuclear attack, developed the Advanced Research Projects Agency Network (ARPANET). It used Internet Protocol (IP) to split up files into packages of data that contained the address of the destination computer. Through this packaging, data could travel in small chunks, each taking the best 'route' to its destination. Should a route be cut off, the data would take another one to get through. Essentially, it was a decentralizing process relying on a collaborative method, linking each individual computer. Since there was no central server – no 'hub' – there was no single target. This is the process on which the Net is based. By the late 70s most academic institutions (familiar with and excited by networking technology) had started to use ARPANET as a means of linking research projects all over the world. Eventually they adopted it as a very simple, efficient way to communicate. In the late 80s the US government set up the National Science Foundation where another network – NSFNET – was launched along the same lines and by the early 90s this was open to commercial traffic. Then came Tim Berners-Lee's World Wide Web.

WWW: THE WORLD WIDE WEB

The Web is the first major graphical Net application. All previous applications were text based. And – as IBM learned with the GUI issue – graphics are user-friendly and user-friendliness is

all. There are thousands of websites, and most of them are free to access. No one owns the Internet and the same is true of the Web. You can source foam plastics in Indiana or have virtual sex on an erotic chatline.

The Web uses a system called Hyper Text Transfer Protocol (HTTP) by which pages of information can be crosslinked in such a way that the user can explore related pages by clicking on a highlighted word or symbol. Web pages – information databases – are linked by the Hypertext system and can be read on screen (or 'navigated') by installing browser software.

Web pages are basically a collection of images, text and often sound which can be accessed by a browser and read on screen. Anyone can design their own Web page and put it on the Net.

Browsers are continually becoming more sophisticated and, since the revolution of 'Netscape 2' in 1996, accessing images as slick as those in film or TV is standard. More exciting still are the plug-ins, softcodes and clips which the manufacturers of Netscape 2 licensed. These have led to the advent of Net telephony – where you can actually speak alongside your other modes of communicating. This means you can not only have a conference call regarding a piece of, say, proposed engineering, but you can have it between Sydney, Boston and Paris (at local-rate call tariffs) and actually edit the design simultaneously on screen. As you can imagine the phone companies are not so sure that this is a great idea. Call up the various Cybercafés listed.

PROS AND CONS

Currently the mean age of all users is 31: 62% are male, 87% white and 65% North American, but the demographics are evening out all the time.

Pros
- The Net is an incredibly useful, practical and inexpensive way of communicating.
- Keep in contact with people worldwide at low cost.
- Access information, from libraries, museums, public companies, anywhere!

- It functions as a 'community service'. Assistance, advice, moral support etc. are readily available: a lifeline for those whose human contact is minimalized by illness, geographical isolation, restricting dependants etc.

Cons
- Time and expense of down-loading information can be frustrating.
- Standard of websites can be variable.
- If you have children, access should be monitored because of the danger of pornography on the Internet.

CREATING A WEBSITE
There are over ten million websites, with thousands more appearing each day – and most are accessed free. Sites used to be written in old-fashioned code but with developments on the graphics front it will soon be easier. If you feel you or your company would benefit from having the cyber equivalent of a magazine you can hire a professional outfit to design it for you. Alternatively if you are a small business and you can't afford to spend much on design, most of the schools or technical colleges in your area are training young people to create websites and they would probably be happy to help. Speak to website publishers like Site City Co UK.
It is important to take note of the security measures when creating a website.

TO GET ON THE NET
You need the following:
- **A computer:** the type is immaterial, either a Mac or a PC with adequate computer memory, 4 megabytes of RAM is the absolute minimum for a basic browser.
- **A phone line:** the Net works by connecting computers through the telephone system at, usually, the lowest local-call rate. (It may depend on where you live.)
- **A modem:** the device that converts data into beeps and whistles which can be transmitted down the phone line. The modem's speed is very important: the faster the modem translates signals sent from your computer to others on the Internet, the faster the information will return.

Right now the most common speed is 28.8K but look for the 33.6K or even 56K modems that are just coming on the market.
- **An Internet Service Provider (ISP)** supplies a local Internet connection to you (see below). It's important to choose one that has a local access number to minimize the cost of using the telephone. Most ISPs will also offer you the option of renting space on their computers or servers where you can house your own website – either as an individual or a company.
- **Software** that allows you to browse the Web, send e-mail and use any of the other myriad Net communications.

MODEMS
- Most new multimedia systems have internal modems fitted.
- If you have an older PC you will need to get a peripheral modem – these are fairly cheap.
- Some laptops now come with built-in fax modems which allow you to get onto the Net. But if yours doesn't, you will need to get a PC Card Modem – a credit card sized device that slots into the side of the laptop. Some of these now have cellular phone capabilities.
- If you have a business, you might be offered an ISDN connection by a telecom company. This is a system of telephony which allows speeds of up to 128,000 bits per second on two channels. The advantage is that if you deal in large files of images (as an artist or graphic designer, for example) you can transmit them at much faster rates but it is expensive.
- Remember, text files take up the fewest bits; image and sound are next (with greater quality of definition increasing the amount); video takes up the most.

INTERNET SERVICE PROVIDERS (ISPS)
There are more and more ISPs being set up, but it's more than likely, given that customer service and billing infrastructures already exist for them, that in the end major telecom companies will provide the most competitive services.

Remember:
- Along with the speed of your modem, the quality

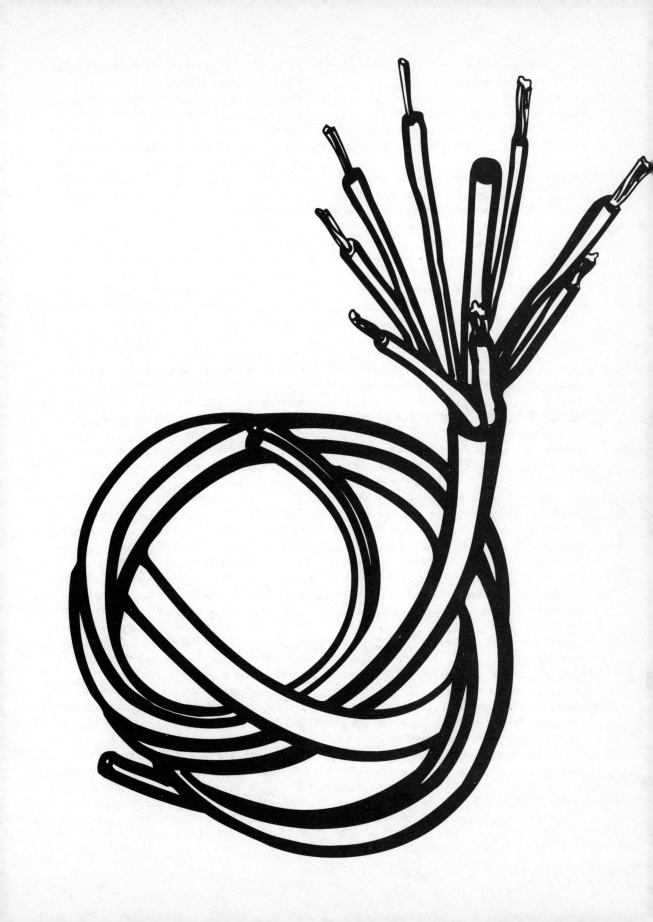

of your chosen server affects how quickly information downloads (i.e. appears) onto your screen.

- Before selecting, thoroughly check Net magazines for reviews and information regarding ISPs.
- Look for an ISP that offers full Internet access at a flat fee per month.
- Any up-front connection fee should be small.
- All ISPs should offer you a package of software (like Netscape or Microsoft Internet Explorer), e-mail software (like Eudora) and some sort of advice and technical support.
- Choose what is called a PPP account rather than a SLIP for your e-mail. This means that you can Telnet in to get your mail from elsewhere.
- If you travel a lot, using a laptop, make sure your ISP has a local phone number wherever you happen to be going. Otherwise you'll rack up major bills.
- If you are abroad a lot, consider getting an account with an online service like CompuServe which has access numbers all over the world.

ONLINE SERVICE PROVIDERS (OSPS)

Online Service Providers like CompuServe are private 'gateways' to the Internet – like websites – which have content and areas that you can only visit if you pay their rates for online time. If the Net were to be compared to a city, online services would be shopping centres with pre-selected shops, restaurants and clubs – all sanitized for your protection. Until now all online services have had their own, easy to use, software, but as the Web is gaining in popularity, almost all are transferring their services to Web-based systems, although they remain behind password protected areas.

Remember, online services:

- give you access to the Net, but not to its users;
- have easy-to-use software, so can be a good introduction to being online;
- have local access points all over the Web;
- are expensive because you pay a flat rate per month plus a certain amount per hour;
- are very slow and demand their own browsing software.

NEWSGROUPS

There are newsgroups on almost any subject imaginable – from breast cancer to Elvis sightings. If you need a hotel in a remote region in India, you can contact a travel newsgroup; if you want someone to translate a piece of Urdu to Finnish you can send messages to the most appropriate newsgroups available and they'll let you know who to call up. Newsgroups are, essentially, linked users providing professional or enthusiast information to anyone who applies to them via the Net.

Remember

- To connect to a newsgroup you need to ensure that your ISP gives access to them.
- Because there are many thousands of them, selecting the ones you would like to connect with or read on a regular basis is arduous.
- Judicious use of newsgroups can be an incredible source of information, but if you send them multiple and inappropriate messages (i.e. perform 'spamming'), you'll be severely ranted at by outraged users ('flamed').
- Newsgroups, because of their incredible power to disseminate information to large numbers of people, are seen as dangerous by repressive governments. China has vetoed ISPs offering access to their customers.

E-MAIL

Electronic-mail or e-mail is the most incredible development in communications since the phone. While wondering at its glory, note that:

- The most popular e-mail software is 'Eudora'. You can download a version free from the Net and, if you like it, get a licence for the pro version. Alternatively, if you use Netscape or Internet Explorer you will be able to use the built-in e-mail software that allows you to see and create e-mail that looks like a web page.
- When you attach a file it needs to be encoded for it to travel to its destination. Your e-mail program will seamlessly handle this process, provided you're set up to work with the right encoders: 'U Encode' for IBM type PCs, 'BinHex' for Macs or 'MIME' for graphics, video and voice on either.
- If you are sending large files (anything bigger than 2MBs), compress it using something like 'WinZip' for PCs or 'Stuffit' for Macs. Sending a

large file to an unsuspecting destination can severely tie up the machine at the receiving end.
- Every new operating system has a built in e-mailer that interfaces with your 'address book'.

INTERNET RELAY CHAT (IRC)

Internet Relay Chat is a way to chat live – i.e. in real time – to users all over the globe via text. As with newsgroups, there are any number of discussions on any topic going on at any one time. Increasingly, there are methods of carrying on Web-based chat straight off a web page – some even allowing you to use speech if you have a sound card and microphone.

AVATARS

These are graphic or iconic representations of 'you yourself' – your proxy in virtual reality. Their use has led to all kinds of debates and ethical questions regarding self-presentation over the Net: behind the avatar of a 20-year-old bloke, for example, may be a 40-year-old woman.

VIRTUAL REALITY MODELLING LANGUAGE (VRML)

Now that we are familiar with the idea of pseudo sensations offered by the goggles and gloves of virtual reality, VRML allows us to create 3-D worlds accessible from all over the Net. Some of these are multi-user – your own and others' avatars interacting in VR space.

INTERNET PHONE

Provided you have microphone, sound card and speakers there are a number of new ways in which you can use the Net like a phone. The main advantage is that you can, for example, access your ISP in London at off-peak, local rates and speak to Washington for the price of a local call.

VIRUSES

These are little programs that can infect and possibly damage your computer operating system or the applications run on it. You can pick them up by loading an infected file from a floppy disk or downloading one from the Net.
- **Note**: protect your PC by running an anti-viral protection program (e.g. Norton or Dr Solomon).

- As with viruses that attack humans, there are new strains all the time so make sure you get regular updates from software manufacturers to ensure full protection.

NETNASTY

Nobody governs or owns all of the Net: as a global enterprise it is ungovernable. This makes it useful for lowlife and criminal activity and there is a lot of dubious stuff on it. 20% of Internet time is used looking at pornography, and setting up rings for those with illegal sexual predilections is disturbingly straightforward online. The laws of whatever land you live in obviously apply to you and your activities but with the Net it is possible to carry on an illegal enterprise which is run from a server in another country altogether. It is becoming a legal minefield and yet another way for lawyers to earn a fast buck.

Remember

- There are ISPs (like BBC Networking Club) that will edit on your behalf.
- Install software like Net Nanny or Surf Patrol to police the websites your children see.
- The law is the law, even in cyberspace. If you get caught, you go to jail.
- The rules of copyright also apply in cyberspace. If you steal someone's work and put it on your website you are doing something illegal. However, geography and borders do complicate the issue.

CYBER HEALTH

Health issues in cyberspace are as real as in any other environment. Net use is isolating, and detachment from social contact can encourage or exacerbate agoraphobic or depressive conditions. Working on (or simply pleasure surfing) the Internet is also very compelling and those with addictive tendencies should take it easy. Visual impairment through over-exposure to VDUs, and Carpal Tunnel Syndrome (where the tendons and muscles of the wrist get damaged) through

prolonged mouse use CAN happen to you.

Remember

If you're working at your computer for long periods:

- Take regular breaks.
- Take walks outside whenever possible.
- Rest your eyes by looking out of the window at all the non-cyber elements of your environment like the birds or trees or the bloke next door.
- Use a wrist rest or interchange mouse use with a trackball or lightpen.
- Don't cut yourself off from real people. Make sure you're interacting with others frequently. If you feel the slightest anxiety about seeing people or going outside, get help – preferably from real (rather than cyber) friends or an actual GP.
- If you find there is a compulsive element to your using the Internet or playing games or if you feel it's dominating your life to the exclusion of most other activities, seek help – again preferably from real people!

TELEMATICS/AUDIO VISUAL CONNECTIONS

- With the Net connecting audio-visual computers, it will soon be possible for multimedia work-stations to be fully operational. That is, working from home – with video-phone connections open, and clients and colleagues on screen for the occasional conference – is about to be truly feasible. Telematics will improve efficiency (fewer interruptions, fewer human excuses for a break), and reduce stress (no rush hour, home comfort). But they may lead to increased depressive and agoraphobic disorders (see above).

GADGETS

MOBILE PHONES

Because it has become such an enormous market, the cost of buying and running a mobile has fallen dramatically in the last ten years. As choice widens further, costs will continue to fall. Deciding on a mobile can be confusing, not because of the phone itself but because the choice of airtime packages, the networks and billing systems almost appear endless. Many

mobiles are subsidized with a network package which makes research critical before buying. The quality for reception, speech and transmission can vary greatly.

THE PACKAGE

The same mobile packages don't vary too much in price from one shop to another. The variety is usually in the cost of each of the four components that make up the package:

1 the phone itself
2 connection to a network (there are three types of network – see below)
3 the monthly subscription charge
4 your phone calls

THE PHONE ITSELF

Before buying consider each of the following factors with regard to your needs:

- **Size/weight:** is it for your car? handbag? pocket?
- **Battery performance:** how often will you have a chance to recharge? Sometimes there's a trade off between weight and battery-life.
- **Features:** nearly all mobiles store numbers for speed dialling but how many? More sophisticated phones have things like one-touch access to features such as voicemail, clock/alarm and data capability. Get the features you need: don't pay for ones you don't.
- **After-sales service:** most mobile deals offer at least one year's manufacturer's warranty. Some come with three.

TYPES OF NETWORK

There are three types of mobile phone network:

1 **Analogue** (Vodaphone and Cellnet): best for people in the UK countryside as it gives you comprehensive coverage.
2 **GSM Digital** (Global System for Mole Communication – Vodafone and Cellnet): best used in urban areas. If you want to use the phone outside the UK then go with GSM.
3 **PCN Digital** (Personal Communication Network – Orange and Mercury One to One): best if you are based in one city and will mainly use it locally. The network operator (e.g. Cellnet, Mercury) is the company that runs the actual system which allows you to make a mobile call. They sell airtime

to companies called service providers, who then charge you for the calls you make and set the terms of your contract. Dealers and retailers generally use service providers to connect you to a network.

To contact the right service provider and so access the best network and tariff for you, the sales person has to be given the following information:

- Approximately how many and what length of calls you are likely to make in a given week.
- Whether you will mainly use the phone 9–5, Monday to Friday or outside business hours.
- Whether you will mainly be receiving calls or making them.
- Whether you will need to use the phone to make and receive calls abroad, throughout the UK or locally.
- Will you need to use the Internet, send faxes etc.
- Whether you will need a message service: ask them whether there's a charge for it, and if so, how much.

BEFORE SIGNING UP

Always read the small print on the contract and make sure to check out the following:

- Full details of the differences between the many services, phones on offer and tariffs. Check the peak times for calling and ask whether Saturday is included as a work day.
- Network coverage: where in the country/ EU/world you can and cannot use your phone.
- Details of extra network services available e.g. CallBack, and the costs.
- If an itemized billing service is available and whether or not you're charged for it.
- If the cost includes insurance against theft, damage and fraud (see below).
- Who your service provider is.
- If there is a trial period.
- What kind of customer care is available (e.g. is a replacement phone offered while yours is out of action?).
- The exact details of the contract, how long it's for, what penalty clauses it includes if you want to end or change the agreement.
- Whether you can upgrade or change network at a later date, and whether you're charged for this.

INSURING YOUR MOBILE

At least 15,000 mobile phones are stolen every month, others are lost or dropped. Insuring against this and replacement costs is essential: phone thieves specialize in long distance calls. Even if your package includes some insurance, check it thoroughly – it may be worth your while taking out a more comprehensive policy. The phone may be cheap initially because it's subsidized by your network agreement, but a replacement phone might cost a lot more.

PAGERS

In the US more than 19 million people carry a pager, but here in the UK they're still quite a novelty. Most are run by telecom companies and the price of the actual pager is your only outlay (approx. £100) as the person paging you pays for the call: examples are BT's Swatch the Beep or Motorola. Alternatively, you can pay monthly rental fees.

Essentially, pagers are little boxes that clip to your belt or sit in your bag, which bleep, buzz or flash when someone's trying to get in touch with you. The number of the caller is digitally displayed and you find the nearest phone and return the call. You can have features such as:

- 24-hour answering service
- voice messaging
- your own home/office answering machine or voicemail service paging you to call in for messages
- auto-timing to specify the hours the pager is on
- locked number recording where pages are banked up until you have returned the call and want to delete them
- silent mode, i.e. a light simply flashes or vibrates – for when you are in meetings, etc.

CONTRACTS

Before signing, find out:

- the range of the telecom networks used: check how far away you the pager can reach
- whether the rental is fixed and competitive
- whether there is a replacement service in the case of loss, theft or accidental damage
- how long the warranty is for and whether insurance is offered

AESTHETICS

As with mobiles, make sure you consider:

- Size and weight: is it for your belt? handbag? pocket?
- Battery performance: how often will you have a

chance to recharge? Remember the trade off between weight and battery life.
• Style and feel.

PAGER V. MOBILE

If you want to be traceable, but don't necessarily want to be tracked, pagers are ideal. They mean that callers can let you know they're contacting you but that you can speak to them (or not) at your leisure. It gives you time to compose yourself before speaking to colleagues, bosses, spouses etc. They are a cheaper, smaller way of being available without being hassled.

LIKELY USERS

Apart from doctors, a lot of former pager users (like contractors, plumbers, electricians, travelling salespeople) have replaced their bleepers with mobile phones. The most obvious candidates now are:
• People operating their own business who can't be tied to the phone.
• Working parents who have children with child-minders/in nursery etc., but are not always available on one particular number.
• Partners of pregnant people who cannot be located at one venue.
• Carers of sick or elderly people who have to be out and about but contactable.
• The young and social: those worried about theft, or wanting to avoid being weighed down by the price and bulk of a mobile.

ELECTRONIC ORGANIZERS

On the face of it, electronic organizers look like an expensive way of keeping an address book and diary but the better ones can be more like mini-laptops.

PALMTOP COMPUTING

Some organizers are the digital equivalent of the Filofax with a few very simple functions featured. They store addresses, numbers and memos very efficiently and allow you to access them by pressing a couple of keys. Information doesn't get crumpled, torn or stained, and outdated stuff is easily deleted. There are no endless crossings out, arrows and scribbled reminders. But on the

other hand unless you can back up your information, if you lose the machine, you lose the lot. The main difference between cheap and pricey organizers is the amount of memory – the more kilobytes(k) the more information can be stored. For around £100 you will get basic memory.

Good personal organizers can feature
• word-processing with spellchecker
• spreadsheet options for financial forecasting
• modem for faxing and e-mail
• web browser
• dictaphone
• alarm mechanism

BEFORE BUYING

As always, only buy what you need: don't pay for features you're never likely to use.

Remember
• Try to calculate how much data you'll want to store. Generally the range is between 32KB to 1MB – but unlike PCs you can't upgrade your organizer with more memory if you run out (though some models do come with mini flash cards for memory and software).
• Talk to as many people as possible who use them on a daily basis: they'll give you the real lowdown.
• Try out as many in the shop as the salesperson can stand.
• Don't be impressed by a handwriting recognition facility as they are all pretty useless.

FAX

Using telecom systems, fax machines transmit and receive images (as opposed to data like e-mail), translating them into sound or beeps for transmission and converting these back into images on reception. The sender dials and feeds the image (written or drawn on paper) into the apparatus. Inside it is scanned and sent out over telephone lines. PCs/laptop computers can have a built-in fax/modem which you can use to send and receive faxes, although it won't receive faxes whilst the machine is turned off.

There are two main types of fax machine:

1 Uses sheets of A4 plain paper: these are quite expensive, £300–£500, and are bulky.
2 Uses special thermal paper: generally cheaper at £200–£400 and more compact.

FAX FACTS

- Faxes are fast, ubiquitous (virtually no office is without one) and simple to use.
- Inexpensive fax machines use thermal paper which comes on a roll and is shiny on one side. It can fade – your document simply disappears – so photocopy anything important.
- On the whole, it is better (though more expensive) to use plain paper fax machines.
- Good models often also function as phones, answering machines, photocopiers and PC printers.
- Remember, since a fax is an image not data you cannot edit or modify it, as you can with e-mail.
- A fax machine is a same-day delivery and reply station.
- A fax can be recognised as a legal document, but must be followed up with a posted hard copy.
- Unsolicited faxes (including junk mail) can be a nuisance. Dial 1471 to trace origin.
- Fax culture is rain-forest hell: a lot of paper is used, often to say very little.

A–Z OF CYBERSPEAK

- **Agent:** search tools that seek out relevant online information or help perform some task, based on your specifications. Also called intelligent agents, personal agents, knowbots and droids.
- **Anchor:** on the Web, the words/images in hypertext to be clicked on to connect to another page/resource.
- **Anchor colour:** the colour on the screen in which the anchor appears. Usually blue because this is the default colour. Also in red and green or combinations.
- **Applet:** mini application or program.
- **Archie:** derived from the word archive, Archie is a Net-based service that allows you to locate files that can be downloaded via FTP.
- **ASCII:** a standard code for upper and lower case letters, numbers, other symbols and including accented letters for various European languages.
- **Authoring software:** software allowing the creation of multimedia or HTML documents and presentations.
- **Avatar:** graphical or iconic representation of a human in a virtual reality environment. Your 'proxy' in the virtual world.
- **Bandwidth:** the range of transmission frequencies a network can use. The greater the bandwidth, the more information that can be transferred over the network at any one time. Also broadly refers to throughput.
- **Baud:** unit of speed in data transmission, or the maximum speed at which data can be sent down a channel. Often the equivalent of bits per second.
- **Bit:** smallest unit of information a computer can hold. Eight bits are a byte. The speed at which bits are transmitted is usually expressed as bps (bits per second).
- **Booting up:** the computer's assimilation and attainment of instructions: the start up routine once it has been switched on.
- **Browser:** software that allows you to navigate information databases (e.g. on the WWW 'Microsoft Internet Explorer', 'Netscape Navigator', 'NCSA Mosaic').
- **Bug:** flaw in the performance of a piece of software. Software is often put on to the Net in alpha or beta versions before it is released in its final version. This is to allow users to put it through its paces, i.e. discover its bugs.
- **Byte:** number of bits used to represent one character of text. Consequently also broadly refers to the space/energy that a disk or machine can store/work up to.
- **Card modem:** credit-card-sized peripheral modem for slotting into laptop PCs.
- **Carpal Tunnel Syndrome:** damage to the tendons and muscles of the wrist and arm through prolonged mouse use.
- **CD-ROM** (*Compact Disk-Read Only Memory*): permanent data storage. Capacity approx. 650MB.
- **CD-ROM drive:** mechanism necessary for accessing CD-ROMs, either built into or peripheral

to the PC.

- **Chip:** short for microchip. Silicon manufactured to function like a complex wired circuit.
- **CPU:** central processing unit, i.e. the processor.
- **Crash:** when a data overload, software malfunction or bug shuts down computer functions.
- **Cursor:** the 'pointer' locating your position on screen, controlled by you via mouse or keyboard.
- **CuSeeMe:** system allowing you to view the person you're communicating with and to present yourself to them. A Connectix camera is attached to your computer and you are connected to a reflector where you can see and be seen by other users all over the world.
- **CyberMall:** describes an electronic site shared by a number of commercial interests.
- **Cyberspace:** coined in a 1984 novel by William Gibson, now used to describe the Internet and other computer networks.
- **Desktop system:** PC hardware configuration designed for the desk.
- **Dial-up connection:** most popular form of Net connection for the home user, i.e. a connection from you to the host computer via standard telephone lines.
- **Digital camera/Digital video camera:** cameras which store images digitally as bits.
- **Direct connection:** permanent connection between your computer and the Internet. Also called a leased-line connection because the line is leased from a telecom company.
- **Docking station:** the peripheral necessary for connecting a laptop to a desktop system.
- **Download:** transferring to your computer a copy of a file residing on another computer.
- **EDE:** Electronic Data Exchange. System allowing linked computers to conduct business transactions (such as ordering and invoicing) over telecommunications networks.
- **E-mail:** electronic mail sent from one computer to another via the Internet.
- **Encode:** often means conversion of pictures/programs to text for transmission.
- **Encryption:** software used to encode very private documents so that they cannot be accessed except by those you intend to see them (e.g. 'PGP' – Pretty Good Privacy).
- **External hard drive:** back-up system which plugs in to your computer and allows you to store your work off the computer hard drive.
- **External viewer:** software used to present graphics, audio and video files.
- **FAQ:** acronym for Frequently Asked Questions. Common feature on the Net: read FAQs before wasting electrons asking obvious questions.
- **Files:** documents stored on floppy or hard disk. Files may be word-processed text, graphic, sound, etc.
- **Firewall:** refers to security measures designed to protect a networked system from unauthorized or unwelcome access.
- **Flames:** unwelcome files FTP'd to your computer in response to your inquiry.
- **Floppy disk:** portable storage that magnetically holds data. Alternative to, or providing back-up copies for your hard drive. Capacity: approx. 1.4MB
- **FTP:** File Transfer Protocol. Allows the transfer of files from one computer to another via a phone line or Internet. Used as a verb to describe the act of doing so.
- **GIF:** Graphic Interchange Format. Commonly used file compression format for transferring graphics files to and from online services.
- **Gigabyte:** also gig, 1,000,000,000 bytes.
- **Gopher:** tool used to locate online resources.
- **GUI:** Graphical User Interface. Information and functions displayed graphically on screen, rather than accessed through codes, e.g. Windows.
- **Hard disk/drive:** storage space, permanently installed in your PC, fits into hard drive.
- **Hardware:** any physical piece of computer apparatus: the VDU, the hard drive etc.
- **Host:** computer acting as an information or communications server.
- **Hotlist:** list of frequently used Web locations.
- **HTML:** HyperText Markup Language. Language used to tag parts of a Web document so browsing software will know how to display links, text, graphics and attached media.
- **HTTP:** HyperText Transfer Protocol. Used to link and transfer HyperText documents.
- **HyperLinks:** HyperText connections between web pages.
- **Hypermedia:** HyperText concept used to include linked multiple media.

- **HyperText:** system that allows documents to be cross-linked in such a way that readers can explore related documents by clicking on a related word or symbol. The Web's infrastructure.
- **IAB:** Internet Architecture Board. The council that makes decisions about Internet standards.
- **Icon:** graphic picture image that represents a functioner program within your machine.
- **IETF:** Internet Engineering Task Force. Subgroup of IAB concerned with solving technical problems on the Internet.
- **Interactive:** able to join in and converse with other computer users, online.
- **Interface:** operational program that allows you to converse with a computer – i.e. what accepts your instructions and makes them readable to the computer mechanism.
- **Internal modem:** i.e. one that is built in to the PC, rather than attached/connected.
- **Internet:** decentralized, collaborative communication network relying on individual computers and their use of telecom systems.
- **IP:** Internet Protocol. Set of standards controlling activity on the Net. An IP address is the number assigned to any Internet connected computer.
- **IRC:** Internet Relay Chat. Like newsgroups, but with spoken communication in real time.
- **ISDN:** Integrated Services Digital Network. Fast, dual operated Net connection offering up to 128,000 baud. For sending large files (e.g. those including graphics, video).
- **ISOC:** Internet Society. Formed to support a worldwide information network. Sponsors IAB.
- **ISP:** Internet Service Provider, i.e. the company that offers you access to the Net, PIPEX. DEMON for example.
- **Java:** programming language that allows you to download an applet to your hard drive on a temporary basis, equipping it to 'run' a program for the required duration. If you need a spreadsheet, for example, you download a spreadsheet applet from a web page and create one – after which the applet 'leaves'.
- **JPEG:** Joint Photographic Experts Group. An image compression format used to transfer colour photographs and images. Along with GIF, it's the best way of moving photos over the Web.
- **Laptops:** portable PCs.
- **Links:** see HyperLinks.
- **ListServe:** running database which will e-mail you information.
- **Mac:** Apple Macintosh computer, including their personal computers.
- **MB:** Megabyte, i.e.1,000,000 bytes.
- **Memory:** see RAM.
- **Menu:** list of available applications/commands displayed on screen for simple program use.
- **Metaverse:** virtual, online representation of reality.
- **MHz:** Megahertz. Clock speed measuring, for example, processor speed.
- **MIME:** Multipurpose Internet Mail Extensions. Allows Net users to exchange e-mail messages enhanced with graphics, video and voice.
- **Modem:** converter of digital systems used by a computer, into audio ones that can be sent down a telephone line.
- **Monitor:** computer screen. See VDU.
- **Mouse:** device, peripheral to the computer keyboard that allows you smooth control over your cursor movement around the screen.
- **Mouse pad:** plastic or foam mat providing better mouse traction and protection than desk surfaces.
- **MPEG:** Moving Pictures Expert Group. International standard for video compression and desktop movie presentation. A special viewing application is needed to view MPEG files.
- **MS-DOS:** Microsoft Disk Operating System. First method of computing for the PC. Uses keyed in commands rather than GUI.
- **Multimedia systems:** text, sound, image, animation, video and interactive 3-D environment in the same package.
- **Netlinked:** connected to the Internet.
- **Newsgroups:** running databases offering insight into virtually any subject, accessed through the Net.
- **NFS:** Network File System. Allows different makes of computers running different operating systems to share files and disk storage.
- **Notebooks:** portable PCs, smaller but not necessarily less powerful than laptops.
- **Online:** part of the Internet, connected and fully operational. Up and running: ready to download, receive e-mail, etc.
- **Online Services Provider (OSP):** offer wide

range of customer-only content, such as online information services.

- **Operating System:** basic software necessary to run computers.
- **PC:** Personal Computer. Computers compact enough to sit on your desk.
- **Peripheral:** device linked to but separate from a computer.
- **Plug-in:** mini software mechanism can be downloaded from the Net and installed alongside running software.
- **POP:** Point of Presence. Service provider's location for connecting to users.
- **PPP:** Point-to-Point Protocol. Where phone lines and a modem can be used to connect a computer to the Net.
- **Processor:** the mechanism that works in conjunction with chips to power computer workings.
- **Processor speed:** the clock speed of the processor, measured in MHz and determining computer capability.
- **Protocol:** a set of standards that define how traffic and communications are handled by a computer or network routes.
- **Pulldown:** a type of menu format where the cursor pulls the options list down from a key word or symbol.
- **QuickTime:** digital video standard developed for Macs but now taken up by PCs. Special applications are needed to run QuickTime movies.
- **RAM:** temporary computer memory, can be both read and written to; information is lost when computer is switched off.
- **Router:** communications device designed to transmit signals via the best route possible.
- **Scanner:** peripheral for scanning documents or images and turning them into data files that can be edited by your computer.
- **Search engine:** allows you to enter words, phrases or names and search the Web for sites that contain them.
- **Service Provider:** see ISP.
- **Shareware:** refers to software available to the public. It is free for a limited time.
- **Shockwave:** application allowing you to download animation, sound and video.
- **Software:** programs, applications. Accessed on disks, CD-ROM or downloaded from the Net.
- **Software package:** everything available from a particular manufacturer in their software deal, i.e. the full extent of applications available through it.
- **Sound card:** internal plug-in hardware allows computer to make more advanced sounds.
- **Storage:** hard disks, floppy disks, peripheral drives.
- **SVGA:** Standard Video Graphics Adapter.
- **Telematics:** multimedia workstations.
- **TELNET:** program used for handling data on a remote system.
- **Track ball:** stationary mouse, without a tail, embedded in your laptop, can also be used with desktops.
- **Upgradable:** hardware with the potential to be added to at a later date.
- **Upgrade:** increase or replace memory, or processor, or add components to computer.
- **Upload:** transferring data from your computer to another via disks or the Net.
- **Utilities:** programs for looking after your PC. They check for errors, organize hard disk to optimize its size and prevent crashes, among other functions.
- **VDU:** Visual Display Unit. The box and screen component of your PC.
- **Video card:** Plug-in hardware to connect computer to monitor, or more recently to connect video equipment to computer.
- **VRML:** Virtual Reality Modelling Language – allows creation of 3-D, virtual reality zones that can be accessed across the Net.
- **Web browser:** software allowing user to access HTML documents.
- **Web document:** HTML document you can browse on the Web.
- **Webmaster:** person in charge of administering a WWW site.
- **Web page:** particular page within a website.
- **Website:** zone on the Web specifically designated to an individual, institution or company.
- **Webspace:** the space created by the WWW.
- **Word-processing:** the manipulation of text through computerized editing.
- **WWW:** World Wide Web. HyperText based Internet service used for browsing its resources.

MONEY

Most of us have to work for a living, but after we've earned our money we then have to navigate our way through personal budgets, savings, mortgages, investments, pension plans, wills and health insurance. Women now earn far more than ever before, and it's increasingly important that we know how to handle our money in order to remain in control of it – rather than the other way around. For many of us, budgeting is an alien concept and we associate money with panic. We may know we overspend, but avoid the details with a vague intention to 'cut back and earn more'. Financial institutions – the people who make all their money out of handling ours – are in fierce competition. But what do they really do? And how should we choose between them?

This chapter will guide you through all major money issues from budgeting, personal borrowing and where to go for good financial advice to tips on claiming benefits or avoiding tax on a six-figure salary. A lot of us feel that until we're high earners, there's no point in trying to organize our finances rationally. Equally, on a tight budget, it can seem a waste of time to start saving or planning for the future. But the opposite is the case. There are ways of doing both – pretty painlessly – to make the most of what you've got. Tackling your finances will free your mind and take the fear out of opening letters in brown envelopes.

BUDGETS

We'd all like to think that we can afford what we want, when we want. Unfortunately, unless we are born with a silver spoon in our mouth, life's not like that! To make the best of your finances you need to have a certain amount of discipline and to budget carefully.

- Write down every item of expenditure (weekly and monthly): overestimate rather than underestimate.
- Split your list into essential and non-essential items. Essential=groceries, non-essential=caviare.
- Make sure you include all the bills you pay quarterly and where you are not sure of exact amounts overestimate rather than underestimate.
- Add in extra costs like heating bills in winter, summer holidays and Christmas and birthday presents (for yourself).
- Work out your cashflow (i.e. what money you have coming in, what you have going out and when) to see when you will need more cash to hand. For example you could find that your gas, electricity and telephone bills all fall due at the same time along with your car MOT and your television licence. This could leave a big hole in your monthly finances and you might need an overdraft to tide you over.
- If you can, rearrange your finances so that you can pay your bills monthly, preferably by direct debit or standing order, so that you can't actually see or feel the money leaving you, and stagger your quarterly and annual payments so they don't hit you all at once.
- Try to arrange for your standing orders and direct debits to be taken out of your account shortly after you have been paid to prevent you getting an inflated idea of your bank balance at any stage. Also arrange for your credit card bills to be paid at this time.
- Work out your average monthly expenditure and your average monthly income. Subtract the former from the latter and see if there is any spare or a shortfall.
- If you have cash to spare, try building up some savings instead of blowing it. Transfer money out of your main account into a savings account before you start spending (preferably by standing order!!).
- Cut right down on non-essential expenditure, (who are we kidding here?) and see if you can make savings in other areas.
- If you find that your outgoings always exceed your income, consider other ways to make some cash (legally) and check whether you are entitled to any State Benefits (refer to section on **Benefits**).
- Try and work more overtime; consider taking on an extra part-time job or letting a room in your house or flat.
- Never buy on impulse. Try not to carry your credit card or cheque book with you: that way you will always have to think twice about a purchase and make a second trip to the shops!
- Credit cards and overdrafts can be useful to help ease monthly cashflow but they are never a solution to bad budgeting (see sections on **Loans/Borrowing**, **Debt** and **Plastic**). Make sure you get regular statements and check them for accuracy.

BANKS
AND BUILDING SOCIETIES

Gone are the days when people automatically opened accounts with the bank that their parents banked with or approached a building society simply because they wanted a mortgage. All financial institutions have become increasingly competitive, selling as wide a product range as they possibly can.

Banks and building societies have become part of the service industry and you should expect the same level of service you would demand from any high street shop, restaurant or hotel. Don't be afraid to shop around and switch your account to suit your changing needs.

The 1986 Building Societies Act widened the scope of the societies' activities significantly and provided the banks with more competition. As a consequence there have been a number of mergers and take-overs and societies such as the Abbey National have been floated on the Stock Market to acquire the same status as a bank.

OPENING AN ACCOUNT

- Personal banking is usually free if you stay in credit and interest is sometimes paid on credit balances in your current account: what rate is currently payable and when is it paid?
- How much is charged for an authorized overdraft (i.e. where you have a pre-agreed overdraft limit), is there an arrangement fee and what interest rate will you be charged if you exceed your limit?
- What is the cost of an unauthorized overdraft? Some banks give you a notional overdraft limit based on your monthly income. They will not take any action if you stay within this limit nor will they necessarily advise you that you are overdrawn unless you exceed your notional limit. In the meantime they will charge you at the unauthorized overdraft rate.
- Some banks will let you have free overdrafts up to a certain amount or for say two or three days. It's worth phoning your bank manager in advance if you know you are going to be overdrawn as they will usually cancel any charges if they have been notified in advance and the overdraft is going to be cleared quickly.
- Check the fees for stopped or bounced cheques, returned standing orders or direct debits or warning letters advising of unauthorized spending. These are often much higher than you would expect (£15–£30 per item) and you should avoid any circumstances that might lead to them being debited to your account.

BANK SERVICES

When you open your account you will be offered a number of basic services as follows: cheque/debit/cash (cheque guarantee) card.

A card will usually enable you to

- Withdraw money from a service till when your correct Personal Identification Number (PIN) is punched in (this should never be revealed to a third party).
- Pay a retailer through the Switch or Delta system, which debits money straight from your account to the account of the retailer.
- Guarantee payment of a cheque up to the limit stated on your card. This is effectively the same as Switch/Delta but the money stays in your account longer if you write a cheque.

CHEQUE BOOK

There is an implied contract between a bank and its customer that it will honour the customer's cheques if there is enough money in the account or an overdraft has been arranged. However if there is a cheque card number on the back of the cheque the bank is obliged to pay it up to the limit of your cheque guarantee card whether there are funds in the account or not.

- If your cheque book is lost or stolen you should advise the bank immediately and they will then be liable if the cheque book is used fraudulently. If you fail to advise them you will be liable for any money taken out of your account and could be charged overdraft interest if you overdraw as a result.
- If you pay by cheque you hold on to your money longer as it takes at least three working days for your cheque to clear through the clearing system. This is good news for keeping hold of your cash but the same time lag applies if you are paid a cheque. So only draw against cleared funds otherwise you could find that you have technically gone overdrawn.

STANDING ORDERS

These are a convenient way to pay regular fixed sums such as annual subscriptions, monthly membership fees or regular payments to an individual. You advise the bank of the details and they make the payments.

DIRECT DEBITS

These are arrangements where you have given a company authorization to make certain charges to your account and you give the bank permission to pay them (e.g. gas or electricity bills). Direct debits can only be used to pay commercial organizations not individuals and it is the debiting party not you that decides how much will be taken from your account each month so you must keep an eye on them.

Both standing orders and direct debits can make paying bills and budgeting much easier and there is usually no charge for private customers. You should make sure however that any alteration to or cancellation of your instructions is put in writing and that you check your statements to make sure that cancelled or amended payments do not slip through the net.

OTHER SERVICES

Telephone banking is now widely available which provides a 24-hour service. All services can be provided over the telephone and approximately 50% of telephone banking now takes place outside conventional banking hours (even on Christmas Day!).

Computer-based banking is also available if you have your own PC and the appropriate modem. This will provide access to your account in real time which means that all information you receive will be totally current rather than showing the position at the close of business on the previous day, which is the balance that you will normally see. The advantage of PC banking is that you can look at your accounts at your leisure and carry out transactions in your own time.

TIPS

- Once you have opened your account try and get to meet the person who will be responsible for handling your business. Keep them advised of any changes in your financial circumstances, if you change your job for example, and always contact them first if you need to arrange a temporary overdraft. In other words show him or her that you are in control of your finances.
- Always give your bank instructions in writing.

- If you get falsely credited with something it is, unfortunately, not yours to keep. Do not spend the money as the bank is entitled to debit your account whenever it wants to!
- You are jointly liable for all debts on a joint account, so if your partner disappears without paying his share, the debt will be your responsibility. It is therefore very important that you understand all the implications of any banking you enter into on a joint basis and make sure that the bank is also aware of your position. You should take independent legal and financial advice where necessary.
- If you are charged for an accidental overdraft or a one-off situation, complain and see if the charges/interest can be waived.
- If you have any complaints that are not dealt with satisfactorily by the branch manager you should take them to the Customer Service Department of the bank or building society and then if you need to go further to the Bank or Building Society Ombudsman.

PLASTIC

Credit cards are readily available from all sorts of retail and financial organizations. You no longer have to be a customer of a particular bank or building society to have one of their cards. So are they a blessing or a curse, or in fact both? It really depends on how you use them and how many you have!

There are basically four different types of card available: credit cards, chargecards, storecards and affinity cards. (Debit cards are slightly different and allow money to be debited directly from your bank account.)

CREDIT CARDS
These are often confused with chargecards. Examples of credit cards are Mastercard and Visa.
- You are not always charged for having a credit card and you are allowed to pay off your balance at the rate you choose with interest accruing on the unpaid balance.

- If you are likely to pay off your balance each month make sure you pick a free card: the interest rate should be of little importance to you.
- Interest rates vary greatly between various institutions, so you should check the APR (Annual Percentage Rate), see **Loans/Borrowing** for comparisons.
- You will have a pre-set limit on your card which should not be exceeded. You can ask for a particular limit but never take more than you can afford to pay back and try to arrange for your monthly repayment date to be just after you have been paid.
- Using a credit card enables you to have an interest-free loan for a number of weeks, if used properly. Once you use your card to buy something your credit card bill will be sent on a monthly basis. This will state when the minimum payment is due, which is likely to be some weeks from the date of the bill so you will only really pay for your purchase on the date the bill is paid. During this time your own money could still be in a deposit account earning you interest.
- However, the loan is only really interest free if you settle it in full on or before the payment date. If you do not, or your payment arrives late, you will be paying interest on the outstanding balance either from the statement date or even possibly from the purchase date.
- Make sure you pay your bill at least three working days in advance of the payment date.
- If you draw cash with a credit card interest can start accruing immediately. Check the terms of your credit card in respect of cash withdrawals and only use this facility in an emergency.
- When choosing a credit card company also check the reward schemes on offer: these are extra bonuses that accrue to you as you spend on your card, ranging from meals out to trips on Concorde for the very big spenders.

CHARGECARDS
Examples of chargecards are American Express and Diners Club: the retailer accepting the card pays for the pleasure!
- These differ from credit cards as customers are not permitted to borrow money on them.
- The full balance must be repaid each month but

the advantage is that chargecards have no spending limit and usually much better reward schemes.

STORECARDS
These are like credit cards but can only be used in certain shops, e.g. Marks and Spencer or the John Lewis Partnership (often where other credit cards are not accepted). They can often be significantly more expensive than credit cards but there may be a reduction in interest rates if a customer agrees to settle a minimum sum per month by direct debit. While there are no reward schemes as such, storecard holders often get extra perks such as free alterations, extra discounts at sale time etc.

CHARITY OR AFFINITY CARDS
These are usually credit cards that support a particular cause, charity or special interest group.
• Approximately £5 is donated to the cause when a card is taken out and then a further 25p per £100 spent. This may not seem a lot but approximately one million pounds per annum is raised in this way and the figure is growing.
• Banks and building societies rarely publicize these cards so you should contact your favourite cause if you are interested.

TIPS
• Credit cards are expensive compared to bank facilities and you should be fully aware of the charges you are likely to incur for late payment, exceeding your limit, obtaining a replacement card and cash advances.
• Don't be afraid to change your credit card company if you are dissatisfied or can get a better deal elsewhere. Some companies may be prepared to take over your existing liabilities.
• Try to limit yourself to one card.
• Consider taking out a card protection scheme in case your cards are lost or stolen. For a small fee you can notify one company of the loss of your cards and they will advise all your card issuers and arrange for replacements.
• If your cards are lost or stolen you are generally only liable for the first £50 and once you have notified the card company you cease to be liable

at all. However you may be held liable for the loss if 'gross negligence' on your part can be proved, e.g. if you kept the PIN numbers with the cards.
• If your cards do go missing you should advise the card company and the police immediately (even if you are not sure if they were stolen). The cards will be cancelled and new ones issued. But beware: if you keep losing your cards you might be refused replacements.
• Some cards offer consumer protection if you spend an amount above a certain limit: check the small print. This means the credit card company is as liable as the retailer for the quality of purchases costing between £100–£30,000 under section 75 of the 1974 Consumer Credit Act.
• If you get into problems with your credit cards contact the card company immediately to try and work out a solution (see **Repayment and debt** in the **Loans/Borrowing** section).
• If you don't have any credit cards you can't get into trouble with them.

CREDIT REFERENCE AGENCIES
If you apply for any sort of credit, loan or mortgage or want to open a bank account or apply for a storecard, the chances are that the company to whom you are applying will check you out with a credit reference agency. Credit reference agencies carry files on almost every adult in the UK and not, as is commonly believed, simply on those who have a bad credit history. The files will cover available details on your financial dealings and other information, much of which is already in the public domain.
• Subscribers to credit reference agencies are those seeking information such as banks, building societies, mobile phone companies or book clubs.
• In order to obtain information they must have a Consumer Credit Licence and be covered under the Data Protection Act.
• Subscribers will only be given 'like for like' information. So, for example, mortgage lenders will only be given information about mortgages and credit card companies information on credit cards.
• Under the Consumer Credit Act 1974 you have the right to know if a lender has consulted a credit reference agency and if so which one. If you are refused credit you should ask the lender

to give you the details provided. In any event, whether you are refused credit or not you are entitled to see what details the credit reference agency holds about you.

- You can obtain a copy of your own file for £1 and the two main credit reference agencies in the UK (CCN Group and Equifax) also provide booklets explaining how the system works.
- You may find that you have been refused credit simply because you are not on the electoral roll at the address you have quoted.
- As credit reference files contain details of every-one at the same address (but only family members) you may find that your rating is affected by someone who no longer lives there.
- You can get your file changed easily if it is out of date, wrong or it contains details about people with whom you have no financial connection. The only way to find out if your file is up to date is to request a copy of it. You will not be given any details over the telephone.
- To back up any requests you may have to change incorrect information in your file, always send the agency copies (never originals) of all correspond-ence with the relevant parties in addition to copies of cheques, receipts, etc.
- If the file does contain mistakes, the agency is required to correct them and advise you what it has done within 28 days. If you are not satisfied with what they have done you can send in your own note of correction of not more than 200 words. This must be added to your file and sent out whenever any further information is requested about you. If you have any complaints about a credit reference agency you should contact the Office of Fair Trading.
- You can also obtain information about all organ-izations which hold information about individuals on computer by contacting the Data Protection Registrar.

ADVICE ON FINANCE

If you win the Lottery, you might want to consider investing some of it. Getting the right financial advice is a must. Alternatively, if you just want to enhance your pension or take out some extra insurance, it's important to pick the right product and the immense choice can make this decision very difficult. So, take good financial advice before you tie your money up and bear this in mind as you read through this whole chapter.

FINANCIAL ADVISERS

Financial advisers work for companies which must be authorized under the Financial Services Act (FSA). (These companies must also be members of a 'regulatory body' which should vet its members to ensure they follow the rules, see below.) In addition the adviser must have passed specific exams to enable her/him to work as a financial adviser.

- Financial advisers must only recommend financial products that are suitable for you.
- They should find out as much as possible about your personal and financial circumstances, e.g. they should check your tax position, your atti-tude to risk, what you hope to achieve from investing your money, i.e. do you want to receive an income from your funds or do you just want to let them grow?
- They will usually fill out an information sheet or questionnaire during a preliminary discussion and you should ask for a copy to check the facts are right.
- Ask friends if they can recommend an adviser, look under 'Financial Advisers' in the *Yellow Pages* or call the regulatory organizations for details of their members. If you know the partic-ular product you want, look for a company that specializes in that field.

- Advisers are either 'independent' or 'tied' and are obliged to tell you which they are and provide you with a 'terms of business' letter before they give any advice.

OTHER FINANCIAL ADVICE

- Independent financial advisers (IFAs) specialize in giving financial and investment advice and are able to pick investment products for you from across the whole market. They are supposed to carry out regular surveys of the market to ensure they are in a position to give 'best advice'. There are fewer IFAs than tied agents.
- Some banks and building societies can offer independent advice. Most banks and building societies are tied to one company.
- IFA Promotion will give you a list of three IFAs in your area with a list of their particular specializations.
- IFAs are regulated by the following regulatory bodies: the Personal Investment Authority (PIA) and the Investment Management Regulatory Organization (IMRO), which under new legislation are all to be regulated under the umbrella of the SIB (Securities and Investments Board).
- Tied agents sell only one company's products. If none of their products is suitable for your requirements they should sell you nothing at all.
- Tied agents are regulated by the PIA.

PAYMENT OF ADVISERS

Generally all tied agents and most IFAs are paid by commission although some IFAs work on a fee basis and some tied agents are salaried. All advisers are required to give full written details of all commissions they will earn and of any other charges payable.

TAKING THE ADVICE

Your adviser will tell you about the products suitable for you and then make a recommendation. If anything is not clear to you, or you require further explanation, ask – it's their job to explain.

- Make sure the product recommended provides you with what you want, i.e. access to your money when you want it, or the level of risk you are prepared to take.
- Always ask what would happen if your current circumstances changed, e.g. if you lost your job.

- Always get advice and responses to your queries in writing.
- If you are confident that you know exactly which product you require, you can buy it without receiving advice on an 'execution only' basis but, be warned, your adviser is not obliged to consider whether the product is truly in your best interests and you will probably have to forgo any rights that exist to protect you if things go wrong.

TIPS

- Read up on the product you are interested in before calling in professional advice.
- Compare fee and commission levels from a number of financial advisers before making your choice.
- Seek advice from a number of different advisers (at least three) before you commit yourself to a product and try to ensure you have a comparison between advice from an independent financial adviser and that from a tied agent. If the advice differs, find out why.
- Always seek reasons for a recommendation and don't be embarrassed to keep asking questions until you are satisfied with the answer.
- Always get recommendations in writing and check for any policy exclusions, especially on medical and sickness insurances.
- Choose a financial adviser you get on with: they are there to help you and it is imperative that they fully understand your needs and expectations if their advice is to be worth while. Find out who will look after your affairs if your adviser is away.
- Ask them about their background, qualifications and training, how long they have been in the business and how many clients they look after.
- Find out how many clients a company has and how it assesses its own performance, charges and commercial strength within the market.
- Ask what criteria they use to select an investment or insurance company. Find out about their internal controls, how and when they audit their client files, how often they will meet with you to review your objectives and how often they review their investments. Do they do this themselves or rely on third-party research?

- Never be rushed into a decision: always take your time and make comparisons with other advisers.
- Do not assume that bigger organizations will necessarily give better advice than smaller firms but be wary of tied agents from firms that you have never heard of.
- Always choose an adviser from a firm that is regulated.
- If financial advice is offered over the telephone do not be persuaded.

COMPLAINTS

If you consider you have been badly advised you should complain firstly to your adviser providing all the relevant back-up information and copies of the appropriate documents. If you are not satisfied, contact the firm's regulator, or if the regulator is the PIA, go straight to the PIA Ombudsman.

SAVINGS
& INVESTMENTS

Saving never seems to be easy; most of us seem to work it the other way around. We take the trip to Florida, chuck it on a credit card and spend the rest of the year paying it off. Saving for a rainy day or for your long-term future is even more difficult. The prospect of it is so dull that most of us switch off as soon as the subject rears its grey little head. However, the trick is to set up regular transfers out of your account so that you don't even know it is happening. Before you know it, loadsa money!

The difference between saving and investment is a question of risk. Investing money in shares might sound glamorous but the value of those shares may go down as well as up and you may actually lose money. Putting money in a bank or building society is safe and boring but you are generally guaranteed to get your money back and should make some money in the form of interest. Before you commit to putting your spare cash anywhere, you should work out a basic

savings/investment strategy and should answer the following questions:
- How much money can you afford to save?
- When will you need access to that money, or at least some of it?
- Are you able to save on a regular basis?
- Do you want to be sure that you will get at least as much out as you put in, or are you prepared to take a risk in the hope that you might get much more?

STRATEGY

Before you start investing, cover the basics:
- Try and ensure that you have an emergency cash fund to hand: in an ideal world you would have at least three months' salary accessible to you at relatively short notice, perhaps in a high-interest bank or building society savings account.
- Consider your pension provisions: you should make sure these are adequate and should top your pension up first before you worry about making other investments.
- Insurance: make sure you have sufficient life and health insurance.
- Once these are covered then you are in a position to consider other savings or investments. Ideally, an amount in the region of 10% of your take-home pay is a sensible sum to save or invest, but don't place all your eggs in one basket. Spread your risk over different types of investments with different maturities and ensure that you always have access to cash in case of an emergency.
- If you are committed to some saving try and organize monthly standing orders to a savings account from your main bank account so that you are not tempted to spend the money on other things.

RISKS

Savings/investment is a trade-off between risk and reward. Controlling the level of risk is crucial to a successful investment strategy. Minimizing your risk might take away the excitement of the 'rollercoaster effect' of the returns from your portfolio but on balance it is better to aim for consistently good returns rather than spectacular highs and lows.

The three main types of risk to consider are:

1 Specific risk (i.e. if a specific company you have invested in performs badly): this can be avoided by spreading your risk, e.g. investing £2,000 in each of five companies rather than £10,000 in one company or alternatively by investing in Unit or Investment Trusts as described below.

2 Market risk (i.e. in general, if the stock market your shares are trading in falls, it will create a negative impact on the value of your investment): this risk can also be reduced by investing in shares traded in stock markets around the world or investing in a range of assets combining shares with cash and other types of investment (see below).

3 Currency risk: there will always be this risk if you have invested in overseas assets. Your income will be converted into Sterling when you want your money back and therefore will be exposed to movements in the exchange rate. If you want to invest in foreign markets make sure you take good advice from a professional fund manager who should reduce your currency risk by spreading investments across a number of different currency markets.

The final points to consider before you start saving/investing are:

• Are you saving for capital growth or investing for income?

• What is your overall tax position?

• If you are currently earning an income and are a long way off retirement, you are unlikely to need investments that provide you with a regular income now. Your aim should be to build up a sufficient fund of capital that will generate an income for you in later life. You will probably be looking at longer term investments that preserve the value of your capital and make it grow. Never underestimate the size of the retirement fund you will need to keep you in the manner to which you would like to become accustomed – the sooner you start saving the better!

• If on the other hand you are nearer retirement and your investment strategy to date has worked, you will probably already have a capital sum saved and therefore will need to start switching your assets from those based on share perfor-

mance (i.e. higher risk) to safer investments which will pay out a more regular income.

• It is extremely important to consider your tax position when choosing your investments, particularly if you are in a higher rate tax bracket, to ensure that you maximize your benefits. As stated below, there are a number of savings and investment schemes which are tax efficient and will give a significant boost to your income.

SCHEMES

Bank and building society accounts

• Instant access accounts are the best place to keep cash you might need in the short term. Interest is usually low and is taxable. At times of high inflation the interest you earn is unlikely to keep pace and purchasing power is eroded. Only keep your emergency funds on this basis.

• Term and notice accounts: with a term account you agree to invest money for a period of, say, one or two years and lose interest if you withdraw the money early. With notice accounts you agree to give a minimum notice period before you withdraw funds, e.g. 30, 60 or 90 days, and you could lose interest if you don't give the appropriate notice period. Interest rates are usually higher than on instant access accounts and there may be a minimum sum that has to be deposited. Interest on these accounts is also taxable.

TESSAS
(Tax Exempt Special Savings Account)

• A TESSA is a tax-free investment available from banks and building societies which does not put the capital sum invested at risk.

• Money can be deposited into a TESSA on a regular or irregular basis over a five-year period subject to certain annual limits and an overall total limit.

• You must be able to keep your investment for five years in order for it to remain tax free.

• Interest rates tend to be fairly high but you may only have one TESSA at a time.

National Savings

• National Savings amount to a Government-backed savings scheme and in effect means private investors lending the Government money.

You can invest in National Savings either by way of a savings account or fixed-term investment bonds, both of which are available at a post office or direct from National Savings. They are considered a risk-free way of investing for income or growth.

- National Savings offers two types of account with fixed interest rates depending on the size of the investment, although better interest rates are usually obtainable elsewhere.
- A number of types of saving certificates or bonds can be purchased which pay out fixed rates of interest if they are held for a certain period, some of which are also tax free. There are also specific bonds available for pensioners and children.
- The most popular National Savings products are Premium Bonds which have a maximum investment level of £20,000 per investor. After these have been held for one month they are entered into the monthly prize draw with prizes ranging from £50 to a maximum of £1m awarded each month. Premium Bonds can be cashed in at any time so your capital sum can always be retrieved (unlike the money you invest in the National Lottery each week!). Interest is not paid on Premium Bonds but there is a probability of you winning 14 times each year if you main tain the maximum investment of £20,000. This works out at a tax-free minimum return of 3.5% which is a good investment for a high-rate taxpayer. Of course you might not win anything at all!

Unit and Investment Trusts

These use investors' money to purchase company shares or other investments such as Government bonds. It is possible for you to invest a small amount of money, say £20 per month, and your investment will be spread across a wide range of different assets.

Unit Trusts: with a Unit Trust you are allocated units according to your contributions which represent your share of the fund. The day-to-day running of the fund is handled by an investment manager and a typical Unit Trust would invest in between 30 and 100 different companies. Unit Trusts are open ended which means that if more people want to buy units in the trust, then the investment managers can create more units and the fund will get bigger. If people want to sell their units and there are no buyers the fund will then get smaller and the investment manager may need to sell some of their investments to pay back those who want to redeem their units.

- Unit trusts offer two different types of units: accumulation and distribution. If you buy accumulation units any income you earn will automatically be reinvested, while if you buy distribution units income will be paid out to you as it is earned.
- You can invest in a Unit Trust by contacting them directly, or you can buy or sell through an independent financial adviser. If you buy directly you will pay a one-off initial charge and then an annual management fee and you should make sure you are fully aware of all the costs and conditions before signing up (see section on **Financial Advice**). If you buy or sell through an independent financial adviser you will probably not have to pay him or her because the unit trust will pay them a commission directly.

Investment Trusts: these trusts invest in the shares of other companies. As an investor you buy shares in the trust and automatically own part of the trust company. The day-to-day handling of the investments is undertaken by an investment manager, as with Unit Trusts, but Investment Trusts are close ended which means that only a certain number of shares are issued. If more people want to buy than to sell, the price goes up until the number of sellers equals the number of buyers. Conversely if there are more sellers than buyers the price will fall.

- You can buy and sell shares in Investment Trusts through a stockbroker, a share-dealing service or an independent financial adviser. It is more difficult to assess the costs associated with Investment Trusts as there is no upfront fee: you simply pay commission to whoever buys or sells shares on your behalf.

Personal Equity Plans (PEPs)

PEPs were established to encourage share ownership and tax-efficient long-term savings. There are limits to how much you can invest in PEPs per annum and to what type of assets can be invested in (e.g. it is possible that a proportion of your investment can be in assets outside the UK).

- PEPs can be invested in Unit or Investment Trusts and these tend to be bought by private investors direct from fund management companies or through independent financial advisers. This has a possible disadvantage that the private investor is not able to switch to a different trust during a tax year, e.g. if they are not satisfied with the returns or the fund managers. An alternative is to use a self-select PEP which allows you to choose the type of investments you hold within your PEP (i.e. shares, Unit or Investment Trusts).
- Other types of PEPs include corporate bond PEPs which effectively mean you are lending money to a company: these are less risky than a share-based PEP but not as secure as a savings based account such as a TESSA, or 'index tracking' PEPs where the remit is to track a particular stock market such as the FT-SE 100.

The market for both PEPs and Unit and Investment Trusts is increasingly competitive with fees and commission levels continually being cut. However, you should always base your investment decision on performance rather than low charges, and while you cannot guarantee future performance it is worth picking your investment from a group which has a proven track record.

With both PEPs and Unit and Investment Trusts you are in a position either to invest in general funds with a spread of interests across the board or alternatively in specialist funds. For example there are a number of ethical investment funds dealing particularly with companies which may reflect your own moral or social attitudes. It is likely that you will need larger sums to invest in these specialist managed funds but check this with your financial adviser or the financial press. Simply buying shares in specific companies that take your fancy may well provide the highest long-term rate of return but you need to be able to tie up your capital for some time. Your strategy should be to hold on to shares for longish periods of time and not panic buy or sell in depressions or booms. You should ensure that you spread your risk across a number of companies in a number of different sectors.

Based on the success and principles of TESSAs and PEPs, the Government have announced their intention to develop a new type of individual savings account that should become available in 1999, so make sure you are aware of all your options when deciding to invest.

MONITORING

- Whatever your investment strategy, and however your portfolio is made up, make sure you monitor the position on a regular basis.
- Take into account changes in your personal circumstances and your future plans when considering any changes.
- Don't make rash decisions if your portfolio has not increased in value over a short period of time, as one year's performance is rarely enough to judge a fund's merit. However, if you are dissatisfied in any way with the performance of your investments and wish to switch or reinvest funds, make sure there are no penalties or additional costs for doing so, and do not let significant discounts tempt you into an investment fund which has not performed well in the past.
- Use the financial press to check share prices and interest rates and always make comparisons of the performance of your assets with other funds in the same sector. Don't always accept the fund manager's word in respect of performance. The annual report provided should show how your money has performed against other types of investments such as a building society deposit account, inflation and various stock market indices. They will not necessarily compare your fund's performance against the competition unless of course it has come out top!!
- Finally, always bear in mind the level of inflation when putting money into savings accounts or making investments for longer periods of time. In order to achieve a real rate of return, the net interest that you are paid needs to be higher than the level of inflation. So in order to achieve real income growth it does not always pay to put all your money in your bank or building society savings account. It may be very safe but it may be losing you money!

LOANS/ BORROWING

All sorts of banks, financial institutions, credit card companies and finance houses are queuing up to lend money these days. However, they are not necessarily doing you a favour! In the majority of cases the lender will be getting more out of the deal than you will, so always be very clear about why you need to borrow and how and when you intend to pay the money back and always deal with reputable lending institutions.

LOANS AND OVERDRAFTS

Interest rates on loans and overdrafts will vary from lender to lender and according to the type of facility you require.

• Ordinary Loans are for a set period of time but the interest rate is not fixed and is usually set at a 'percentage over Base Rate' (Base Rate is set by the Bank of England) so you end up paying more if interest rates rise (and less if interest rates fall). It is possible to make fixed repayments and also to have the flexibility to make lump sum reductions.

• Personal Loans are moneys lent over a set term at a fixed interest rate with a fixed repayment schedule. If interest rates are starting to rise this may be the best option.

• If you want to repay a loan early you will not only have to repay the outstanding balance but also some of the interest the lender expected to receive over the full term of the facility ('early repayment penalty'). The lender will give you a rebate on the full amount still owing which is calculated by using a formula set down in law. If the small print of your loan allows it you should repay all but a few pounds of the balance and then a month or so later repay the loan in full. The amount you settle is based on the amount you still owe.

• Generally you will not receive statements on loans unless you ask for them. Check that there is no charge.

• Overdrafts are subject to fluctuations in interest rates, are usually more expensive than loans but have the advantage of flexibility. Money can be paid back at any time in any amount and can be redrawn providing the overall overdraft limit is not exceeded. You will only pay interest on the outstanding balance and if interest rates are starting to fall an overdraft may be more suitable.

• For larger purchases, such as a car, most lenders would prefer to see the borrowing on a fixed repayment schedule as with a personal loan.

INTEREST-FREE LOANS

Why borrow to pay for something if you are offered interest-free credit terms by the seller? 'Buy now, pay later' deals sound like a good idea and can be if the loan really is interest free.

• Interest-free deals are often available when buying larger consumer goods such as furniture or cars and really do not cost anything provided the price of the goods is not higher than you could find elsewhere.

• You should always check that the cost of the interest has not simply been added to the original cash price. If the total cost is higher than you would pay for cash then the chances are that the amount of interest that would have been due, or at least part of it, has been added to the overall price.

• Salespeople will always focus on the fact that you pay nothing for 'x' months and 'y' for so many months, i.e. with the emphasis on monthly cost rather than the total. You must focus on the total cost.

• Deals are often better still if you can afford to pay part of the cost as a deposit with the rest over say 6–12 months. Try and negotiate a deal with a flexible repayment plan that allows you to pay cash at any time over the life of the loan.

• Make sure you know the full details of the deal before you enter into it and be wary of interest-free deals that seem too good to be true.

• If you were prepared to pay in full for something and then take an interest-free loan, make sure you keep the cash to earn you interest and to make the repayments rather than using it to buy something else.

• If you buy on credit, the goods you have bought are yours immediately even while you are repaying the debt. If the goods you bought are faulty do not stop making the repayments while you complain, as you could lose your rights if you fail to keep to your side of the bargain.

- If you cannot make the payments, the company you have bought from must give you seven days' notice in which to pay, after which they can reclaim the goods. But if you have paid over one third of the credit price, the company can only reclaim the goods with a court order.
- If you fail to repay the credit loan when it falls due, the chances are it will be swapped to a hire purchase deal (see below).

HIRE PURCHASE (HP)

This is a system by which a hired article becomes the property of the hirer after a set number of payments. Hire purchase agreements are often offered to help fund an impulse purchase and should be treated with caution.

- Unlike buying on credit, goods bought on HP remain the property of the seller until they have been paid for in full. If you do not keep up with the payments the goods can be repossessed.
- Once the cancellation period for the HP agreement has passed you cannot get out of the agreement without returning the goods and paying a sum in the region of half the value (you would also have to pay for any necessary repairs if the goods returned were not in perfect condition).

Under the Consumer Credit Act 1974, the supplier of credit also carries liability for the goods. If you have paid for faulty goods (with a value between £100 and £3000) using a credit card, bank loan or HP, you can sue the company who supplied the credit. This is particularly useful if the trader in question goes bankrupt. See **Law** chapter for legal advice.

PAWNBROKERS

This is a desperate way to raise money and not recommended. The pawnbroker lends you money on the security of an article you leave with him. If you cannot pay a pawnbroker back by a certain date you will either have to pay interest (likely to be very high) or lose the object pawned.

INTEREST RATES

- If you borrow any sum up to £15,000 you must, by law, be quoted the Annual Percentage Rate (APR). This is the actual cost of borrowing and must include the interest rate and any fees or additional costs.
- The APR should be a way of comparing credit costs between various institutions but the method used for calculating the APR for an overdraft is not set by law and often lenders will omit fees from their calculations.
- When a written quotation for a loan is given it will state a monthly or annual interest rate and the APR. If a monthly APR is quoted this will be higher than an annual figure because it will take into account how quickly the loan is repaid.
- Not everyone pays additional fees or charges so always ask for a written quotation so that the APR is specific to you.
- The courts can reduce extortionate interest rates but there is a fine line between extortionate and high: if in doubt check with the Citizens' Advice Bureau.

CREDIT AGREEMENTS

- Personal borrowings below £15,000 are governed by the Consumer Credit Act 1974. Always obtain a written quotation for your loan facility and read the small print carefully. Check for security or additional insurance requirements and penalties for early repayment.
- Be sure you can afford the repayments and ensure that the repayment schedule does not extend beyond the life of what you intend to buy (i.e. don't pay for a holiday over three years!).
- Before you sign up for a loan, particularly if you are away from the lender's main place of business, you will also be given a cancellation form if you wish to change your mind. If this is the case advise the lender, in writing, as soon as possible that you no longer wish to proceed.
- Make sure you keep copies of all agreements, receipts and associated correspondence in case there is a problem over the life of the agreement.

REPAYMENT AND DEBT

- Once you have taken on extra commitments, do not forget them! Make sure you keep up with your repayments and if possible arrange to have standing orders set up at your bank timed just after you receive your salary to ensure the payments are made.

- If you fall behind with your payments never ignore chasing letters as this can lead to debt collectors and court summonses. Don't panic! Speak to the lender in question and explain your circumstances and why you are having difficulty with your repayments. They are far more likely to be reasonable and helpful if you contact them rather than ignore the problem.
- It is a lot of hassle for banks, building societies and other lending institutions to call in debts and get solicitors or debt collectors involved (but they will do it if they have to!). They would rather have reduced repayments for a longer period of time than nothing at all.
- Work out a realistic plan of what you can afford and then offer the lender an alternative repayment schedule. Be 100% sure that you can stick to your revised schedule. It is better to offer less knowing that you can manage rather than have to go back to revise the repayment plan again.
- Always keep details of all correspondence to and from the lender and a record of who you have spoken to on the telephone.
- If the situation gets worse, seek help from your local Citizens' Advice Bureau or call the National Debt-Line.

MORTGAGE

The single largest purchase you are likely to make is your own home but before you dive in you should plan ahead. Budget for what you can afford and check that this is realistic when compared with property prices in the area in which you want to live.

- Firstly you should find out how much you can borrow either by consulting a financial adviser (who specializes in giving mortgage advice) or speaking to your bank or building society.
- Most lenders will not lend more than 95% of the valuation or purchase price of a property, whichever is the lower. You should expect to have

to find at least 5% of the total purchase price yourself along with all the additional costs and expenses which are discussed below. The higher the mortgage/property value the smaller the lender's contribution, i.e. for a mortgage of £300,000 you would be more likely to have to contribute 15% than 5%.

- You can usually borrow up to three times your gross annual salary if you are borrowing on your own and in the case of joint borrowers up to three times the largest income plus the total of your partner's income or up to two and a half times your combined gross incomes. Gross income counts as your basic salary and guaranteed bonuses or overtime and you will almost certainly have to provide proof of these amounts.
- If you are self-employed lenders usually want to see your trading accounts for the past three years in order to calculate your average income.
- Once you have worked out what you can afford you then need to focus on which type of mortgage is the most suitable for your requirements.

There are three basic choices:
1 endowment
2 repayment
3 pension

ENDOWMENT MORTGAGES
- Endowment mortgages are linked to life assurance policies. Your monthly payments are split, with one part going to cover the interest on the capital sum, i.e. the original sum borrowed, and the other part payable as the premium for a with-profit or unit-linked insurance fund (see **Insurance** section). The intention is that this investment policy will mature at the end of the mortgage term and produce a lump sum sufficient to repay the capital and possibly also leave you with extra cash. However this is not always the case and you should be very clear about what you can expect from your endowment policy and any limitations it may have.
- An endowment mortgage also has the added advantage of life assurance so that if you died during the term of your policy your mortgage would be repaid. If you decided to move property during the term of your endowment policy it can

be transferred to your new home, although a small fee may be charged.

REPAYMENT MORTGAGES

- Under this type of mortgage you make straightforward monthly repayments of the capital sum and interest charges over the term of the mortgage which can be up to 30 years. Over the initial years the repayments consist mostly of interest but as the outstanding amount falls so does the interest as a proportion of your monthly repayment with the capital sum being repaid in full effectively towards the end of the mortgage term.
- Life assurance is not included with this type of mortgage and you will be required to take out additional assurance as a condition of your mortgage. Critical illness insurance should also be an option (see below).

PENSION MORTGAGES

- This type of pension-linked mortgage might be more appropriate if you are self-employed or an employee who is not a member of a company pension scheme. It is similar to an endowment mortgage whereby your monthly repayments go to cover the interest due on the loan with a separate payment being made towards a pension plan. When your pension matures at the end of the mortgage term it should provide a sufficient tax-free lump sum to repay the capital.
- A pension mortgage does not include life cover and therefore you would have to take this out as a condition of the loan. Again critical illness cover should be considered.

It is possible to have other types of mortgages particularly where you have other forms of income which can be used to repay the capital sum. In some instances you can have an interest-only mortgage and pay the final amount on the maturity from your own resources.

INTEREST RATES & SPECIAL DEALS

As with all areas of the financial sector, providing mortgages has become a competitive business. Lenders are constantly trying to poach customers from other institutions and it is no longer necessary to view a mortgage as a single long-term buy.

It is now much easier to shop around to get a better deal.

One particularly competitive area of the market is in respect of interest rates; there are basically two options but there are always a number of special offers around, particularly for first-time buyers.

VARIABLE-RATE MORTGAGES

If you choose a variable rate the interest charged by your lender will alter from time to time in accordance with market conditions. Your payments will rise when interest rates rise and fall when interest rates fall. This obviously has its pros and cons and can make trying to budget more difficult.

FIXED-RATE MORTGAGES

- Fixed rates are offered on all types of mortgages from time to time and can be fixed for any period of time usually ranging from one to seven or more years.
- On expiry of your fixed rate you may be offered another fixed rate or alternatively your mortgage will be switched to your lender's variable rate. A fee is often charged on fixed-rate mortgages.
- If you take out a larger mortgage you will often get a better rate whether it is fixed or variable and it may sometimes be worth considering borrowing a little more if it would take you into a lower interest-rate bracket.
- Special deals are more likely to apply to new borrowers or borrowers who agree to switch from one institution to another. You should ensure that you always read the small print carefully and are fully aware of the possible additional costs of switching lenders, i.e. arrangement fee, valuation fees, legal costs.
- You should also check what penalties may be incurred for leaving your existing lender (early redemption penalties). If you decide to switch to a new lender always check how long you will be locked into the deal or what would happen if, for example, you wanted to reduce the amount of your mortgage during the initial term.

MORTGAGE STATEMENTS

- These are usually produced on an annual basis. The statement for a repayment mortgage should show a reduction in the closing balance, however small, during the early stages. A statement for an endowment, pension or interest-only mortgage should show the overall capital sum staying the same.

- Your statement will not confirm to you whether you are paying enough into your endowment, PEP or pension policy to have sufficient to repay the capital sum and if you are in any doubt about this you should ask for confirmation from your mortgage lender.
- Some lenders do not credit any extra payments you may make to reduce the amount of your mortgage until the end of the year, so your interest charges will not be reduced in the meantime.
- If you want to make reductions to the outstanding balance either ask your lender to credit your repayment to the capital sum immediately or alternatively keep it in an interest-bearing account until the end of the year and then transfer it to your mortgage account.

NB. Some lenders may only be prepared to accept a minimum sum for early repayment or alternatively there may be a penalty clause, particularly in the case of fixed-rate mortgages.

ADDITIONAL EXTRAS

See **The Buying Process** in **Home** chapter for a more detailed breakdown of costs.

Your mortgage lender will require a valuation report on your property to ensure that it represents adequate security before they lend you the money. Valuation provides basic information on the structural condition of the property and will point out any major defects.

A surveyor's report is far more comprehensive and should reveal all major and minor defects. If a surveyor fails to note any existing problems that later come to light s/he will be liable to you for compensation. As a consequence you may find a full structural survey quite depressing on first reading as it will cover every negative feature in great detail! Full structural surveys are considerably more expensive than valuation reports and therefore it pays to shop around and get quotes

from various surveyors. Your mortgage lenders might be able to recommend somebody with whom they have a special deal. See **The Right Survey** in **Home** chapter.

LOAN TO VALUATION FEE

If you borrow a high percentage, say, 80% or more, of either the value of the property or its purchase price you may have to pay an additional fee to cover the increased credit risk. This fee will reflect the total percentage advanced and can be added to your loan if necessary.

STAMP DUTY

This is a Government tax which is payable if your property costs £60,000 or more. If this is the case, you have to pay an additional 1% of the total purchase price by way of stamp duty. This will be dealt with by your solicitor and will be included in her/his final bill.

LEGAL COSTS

Your legal costs will depend on whether you are simply buying a property, or selling one property and buying another.

- You should appoint a solicitor or a licensed conveyancer once your offer to purchase a property has been accepted.
- Conveyancing is the term used to describe the legal process by which ownership of the property is transferred from the existing owner to you.
- It is the role of your solicitor or conveyancer to ensure that all legal aspects of your mortgage transaction including the title deeds and/or lease are in good order. Your mortgage lender may even have a list of approved firms with whom they have negotiated special rates.
- In the absence of such recommendations you should obtain a number of quotes for the work to be done but bear in mind that, depending on the complexity of the transaction, the final bill may be higher than your initial quote. If you are buying and selling try and negotiate an all-in fee for both.
- See **Solicitor/Conveyancer** in **Home** chapter.

ESTATE AGENT'S FEE

This will be charged if you are selling your

property and have advertised it through an estate agent. The cost of employing an estate agent varies considerably but can be as much as 3% of the final sale price of your property. You should obtain a number of quotes and don't be afraid to bargain with an estate agent to get a better deal.

RENTING YOUR PROPERTY

If you decide to let out your property check with your lender first.

- Find out whether your mortgage rate will be increased once you have been given permission, as many lenders will add 1% or 2% to their rate if the mortgaged property is let.
- It may be tempting not to tell your lender but if you don't you will probably be in breach of your mortgage contract which would enable your lender to force you to stop renting out the property and would almost certainly make them increase your mortgage rate.
- You are required by law to notify the Inland Revenue if you actually receive rent. However, as you can offset mortgage interest paid against any rental income you receive, there will be little or no tax to pay on the funds you receive if the amounts involved are similar.
- If you have no experience of letting property you can transfer the responsibility to experienced letting agents who, for a fee, will be responsible for finding tenants, making inspections and charging for damage.
- Always have a proper tenancy contract drawn up. If you have a group of tenants make sure they are all named as joint tenants so they will all be responsible for paying the rent in full in the event one leaves without paying their share.
- Transfer the utilities (electricity, gas, water, telephone and council tax) to the tenants' names so you don't get landed with the bills.
- Always make a full inventory of all the furniture, fixtures and fittings that are being left in the property, taking photos if necessary, so that there can be no argument as to who pays for damage.

TIPS

- If you buy a property with a partner you are joint tenants. If you are married your share will auto-matically pass to your spouse on death. However, if you have bought a property with your partner or a friend and have now split up you will be responsible for the whole debt unless you have made separate financial arrangements. Unless you make a will, your share of the property will not automatically pass to your partner on death.
- You do not have to borrow by the same method if you want to top up your mortgage. For example if you already have an endowment mortgage and then move to a larger property it is possible to keep the endowment and have the top-up portion by way of a repayment mortgage.
- Endowment policies that are no longer required can be cashed in for their surrender value. However the surrender value may well be less than the amount paid in if the policy is cashed early in its term.
- Flexible mortgages are becoming more popular where it may be possible to overpay your monthly repayments in times when you are better off and underpay in periods when money is tighter, e.g. if you are out of work or on maternity leave.
- If you are considering changing your mortgage always check the small print first. Ensure there are no penalties for redemption imposed by your old lender and confirm what costs will be covered by your new lender.
- If you get into financial difficulties and are struggling to meet your mortgage repayments speak to your lender straight away. It is much better to work out a solution with your lender than just hand back the keys. You can also seek advice from your local Citizens' Advice Bureau or contact the National Debt-Line.

If you have any problems with your mortgage that cannot be sorted out by your mortgage lender you can take your complaint to the building society or banking ombudsman.

PENSIONS

People spend an average of 20 years in retirement and almost a quarter of all working adults make no pension arrangements and rely entirely on the State to look after them in their old age. Few people have sufficient savings to rely on throughout their retirement and it is now recommended that you put aside the equivalent percentage sum to half your age if you want to maintain your standard of living in retirement, i.e. 15% of income for a 30 year old, 20% for a 40 year old etc! It is a horrible thought but the sooner you can start saving for your retirement the better: the interest your savings will generate will give you far more pension power.

Women play an increasingly important role in the work-place and as their financial role increases within the family more emphasis must be put on how to replace or supplement that income when they retire, particularly as women generally live longer than men, so their income can be more severely eroded by inflation.

There are a number of different pension schemes enabling you to make different choices for your future. However, if you decide to make extra provision for your pension, ensure that you take adequate financial advice from a specialized pensions adviser (see section on **Financial Advice**).

There are three main types of pension plan:
1 basic state pension
2 company pension scheme
3 personal pension plans (PPPs)

THE STATE PENSION

This operates under two schemes:
• the basic state pension
• the State Earnings Related Pension Scheme (SERPS)

The basic state pension

• This is paid through National Insurance contributions (or credits if you are unemployed) and anyone with a full record of contributions will receive a full state pension.
• If you do not have a full record you may receive less. This is historically the position in the case of women as a good portion of their working lives may have been taken up by raising a family or working part-time. Fewer than 20% of those at pensionable age receive the full state pension.

Currently women receive the state pension at 60 and men at 65 but from 2010 women will have to wait until they are 65 too. There is no allowance for receiving the state pension on early retirement.

SERPS

• SERPS is an additional pension linked to your full or part-time earnings. It is also paid through National Insurance contributions but there are no credits for the unemployed.
• If you are self-employed you will not participate in SERPS but if you are an employee you will automatically pay into SERPS unless either your company scheme is 'contracted out' of SERPS (i.e. agreed not to be part of SERPS) or you have decided to take out a personal pension plan in which case your SERPS contributions will be redirected to this plan.
• If you reach 60 in or before the year 2000 your SERPS pension will work out to be 25% of the average of your highest wage level over the best 20 years of your working life adjusted for inflation. If you hit 60 after the year 2000 the SERPS pension will be lower with the maximum percentage being reduced over a ten-year period to 20% in the year 2010. In addition it will be calculated on the average of lifetime earnings, not your best 20 years. This will particularly affect women who have taken career breaks or worked part-time as the less well paid years will drag the average down and reduce the overall SERPS benefit.
• It is possible to 'contract out' (i.e. not be a part) of SERPS but there is no guarantee that the benefits will be as good as SERPS. 'Contracting out' does have benefits however if your employer offers a contracted out final salary pension (see below), or you obtain better benefits under a contracted out personal pension scheme such as payment of benefits before state retirement age or a lump sum on death or retirement.
As SERPS is a Government run scheme and the benefits have already been reduced once in 1988, it is always possible that they could be reduced again. SERPS is linked to earnings but is

unlikely to bring all the benefits you would ideally like; therefore it is important to consider alternative or additional means of ensuring future financial security. The current state pension works out at a basic 17% of the national average wage, so depending on the state to look after you in your old age is a recipe for poverty.

TIPS

- If you have any queries regarding your state pension call the State Pension Entitlements Helpline.
- If you can afford to, defer your state pension. It is possible to defer it for up to five years. For each seven weeks deferred its value increases by approximately 1%.

COMPANY PENSION SCHEMES

Company schemes are run by trustees or managers who, by law, must keep you informed about both the scheme and your rights.

There are basically two types of company pension scheme:

1 final salary or defined benefit schemes
2 money purchase or defined contributions schemes

FINAL SALARY SCHEMES

- These undertake to pay you a pension expressed as a proportion of the salary you are earning at or near retirement.
- The benefits depend on how many years you are a member of the scheme with most schemes providing for 1/60 or 1/80 of your final salary for each year you have been included in the scheme with a maximum permitted benefit of 40/60 or 2/3 of your final salary.
- Some earnings such as overtime and bonuses may be excluded from pension calculations.
- When you retire you may be allowed to take some of your entitlement as a tax-free lump sum.
- The retirement age will be fixed by your employer and final salary schemes may permit the opportunity to take early retirement although this will mean a smaller pension.
- Many final salary schemes are contributory, i.e. you have to make a contribution, usually in the region of up to 5%, with your employer paying the remainder to cover the cost of all your

pension benefits. Some schemes are non-contributory, i.e. your employer pays all the costs. If you do contribute you will get tax relief on your contributions.

- Most company schemes also provide for benefits for your dependants if you die. These can be in the form of pensions and/or tax-free lump sums.

MONEY PURCHASE SCHEMES

- Contributions are paid into a fund by you (if the scheme is contributory) and your employer which is invested in stocks and shares (equities) and property etc.
- The fund builds up over a number of years and although all members' 'contributions' are pooled and invested together those funds invested by your employer on your behalf are identified as your retirement fund.
- The amount of your pension cannot be calculated in advance but on retirement part of the accrued fund can be taken as a tax-free lump sum. The remainder must be used to buy an annuity from an insurance company (i.e. you pay a lump sum and in return you receive a guaranteed income for the rest of your life). The amount of income will depend on the 'annuity rate' at the time. These rates depend on both the current and expected interest rates, your age and gender.
- Once you have paid a lump sum for your annuity you will not receive any refund of capital even if you die within a short time. However there is usually an option to have your pension guaranteed for a period of time, say five years, so even if you die within that time your dependants should receive the remainder of your pension over that time.

Benefits for dependants are usually provided if you die in service but if you die after retirement any arrangements for a dependant's pension should have been arranged by you on retirement.

Comparison

- Final salary schemes make financial planning for retirement easier as you will have a good idea of the amount you will be entitled to.
- Your employer takes the investment risk in a final salary scheme so if the Stock Market crashes it is

unlikely your benefits will be affected. However if investment returns are extremely good it is possible that a money purchase scheme can provide higher benefits.

- Money purchase schemes offer more flexibility in terms of the benefits they offer, e.g. a single person with no dependants may prefer more contributions to go towards his/her pension and less towards death benefits.

TIPS

- In general company pension schemes offer better benefits overall than PPPs. Don't be tempted to transfer without taking proper financial advice.
- If you have any spare cash consider making AVCs (additional voluntary contributions), see below, as you near retirement age to use up your tax allowances. This is the most tax-efficient way of saving and is totally protected from your creditors if you were made bankrupt!
- Make sure you receive regular trustees' reports from your company pension scheme and pay attention to how the risk is spread throughout the fund.
- If you die before retirement age your company scheme will usually pay out a lump sum to your dependants. You should make very clear who these moneys should be paid to, particularly if you have had more than one partner, as the trustees of the pension fund have the power to overrule your wishes, particularly if you have not nominated a dependant. If you have a complaint about your company scheme and cannot resolve it with the trustees or managers, approach the Occupational Pensions Advisory Service (OPAS) before you go to the Pensions Ombudsman.

PERSONAL PENSION PLANS (PPPs)

- Since 1988 the self-employed and those who are not members of a company scheme can have their own personal pension plan.
- You cannot have a PPP and a company pension unless you have two different sources of income, e.g. two part-time jobs.
- PPPs are normally sold by insurance companies and involve paying contributions into a policy in your own name. The fund is then invested at your choice and accrues until retirement.

- You can pay into a PPP on a monthly, quarterly or annual basis or contribute a series of lump sums, but the amount you can invest per annum is limited to 15% of your gross income.
- You are likely to have a number of investment options for your fund offering different degrees of risk. The higher the risk, the higher the potential reward but don't forget investments can go down as well as up, so it is sensible to have a spread of different types of investment.
- Your investments should reflect your personality, your attitude to risk, age and personal circumstances: if you like to play safe or can't afford to take risks building society accounts or deposit based funds are probably the best bet;

  if you are braver you could have a fund that is invested entirely on the stock market through a unit-linked or managed fund. Your funds alone are not likely to be sufficient to invest on the Stock Market so you can buy units in a pool of funds which will be managed by a fund manager. You will always retain your entitlement to your share of the pool but the price or the value of the units will go up and down in line with the prices of the stocks and shares the fund manager has bought.
- You can buy into many different types of fund: some have a mixture of UK and foreign equities with some property and Government stock thrown in, or you could buy into a fund which specializes in foreign equities or ecologically friendly companies, etc.
- If the above options don't appeal you could take out a 'With-profits' insurance policy. This is like the unit-linked alternative but without so much of the risk. Your contributions are pooled as before but the insurance company protects you from the full extent of any negative fluctuations in the Stock Market and conversely you will not receive the full value of any positive swings in share value either. You will be guaranteed a modest rate of return but using their investment expertise the insurance company will try and achieve a better return for your money which it will pay to you in the form of annual bonuses. These cannot be taken back once declared. Whilst fluctuations in the world stock markets will affect the amount of the bonus, insurance companies will try and declare bonus levels that they think they can maintain in bad times as well as good.
- On retirement you can take a cash lump sum and the rest can be used to buy your annuity or pension. This does not have to be bought from the same company to which you paid your contributions, so you can shop around to get the best deal (NB take financial advice!).
- The amount you receive depends on how long the fund has been invested, the performance of the fund, the charges levied and the type of annuity you choose to buy. For example, you could choose to have a guaranteed pension increase or a widower's or dependants' pension in addition to your own but these extra benefits would mean that your pension starts at a lower level.

TIPS
- Make sure your PPP has an 'open market' option so that you can choose the best company to provide your income when you retire, i.e. not necessarily the one you have been contributing to.
- Make sure you can swap funds without penalty if your fund manager retires or moves on. It is possible that your fund may not perform so well without him/her managing it (although it may perform better).
- Ensure that you understand all the options, how you will be paying and if the plan suits your circumstances.
- The longer you leave any pension policy the bigger the benefits when you do take it. So, if possible take out a PPP in a number of policies which can be activated separately as you need more income.
- There can be enormous differences between companies selling pensions. Surveys are published periodically in newspapers and *Which?* magazine.

ADDITIONAL VOLUNTARY CONTRIBUTIONS (AVCs)
- As the name suggests these are extra contributions you can choose to pay towards your pension if you are a member of a company pension scheme in order to top up your benefits.
- AVCs can be used to increase your benefits on normal retirement or if you want to make provision for an event that would otherwise reduce your benefits such as part-time work, early

retirement or a break in service for maternity leave for example.

- Total pension contributions cannot exceed 15% of your salary including any contributions to your company scheme, so if you are paying a 5% contribution already the maximum amount of AVCs you can make is 10% of your salary.
- You will have a choice of joining the company AVC scheme which is likely to be a money purchase scheme (see above) or making 'free-standing' AVCs. These schemes are all money purchase schemes and involve funds being paid across to another financial institution outside your company AVC scheme.
- The advantage of free-standing AVCs is that you do not have to change your scheme if you change job although the charges of a free-standing scheme could well be higher than under your company arranged scheme.

CHANGING JOBS

If you change your job you have three choices:

1 Leave the funds continuing to grow in your old scheme. They will then become payable at normal retirement age.
2 Transfer your existing pension to the new company scheme.
3 Transfer the money to a PPP.

In the latter two cases the transfer value of your pension will be calculated by the actuary of the old scheme.

If you lose track of pension benefits you have left with previous employers, the Pensions Registry, a free Government service, can help trace your entitlements. The Pensions Registry can be contacted through OPAS.

TAX

It's very depressing when you look at your pay-slip and see how much of your hard-earned cash has gone in taxation. Taxation is the means by which the Government, through the Inland Revenue, derives the bulk of its income and you don't just contribute through your wages. Tax is charged in one of two ways: direct or indirect.

- Direct tax is charged on: income earned (income tax); capital gains, i.e. on disposal of a valuable asset like a second home; inheritance, i.e. assets at death (see below).
- Indirect taxes are levied through Value Added Tax (VAT) on everyday goods and services, vehicle excise duty (road tax) and council tax, for example.

Personal taxation can be very straightforward for those in steady employment with a limited amount of savings. However, tax matters can be extremely complicated and professional advice should always be sought in these cases to ensure you pay the right amount of tax.

The Inland Revenue provides masses of free information on all aspects of tax affairs which can be obtained through your local tax office listed in the telephone book. Remember, tax avoidance means lawfully planning your financial affairs to reduce your tax liabilities, but tax evasion to avoid an assessment of your true tax position is totally illegal and could lead to a prison sentence. The Inspector of Taxes is responsible for assessing the amount of tax that you pay and it is the responsibility of the Collector of Taxes that you pay up.

Your tax affairs are dealt with at the office of your tax district which will not necessarily be the nearest one to you geographically. If you are an employee or pensioner it will be the office in the area where your company's headquarters or wages office is situated.

The tax year is from April 6 of one year to April 5 of the following year and you pay tax in the forth-coming year based on what you earned in the previous year with any adjustments for under- or over-payment in the previous year being taken into account.

Previously, in order to work out how much tax you were required to pay (if any!) you may have been required to fill in a tax return detailing all information about your income. But you may never have received a tax return, particularly if you have received a steady income which the Inspector of

Taxes already knows about through your employer. However the UK system for assessment has now changed putting more onus on the individual and therefore there is more likelihood of you receiving tax returns in the future (see below, **Self-assessment**).

- There are currently three rates of taxation on income: lower, basic and higher. These can change on an annual basis and any changes are announced in the Budget prepared by the Chancellor of the Exchequer. Changes in the levels of indirect taxation are also announced at this time.

  Income is split into three groups:
  1 liable to be taxed
  2 already had tax deducted, e.g. if you have a building society savings account or you are an employee on PAYE (see below)
  3 not liable to be taxed. This includes premium bonds, tax-free savings schemes such as TESSAs and some state benefits.

WHAT COUNTS AS INCOME?

- **Employment**: wages or salary, tips, expenses, commission, bonus, etc. If you work for someone else you are probably on PAYE (Pay As You Earn) which means that your employer will have deducted the tax due on your earnings according to your tax code (see below) before you are paid. If you are self-employed you pay tax in a slightly different way to an employee by submitting a return for the profits you made in the previous financial year.
- **Pensions**: the retirement pension and widow's pension are liable for tax and if you have a pension from your former employer this is likely to be taxed through PAYE.
- **Interest on savings**: most banks and building societies deduct tax at the basic rate before interest is credited to your account. If you have offshore accounts where tax is not deducted (and are permanently resident in the UK) or National Savings accounts, for example, you will have to show how much interest has accrued during the tax year, including accounts that you have closed during that period.
- **Investments**: any annuity, dividends from shares or profits.

- **Property**: if you let out any land or rent your home. (If you let out a room in your home you may not be liable for tax if you meet certain conditions.) Any rental income must be backed up by proper accounts and invoices as you may be able to offset some of the associated expenses from this income.
- Maintenance payments for you and your children from an ex-partner are not taxed.

TAX ALLOWANCES

Whatever the amount or source of your income everyone automatically gets a tax allowance or effectively a 'tax-free zone'. This depends on your age, marital status and any special circumstances. But there are currently three main types:

1 **Personal allowance**: everyone is entitled to this.
2 **Married person's allowance**: this can be used by either partner or split jointly between the two to suit your tax circumstances.
3 **Additional personal allowance**: mainly for single parents. There are also other special allowances, e.g. widow's bereavement allowance or blind person's allowance.

TAX RELIEF

In addition to claiming your allowances you may also be entitled to claim tax relief on certain outgoings.

The most common forms are:
- Mortgage Interest Relief (MIRAS) if you've taken out a loan to buy your main home (whilst MIRAS is still a benefit, this allowance has been reduced over the years and could be phased out altogether, so don't count on it!).
- Tax relief to buy equipment for your work.
- Tax relief to buy or improve property you rent out to tenants.

TAX CODES

At the start of every tax year you will be sent a Notice of Coding by the Inland Revenue stating your new tax code. This will show all the allowances and tax relief that the Revenue think you are entitled to and all the deductions they think they are entitled to make by taking the second set of figures from the first. The Revenue can then calculate your code, which represents the sum of money you can earn 'tax free' before they will start deducting tax. You will also get a letter after your code which denotes your tax status in terms of your personal allowance. If you have concerns about your coding notice you should inform the Revenue and explain why.

SELF-ASSESSMENT

This came into effect for the tax year 1996/1997 and involves a role reversal. Instead of filling in a tax return and the Inland Revenue advising how much you owe them, you will complete the paperwork, work out how much you owe and send the Revenue a cheque. You will be responsible for obtaining your forms and there will be penalties imposed for late submission and late payments. Instead of having one form to cover all eventualities there will be separate schedules to cover separate possibilities, i.e. one for pensions' income, one for savings' income and a separate schedule for the self-employed, so in theory life could be much simpler. It will still be possible to have the Inland Revenue do the calculations for you but you will have to provide the relevant information to them earlier than under the previous regime. You can call the Self-Assessment Line at the Inland Revenue or your local tax office for advice on your tax position under the new scheme. If this all sounds too much for you then you can always ask an accountant to sort matters out for you, but this will involve a fee of course.

TIPS

• Keep good financial records, i.e. copies of pay slips, details of other income, payments and expenses and any information to support statements you are making on your tax return, e.g. record of business miles travelled in company car.
• Keep accounts as you go, numbering bills consecutively to match numbers in accounts.
• Keep copies of the following forms: P45, the form given by employers to the Inland Revenue and staff when they leave employment; P60 given by employers to staff at the end of each tax year showing total pay in that tax year, the amount of tax paid and the employee's PAYE code; P11D

given by employers to the Inland Revenue showing expenses payments and benefits in kind.
• Always quote your National Insurance number in correspondence.
• Always ask for a written explanation if you have any queries and ask for a meeting or to speak to an Inspector if necessary.
• Tell your tax office when you get married and consider transferring some of your income-bearing assets to a non-earning or low-income earning spouse.
• Take advantage of tax-free investment or savings schemes, e.g. TESSAs or PEPs.
• If you are a non-taxpayer make sure you don't pay tax on your savings.
• Make sure your tax coding is correct.
• Make sure you claim all possible allowances and tax relief.
• If you overpay because you forgot to claim an allowance, for example, you can claim a rebate up to six years later.
• If the Revenue is late in asking you for payment it is possible that they may waive some of the moneys due if they were at fault.
• Don't forget that tax relief and allowances can change on an annual basis so make sure you have up-to-date information to hand.

CAPITAL GAINS TAX

This is paid on the profits you make from the disposal of assets. The tax is payable on gains made from the sale of property, e.g. a second home, and the sale of assets, e.g. works of art, stocks and shares or gold. Fortunately it is not charged on the sale of your main residence, your private car or the fortunes you win on the Pools, the National Lottery or from horse racing (although there is gaming tax on winnings).
• Capital gains tax can in some circumstances be charged on gifts over a certain value but will not be charged if the gift is to your spouse.
• Advise your tax office when you get married and consider transferring some of your income-bearing assets to your spouse if he does not take full advantage of any or all of his tax allowances.
• The Inland Revenue allows the reduction of your capital gains bill each year by allowing you to

offset your losses against your profits and applying the tax to the net gain.

INHERITANCE TAX (IHT)

- After you die your estate is treated as though you have given everything away and will become subject to IHT after deduction of your allowances. The tax due will come from your estate but if you have made gifts within the previous seven years the beneficiary will have to pay the IHT due. IHT is not payable on property that passes to the remaining spouse.
- Inheritance tax is a tax on gifts and for the majority is easy to avoid. Once again there are allowances announced by the Chancellor that can be used without attracting tax and your estate after death will only attract IHT if it has a net value over a certain sum.
- The first way to avoid IHT is to ensure both you and your spouse make a will. This would enable a couple to have the benefit of a double IHT allowance to cover their estate before their heirs became liable for tax.
- If you make use of your gift allowance this can also bring down your IHT liability. Gifts made at least seven years prior to death and gifts to a spouse are tax exempt but you should beware of giving too much away and not having enough to live on yourself.
- You cannot, however, give something away and then continue to benefit from it, i.e. you cannot give your house away and then keep living there rent free.
- IHT can be a heavy burden on your survivors and therefore if you are likely to be affected it pays to take expert tax advice.

INSUR-ANCE

You can insure against almost anything happening: a footballer breaking his leg, a film star being kidnapped and companies can now insure against syndicates of their employees

winning the Lottery. However this section focuses on the more mundane side of insurance and those events that you are likely to want to insure against in everyday life (except for car insurance which is covered in the **Cars** chapter).

A lot of insurance is taken out with telephone-based insurers such as Direct Line, putting the onus on you to phone around for a number of quotes. Alternatively, and for a fee, you could appoint an authorized insurance broker to advise you on the best (but not necessarily the cheapest) insurance – contact the British Insurance and Investment Brokers Association (BIIBA) or the Institute of Insurance Brokers (IIB) for free lists of general or specialist brokers.

LIFE ASSURANCE

Life assurance is the technical name for Life Insurance on the basis that you can only 'insure' against something that may not happen – and death certainly will! Life assurance is therefore actually something of a misnomer as a Life policy offers protection against death not life.

- Life assurance is most commonly sold when you take out a mortgage and the benefit of the policy decreases over the term of the mortgage as the amount you owe falls over the years.
- Life cover is extremely important if you have children or other dependants or if your spouse/ partner would be in financial difficulty if you died. In addition, if you have debts in excess of your assets which would need to be repaid when you died, a life policy could cover this liability.
- Single people with no dependants have no real need for life cover.
- Premiums on life assurance will vary according to age and sex. (Women live longer and therefore on average the cost of a policy for women is the same as that for a man four years younger.)
- There are two basic types of life assurance: term assurance and whole life assurance.

TERM ASSURANCE

- Term assurance pays out a lump sum if you die.
- You choose how much that lump sum will be and over what term you want to pay: the time period is often 25 years in order to cover the average length of a mortgage.
- If you die within this period your dependants get a cash sum tax free. If you haven't died within the agreed period you get nothing. Once you stop paying, on expiry of the term, the insurance stops.
- As there is no investment value under such policies you should choose the cheapest cover available.
- Level Term Assurance permits a set sum to be fixed on inception of the policy which will provide a fixed amount of life cover over the term of the policy.
- Increasing Term Assurance: under this type of policy beneficiaries would receive more in year five than year four, more in year six than in year five, etc.

WHOLE LIFE ASSURANCE

- A whole life policy guarantees to pay the sum assured on the death of 'the life assured', whenever that may be.
- As the assurance company knows it will have to pay out at some point, part of the premium is invested to build up the funds that are eventually paid out.
- Unlike term policies, whole life policies do carry surrender values so that you can get something back if you stop paying premiums after a few years. However, as the fund element grows very slowly, surrender values will be very low in the early years.

Some examples of whole life policy include:
- **With profits:** these cost more but beneficiaries will also receive a share of the profit of the investment fund through payment of annual bonuses.
- **Unit-linked policie**s where the investment part of each premium is used to buy units in managed funds, the value of which will go up and down in accordance with the market value. You can choose which type of fund you want to invest in depending on the level of risk that you are prepared to accept. Payment made under the policy will be either the sum assured or the value of the units, whichever is the greater.

OCCUPATIONAL/MEDICAL HISTORY

- If you have an existing medical condition, you

may be refused cover or your premiums may be loaded to match an increased risk of claim.

- If you are requesting more than the set amount of cover, it is quite possible that insurers will ask you to have a medical and if you are a smoker your insurance is likely to cost more than a non-smoker's.
- Most life insurance companies include questions about HIV/Aids on their application forms and will ask about positive HIV/Aids tests. When concern about the risk emerged, insurers increased their premiums significantly. However, as there have been far fewer Aids-related deaths than expected, premiums are now falling.
- Many people are given life cover as part of their personal or company pension plans and this should always be taken into account when working out how much life cover is required on a new mortgage, for example. It is suggested that people with families should have life cover worth the approximate equivalent of 10 years' wages.

A series of leaflets on life cover is provided by the Association of British Insurers.

BUILDINGS INSURANCE

- Buildings insurance covers the cost of rebuilding your property from scratch including site clearance and architect's fees. It is not the same as the market value of a property and is likely to be significantly lower.
- This type of insurance is usually a condition of your mortgage offer but you are under no obligation to buy the lender's own buildings insurance unless, of course, this is a condition of a special mortgage deal. Be aware, however, that your mortgage company may charge you an administration fee for the extra work involved in accepting somebody else's insurance policy.
- Buildings insurance covers all buildings and out-buildings and most things which are fixed and part of the house and its grounds including swimming pools, paths, walls, drives and gates.
- The cover will include almost all accidents which could befall a home such as flood, fire and subsidence, and will also cover your liability if someone is injured on your property because you didn't maintain it properly.

- Check your policy thoroughly for any exclusion clauses. If someone fell through your floor because of dry rot your liability would not be covered if dry rot was specifically excluded from the policy.
- Check also for excess charges. An excess is when you have to pay a certain amount before the insurers will pay the balance.
- This is particularly prevalent when it comes to subsidence of a building which has already been underpinned. You should consult with the Subsidence Claims Advisory Bureau for the best type of insurance.
- The building survey completed for your mortgage lender will advise as to how much building insurance you require. This will depend on the size and the square footage of the house and also the quality of the fixtures and fittings.
- The Association of British Insurers issues a guide as to what rebuilding costs would be for various types of property in differing areas. If, however, your house is unusual in any way you may need more specialist advice which can be obtained from the Royal Institution of Chartered Surveyors or the Incorporated Society of Valuers and Auctioneers.

CONTENTS INSURANCE

- Although this is not compulsory it is strongly recommended.
- House contents insurance can cover many different types of risk. It can vary considerably in cost to the extent that premiums can be so high that some people don't insure or under-insure their property. Cost of premiums may also depend on the security and situation of your home.
- Your contents should be insured for the total replacement cost less wear and tear for items such as linen and clothing.
- There is no short cut for working out the amount of insurance you need. Basically you must list the contents in every room and count up the value. Be totally realistic. Be aware if you under-insure items then the insurance company may well refuse to pay the full replacement cost.
- Usual minimum sums for contents insurance total about £10k–20k although companies are becoming more flexible.

- Greater emphasis is now being put on home security, and if you install approved security equipment the insurers will pass the benefits on to you by way of cheaper premiums.
- Discounts are available for burglar alarms, window locks, heavy-duty door locks and properties in Neighbourhood Watch areas where someone is likely to phone to report an alarm ringing rather than just letting it ring and ring.
- Installation of security equipment must be of the highest standard and acceptable by the insurers who may well send somebody out to complete a survey of your property.
- Burglar alarms must be regulated by NACOSS (National Approval Council of Security Systems) and must be maintained annually by a NACOSS operator. It should be noted, however, that while alarms give an added sense of protection they will not recover their costs by premium reductions in the short to medium term and your policy may be invalidated if an alarm is not set when property is unoccupied or the occupants are in bed.
- Discounted premiums are also available for older people or households where somebody is usually at home during the day when most burglaries take place.
- Contents insurance covers your furniture and other belongings in your house. You can also pay an extra premium for personal possessions insurance which covers your belongings when they are outside the home. When you take out this additional cover make sure you insure for the maximum amount you might take away from your home, on holiday for example.
- You should choose an index-linked contents policy so that cover rises with inflation and always inform the insurers of any changes in circumstances or any additional significant purchases.

KEEPING COSTS DOWN

The easiest way to save money on your insurance is to switch to a cheaper company. Make sure you are getting good value, and a month or so before your insurance is due for renewal get quotes from a range of insurers to ensure you are getting the best deal.
- Check that you are insured for the right amount and ask for a reduction in your premiums if you are over-insured. However, if the difference is marginal don't risk being under-insured.
- Consider taking out standard cover rather than accidental damage cover. Standard cover protects you for a list of specific events such as storm or flood damage, escape of water, theft or vandalism, whereas accidental damage provides additional cover if, for example, you break some china, glass or drop your television.
- Make sure you have the benefits of all additional security measures you have taken.
- Consider taking a voluntary excess, i.e. agree to pay an amount of each claim before the insurers have to pay the balance.
- Consider a policy with a no-claims discount. This type of policy discourages you from making a lot of small claims and gives you the benefit of reduced premiums for not having claimed.

CLAIMING
Immediate tasks
- Take photographs of items that have particular value – either monetary or sentimental.
- Make sure your policy covers these valuables against all risks. Most claims are not settled in full if items weren't adequately covered within the policy.
- Keep an up-to-date, accurate record of how much your belongings are worth (keep receipts). Valuations from jewellers/auction houses etc. can make life far simpler when it comes to claiming.
- Check the exclusion clauses: what conditions you are required to meet. It will affect your right to claim if these are not followed.

When you make a claim:
- Advise the police as soon as possible if you have been burgled. Keep a record of the name and number of the police officer who will also give you a reference to quote when making a claim.
- Check that the item you want to claim on is fully covered by your policy and whether the event that caused the damage is covered. This information will be set out in your policy booklet.
- Contact your insurer and request a claim form.
- Complete the claim form in detailed fashion as soon as possible and make sure you have included all the information requested, e.g. estimates for repairs. If you are not sure you have

remembered all the items lost or stolen please advise the insurers of this on the claim form.

- Keep a copy of all correspondence, and, if you have to buy replacements before your claim is settled, try to obtain confirmation in writing that your claim will be met.
- Some policies offer to replace items instead of paying cash. If you don't want a replacement, if an item has a mainly sentimental value, for example, you should demand cash. Do not accept anything but the full replacement value.
- If an item is separately insured do not accept less than the specific amount detailed in the policy.
- Resist any attempts to scale down claims because insurers argue that you are under-insured and offer to increase future cover if necessary.
- If you have an indemnity policy whereby insurers pay out cash they will often try and make a blanket reduction on replacement costs for wear and tear. Don't automatically accept this and be aware that some items such as jewellery can appreciate in value.
- It may take some weeks to settle a claim and the larger the claim the longer it is likely to take.
- For larger and more complicated claims, insurers often employ loss adjusters which adds another link to the chain and, therefore, may delay matters further.
- However many parties are involved, it is wise to telephone the loss adjuster and the insurer on a regular basis to ensure things keep moving. (Keep notes of dates and the name of the person spoken to.)

LOSS ADJUSTERS

- Quite often a loss adjuster is appointed to deal with the claim, to investigate and check the claim is genuine. The bill for this is covered by the insurers. If the loss adjuster rejects the claim, ask for a written explanation. Complain to the insurance company if you have any problems or contest the loss adjuster's evaluation of your claim.

HOW TO COMPLAIN

- Your policy document should tell you how to complain. Most insurers belong to the Insurance Ombudsman Bureau and you can take the

problem to them. The ombudsman can make financial awards of up to a certain level which are binding to the company.

- If you are still not satisfied you can take it to the courts. Some insurance companies belong to the Personal Insurance Arbitration Service, which offers less protection for you. This is because you need the insurer's consent to use it. You will not be able to take the insurer to court at a later date if you use this method.

PET INSURANCE

- This can be taken out to cover the cost of vet bills, which should never be underestimated.
- It is usually only available for cats and dogs but can also be taken out for more exotic pets and horses. In addition the insurance can cover the possibility of claims made against you for injuries or damage caused by your pet.
- Don't wait until your pet is getting old before you take out the insurance as most companies don't insure old animals for vet's fees.
- Check the terms and conditions of each policy carefully. Some policies have upper limits on vet's bills, expressed on a 'per claim' basis, whereas others have limits based on a 'per year' basis.
- Excesses on these policies vary. They can be a fixed amount or a percentage of the claim.
- If you own one of the breeds of dog defined in the Dangerous Dogs Act ensure that your policy covers any liability if your dog injures a person. It is also useful to have a policy that has a 24-hour legal advice service.
- If you tend to travel a lot try and choose a policy which covers you for cancelling your holiday or your trip abroad if your pet has to have emergency surgery.

WEDDING INSURANCE

- Unfortunately this does not pay out if your partner gets cold feet!
- For a one-off premium it does cover other circumstances beyond your control such as theft of wedding presents, cancellation of reception or perhaps negligence of a photographer which means that you have to have your photos retaken.
- Details of this type of insurance are most readily found in magazines specializing in weddings.

SCHOOL FEES

- Private schooling is expensive and school fees have risen far in excess of the rate of inflation.
- While you may be one of the fortunate who can accommodate all fees within existing savings or income this is unlikely to be the case for the majority, and flexible tax-efficient school fee planning should be started as early as possible.
- There are a number of types of school fee plans available but these can be expensive and difficult to get your money out if you change your mind about private education. For those who start early enough it is often cheaper and more flexible to save for school fees through normal saving methods such as TESSAs, deposit accounts, National Savings or PEPs.
- Insurers can provide a package of endowment policies with maturity payouts coinciding with annual school bills. Parents pay regular premiums and while returns are only average they involve little risk. There is no obligation to use the money to pay for private schooling on maturity if this is no longer an issue.
- Some schools run schemes themselves called 'composition schemes'. Parents pay a lump sum before their children start school and this is invested by the school and used to pay bills as they arise. You should check what rate of return a school needs to earn to pay for the fees and what will happen if that is not achieved. Parents will also be penalized if the child does not attend the school chosen or leaves early.
- Educational trusts are more flexible than composition schemes as it is possible to switch payment from one school to another with a guarantee that money will be repaid if the cash is no longer required for school fees.
- The Independent Schools Information Service (ISIS) can provide the names of companies offering such policies as can the School Fees Insurance Agency.
- If you haven't taken out insurance early enough you can make last-minute arrangements through banks who have schemes for school fee loans on terms which allow repayment over a long period of time. They will also require you to take out life assurance to guarantee repayment in the event that you die.

- If you already have life insurance you may also be able to get a loan from the insurance company against this policy which does not affect your life policy provided the loan is repaid.
- In all instances though you should ensure that whatever the insurance scheme you choose for school fees it allows you to use the money for something else if your circumstances change.

Insurance is a very necessary part of life and should be regularly reviewed to ensure that your overall insurance package is suited to your particular needs as they change throughout your life. Always ensure that you read the small print carefully and are aware of the things that aren't covered as well as the things that are.

HEALTH
INSURANCE

The probability of suffering some form of critical illness or accident and surviving is much higher than of dying, yet, ironically, we take out more life assurance policies than insurance policies to protect us against ill health. Health insurance policies have made a far more recent appearance on the market and they are becoming increasingly important in view of the fact that the state is no longer in a position to fund all benefits to support those with long-term illnesses or disabling injuries.

The best way to obtain the main form of health insurance is to join your employer's company-paid scheme, if one exists. However, if you have to go it alone the main types of insurance are:

- private medical insurance (PMI)
- permanent health insurance (PHI)
- critical illness (or dread disease) cover

PRIVATE MEDICAL INSURANCE

The spending on private health insurance rose by 0.3 billion pounds to 1.6 billion in 1993 alone. PMI covers the cost of medical treatment for acute medical conditions (i.e. short term or curable). It does not provide cover for chronic (i.e. lasting or recurring) illnesses. It aims to make private treatment affordable and covers the cost of hospital charges, fees for consultants, surgeons, etc. PMI will sometimes cover the costs of outpatient treatment depending on the type of policy. In reality if you require emergency treatment you will probably receive this on the National Health Service, but PMI allows you to avoid waiting lists and gives you more choice as to timing of when you go into hospital and indeed which hospital you go to (some are more like hotels).

GENERAL TIPS

- There are many different types of policy and you usually get what you pay for. Standard policies cover the treatment mentioned above and some policies allow you a cash allowance if you have to stay in an NHS hospital.
- Most policies exclude dental treatment, elective cosmetic surgery, childbirth (apart from complications arising from or during childbirth) or infertility treatment, Aids-related illnesses and kidney failure. If you buy a top-of-the-range policy, extra cover for dental treatment, for example, may well be provided.
The top-of-the-range policies cost significantly more than a standard policy. At the other end of the spectrum there are budget policies which provide a lower level of cover and may restrict payouts to
1 circumstances where the waiting time for NHS treatment is longer than six weeks,
2 certain illnesses only.
- Another way to reduce costs is to opt for a policy that restricts access to a limited number of hospitals.
- In some instances you may be required to complete a detailed medical history before you are insured.
- However, if you have been told by your doctor that you have a specific illness within, say, the previous five years, this is likely to be termed a 'pre-existing condition' and it is unlikely that you will be given immediate, or indeed any, cover for treatment for this condition. Check this with the insurer.
- There is generally little cover for alternative treatments such as osteopathy, acupuncture or homoeopathy, although insurers are becoming more flexible. Usually these treatments have to be recommended by a hospital consultant before the insurer will pay for the costs, although some insurers now only require GP referral.
- PMI is not cheap and premiums depend on your age, sex and occupation. There is no financial benefit in taking out PMI when you are young as premiums will generally rise with age due to the fact that older people make more claims. Some companies are cheaper for different age groups so you should ask for quotes for an older age group as well so that you can see what you are likely to have to pay in the future.
- Premiums can be cut by requesting a 'No claims discount' or it may be suggested that you accept a voluntary excess in return for a cheaper premium.
- Before taking out a PMI policy, you should take specialist advice from an independent adviser who specializes in PMI, e.g. the Private Healthcare Partnership, Healthcare Matters or the Medical Fees Insurance Agency.
- You should consult an adviser if you are considering switching your policy as this may be one instance where shopping around for a cheaper deal may not be beneficial to you, particularly if you reduce the level of your overall cover or the conditions attached to the new policy are less favourable.
- If you must undergo treatment, ask your doctor for an estimate of the costs involved to ensure that these are covered within your policy limit. It may also be a condition that your insurer has to pre-approve any treatment so you must ensure that this approval is obtained prior to making a claim under your policy.
- Check the small print. A 1992 *Which?* survey showed that 1 in 7 patients (of a survey of 660) had to cover some of the costs themselves. It is essential to check the small print of any medical insurance policies carefully: some include loopholes or ambiguities designed either to severely limit the claim, or prevent you from making claims altogether. Small print clauses exclude
incurable or chronic diseases (unfortunately this is standard)
ordinary dentistry
cosmetic surgery

normal pregnancy
infertility treatments
injuries caused by dangerous sport
'addictive conditions' (open to interpretation and abuse on the insurer's part) has recently replaced 'alcoholism'

- You may have to put up a fight: by drawing out the process, insurance companies hope to tire the claimant into either accepting a smaller sum or giving up altogether. The support of a GP or consultant is invaluable. However, you may need to resort to arbitration or the courts (providing you have a big enough claim). Concern over bad publicity leads virtually all insurance companies to settle before the dispute reaches the open court.

PERMANENT HEALTH INSURANCE

- Permanent health insurance pays you a regular income if you cannot work through illness or disability. Payments will continue until you return to work or reach the normal retirement age.
- Most policies will pay up to 75% (they are not permitted to pay more by law) of the sum you earned prior to becoming unable to work, less any state benefits for which you are eligible and any other income. In the case of the self-employed insurers will usually base the level of cover available on previous taxable income.
- Different policies pay out under different levels of disability and the distinction can also vary according to your occupation.
  The three definitions are:
  1 an inability to do your own job
  2 an inability to do your own job or a similar job for which you are also qualified
  3 an inability to do any sort of paid work.
  A policy which pays out on the first definition is clearly preferable.
- PHI can be very expensive and most policies will have a waiting period of at least four weeks after you stop work before they will start paying out. One way to reduce your premiums is to extend this period for up to 26 or even 104 weeks, which cuts the cost of premiums but also the likelihood of being able to claim. If you are a member of a company sick-pay scheme which would continue to pay out for the first six months, for example, it

would then make sense to choose a deferred period of at least 26 weeks.

- Another way to reduce your premiums is to reduce your actual cover. As previously stated, most policies will provide cover for up to 75% of your earnings, but you don't have to insure for this full amount if you feel you would be able to survive on less or have sufficient savings to cover any deficit. You should, however, take out cover for at least the level of your basic outgoings/expenses.
- Check whether your premiums and the level of cover guaranteed are reviewed periodically. You may find that a policy with low premiums is subject to an annual review and therefore the premiums you pay may rise steeply.
- As with PMI there are a number of exclusions which are common to most PHI policies. These include disability resulting from alcohol or drug abuse, pregnancy or childbirth, HIV and Aids-related illnesses and intentional self-inflicted injury.
- Before taking out a PHI policy you should check out what benefits (if any) are covered by your employer and get quotes from a number of companies particularly if you are in a high risk occupation. You should also take advice from an independent adviser.

CRITICAL ILLNESS (DREAD DISEASE) POLICIES

- While PHI pays out a regular income to those unable to work due to illness and injury, critical illness policies provide a tax-free lump sum in the event that you are diagnosed as suffering from a life-threatening illness.
- Most critical illness policies cover major organ transplants, heart attacks, strokes, cancer and renal failure.
- While the chances of suffering such a critical illness have increased, more people are recovering from life-threatening illnesses and so this type of insurance is becoming more popular.

ALTERNATIVE HEALTH INSURANCE

- Personal accident insurance: provides for a one-off payment in the event of a specified injury or accident, or upon death. Premiums are generally low but cover is restricted. This type of insurance ranks between PHI and life assurance.

- Long-term care insurance: this is in its infancy and therefore it is difficult to assess standard criteria. It is for those who are unable to cope without professional care either in their own home or in a residential nursing home. The definition of 'coping' means that you are unable to carry out a number of tasks defined as the 'activities of daily living' (ADLs). ADLs cover washing, feeding, dressing, general mobility and using the toilet. Benefits are paid until death, recovery or until expiry of the specified term. Like PMI and PHI, premiums increase with age and are generally relatively expensive.

- Anyone with savings or assets in excess of a certain amount is required to pay for long-term care costs in nursing or residential homes themselves. Once your savings fall below this figure local authorities will contribute part or all of the fees, although it is only a certainty that all fees will be paid when you have minimal savings. This is a thorny issue and one that is likely to stay at the forefront of the political agenda for some time so keep yourself well informed.

- Dental insurance: free dental care is no longer the norm. It is now available only to children, women who are pregnant or who have just had a baby (within the last 12 months), and people on state benefits. Dental health insurance can be taken out to cover accidents or specific treatments, or alternatively you can pay premiums dependent on the standard of your oral health. A few employers offer dental insurance as an additional perk but this is exceptional and you are only likely to see dental health cover if you take out the Rolls-Royce of PMI insurance policies.

GENERAL TIPS

- Choose a policy that provides the right cover.
- Check wording carefully, particularly for exclusions and excesses.
- Check for limits on the total amount you can claim during the life of the policy or in 'one policy year' in the case of PMI.
- If you don't understand any terms of the policy get them explained by the insurer or by your financial adviser.

- Always obtain several quotes and ask for quotes for different age groups.
- Always keep your insurer up to date with the state of your health to ensure that claims are not dismissed for non-disclosure of facts.
- If you are dissatisfied with the service you have received over a disputed claim you should contact your insurer in the first place and the Insurance Ombudsman Bureau (IOB) if your insurer is a member. Some of the larger insurers are not members of the IOB and therefore you may have to go to the Personal Insurance Arbitration Scheme (PIAS).

MATERNITY FINANCE

Having a child has massive implications, particularly on family finances where the loss of one income for a period of time can have a serious impact on your budget.

It is estimated that having a baby can cost between £2,500 and £6,000 in the first year and in any event it will always be more expensive than you think. Therefore, it pays to plan ahead. If you are thinking of starting a family you should consider the following:

- Try and save as much as you can to cushion the effect of losing your income for a time.
- Pay off any loans or credit card bills that are outstanding.
- Make sure that you have an up-to-date will. If you die intestate (without a will) your spouse will receive an initial sum of money and your personal belongings and your children will receive the rest.
- Check that you have sufficient life assurance and perhaps consider taking out private health insurance.
- Check out the implications of maternity leave on your pension contributions, particularly if you are in a company scheme. Five years out of work could cut your pension by as much as 20%. Therefore you should try and make up any gaps while you are on maternity leave, i.e. additional voluntary contributions (AVCs), see **Pensions**.

MATERNITY BENEFITS

- As soon as you start work for a new employer you are entitled to a minimum of 14 weeks' maternity leave. This period must include two weeks after the birth. (Details of your maternity rights can be found in booklets available from a Citizens' Advice Bureau, local library or job centre.)
- If you have been working continuously for your employer for a period of time you will be entitled to a longer break with the maximum totalling 40 weeks (up to 11 weeks before the expected birth and up to 29 weeks after the date of birth) provided that you have been working for this employer continuously for over two years. You will be required to provide your employer with a doctor's certificate advising of the expected date of confinement.
- Some employers, mainly the larger ones who place more value on specially skilled labour which is difficult to replace, have more generous packages and you should speak to your personnel department to find out your entitlements.
- Statutory maternity pay (SMP) amounts to 90% of your total salary for the first six weeks of maternity leave, then a sum fixed by the Government for the next six weeks.
- The self-employed and unemployed can claim maternity allowance up to a maximum figure depending on the amount of National Insurance contributions made. You should check this with your local DSS office or Citizens' Advice Bureau.
- While you are on maternity leave your job must be kept open on the same pay and benefits (including membership of the company pension scheme). If you are taking a full 40-week break you may not be given your old job back but one of similar status and responsibility and on the same terms must be made available to you.
- All parents are entitled to claim Child Benefit until your child reaches the age of 16 (or later if still at school). The amount is set by the Government and is slightly larger for the first child than for the second and subsequent children. If you claim Child Benefit you will also get National Insurance credit towards your basic state pension to cover the period when you are not working.
- It is unlawful to discriminate against an employee for any pregnancy-related reason and if this occurs you have an automatic claim for unfair dismissal. See **Unfair Dismissal** in **Work** chapter. This has limited compensation awards if you take your employer to a tribunal. If, however, you are discriminated against in areas regarding promotion, pay or fringe benefits due to your pregnancy you may submit to a tribunal for sex discrimination in which case the awards are unlimited. See **Sex Discrimination** in **Work** chapter.

TAKING A LONGER BREAK

- If you decide to stay at home and look after your child for a period longer than your statutory maternity leave, your finances are likely to need more substantial reorganization.
- It is now possible to obtain mortgages with a 'baby break' where payments are reduced over the period of a maternity break, for example.
- Some building societies may also be willing to extend the term of a mortgage or change the terms from a repayment mortgage to interest only or perhaps suspend payments for a period of time.
- Some institutions may also suspend payments or at least reduce them on regular saving schemes such as PEPs, endowment policies or pensions.
- If you are no longer a taxpayer you should make sure your bank and/or building society interest is paid gross.
- You and your partner should also consider transferring investments to your name so that you can both take full advantage of your personal tax allowances.

RETURNING TO WORK

- On deciding whether to return to work you should consider both the financial benefits and your personal well-being. While your net income after paying the costs of returning to work may not be substantial it may well be worth it to preserve your sanity!
- Child care can be very expensive. Nannies are more flexible and generally more experienced but expensive, whereas au pairs are cheaper but may not have the necessary experience to deal with very young children. (See **Child Care** in **Babies** chapter.)

- Probably the cheapest form of child care is to leave your child with a registered child minder or at a nursery. Your local authority will be able to provide you with a list of approved child minders. You should check their pricing policy carefully and find out if you will be charged when you are on holiday or if your child is sick.
- When you employ a nanny you are responsible for paying the tax and National Insurance as you are their employer. Whatever type of extra help you take on you should also take into account additional food bills, possible car expenses, telephone bills, etc.

If you are returning to your old job or even seeking a new job don't be afraid to negotiate the terms of your employment. For example if you want to work more flexible hours or part time and would rather forgo one benefit in favour of another, i.e. no company car and more holiday, you should ask. More and more employers are prepared to be flexible now that the female workforce has increased in value. It may well be better and more cost effective for your employer to have you back to work on slightly different terms than have to retrain or recruit someone to replace you. So if you want to work part time or can find somebody with whom you could 'job share', approach your employer and ask – if you don't ask you don't get! See **New Ways to Work** in **Work** chapter.

One very real option for a number of women is self-employment, particularly if the costs of going back to work outweigh the benefits. This has the added advantages of flexibility to fit around family life and of being your own boss. However, it is certainly not an easy option and, therefore, requires careful consideration.

BENEFITS

Benefits are not gifts, they are paid out of a State reserve fund we all contribute to through taxes and National Insurance (NI) contributions. Most people do not get all the benefits they are entitled to simply because they don't claim them or they are not actually aware that they are entitled to them. Unfortunately it is often the most deserving cases that go without.

TYPES OF BENEFIT

- Most working people between the ages of 16 and 65 have paid contributions to the National Insurance scheme which help you to qualify for certain benefits, e.g. Incapacity Benefit, Unemployment Benefit, Retirement Pension, Maternity Allowance and Widow's Benefit.
- You can only get these benefits if you, or for some benefits, your husband, have paid or have been credited with the right class of NI contributions at the right time. You should always quote your NI number when claiming.
- There are many types of benefit available from the State. The Benefits Agency, which is an office of the Department of Social Security (DSS), publishes a general guide to the benefits available in addition to many specialized leaflets regarding individual types of benefit. These leaflets are freely available in post offices, social security offices and your local branch of the Citizens' Advice Bureau. Information can also be obtained from Freeline Social Security or the Benefit Enquiry Line.
- Advice is available in a number of languages including Hindi, Punjabi and Welsh, for example.
  In addition to those listed above other benefits are available: Income Support, Family Credit, Benefits for Illness, Disablement, Infirmity, Invalid Care Allowance, Child Benefit/One-Parent Benefit, Housing Benefit, Widowed Mother's Benefit, Victims of Industrial Accidents, Residential Care, War Pensioners, benefits for those doing voluntary or part-time work and NHS assistance benefits for those working with the disabled.

CLAIMING BENEFITS

A number of benefits are means tested, that is to say that if you have a certain amount of savings your entitlement may be cut so that the savings are utilized first. This is particularly the case with Family Credit or Income Support or where assistance is being sought for nursing home or residential care expenses.

- To claim benefits you should fill in the forms available from the post office or go to the social security office or Citizens' Advice Bureau who will provide assistance in completing the paperwork.

- Officials may not tell you all the benefits you are entitled to, so check with Citizens' Advice if unsure.
- If you apply for benefit within a year of being entitled to it, it is possible to get back all the money from the date you were entitled. In special cases your benefit could be backdated further but not knowing you were entitled to the benefit does not count as a special case.
- You are entitled to appeal against any decision in respect of the award of benefits and you can also appeal if you have been paid less than you think is due.

THE SELF-EMPLOYED

- If you are self-employed you will pay a different class of NI contributions (there are five classes altogether) and for all parties it is possible to pay additional voluntary contributions to ensure that your right to claim the above mentioned benefits is not compromised.
- An increasing number of benefits are now available to the self-employed but the able-bodied who are not caring for dependants and are claiming benefits due to lack of work must be seen to be seeking employment.

THE CHILD SUPPORT AGENCY (CSA)

It is a Government agency which deals specifically with child maintenance and ensuring that absent parents contribute to the financial support of their children. A formula is used to work out how much maintenance is payable, taking account of each parent's income and essential outgoings and is reviewed every two years. In order to obtain child maintenance you must first request an assessment and possibly give the CSA authority to recover maintenance from the absent parent. For further information you should contact the Child Support Agency National Enquiry Line.

WILLS

If you die without making a will, you die 'intestate'. The Rules of Intestacy are very strict and make no allowance for any special circumstances or personal wishes. The Rules only recognize blood relations and make no allowance for unmarried or cohabiting partners. Spouses will not automatically inherit the entire estate if it is valued over a certain figure and if there are children to consider. It is therefore very important to set down who you want to benefit from your estate when you die.

- To be legally binding the will must be properly drawn up and witnessed. A beneficiary of the will is not allowed to be a witness.
- You should ensure that both you and your partner make a will. This is all the more important if children are involved. If both you and your partner die intestate at the same time the Rules of Intestacy assume that the older dies first. This could have significant implications for your estate.
- Your will should state how you want your estate divided up and who you are appointing as your executors, i.e. those who will administer your estate. (Executors are allowed to be beneficiaries, unlike witnesses.) Banks and solicitors offer professional executor services but these are expensive (they will either charge an hourly rate or a percentage of the total estate), and may not be as quick and efficient as you would like.
- Your will should also appoint guardians for your children and make adequate provision for the guardians to bring up your children as you would wish. (Make sure your chosen guardians are pre-warned of your wishes and agree!)
- If you marry after you have made a will it is automatically revoked (cancelled) and you should make a new one. If you divorce, your will will not be revoked but your former spouse will drop out of the will as if they had died. They will not be able to act as executor or benefit from your will and if they were the sole beneficiary your estate will be treated as if you had died intestate. If you want them to remain involved you will have to draw up a new will.
- You should consider drawing up a new will if there is any change in the circumstances of you and your partner.
- When someone dies all their assets are frozen until probate is granted (see below). This allows the executors, or administrators (see below) in

the case of the Rules of Intestacy, to administer your estate. However, if your estate is sufficiently large it may be liable for inheritance tax which will have to be settled before probate is granted. If your estate is likely to incur inheritance tax it pays to give this consideration at an early stage (see **Tax** section) so that the tax burden does not fall on your survivors at a difficult time. Specialist tax and/or legal advice should be taken.

- Make sure you keep your will in a safe place and advise your executors where it can be found. Most banks and solicitors store wills for free.

EXECUTORS/ADMINISTRATORS
These are the people appointed to wind up the estate of the deceased. If there has been a will, executors should have been appointed. They are usually the beneficiaries of the estate, and often those closest to the deceased. It is obviously in their best interests to wind up the estate in the quickest and most inexpensive way possible. If there is no will, those appointed to wind up the estate are known as administrators.

PROBATE
Whether you have been appointed an executor in a will, or are an administrator of the estate, you will have to apply to the Probate Division of the High Court for a grant of probate. This essentially gives you the legal authority to act, and in both cases is known as the 'grant of representation'. A leaflet is available from the Lord Chancellor's Department setting out the whole procedure. The Probate Registries are listed with their addresses in booklet PA2. An interviewing officer will be assigned to help you through the whole procedure, but they cannot help with the administration of the estate. Once probate is granted, the will is made public, and will be available to anyone who applies to see it.

WHO SHOULD WRITE YOUR WILL?
- Solicitors are a safe option as they can be sued for compensation. All solicitors should be covered with an indemnity insurance against negligence.
- Banks, building societies and some life insurance companies offer services but many insist on being appointed the executors, which they charge for.

- Large charities offer services, usually in the hope that you will leave them something.
- Professional will writers can be a cheaper alternative to solicitors, although they are not required to have legal training, which can lead to problems. The more reputable firms will carry an indemnity insurance, but always check. The Institute of Professional Will Writers acts as a governing body, but membership is optional.
- DIY packs are widely available in stationery shops. However, there are dangers. Some packs neglect to mention the necessity for witnesses, or fail to warn that a beneficiary acting as a witness invalidates their claim.

LIVING WILLS

Adults of sound mind can make the decision in advance that certain medical treatments (which include those that can save lives) should not be used on them. However, although the document may be valid in preventing the specified medical procedures at a point when the patient is no longer able to articulate her/his wishes, it cannot give legal authorization for euthanasia. An enduring power of attorney cannot be used with regard to a person's health. Documents and information are available from the Terrence Higgins Trust and the Voluntary Euthanasia Society.

LEGAL AID

Legal advice and the facilities for preparing a will are available should your circumstances meet the requirements for obtaining Legal Aid. However, it is important to remember that if the beneficiary is on social security, the legacy is liable to be removed following a means test. See **Legal Aid** section in **Law** chapter Special help is available for those who need to set up a trust for a handicapped person. Contact organizations such as MENCAP.

CARS

Women and cars are the butt of a thousand bad jokes, and 'bloody women drivers' has been a metaphor for poor road skills for as long as women have been behind the wheel. A lot of us actually believe the bad press, and leave everything under the bonnet as unexplored territory. This can make us dread ever breaking down, and, financially, puts us at the mercy of the garage mechanic.

However, statistics illustrate that women are actually *more* competent behind the wheel, have fewer accidents and commit fewer motoring offences than men. But while cars and motorbikes are liberating, there is also a growing awareness of the impact they are having on our environment and health. The government predicts that road traffic will double by 2025. Almost half of all car journeys are under two miles. Towns, cities, shopping and working areas are becoming more hostile to pedestrians as they are increasingly planned around car use. It is essential to weigh up these issues carefully when buying a car. If you're determined to drive, sharing schemes are one option which allow freedom but curtail environmental damage.

You don't have to take a course in mechanics to become more aware of how a car works. This chapter covers buying, selling, repair work, basic maintenance, what to do in an emergency and how to make the best insurance and finance deals.

LEARNING TO DRIVE

PROVISIONAL DRIVING LICENCES

- You are legally allowed to drive when you are 17.
- You will need a provisional licence. Pick up the form from your local post office, fill it in and send it off to the DVLA (Driving Vehicle Licensing Authority), costs £21.
- **Important:** when learning to drive you must always display L-plates and be accompanied by a fully licensed driver over 21 years old. The car must be insured for a learner driver.
- You must be able to read number plates at a distance of 67 feet.

DRIVING LESSONS

Learning to drive can be expensive: an average learner may need around 30 lessons to prepare for their test, especially without much practice in between. Driving-school costs vary and average about £14 per hour. Most driving schools are small and independent, although there are two main national bodies, the BSM (British School of Motoring) and the AA Driving School. It is important that you select your instructor carefully; sitting in a car with someone is an intimate business and you should feel confident and relaxed. Professional instructors must be qualified and display an ADI (approved driving instructor) green licence in the windscreen. If it is red it means they are still only trainees. Insist on a fully qualified person. If you have a complaint about the instructor or the driving school, contact the Driving Standards Agency who will investigate on your behalf.

If you own or have access to a car, it is advisable to practise with a dependable friend in addition to the lessons. You will find you are ready to take your test much faster. If you live at home, practising with one of your parents is usually the most convenient, but if they are very uptight you might do better trying to find a more objective tutor.

STUDY THE HIGHWAY CODE

Learners have to pass a two-part driving and theory test before qualifying for a full driving licence. The theory covers the Highway Code, driver attitude and driving conditions. There are 600 possible questions and you have to answer 35 multiple-choice questions. You have to pass the driving theory first before applying for the practical driving test. (See Directory for good guides to theory tests.) The Highway Code is available from post offices and most newsagents.

APPLYING FOR THE TEST

The two-part test costs £43.50. You can apply for a test via your instructor or direct to the Driving Standards Agency or local testing centre. You may take the test anywhere you choose, provided you send the fee and the application off to the appropriate traffic area office. You may have to wait up to three months to get a test date. You will receive an appointment card within two weeks. If possible request cancellation dates which can get you an earlier test at short notice.

TIPS FOR THE TEST

About 30% of people pass first time. You don't have to be brilliant to pass a test but you must show that you are competent, safe and considerate.

- Most people take their test in the car they have learned to drive in as they are used to it. The car you take the test in must be in a roadworthy condition, including working seat-belts, brake lights, indicators, etc. If the car breaks down your test will be terminated.
- Arrive early so you have time to relax and park in the easiest place.
- The test takes 30 minutes but it only takes the examiner a few minutes to get a good idea of your standard, so how you begin is very important.
- You must show your provisional licence and a photo ID is now required.

ADVANCED MOTORIST TEST

To get 20% off your insurance, you can take the advanced motorist test. Contact the Institute of Advanced Motorists who will direct you to a local training school. Most serious accidents involve a loss of control and it is possible for you to take specific training in order to reduce the danger on the roads. Skid School at Silverstone Circuit runs courses on coping with skidding.

Important to note: the Road Traffic (New Drivers) Act 1995 states that new drivers who get up to six or more penalty points on their licence within two years of passing their driving test will be forced to become learners again (i.e. re-pass the theory and practical tests).

TAX, MOT ETC.

Apart from a valid driving licence you need to have a road tax disc, MOT certificate, car registration document and insurance.

- **Road tax disc:** you must pay annual road tax for any vehicle whether it is roadworthy or not. You have 14 days' grace after your tax disc expires but only if you have applied for a new disc before the old one expired. During this period, you must display your old disc. It is a serious offence to display a tax disc which has been taken from another vehicle even if there was time left on the disc and the other car is no longer in use.

- **MOT certificate:** as soon as a car is registered for more than three years, it will require an MOT certificate. Imported cars also need an MOT as soon as they are three years old – NOT three years after the date they arrived in the country. You can be asked by the police to produce your MOT certificate whenever you are asked to produce your licence.

- **Registration document or log book:** the registered keeper of the car is shown on the registration document (the registered keeper is not necessarily the owner). In other words, while the registration document should be handed over when selling a car, it is not proof of ownership of the car. Details of the number of former owners, and the name and address of the last owner can

be obtained by the registered keeper by applying to the DVLA. There is no charge for this.

- **Insurance:** the laws concerning motor insurance are essentially quite simple, and were set up to ensure that anyone injured in a motor accident would be financially compensated for it. All motorists therefore, must by law have third-party liability. In other words, they must insure against injury to other people, which includes passengers in any car. See **Insurance** below.

CAR CARE

BASIC CHECKS

There are a number of simple maintenance tasks you can do yourself without much hassle. Obviously, don't do them while the car engine is running or immediately after the car has been used as the engine might be extremely hot.

- **Check the oil every month:** running out of oil will ruin the engine which must be kept lubricated. Use your car manual to locate the dipstick. This measures the level of oil. There are minimum and maximum marks on the dipstick and the correct level should be somewhere in between the two. If it is not, you should top it up with the appropriate oil. Once or twice a year you should completely change the oil according, to the manual advice, as it accumulates dirt. Undo the plug (indicated in handbook for the car) and drain the oil into a large container, then refill the tank with the appropriate oil for your car. Wear gloves because it can be pretty messy. To dispose of the oil, call up your local waste services who may have a collection service. Otherwise, dispose of it thoughtfully. For more information on the impact of cars on the environment contact Transport 2000.

- **Maintain your car's cooling system:** the intense heat created by the engine is usually cooled by the water from the radiator. Use your handbook to identify your radiator and make sure there is plenty of water in it. Top it up with tap water if it seems low and add antifreeze to prevent it icing up in winter. Follow the instructions on the bottle which you can buy at any garage. The radiator needs to be flushed out by your garage about every three years, as water can become corrosive and damage the engine. If you have bought a used car you should get it serviced and have the garage include a radiator flush. Never check the water tank when the engine is hot.

- **Battery check:** check that the level of water is adequate in the battery cells and refill them with distilled water if necessary. Use your manual to locate the battery and wear gloves as leaking battery acid could burn your skin. If the battery is leaking it should be changed.
- **Regularly check the tyres:** tyres should be filled to the manufacturer's recommended pressure which should be listed in the handbook. Every garage forecourt has facilities for testing and inflating tyres. Underinflated tyres increase fuel consumption and can be dangerous. It is illegal to drive your car if your tyres have severely worn treads – the grooved rubber that enables the tyres to hold the road. New tyres have 7mm grooves and should be replaced before they reach 3mm.

BASIC UPKEEP

A clean and unscratched car will fetch a better price second hand. Regular cleaning can also help keep the paint clear of corrosion. Cleaning the underside with a jet washer 2–3 times a year, particularly during the winter, helps reduce corrosion.

CLEANING TIPS

- Clean and shine chrome with polish
- Vinegar and newspapers for cleaning windows
- Washing-up liquid for the paintwork
- Car wax for all over shine
- Sponge clean and vacuum interiors

MOT TESTS

- MOT tests come around once a year and can only be done by an approved MOT-testing centre. You must take your old MOT and car registration documents with you. It costs approximately £30, takes about 30 minutes and looks at the following things: lights, steering, wheel bearings, suspension, shock absorbers, brakes, wheels, tyres, wipers, washers, horn, exhaust, chassis structure, seat-belts, fuel tank, mirrors, number plates, rear fog lamps and exhaust emissions.
- Before you go for an MOT, check as many things on the list as you can. If you find things are not working properly, have them fixed in advance so you don't find yourself in a situation where you have to pay the MOT garage above the odds to fix them for your car to pass. If the car fails, you will be given a form which lists the reasons for failure. If you feel that the result was unfair, you can appeal using form VT17, available from the MOT testing centre. The centre will tell you how to appeal and how long the procedure will take. You have to pay for the retest, but you may get money back if appeal is successful.
- Remember, an MOT is not a mechanical guarantee of roadworthiness. A service is a more thorough examination.

SERVICING

Most cars should have a service record book which indicates the type of service required at particular mileages or time intervals. While it can seem expensive to follow their guidelines when your car is working fine, it is a good investment and may actually be required to maintain a manufacturer's warranty. It is also a very valuable asset when you sell the car as the buyer can see how, when and where the car has been serviced. Costs of a service vary enormously. You do not need to go to the garage where you bought the car, but most garages will specialize in certain car models.

GARAGES

SHOP AROUND

- Choose specialized garages for special jobs.
- Look for garages that have membership of the various trade associations. This will ensure that there is a code of conduct in place and that you have some comeback if you are dissatisfied with the work. e.g. AA, RAC, the Retail Motor Industry Federation, Vehicle Builders and Repairers Association.
- Roughly identify the problem, then shop around for a price for the repairs. The quote will be more accurate if the garage has looked at the car.

- Use the *Motorist's Guide to Car Repair Costs* to get an exact price for replacement parts or refer to the *Parts Price Guide* published by the Thatcham Motor Insurance Repair Research Centre.
- Remember to check whether the work is covered under warranty.

FINDING THE RIGHT GARAGE

There are four traditional ways of servicing your car:

1 Franchised dealer or main agent: for the first couple of years take your car back to the garage that you bought it from (if you have a good relationship with them). A consistent service record contributes to a car's resale value (even if the service is slightly more expensive).

2 Non-franchised garage or reputable specialist: these are experts in a particular make or model of car. Find out the best ones from friends who have the same or similar cars or refer to owner's clubs.

3 Fast-fit centre: these started as tyre and exhaust specialists and have moved up into servicing. The more sophisticated the car, the less appropriate this option is, but they can be fast, friendly, convenient and cheap. Mechanics may be paid commission for the parts they sell, so don't get fooled by sales talk. The *Which?* guide of September 1995 recommends Halford's as the best in terms of advice given.

4 Back-street garage: smaller operations may be less able to afford the latest diagnostic equipment, but they can be honest and offer a good and economical service. If you have a popular make of car and the garage has been recommended, it is worth a shot. However, there are lots of cowboy operations out there.

DEALING WITH GARAGES

- Always write down the list of things to check.
- Describe any noises or problems you are aware of.
- Ask the mechanic to be specific about the repairs.
- Get several quotations from garages and make sure they include VAT, parts and labour. Ask for a labour rate per hour as this can vary from £15 to £50. Consult the *Motorist's Guide to Car Repair Costs* for standard replacement part costs.
- Get a written quotation, not a verbal one. A written quotation is legally binding.
- Franchised dealers should always quote a price based on the manufacturer's recommended service schedule. Get guidelines from them as to the labour time and approximate cost.
- If you go to an independent garage make sure they base the service and the quote on the manufacturer's service schedule. This should be in your car handbook.
- Make sure you have a list of any extra work needed, and request an exact costing on paper including labour and costs for parts.
- Ask the garage to keep all the old parts that they replace: they'll think twice about unnecessary replacement.
- Get the service book of your car stamped with the mileage and date of service: important for records when it comes to reselling the car.
- Check the final invoice before paying the bill and keep any bills/correspondence between you and the garage. You may need this if you have a problem with the garage later on.
- It is cheaper to do the simple DIY aspects of the service yourself, like changing bulbs on the car, for which you might be charged £15–£50 per hour.
- Check the work done is under some sort of guarantee in case of recurring problems.
- If you have an older or classic car, join the relevant car owners' club and source a garage through that network.

TIPS BEFORE YOU PAY

- Test drive the car.
- Ask the mechanic to go through the problems with you and show you the old parts.
- If you are dissatisfied, speak up then and there.
- Many garages charge flat rates for standard repairs even though they can be done in less time. Ask if they only charge for the actual time if it's lower than the flat rate.
- Check your car warranty if you have one to make sure that some of the work you are authorizing

isn't already covered under your warranty. Dealers are obliged to do this work for free.

- Check the parts replaced are not reconditioned old parts rather than new ones as they won't come under warranty.
- Ring up your car manufacturer's information department: they have guidelines for the items, times and costings involved in mending different parts of the car.

IF THERE IS A PROBLEM

- Go through the paperwork carefully with the garage and try to reconcile the differences.
- Know the basic legal basis of your claim, so they know you mean business.
- Speak to the person in charge.
- Keep a written record of what you do, and when you did it.
- Follow up your complaint by letter, keep to the point and make it as brief as possible quoting relevant laws. State what you want. Use recorded delivery and keep copies of all correspondence.
- Get evidence, other estimates and other trader's comments as to reasonable charges, photographs of the damage, etc.
- Remember, legal responsibility rests with the garage, so do not be fobbed off onto the manufacturer.

THE LAW

- The **Sale of Goods Act 1979** offers protection when buying goods, spare parts.
- The **Supply of Goods and Services Act 1982** offers protection when using the services of a trader to repair or service your car:
  to carry out the service with reasonable skill and care;
  to carry it out in reasonable time;
  to make reasonable charges;
  to use materials which are fit for their purpose under the Sale of Goods Act 1979.
- If work by the garage fails or breaks, the garage is obliged to replace the parts and redo the work under warranty. If this fails you have three options:
1 **Conciliation service:** if the garage is a member of any of the trade associations mentioned earlier, check whether they have a conciliation scheme which you can apply to. The Society of Motor Manufacturers and Traders (SMMT) and the Motor Agents' Association (MAA) are bodies which have produced a code of practice setting out minimum standards to govern the repair work on cars. If a member is reported as falling below standard, they can investigate independently. The outcome of conciliation is not legally binding and the trade body cannot force its members to reach a compromise.
2 **Arbitration schemes:** these are offered by the trade bodies or independent bodies such as the Chartered Institute of Arbitrators (a more expensive option). Both sides have to agree to refer the matter to arbitration and there is a small charge. Arbitration generally uses written evidence only. You cannot present your case in person, so you have to give all your evidence in writing.
3 **Small claims court:** claims of £3000 or less are referred to 'small claims arbitration' and are heard by a district judge. You will represent yourself, so costs are relatively low. You have to write to the garage first, stating that you will issue a county court summons: this is called 'a letter before action'.

BREAK- DOWN TIPS

There are two kinds of breakdown: either the car stops or the car doesn't start. Either one is most unwelcome. It is a must for women to join a breakdown service: the AA, RAC, etc., but shop around as they all offer different deals. Your insurance package also might offer a discounted membership when you sign up to certain services, so check it out first. Most of the reasons why cars break down are very straightforward and with a bit of detective work you can sort them out yourself.

KEEP IN YOUR CAR

Things to keep handy in the car: even if you don't know how to use the equipment someone with you, the AA/RAC person or another helpful motorist, might.

- jack
- spare tyre/wheel (by law): make sure it's in good condition
- wheel-nut wrench
- rags, gloves and an old piece of carpet
- torch with fresh batteries – getting one that can sit on your head like a miner's keeps your arms free and means that other motorists will see you in the dark
- tow rope
- jump leads: get a heavy-duty set as the thin ones are unreliable
- selection of bulbs: headlamp bulbs, indicator bulbs, etc.
- selection of fuses – check your car's manual for fuse types
- insulation tape to patch up holes in the exhaust
- empty can for petrol
- water-repellent spray like WD40
- set of screwdrivers: slot-head and cross-head
- pliers and wire cutters
- warning triangle
- a warm coat and walking shoes
- a throw-away camera to record accidents
- first-aid kit
- a can of the right oil, and water

THINGS YOU SHOULD KNOW

Changing a flat tyre

75,000 people called the RAC last year to get help changing a tyre. Be prepared when you take to the road. You can buy a long-handled wheel wrench from car shops for about £10. This will help you undo tight nuts. Keep it in your car boot with a piece of old carpet for resting your knees on. You don't want to get your clothes dirty changing a tyre on the M4. Refer to your handbook for instructions.

Flat battery (see right)

If your car doesn't start and your lights don't work you probably have a flat battery. Use your handbook to locate the battery and find another motorist to help you jump-start your car. You will need jump-leads which are a pair of red and black wires with clips attached at either end.

- Drive the other car close to yours so that the leads can reach between batteries.
- Place the cars in neutral and put the brakes on.
- Attach each end of the red lead with the clips to the positive terminal of each car battery (+). (Don't let the two lead clips touch each other otherwise sparks will fly.)
- Attach the black lead in the same way to the negative terminals of both car batteries (–).
- Start the other car and have the driver rev the engine a bit.
- Start your own car – the engine should ignite but if it doesn't, let the power run through for a few minutes before trying again.
- Keep your car's engine running and don't switch the engine off while you are disconnecting the leads.
- Turn the other car's engine off and carefully release the leads and clips, starting with the black one.
- If jump-starting doesn't work, the battery leads could be faulty or the battery may need replacing.

Charging a Flat Battery

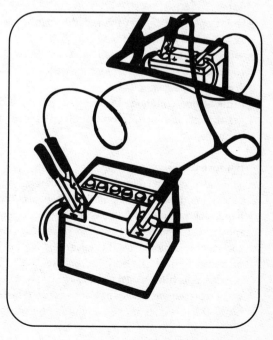

Damp distributor

Some engines are susceptible to damp and a liberal spraying of water-repellent WD40 (bought from the local car shop) might do the trick. Open the bonnet and spray it around the electrics, wait a couple of minutes and try again. Otherwise you may need to dry the distributor, which has several leads connected to it – use your manual to locate it. Undo the clips, spray WD40 onto it and wait a few minutes before replacing it.

Overheating engine

There is a temperature gauge on the dashboard. If it is up in the red area your car may be overheating, although it can mean that your gauge is broken.

- Turn on the heater in the car to divert the heat away from the engine.
- Drive to a safe place and turn on your hazard lights.
- Turn off the engine, open the bonnet and wait for the engine to cool down.
- Take your time, be careful and consult your manual.
- If it looks like there is water all over the engine, you may have a split hose, in which case you should call the AA or the RAC. If you can identify where the leak is coming from you may be able to patch it up with insulating tape and get to the nearest garage.
- If your engine looks dry you probably just need water.
- Don't open the cap on the radiator immediately as you could be scalded very badly.
- When the car has cooled down, add water (distilled if available) to the water tank.
- Try driving it again.
- If the engine continues to overheat you need to get to a garage as it could be something more complicated.

If a fuse blows

The electrics for your car's lights, wipers, indicators, windows/sunroof, all require fuses. Your handbook will identify where the fuses are and the correct replacement fuse. In newer cars you can identify a blown fuse because they are made of transparent plastic and you can see that the wire inside is broken, like a faulty lightbulb. If you carry replacement fuses, they are easy to replace; but if the fuse fails on something important like the lights you can replace it with a similar fuse from another part to get you to the garage. Buy replacements ASAP in a car shop.

Motorway breakdown

If most of your travel is done at night, get a mobile phone.

- Get on to the hard shoulder and if you are alone lock all the doors apart from the front passenger door (use this one to exit the vehicle).
- Put your hazard-warning lights on.
- Mobile phones are a godsend in these situations, but if you don't have one, get to the nearest emergency phone box – usually placed 1 mile apart.
- If you need to walk to the telephone box, remember that the arrows on the marker posts point to the nearest one. You don't need money to make the call and you will automatically be put through to police control who will take your details.
- When you've made your emergency call, stand on the motorway embankment if weather conditions permit – the main danger being from passing traffic.
- If you are alone and an unidentified car pulls up, immediately get into your car and lock the passenger door.
- Keep warm.

CAR SAFETY & THE LAW

95% of accidents involve driver error. Keep alert, keep your eyes open and anticipate what might happen next. These simple actions save lives.

ACCIDENTS

The Road Traffic Act 1991 lays out your responsibilities under the law in case of an accident.

You must:
- Stop.
- Call the police and emergency services if someone has been injured.
- Give your name and address, or that of the owner of the car if it is not your own. If you can't give your particulars to anyone for whatever reason, you must report the accident at a police station within 24 hours.

TIPS IN AN ACCIDENT

- Avoid making a statement to the police immediately – you are bound to be shaken. Your comments will be written down, and could be used by the other driver's insurance company. Be polite, give your details and supply any paperwork requested, and tell them you will make a statement later. Note the number of the police officer.
- Be civil, but don't apologize or admit guilt if you feel it wasn't your fault: don't abuse or attack the other driver.
- Note the speeds at which you were both travelling and whether seat-belts were worn.
- If they drive away without stopping, get their licence number if possible.
- Take the names and addresses of any witnesses – write down their comments. If you do not manage to speak to them, take their licence numbers. They may need to be contacted later.
- Write down the time, date and place of the accident.
- Write down everything that could have contributed to the accident.
- Make careful notes of injuries to anyone involved.
- If they are serious, seek medical help. If you go to an accident and emergency ward, make a note of the doctor who treated you.
- Make detailed notes of everything you can remember as soon as possible. Before moving your car, sketch or photograph all the details of the scene, including the positions of cars and roads.
- Contact your insurance company as soon as possible – most have a time limit of seven days – but don't wait for them to contact whomever is responsible. Do it yourself – in writing.

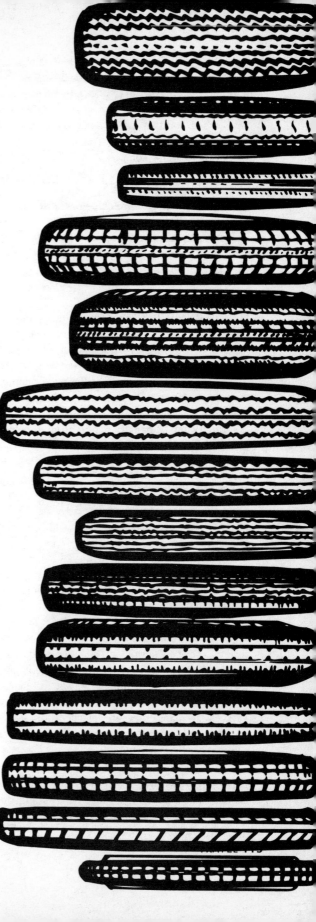

If you have been injured in an accident (any accident, it needn't be related to driving), the Accident Line run by the Law Society will give you legal advice in a free first interview. Your case will be assessed, and they can advise you on the likely cost of the case and on your chances of making a successful claim for compensation.

DRIVING OFFENCES

Many driving offences are actually considered to be criminal offences. Unlike other crimes, whether or not you intended to commit the offence is irrelevant. Fortunately, only major offences lead to criminal records.

MOTORING LAW

Most of the 36.9 million drivers already have a pretty good idea of what the law is and what their rights are. The Highway Code's latest edition not only outsells the Bible but has a simple guide to basic law. Speeding is the most common motoring offence. It is left to the magistrates courts to deal with the discretionary aspect of the law. Tot up 12 penalty points or more over a three-year period and you will be banned for at least six months.

CAR PROTECTION

Head-on crashes cause about 50% of all car deaths and serious injuries. Consider the following:

• Design, size and weight determine how much impact the car can absorb in an accident. The heavier the car, the less likely you are to be injured. Tables of statistics of accidents and car models are now published annually and the results can be surprising: cheaper does not necessarily mean less safe. However these figures do not take into account the way particular models are driven.
• Every year many cars are recalled for safety related defects and some models have better safety records than others.

Extra safety features
• Air-bags which protect the face from hitting the steering wheel are becoming standard but if your front seat has an air-bag, don't put a baby in there as they can suffocate if the air-bag releases.
• Safety-glass windscreens shatter but don't break.
• Anti-lock brakes reduce the chance of the car skidding.
• Childproof locks prevent your child from opening the door while you are driving.
• Consult the *Which? Car* for safety ratings.

KIDS IN CARS

Every year over 9,000 children under the age of 11 are killed or injured in car accidents, according to the *Which?* car guide. By law children under the age of 14 should always sit in the back of the car unless they are babies in a properly fitted back-facing seat. Seat-belts are a legal requirement for anyone travelling in a car.

Tips for child car seats
• Check the seat fits into your car.
• Use the right seat for your child's age and weight.
• Babies under 10 kg should face towards the back seat. The seat is held in place by the seat-belt and the baby is held in the seat by a separate set of straps. Toddlers and older children sit facing forward in a seat that is held by the existing seat-belt.
• Make sure the seat-belts are tight enough to hold the seat rock steady. You can buy kits which attach special straps to anchor points under your car's rear seats for extra support.
• Adjust the straps before every journey.
• Avoid buying second-hand seats.
• Junior travel pillows designed for children to sleep with support cost £3.99 from AA shops.
• Get the RAC child safety video and the leaflet *Childseat safety, a parent's guide.*

SEATS, WHAT TO LOOK FOR?
• harness adjusters well away from the child's neck for comfort

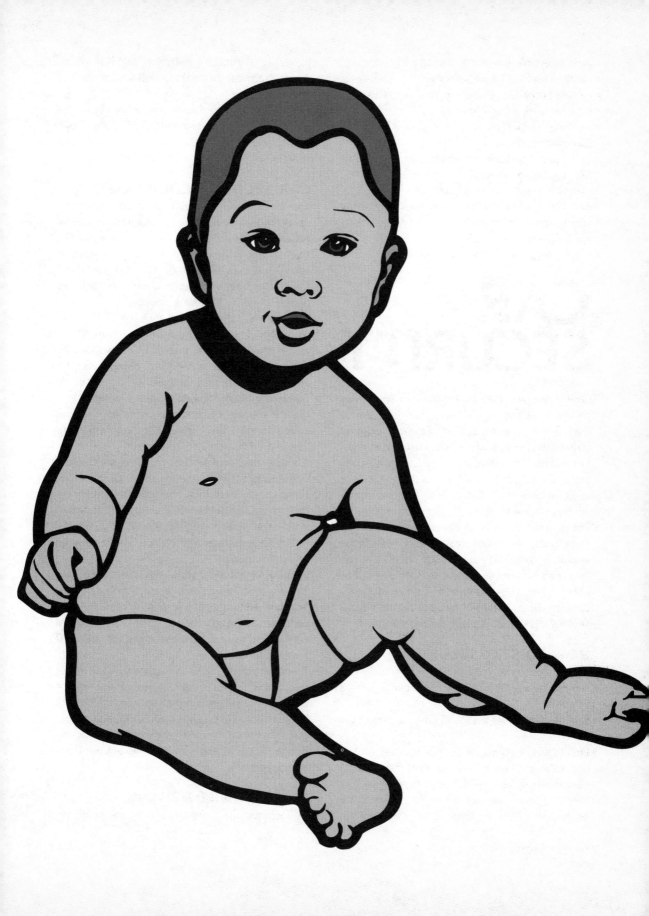

- easy adjustable harness and head pad
- easily assembled harness buckle
- harness buckle over thighs and hips (not stomach)
- machine-washable covers
- reclining mechanism on some stage-2 seats for improved comfort
- seat fitted with your car's lap and diagonal seat-belt, lap belt or fixing kit
- seat-belt buckle well clear of frame
- seat fits tightly in car, very little movement from side to side
- approved mark 'E' or 'BS'
- easy to install with clear instructions

CAR SECURITY

Over 2.5 million cars are broken into and stolen each year, one every 13 seconds. Is your car at risk? Some cars are easier and more popular targets than others. Most thefts happen at night to cars that don't have an alarm. Cars are usually stolen for a purpose, whether that is joy-riding or as a getaway car. Only 25% are stolen by professional car thieves. The Association of British Insurers has a list of certain approved car security devices – contact them for a copy. Some insurance companies give you a discount if you have one of their approved devices fitted. The Motor Insurance Research Centre security department in Thatcham has graded the various security devices – call them for the categories.

HOW TO STAY SECURE
- Buying a more secure car is the first thing you can do. Look at Which? Car for security ratings of cars.
- Park in a well lit area: 25% of crime occurs in car parks.
- Don't leave anything on view in your car. Mobile phones account for 60% of car theft crimes. Get a removable radio cassette and don't get lazy. Hiding it under the seat is the oldest trick in the book.

- Never leave vehicle registration or MOT documents in the car or anything with your name and address on it.
- Use visible security devices: the more visible the alarm, the more of a deterrent to the casual thief.
- Talk to your local crime-prevention officer about security on your car.

CAR SECURITY EQUIPMENT
You can spend from £20 to £500 depending upon the risk that you feel your car is under. The police recommend that the longer you delay the thief in taking the car, the less likely they are to succeed. A multi-layered security plan is advised:
- **Central locking** – it sounds obvious but a lot of people forget to lock back doors.
- **Car alarms** – there are two types:
1 those built in or fitted by the manufacturers;
2 an off-the-shelf alarm system which is fitted by the car dealer or garage but should also be approved by the manufacturer.
- **Electronic immobilizers:** these are installed into the car's wiring system and you need a special device to start the engine. They cost anywhere between £100 and £400.
- **Clamps and locks:** choose between steering wheel to pedal lock, steering wheel clamp, wheel clamps, gear-lever lock and gear to handbrake lock. They cost between £10 and £150 and their main value is as a visual deterrent. The Which? report tested them and reported that they all came off quickly.
- **Locking wheel nuts:** alloy wheels are targets for thieves, so it's worth locking them individually.
- **Window etching:** getting your windows etched with the car's registration number is a cheap and easy way to put off a professional thief (£5–£10 for each window).
- **Tracker systems**, sold through the AA/RAC: a radio transmitter is hidden in the car and when it is stolen the police can pick up a signal to track the car. They cost upwards of £200. You should put a sticker on the car to say you have a tracking device fitted to deter thieves who would not otherwise know.

SAFETY WHILE DRIVING
Attacks while the driver is in the car are increasing.

- **These are some simple precautions:**
- In town, lock the doors and keep the windows only partly open.
- Keep your bags out of sight.
- When you stop at traffic lights, leave enough space between your car and the one in front to allow you to pull out quickly if anyone tries to attack you.
- If someone tries to get into your car, beep your horn and drive away.
- Ignore anyone who signals that there is something wrong with your car and don't get out of it under any circumstances.
- If you think you are being followed, drive to a busy place like a petrol station.

BUYING A USED CAR

Four million used cars change hands each year. 400,000 of them are duds.

CHOOSING A CAR

Define your needs by writing your own specification.
- How much can you afford to spend and how long do you intend to keep it?
- Do you need a hatchback, soft top, four doors or two? If you have three children needing car seats, will they all fit in the back? (Some cars have much narrower back seats than others.)
- Do you drive in harsh conditions?
- What power features are important to you (e.g. power steering)?
- What sort of mileage does it do to the gallon and is it fitted with a catalytic converter?
- Do you want diesel or petrol?
- Does colour matter?
- What insurance bracket can you afford?
- Think about comfort and luxury. Do you want orthopaedic seats?
- Do you want a warranty with the car?

- How much money do you have for maintenance, servicing a year?
- Does car safety protection concern you?
- Do you want a classic car? Approach the relevant owner's club for advice and sources of well-known cars that have been looked after.

When you have a picture of the kind of car you want, then start to look for something that fits the bill. Check out car showrooms, ask your friends and take details of cars generally. Good sources are magazines such as *What Car?*, *Which? Car*, *Autocar* and *Top Gear Magazine*. First check in *Parker's Car Price Guide*, a booklet available from local newsagents, which gives current second-hand car prices, so you'll have an idea of the price. Now to track the car down.

PHONE TIPS

Utilize your time by phoning people, don't spend it trailing from Hereford to Hackney before finding out the car's the wrong colour. The following questions will help you assess a car's potential. Have realistic expectations.

- What make and model?
- How old and how much?
- Automatic or manual?
- How many owners?
- Why are they selling?
- Are the registration date and valid papers to hand?
- When was the last MOT and when does the tax expire?
- How many miles are on the clock?
- Has the car been garaged?
- Does the car have a full service history?
- Has the car been reconditioned, i.e. has it been in a crash and repaired with second-hand parts?
- What's the condition of the bodywork?
- Has any of it been replaced and is there any rust?
- What is the colour of the exterior: metallic or matt?
- What is the colour of the interior?
- Does the car have a catalytic converter fitted that takes the carbon monoxide out of the exhaust fumes (standard in all new cars)?
- Does it take leaded, unleaded or diesel?
- Does the car have an alarm or an immobilizer?

Some insurance companies require them.
- Does it have a sunroof, air-conditioning, electric windows or central locking?
- What about a radio or cassette?
- Check that it has all the seat-belts, front and back.
- What condition are the tyres in and when were they last replaced?
- Car safety: what is its record? (see **Car protection** section).
- What insurance bracket is the car in and who insures it?
- What does the average service cost?
- Ask if they have any other comments about the car. **Remember, always buy in the cold light of day.**

BUYING FROM DEALERS

The classic image is of the cowboy dealer who's slick and smarmy. Obviously they're not all like this. Go to dealers who are members of a trade association like the Retail Motor Industry Federation. Sales of used cars are subject to the Sale of Goods Act 1979, which means the condition of the car has to be made very clear to you. However, many second-hand cars are not covered by this Act as they are bought and sold by private individuals rather than motor traders. Look out for a trade association sign: this provides you with some legal comeback. All information should be made available to you: service history, repair invoices, handbooks, MOTs and a reasonable guarantee of recorded mileage (there are private companies that can do mileage checks for you). Most dealers will offer warranties (mechanical breakdown insurance), but you should read the small print and find out exactly what they cover. Be prepared to walk the forecourts comparing prices as they can differ enormously.

There is now a voluntary code of practice among the Association of Car Dealers. This includes quoting prices with VAT and giving you a copy of the checklist that was used when the car was inspected by their mechanics. You also have legal protection if things go wrong. Your local Office of Fair Trading produces a free booklet listing your rights (see **Consumer law** in **Law** chapter for more advice).

BUYING PRIVATELY

- This is often where you get the best deals, but legally the least protection. There is now a large selection of car magazines to choose from, especially useful if you're looking for a vintage or classic; otherwise Loot, *Exchange & Mart* and the national press at weekends have huge listings.
- There are also computer sales services which match sellers to buyers. The downside of private sales is that the consumer protection laws don't apply: the car need only be as described in the advert.
- Sometimes traders advertise as private sellers in the local press. You can tell because you will see ads with the same phone number next to several different cars. When you ring up refer to 'the car'. If they ask which one, it means they are probably a trader.
- When going to see a car, insist on meeting the seller at their home; not a motorway service station. Take a friend with you and a mobile phone for security. If you go alone leave the address and number of where you are visiting with a friend.
- Check the registration document in the light – it should have the DVLA watermark, and check that the owner's name is on all the relevant paperwork.

CAR AUCTIONS

You could be paying up to 25% less than for the same car in a forecourt, but you really have to know what you are doing. You buy as seen and have fewer legal rights. Go to one which is a member of the Society of Motor Auctions. There are about 60 car auction sites: British Car Auctions, Central Motor Auctions and National Car Auctions are the main ones. It's important that you learn to identify cars that are old company, rental or leasing cars. Read the catalogue thoroughly and have a few dry runs before the final bidding. Use the tips in 'Choosing a car' to build up a picture of the car and its merits. The auctioneer's conditions of business should be read with a magnifying glass.

CHECKING THE CAR

Try checking the basics yourself before you call in the professionals. You've narrowed it down over the phone, but don't leave your checklist at home. Take a camera to record, a torch to investigate and a magnet to identify any plastic filling.

- Listed below are basic DIY checks to make. The ultimate test is to have a garage that you know and trust give the final once over. This will cost in the region of £25–£50. Find a garage specializing in the make of car you are buying. Owners' clubs and specialist garages are very useful sources of information for older, classic and second-hand cars. The AA or the RAC can also check it over thoroughly: costs for checking a car are from £100 to £275 depending on the type and make of the car. It is cheaper if you are a member of the RAC or AA. If the owner starts to get tetchy at having it so thoroughly tested – walk away. It isn't the only car for sale.
- There are two companies that keep databases of cars that have been in severe accidents and have been written off by the insurance company, have outstanding financial payments still due or are stolen. It is advised to check with them before buying the car. Contact HPI or CCN, it costs about £30 and it can be done over the phone.

BODYWORK
- Look carefully for signs of rust: under the carpets, under the car and inside the bonnet as well as on the bodywork and headlamp reflectors. Rust is more dangerous and potentially more expensive to repair beneath the car than anywhere else.
- Little bits of rust can easily be sanded down and repaired but look out for patches which have been painted over (they will have a bobbly surface). If you think there has been a lot of repainting try the magnet test: anywhere it doesn't cling has rusted, been sanded, filled and resprayed. Beware, you don't want to buy a sponge on wheels.
- Don't be put off by small dents: you might be able to argue the price down and they don't always mean any real damage. Besides, living in a large city it's almost par for the course.
- Check the tyres, including the spare; for wear and condition.
- Check the floor, sills, exhaust and brake system for any damage, corrosion or leaks.
- Look carefully at the number plate to make sure it

hasn't been ground down and restamped (if it has, the car will most certainly be stolen), and that it's the same as on the registration document.
- Stand 15 feet away from the car, half close your eyes and check the alignment of the doors, bonnet and tyres. If it's a little out it has probably been in a crash.
- Put your fingers behind the back of the two front tyres; the space between the tyre and the body should be the same on each side. If it is not, the car could have been in an accident.
- Push down firmly on each corner of the car: it should bounce back and return to its normal position immediately. If not, the dampers or shock absorbers need replacing.

INTERIOR
- Check all the electrics: lights, washers, wipers, warning lights, electric windows, alarms, locks, sunroof, stereo, radio, heater, air-conditioning, horn, fan, rear-window defogger, clock, oil pressure and alternator lights.
- Look at the upholstery for wear and tear including the carpets and what's underneath.
- Make sure all the windows work and that the seats and seat-belts slide smoothly back and forth.
- Make sure the doors and door-handles are in good working condition.
- Check there is a jack and a spare wheel and the keys work in all locks.
- Finally, look closely at the milometer. If the numbers are not perfectly in line, it's been reset. If you're not sure, look at the pedals for wear: under 30,000 there shouldn't be much. Average annual mileage is around 10,000 miles.

UNDER THE BONNET
- An old trick is for the seller to warm up the car prior to your arrival. Most mechanical problems can show up when you attempt to start up a car from cold.
- Look for leaks, slack belts or worn cables.
- Check the exhaust for excessive noise and smoke (blue smoke means it's burning oil, i.e. worn piston rings or valve guides).
- Check the battery for signs of leaks or corrosion.
- Run the car with the radiator cap off: if bubbles appear, the head gasket may have gone (expensive).

- Remove oil dipstick and look at the colour of the oil. If it is creamy brown rather than black, it is likely the engine has serious problems.
- Look for the VIN (vehicle identification marks, the chassis and engine number) on a metal plate under the bonnet. Real ones tend to be stamped into the bodywork and phoney ones printed and welded on. The VIN and the engine number should be checked against the vehicle's registration document. Observe carefully, it could be a stolen motor.

TEST DRIVING
- Listen for backfiring, brakes squealing, clutch or gearbox whining, rattling or squeaking suspension.
- Feel the brakes for any pulling. Do they work in an emergency stop?
- Then check the steering for any pulling away from the straight along a clear stretch of road. Brake gently. If the car pulls to one side there are worn discs or unbalanced brakes.
- Feel for any slipping or difficulty in engaging gears. In a large clear space, put the car in full lock. If there is knocking or hissing and groaning, then the axles are in trouble.

THE NEGOTIATION
You love it and want to buy it. There are various factors that alter the car's value significantly. If the condition is less than perfect subtract 10–30% off *Parker's Guide* price. The effect of high mileage differs according to the model and its age: calculate it carefully on an average of 10,000 miles per year. Do not let extras sway you into buying a car. Used car extras lose virtually all their value very quickly. Don't make a financial allowance for them. Remember to get a signed, dated and addressed receipt for your money. If you give a cheque, the seller won't necessarily give you the log book until your cheque has cleared. Send the registration slip to the DVLA.

Don't forget your insurance.
Both the buyer and seller must notify the DVLA immediately a car is sold (the seller should fill in the detachable part of the document). If you don't supply this information you could be liable for someone else's motoring offences.

BUYING A NEW CAR

A new car has the obvious advantage of being in pristine condition. It should be totally reliable and have a manufacturer's warranty. The cost of servicing and maintaining a brand new car will almost certainly be lower than for a second-hand car. Before you choose, write down exactly your motoring needs: power steering, central locking, hatchback, saloon, estate. Saloon and hatchback are the most popular cars.

TIPS FOR CHOOSING A NEW CAR
- Work out what you can afford, how you can pay and stick to it.
- Work out the type of car you need and what you want from it.
- If you have a car to part exchange, get it valued independently. (The AA offer a service for this or check **How to Sell your Car** in this chapter.)
- Think about running costs, such as insurance, road tax, servicing.
- What is the petrol consumption like?
- How big is the boot, back seat and how many doors.
- Car safety protection – see **Car Safety and the Law**.
- Check market write-ups of the car you are interested in, ask friends, mechanics, etc. Do your research well, read up on cars available.
- Do not buy on emotion alone, be practical.
- *Which?* offer a phone service for helping to choose a car, called *Which? Car Line*. Calls cost 39p cheap rate and 49p per minute other times.
- The Ability Car Team offer fact sheets recommending cars for the elderly and disabled. (The factsheets cost £5.)

Depreciation can vary, depending on the make, image and quality of your car. Cars depreciate heavily in their first year, so you save money if you buy a car that's nearly a year old. For sourcing nearly new cars, try the dealer's own stock of demonstration models. Also check the manufac-

turer's own fleet as their stock of company cars tends to be turned over very quickly. Rental cars are also changed frequently. They are usually sold at auction and are bought by franchised dealers.

Things to consider to minimize the rate of depreciation of your car:
- Buying from a dealer gives them the first chunk of depreciation in the form of a profit margin.
- Buy a current model shape: when a new shape appears, old shapes become less desirable and values fade quickly. Hatchbacks are more desirable than saloons.
- Choose a car with a good mechanical reputation, reasonable servicing costs and a fashionable image.
- Attractive colours such as red or black are always more desirable. Colour can represent as much as 20% of a car's value.
- Engine size is important: bigger engine size is usually more popular for resale.
  Top Gear: *The Good Car Guide* has a new car A–Z which is a good way of studying what's available.

TERMINOLOGY
- **Special edition:** this usually means that a basic model has been given a few extras such as a sunroof and fancy graphics. Discounts are hard to negotiate and resale is harder. Dealers will go back to basic model price as a guideline.
- **Run-out model:** when manufacturers upgrade a car, dealers sell the out-of-date models cheaper.
- **On the road:** make sure you get the precise on-the-road-cost. The list price does not include the on-the-road charges, which are delivery, pre-delivery inspection, number plates, road fund licence, fuel and possibly a charge for the first service. These elements can add up to around £400–£500.

WHERE TO BUY A NEW CAR
Franchised dealers
Most reputable dealers belong to a trade association such as the Retail Motor Industry Federation or the Motor Agents Association and have a code of practice that protects you. They are appointed and approved by the car manufac-

turers and are on a fixed sales price. You can shop around the UK for the best deal but the dealer's margin has been substantially reduced over the years to around 5–10%, so room for negotiating is limited. Two or three days before a month's end the salesman will have a good idea whether that month's sales targets are likely to be met. If they have had a bad month they may offer extra discounts. Certain times of year are better for discounts. January and August are the worst months for negotiating discounts. Cash always improves your negotiating position.

Check the number of servicing outlets in your area. You don't want to have to travel miles for a service. Not all manufacturers have large servicing networks.

Car brokers
Brokers are middlemen who obtain brand new cars from franchised dealers. Because they buy a lot of cars, they get the best discounts, which in theory they pass to you. Find them in the *Yellow Pages* and ring them for an on-the-road quote. There is an element of risk: some brokers have no more than a telephone and a book of contacts, so it is not as secure as going through a dealer. Make sure you pay the dealer, not the broker, and get all the proper receipts. You can use broker prices as a guideline when negotiating with any dealer. Brokers won't accept part exchange, just cash sales, so you'll have to sell your car first.

NEW CAR NEGOTIATIONS
Worth asking for (they can only say no):
- A discount of around 7–8%.
- Which cars are currently attracting the best manufacturer's bonus. This is a series of payments made to the dealer as an incentive to sell a particular model and can range from £50 to £1500 depending on the car.
- A discount on any factory-fitted items you want.
- A discount on the on-the-road costs.

BUYING A FOREIGN CAR
- You must read the Department of Transport notice on 'Permanent Import of Cars into GB', form P11, and contact the DVLA about their requirements.
- Contact the commercial department of the

embassy in London for the country where you intend to buy the car. It can provide a list of distributors or garages.

- A personal import will always appear on the registration document. This can put subsequent buyers off and affect second-hand value.
- Car may have continental specifications: headlamps dip to the wrong side, left-hand drive.
- Warranty can differ; may not be covered by a British warranty.
- You have to pay VAT at 17.5% plus the cost of shipping and variable exchange rates.
- The AA lists established dealers, has a leaflet on how to import a car and runs an import service.

BUYING A NEW CAR? WATCH OUT FOR . . .

- **The disconnected speedometer:** check that the car hasn't been driven miles before you buy it.
- **Check the price:** sometimes a couple of hundred pounds is added to the invoice. Make sure the dealer writes the total for the on-the-road price when you make your order.
- **Delivery charge:** this is an unfair addition which is borne by the customer and covers the delivery and predelivery inspection costs. It can be as much as £400.
- **Minimum part exchange:** hard to know exactly the price you'll be getting for your old car, better to know that you are getting a fair percentage off the list price for your new car rather than some artificially inflated price for your old car.
- **Inadequate warranties:** check that the warranty covers all manufacturer's faults and defects for the full time; the warranty cover in some cases might be reduced after the first year. The warranty also may be subject to regular servicing at your expense.
- **Extended warranties:** dealers make a profit by selling extended warranties. Any form of cover on your new car is a good idea, but press for it to be included in the price because all manufacturers are looking towards offering extended warranties as standard.
- **Predelivery inspections:** the Motor Agents Association code of practice states that every new car must have a predelivery inspection with

written details available to buyers. Look at the PDI before purchase to cover problems that might arise shortly after the deal.

CAR FINANCE

New cars are expensive and few people have the cash to cover their purchase. Financing can be done through a bank, building-society loan, hire purchase, personal contract scheme or personal leasing-plan.

Ask yourself
- Can you afford to pay cash?
- How much will borrowing cost you in total?
- Can you afford the running costs of the car on top of the loan, at least £115 per month?
- Have you researched all the options for financing the car?

USEFUL TERMS TO KNOW

- **Rate of interest:** this is a charge made for borrowing money and is a percentage of the total loan.
- **Flat interest rate:** this is usually the rate on which HP and personal loans are calculated. It remains constant for the duration of the loan.
- **APR:** yearly rate of interest charged on a loan. It acts as a measure of the costs of different types of agreements from different sources.

WHERE TO GO FOR FINANCE

- **Hire purchase:** you can only get HP through dealers who have a consumer credit licence, not a private seller. Monthly repayments for HP can be either higher or lower than other financing arrangements. Car dealers can arrange HP for you, but they are not always impartial, so shop around. Normally you pay a deposit of 10–40% of the cost of the car and a little bit more for used cars. The more you pay up front, the cheaper your monthly repayments will be. It will probably take from one to five years to pay off the cost of the car. You don't own the car until you have completed the payments and it can be repossessed if you don't keep them up. You cannot sell it on without first settling up with the finance company. By law you must get a written quotation, including APR (annual percentage rate), total cost of credit being charged, the frequency, number and amount of payments and charges involved. They must provide you with one by law under the Consumer Credit Act.

- **Personal contract schemes** have been around since 1992. Their advantage is low monthly payments and you can have use of a new car that otherwise you couldn't afford. Plus you can always replace your car every two or three years. Watch for the total costs and look at the mileage-limits, which may be inconvenient. Similar to hire purchase, but instead of paying off the whole cost of the car during the repayment period, some of it gets deferred. This is known as the MGFV (minimum guaranteed future value) and is an estimate of the car's worth at the end of the contract. Deposit is 10–40% of a car's value. The MGFV and the deposit are then deducted from the selling price and the monthly payments are based on the remaining balance, plus interest. Payments are lower than other types of finance deals because you're not paying off the MGFV, you just pay interest on it.

At the end of the agreed period you will have three options:

1 Start all over again: trade the car in, pay the MGFV and get a new one, or sell privately.
2 Return the car and walk away, provided the car is in good condition.
3 Keep the car, paying the MGFV.

- **Personal leasing-plans:** until recently leasing cars was restricted to business use, however, since VAT leasing charges were abolished, opportunities are increasing. Taking out a personal leasing-plan (PLP) is similar to hiring a car for a long time: you won't own it and you can't buy it at any stage. You pay a deposit equivalent to about 3–6 months' rental charges and then make monthly payments. These do not include servicing, repairs or membership of a breakdown organization.

- **Manufacturers' deals:** most offer finance through their own credit companies: check the total figure. Deals can differ depending on the dealer. Often they offer a year's interest-free credit, if the repayment period is short. They can reclaim the car if you don't make the payments, don't keep your insurance up and don't keep the car in good condition. Make sure that the price of the car is not subsidizing the free interest offer. They also ask for a high deposit. They sometimes offer 50:50. This lets you pay 50% of the car's price before driving it away. There's no interest charge, and you pay the other 50% after a number of years.

- **Banks:** most banks and building societies will offer unsecured and secured loans. Unsecured loans usually have a fixed rate of interest and levels of borrowing are lower. With secured loans the rate of interest can be variable but the minimum you can borrow will be higher. Beware if you default on payments: they can force you to sell your security. Shop around as they vary greatly. You choose how much you want to borrow and for how long. You can also sell the car before you've finished paying off the loan if needed. They usually charge an arrangement fee, usually 1%.

- **Cash:** if you can afford to, it is worth paying in cash, as the cost of borrowing will be higher than the interest you get on your savings.

FINANCE FOR AUCTION PURCHASES
Don't be put off buying at auction because you need help with finance. Payment can be arranged.

Things to do
- In advance, arrange with your chosen finance company the time scale and agree the planned method of payment etc. They should, with all the relevant information, agree to releasing a cheque on the day of the auction.
- Be sure to talk to the auctioneer's general manager a day before the sale begins, so they are aware of the situation and advise you accordingly.
- Make sure they have all the relevant information about the finance company involved.

- Find out how much the deposit is and have it available, but take a trial run with the car before you hand it over.

GENERAL TIPS ON FINANCE

- Compare the deals, checking the relative merits of each option.
- Every lender has to state the annual percentage rate because they each calculate their loans and interest rates in different ways. You must compare one loan with another in detail. The shorter the period of loan, the higher the APR.
- Calculate the total cost of credit, i.e. how much you will have to pay on top of the cash price of the car.
- Sometimes lenders will add documentation fees known as an administration fee/set-up cost. It'll vary from lender to lender. You can try to negotiate them down on this fee.
- Direct debit is the preferred method of payment for most lenders. This way you also avoid the danger of late payments and any possible bad credit reputation.
- Loan protection insurance: if you pay a small monthly premium you can protect your loan in the event you can't make payments. This will cover you in sickness, non-voluntary redundancy and death.
- Credit cards sometimes offer big discounts on new cars. Some major credit cards and major manufacturers have teamed up together.
- Cash-back schemes are sometimes available from manufacturers: they pay you cash if you buy their car.
- 0% APR finance is sometimes available whereby the manufacturer subsidizes the finance company lending you the money for the car. See **Money** chapter.
- If you wish to terminate your loan: the Customer Credit Act 1974 allows the customer to end the agreement and return the car to the finance company, but only if they have paid at least half of the credit price of the car. So you are forced to pay for half of the cost of the car with nothing to show for it.
- If your new car develops a fault, you can take it back to the dealer to repair. You can seek a refund or exchange the car (as long as the car's problems are clearly to do with the car and nothing to

do with you). It is very important that you are still paying your instalments. If you want to repay the loan early, check if you will be charged a proportion of the extra interest and charges of the longer term agreement.
- Don't pay full price: bargain.

SELLING A CAR

You have two main options, the first is to go back to the dealer and part exchange your old car for a replacement. The other is to sell the car yourself and buy a new one outright. There are advantages and disadvantages to both.

Selling to a dealer
- A dealer might buy the car outright without the need for a part exchange. Garages selling new cars of the same make are likely to be interested as long as the car isn't too old, i.e. over three years old. Or look for the used-car dealer that specializes in your particular make of car.
- Part exchange: this is the easiest solution. You don't have to go to the expense of advertising or waste time dealing with potential car buyers. However the money you get is usually less than you could get if you sold privately. By doing a little research you can win at the part-exchange game. Find the lowest retail price for the new/second-hand car you want and the trade price of your own car from *Parker's Car Price Guide*, which is available at most newsagents. The difference between the two is what you want to pay: this is called the 'price to change'.
  The best tactic is to negotiate the discount on the new car without mentioning the part exchange. Once you secure the discount then introduce the part-exchange car.

Selling privately
You can achieve a better price this way. Determine your car's average retail value through *Parker's Car Price Guide* and be competitive with price.

Classified ads

Outlets for these are enormous but select the right one for your car. If your car is a prestige car you should go for nationwide cover – the *Sunday Times* is the market leader. It costs more but you are more likely to sell. For classic cars go to *Classic Car Weekly*. Use local newspapers to sell cheaper cars. In *Loot*, you pay nothing for the ad but you have to remember to fax it in to them each day. *Auto Trader* and *Exchange & Mart* have the biggest circulation and an ad costs an average of £50. Some magazines will include a photograph of your car for free. Ad should include: make/model, year, mileage, condition, full service history, additional features such as CD, stereo, metallic finish, is it a convertible? Price, phone number and times to call. Make sure you put on your answerphone.

Auctions

Contact a local car auction for auction dates. The auction house usually charges between 8–10% plus VAT. You can put a reserve figure on the car so if it doesn't reach a certain price it can be auctioned again. It is a good way of selling cars quickly but you won't necessarily get the best price. Prices tend to be close to trade price.

Computer bureau

Computer bureaus claims to match your car to potential buyers who are registered with them. The seller pays a fee and waits to be contacted by the buyers. Bureaus don't have a good track record.

Car marts

Basically you arrive with the car, pay £15 to park and wait for potential buyers to turn up. Check out the car mart first for the interest it generates.

Owners' clubs

Advertising in an owners' club magazine will ensure you reach the enthusiast, especially if it is an unusual or a classic car.

WHAT IS YOUR CAR WORTH?

Check *Parker's Car Price Guide* for an approximate price. The value of the car is firmly linked to the specification of the precise model. The nominal value will be adjusted to account for variables, which you can investigate and add or subtract accordingly.

Factors

- **Colour:** Red, black and white are good sellers.
- **Registration letter:** if registered after August of that year the car will be worth more.
- **Mileage:** average mileage per year is around 10,000 miles, below or above this amount will affect the price.
- **Time of year:** in spring, summer and September used-car values are higher. Winter is a bad time unless you are selling a four-wheel-drive. Summer is the best time to sell convertibles.
- **Engine:** diesel cars are worth more than petrol cars.
- **Extras:** values linked to extras are pretty worthless other than the psychological effect on the buyer.
- **Advertise** at 10–15% above the rock-bottom price you'll sell it for.
- **Show the car at its best**: make it shine. First impressions last.

Things to do

- Either pay the professionals who will already have the correct cleaning materials or DIY.
- Have your documents ready: owner's manual, service records, any warranties remaining, registration document, MOT and all the service bills in order.
- Steam clean the engine compartment (have it done by a professional).
- Wash the exterior: do wheels thoroughly, clean inside the doorjams, the undercarriage.
- Re-chrome the relevant parts.
- Touch up paint on scratches (dealership and autopart shops carry tubes or bottles of your paint colour). The key is to use as little paint as possible. Spray paint is difficult and needs the experienced hand.
- Polish with wax after.
- Vacuum the interior and shampoo the upholstery, use a toothbrush to get the dirt out of the cracks.
- Fix the tears, scratches.
- There is little point in replacing major components unless they are very badly worn. Better to renew any cracked or broken hoses, fan belts.

- Check the battery fluid, change the engine oil and filter (see **Car maintenance** section).

HANDLING PRIVATE BUYERS

- Always get a contact number from them and ring back to check whether they are genuine or not. Don't take mobile numbers as a guarantee.
- Patience is important and having all the information ready to hand makes you appear to be a caring and professional owner.
- Be open about the car's faults.
- Show the car in daylight.
- When handling the test drive, make sure they have the right insurance cover, comprehensive insurance. Go along with them for the ride so they don't disappear.
- Be prepared to negotiate to within 10% of what you want.
- If they want a professional inspection, it is fair to ask for a returnable deposit because you will be reserving the car for them and preventing others from buying it.

PAPERWORK & LEGAL OBLIGATIONS

As a seller you are bound by the Sale of Goods Act 1979. It is a criminal offence to make false statements about the goods: this covers the physical characteristics and statements about the size, performance.

- If they do not have full payment on the spot, ask for a 10% non-refundable deposit. You may write out a receipt for this, specifying non-refundable.
- Keep car until full payment is made.
- Let the cheque clear before handing over the car.
- Give a sales receipt at the end of the transaction, including name and address of buyer and seller, the car make, model, year and description, car identification number, price, date, condition it was sold in and both signatures; duplicate it and keep the original.
- Give the service-history records, send off registration documents.
- See **Obligations of the seller** in **Law** chapter for details on legal rights.

CAR INSUR- ANCE

Driving without insurance is a serious offence. All cars must be insured whether they are on the road or stationary. Motor insurance is a complex business and policies differ to such an extent that it is worth shopping around for the best possible terms. More than 366,000 motorists were involved in accidents last year costing the insurance business £433 billion, the average claim being about £1182. Getting the full benefit of a policy requires a full understanding of the claims procedure.

PREMIUM PAYMENTS

You must divulge all the relevant facts to the insurer so they are able to assess what premium you should pay. It is based upon the risk of your making a claim. They calculate it on the following:

- Your age: under 25 is more expensive. The older you are the cheaper your insurance gets provided you don't claim. The excess is considerably more for the under-25s.
- Driving experience: a person who has driven a car for less than 12 months is regarded as inexperienced and is considered a high risk for insurers.
- The cubic capacity of the car's engine: faster cars cost more to insure.
- The age and value of the car is significant as the relative costs of repairs or replacements are correspondingly more expensive. There are cheaper policies available for veteran or vintage cars which have limited mileage and other requirements.
- Whether it is used in the city or the country is also taken into account. Insurers have developed a ranking system for different areas of the UK: Cornwall, Suffolk and Dyfed being the cheapest, and London, Liverpool and Glasgow being the most expensive.

- Your history: a good record with no claims can reduce your premium.
- Your profession is taken into account: doctors and civil servants are considered less risky than those in jobs connected with entertainment, media and sports which are considered high risk.
- Drink-driving offences can affect premiums for up to ten years.

VOLUNTARY EXCESS PAYMENTS

Most insurance companies have a 'Voluntary Excess' scheme whereby you pay the first part of the cost of each accident claim.

NO CLAIMS DISCOUNT/BONUS

All insurance companies give large discounts if no claims are made on the policy. This can be as much as 30% for the first year, then up 10% annually until the maximum is reached of around 60% depending on the company. These 'no claims discounts' are transferable from company to company. If you do have to claim from your insurance, your no claims discount may be affected. You can also get your no claims discount protected. When you have reached the maximum discount of 60% it can be maintained whenever you claim, but there are certain restrictions, e.g. a limit to the number of claims that you can make.

If your car is a write off you will get paid according to the small print, so read it carefully. It could be either the value of the car before the accident or the cost of buying a new one.

CAR GROUPS

There are 20 car groups for insurance and these have great bearing on the cost of the premium. Groupings are largely based on cost and availability of spare parts as well as the potential speed of the car.

The size and power of the car affects its classification, e.g. a two-litre Golf Gti is **Group 14** but a Golf 1.4CL is **Group 6**.

Here is a sample of cars and groupings:
- **Group 1**
a Mini is the least costly
- **Group 3:** small cars such as
Fiat Uno
Nissan Micra 1.0
Fiat Punto 55
- **Group 6:** small/medium cars including
Citroën ZX 1.1I
Ford Fiesta 1.3LX
VW Polo 1.6L
- **Group 9:** family cars including
Rover 124SEi
VW Golf 1.8
Renault Laguna 2.2D
- **Group 12:** large family cars including
Honda Civic 1.5LSI
BMW 318SE
- **Group 15:** executive saloons including
BMW 525iSE

SECURITY

Contact the Motor Insurance Research Centre for published lists of approved security systems that may entitle you to a discount with your insurance company. Each new car is judged on a number of features, including alarm systems and high-security locks. Some companies specify particular security devices and then offer a discount.

LEVELS OF INSURANCE

There are three main levels:
- **Comprehensive:** this includes the damage to the insured car, third-party liability (covers the cost of repairing the other car), legal costs for defence if necessary, repairs, personal accident cover, medical expenses, personal effects.

- **Third party, fire and theft:** covers the cost of repairing the other car, loss or damage due to fire or theft, as well as your legal requirements to other people.

- **Third party only:** this is the compulsory minimum which only includes cover for the damage to the other car, its driver and legal costs.

INSURANCE FOR DISABLED DRIVERS

The applicant must describe all alterations to the car if any are made. Costs are assessed according to type of car, whether there is any no claim discount, the area and the age of the driver.

Some companies offer personal accident policies as a supplementary cover to the car insurance, including getting you home if you have a breakdown. Contact the Department of Transport Mobility Advice and Car Information Service (*The Mavis pamphlet*).

CUTTING COSTS

- Limit the drivers and save up to 20%.
- Pay voluntary excess on each claim made and your overall premium will go down.
- Limit your car to social, domestic and pleasure use.
- Garaging the car overnight may make a difference, particularly if it is a classic car.
- Limit the mileage that your car will cover in a year.

HOW TO BUY INSURANCE

In their adverts insurance companies will claim to give you the cheapest quote. Don't take this seriously but get a quote from them anyway.

- **Brokers**

A broker can represent many insurance companies. Some brokers specialize in younger drivers, older drivers, sports cars, etc. Look in the local directories, but for your own protection check to see if they are members of the Association of British Insurers. Ask how many insurance companies they represent. It can be anything from five to 200 and the more choice, the more competitive their prices. Brokers who have access to Lloyd's Insurance market through syndicates can be cheaper.

- **By telephone**

Direct sellers are usually part of a major insurance group and will be selling you parent-company policies in one form or another. They may not be keen to take high-risk people and as always, make sure they are members of the Association of British Insurers.

- **Classic car insurance**

Great deals are available for cars over 20 years old. You can either belong to a car club or have it insured by specialist insurers. There are limitations on mileage and drivers and your car may have to be garaged.

QUESTIONS TO ASK

Always write down the name of the person with whom you are speaking and keep notes of all that is discussed.

- Find out how many companies the broker's search will cover. More companies means a better chance of lower quotes.
- Make a note of any compulsory excesses to the policy.
- Ask if the insurer is a member of the Insurance Ombudsman scheme (can help you if you have a dispute with your insurer).
- See whether the premium can be reduced.
- Specify the exact cover you will need.
- If you are high risk, contact at least five brokers, as well as a broker who has access to the Lloyd's market.
- If you want help in finding a registered broker in your area, get in touch with the British Insurance Investment Brokers' Association or the Institute of Insurance Brokers.
- Ask the brokers what their fee is. They are required by law to answer this.
- Also, ring the same company twice, once in the morning and once in the afternoon, to check that they give you the same quote. Sometimes there can be huge discrepancies, depending on the time of day, who you speak to and their pressure to fill quotas.
- Check whether the insurance company is a member of the Chartered Institute of Arbitration scheme, see **Accidents and claims**.
- What's the fee for cancelling the policy?
- Ask for a policy booklet before accepting the price so you can check the terms and conditions. Is it possible to transfer the policy to a new car should you wish to; if yes, is there a transfer fee?

ACCIDENTS AND CLAIMS

If you are involved in an accident where someone has been injured, or the accident has caused congestion or there is a dispute, by law, you have to report to the police, then to your insurance company. More than 220,000 cars are written

off each year according to the Association of British Insurers.

- Some insurance companies have knock-for-knock agreements with each other, which means each insurance company will pay for their own claimant and this can affect your no claims discount. You will have to prove that the accident was the fault of the other person in order to avoid this.
- If the insurance company refuses to pay and you feel that you have a strong case for a legitimate claim, contact the Personal Insurance Arbitration scheme run by the Chartered Institute of Arbitrators. They will assess independently, and at no cost to you, whether the insurance company is liable. The insurer has to be a member of the scheme to begin with.
- If you have a drink-drive conviction your premium will increase up to 100%.
- If you are in an accident and are not wearing a seat-belt, compensation will be reduced.
- If you have an accident involving someone who is not insured, the Motor Insurers Bureau has a fund which compensates people. Of the 50,000 people who apply each year, half are successful.
- You can also negotiate with insurers when you get valuations on accident repairs for you car.
- As the car gets older check that your comprehensive insurance is not too high. It can cost more than the value of the car.

BIKES

The number of women bikers is rising by more than 20% per year. The rise in popularity of motorbikes, mopeds and scooters is not surprising as traffic mounts in major cities around the country. They are cheap, flexible, efficient and more environmentally responsible – they use one tenth of the space and fuel used by a car.

CHOOSING A BIKE

When choosing it's very important to assess the following: performance, reliability, economy, and your weight and height in relation to the bike.

There are three general types of bikes:

1 **Moped:** this is the smallest bike available, with around 30 models to choose from. They go up to 30mph and have no more than a 50cc engine. They can be stylish and easy to ride and are mostly automatic.
2 **Scooters:** they start at 50cc up to 200cc, but most of them are 125cc. They offer some protection from the elements and many of them are automatic. On the continent they are the bike of choice, e.g. Piaggio.
3 **Motorcycle:** there are generally two types.
Trial bikes: they are small and light and ridden in an upright position which can be more comfortable. They have an engine size of 125cc up to 1000cc.
Road bikes: can be a racing bike or a standard commuter bike with an engine size from 125cc up to 1300cc.

'cc': cubic capacity means the internal volume of the engine, the higher the cc the bigger the engine, which means the more powerful it is.

You will need to be aware of licence requirements for each bike as they vary; see **Directory** for contacts for further advice.

LAW

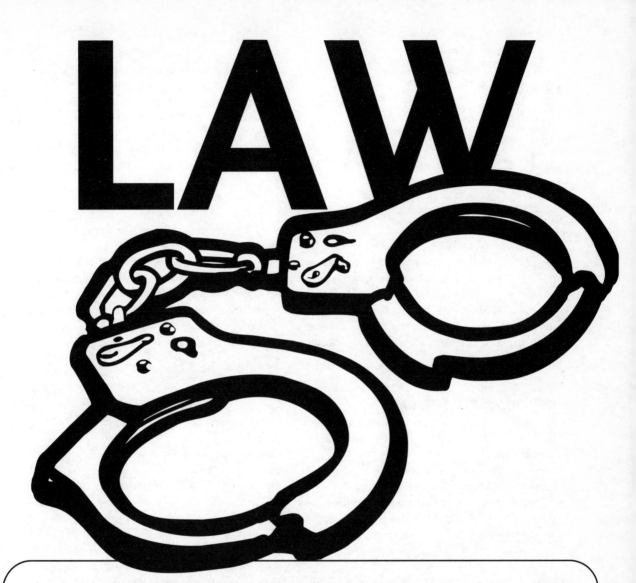

For most people the law is unknown territory – to be avoided until absolutely necessary. TV dramas suggest that the legal system revolves around witty barristers dealing justice to slavering criminals in atmospherically lit courtrooms. But while criminal law may yield more entertaining plots, in reality only a very small proportion of the population ever comes into direct contact with it. Criminal law is enforced by the State and deals with behaviour which is 'threatening to the person or the community'. Civil law outlines the rights as well as the obligations of each individual in this country. It governs virtually every detail of our lives, from birth to death, and for this reason, the civil branch of the law is largely the focus throughout this book. Legal issues crop up everywhere, and you'll find them in each chapter wherever they're most relevant.

This chapter gives a rundown of how the system works, who's who, where to look for advice, and includes a section on criminal law. While the complexity of the law can seem daunting, it isn't difficult to grasp the principles, your basic rights and how to find the right help when you need it most.

THE LEGAL SYSTEM

Britain has no single written constitution defining citizens' rights. The legal system here is based on 'common law' which has evolved over centuries. Parliament makes new laws which are enforced by the courts; judges then have to 'interpret' the law (giving them considerable power), and their rulings on particular cases set precedents, which are followed unless they are subsequently over-ruled. This means that while the basic guidelines defining right from wrong remain fairly steady, the finer details of the law are constantly changing.

REFORMS TO THE LAW

- Parliament is responsible for the ultimate legislative changes, but it can be influenced through several routes.
- MPs can rally for changes, and (at least theoretically) reflect the views of their constituents.
- Pressure groups can be formed by members of the legal profession or general public to instigate change (see **Politics** chapter for advice on approaching your MP and forming pressure groups).
- The Law Commission is a body specifically set up to advise the Government on legal issues. Headed by a High Court judge, the Commission publishes reports outlining specific proposals for law reform.
- Royal Commissions are appointed by the Government to investigate specific areas within the law which require urgent updating.

WHO'S WHO?

The term 'lawyer' is generally applied to anyone versed in law and includes the familiar solicitors and barristers; judges are also lawyers.

SOLICITORS

- A solicitor's full title is 'Solicitor of the Supreme Court'. They are bound by duties to the court which can take precedence over their duties to their client (e.g. a solicitor would be committing an offence by asking a client s/he knows to be guilty to plead 'not guilty').
- Working solicitors must have a valid 'practising certificate'.
- They generally practise in partnerships.
- They are personally liable for (and have to be insured against) negligence.
- They are governed by the Law Society who set and monitor standards of conduct.
- Until 1990 only barristers were allowed to represent clients in the higher courts (the right of audience). Now, solicitors with additional training can become a 'solicitor advocate' and represent his/her clients in all courts, though not many do so.
- Nearly half of all recently qualified solicitors are women.

Solicitors' work is generally divided between 'contentious' and 'non-contentious' cases – the vast majority being 'non-contentious'.

- **Contentious work** involves a conflict between two parties and may involve litigation (court proceedings). Contentious work includes criminal and matrimonial cases as well as some civil disputes. In most contentious cases the solicitor will prepare the case and then brief a barrister for the court appearance. Solicitors can also negotiate for out-of-court settlements.
- **Non-contentious work** includes writing 'solicitors' letters', house conveyancing and the drawing up of wills.

BARRISTERS

- Barristers are very much in the minority: there are about seven times as many solicitors.
- Only Gray's Inn, Lincoln's Inn, Inner Temple and Middle Temple (the four Inns of Court) have the right to appoint barristers; all barristers must be a member of one of these inns.
- When barristers are appointed, they are said to have been 'called to the Bar'. The General Council of the Bar (the 'Bar Council') is their governing body.

- They work in 'chambers' – rather than offices – of which they are tenants.
- Barristers must operate independently – they cannot practise within a partnership (although this is under review).
- Members of the general public can only instruct a barrister through a solicitor. Any information the barrister may need from the client must be obtained by the solicitor, extending both the process and the bill.
- 'Direct professional access' means that members of professions approved by the Bar Council, including architects, chartered accountants and engineers, can instruct barristers without resorting to a solicitor.
- Barristers are not supposed to discuss money. They employ a clerk (who effectively acts as an agent) to negotiate jobs and fees with solicitors.
- Barristers may take on cases, without charging, which represent the public interest. Encouraged by the Bar Council, this is known as *pro bono* work.
- Queen's Counsel (QCs – in silk rather than cotton gowns) make up roughly 10% of barristers – they are generally more experienced. Since 1977 QCs can appear in court without a junior barrister, although this is still discouraged. This means that although the team is doubled, the fees increase accordingly.

JUDGES

There is a hierarchy of judges which reflects the trial system in this country.
- District Judges are usually solicitors and only deal with 'minor' cases in the County Court such as small claims.
- Circuit Judges are barristers or solicitors who have been practising for at least 20 years. They try the less serious Crown Court cases and the county cases.
- The Lord Chief Justice heads the High (or Crown) Court where serious criminal offences such as treason and murder are tried.
- The Master of the Rolls heads the Court of Appeal and 27 Appeal Court judges: the Lord Justices of Appeal.
- The 'Law Lords' are the most senior judges in Britain. They sit in the House of Lords under the Lord Chancellor.

The Lord Chancellor (the most powerful) is politically appointed and has a seat in the Government. The Lord Chancellor appoints all but the most senior judges. The most senior are appointed by the Prime Minister, based on the advice of the Lord Chancellor.

MAGISTRATES OR 'JUSTICES OF THE PEACE' (JPs)

Often don't have a legal background and are chosen from the local community by the Lord Chancellor. They work in small groups to hear cases, and have to take advice from a qualified lawyer.

GETTING LEGAL ADVICE

A previous Lord Chancellor has identified cost, complexity and time as the major deterrents for people who might otherwise consider taking legal action. However, there are some things you can do to minimize the expense and the hassle. But remember, if you do start proceedings against someone and then 'change your mind' (for whatever reason), not only will you be liable for your own costs but theirs as well. Think very carefully before acting. Check if any of your insurance policies include legal cover or have legal advice lines.

ACCIDENT LINE

Free legal advice on personal accidents is available by calling Freephone 0500 19 29 39. The Accident Line is run by the Law Society and they will give you a free 30-minute interview and put you in touch with a specialist solicitor. Up to 85% of people who could claim injury compensation don't bother.

CITIZENS' ADVICE BUREAUX

Financed by central and local government grants, Citizens' Advice Bureaux are staffed by skilled professionals and local volunteers who offer free advice, guidance and even practical help such as the drafting of letters. They should be your first stop when trying to get advice. Essentially, they can help you define the nature of your problem, and even if they can't solve it they can refer you to a more appropriate body. If you have a legal problem they can help you find a free legal advice scheme or an inexpensive lawyer and they may even be able to offer some opinions on your rights or what courses of action might be open to you. They cover many of the issues which have been marginalized (for obvious financial reasons) by private solicitors' practices such as debt, housing, social security, immigration and employment. They produce a range of leaflets in several languages and they are nationwide. You'll find your local CAB in the phone book. Though much of the work carried out by Citizens' Advice Bureaux is legal in content, they are independent of the Legal Aid system so clients are not means tested or expected to pay a fee.

LAW CENTRES

There are about 60 law centres in England and Wales; most are found on the high streets of inner-city areas. They generally focus on social welfare law which includes benefit claims, housing and immigration: again areas not adequately covered by solicitors in private practice. They are usually funded by local authorities and run by volunteers who refer to one duty solicitor. Some may be better equipped than others to deal with a particular problem, in which case they can make a referral to another centre or solicitor (local referral schemes). They will give at least an initial interview for free, and will work on Legal Aid schemes for which they will assess eligibility.

LEGAL ADVICE CENTRES

Often run by churches and charities; free legal advice is offered by volunteer lawyers on a certain evening each week. The type of advice will depend on the individual. Your Citizens' Advice Bureau will have details of centres in your area.

LEGAL AID

Legal Aid was originally introduced to allow 'universal access to justice'. However, since 1950, when 80% of the population were eligible, funding has been severely restricted, reducing those who qualify to 48%. Now, you must earn less than £2,563 per year in order to qualify for full Legal Aid. You may qualify for some help (on the 'Green Form Scheme') if you earn less than £7,595 per year, but anyone earning more than this is ineligible. This has made covering legal expenses extremely difficult for all those but the very poor and the very rich. Often a contribution to the costs of a court case won on Legal Aid is demanded, so it is essential to work out beforehand (with the lawyers) whether or not your case makes financial sense. A booklet is available from the Legal Aid Head Office which explains how Legal Aid works, how to assess whether or not you are eligible, and how you can get in touch with a solicitor approved by the Legal Aid Board.

CONDITIONAL FEES

In an attempt to make the law more accessible to the general public, some lawyers are now operating on a 'no win – no fee' basis: in other words, you will only be charged if you win your case. Predictably, lawyers are only prepared to take on 'no win – no fee' cases if there is a high chance of success. The previous government severely reduced the amount of Legal Aid available, and encouraged the conditional fee scheme. This has left a lot of those who would have previously qualified for Legal Aid out in the cold.

LAWYERS FOR YOUR BUSINESS

Inexpensive legal advice is available for small businesses. Contact the Law Society for details.

TRADE UNIONS

Trade unions often provide their members with free legal advice on any legal problems related to work such as unfair dismissals or accidents. They may also underwrite legal fees. Check the union application form: you may be restricted in your choice of solicitor. More information is available from the Equal Opportunities Commission and the Commission for Racial Equality.

FINDING A LAWYER

CHOOSING A LAWYER

Choosing a lawyer can be a tricky business. Word of mouth is a good way to begin, but a great divorce lawyer will not necessarily be able to help you fight a case of medical negligence. A lawyer who specializes in the particular field you need will usually be faster than someone who doesn't, and yet may charge the same hourly rate, saving time and money. Always check this out before taking your first appointment. Ask the hourly rate, who will supervise and who will have day-to-day charge of the matter. Lawyers are under obligation to provide a client case letter including the above and outlining the firm's complaints procedure.

GUIDES AND DIRECTORIES

- *The Solicitors' Regional Directory*: available in libraries, town halls and advice centres, lists most solicitors' firms and outlines the kind of work they do. It also indicates which solicitors will give free or low-cost interviews. It does not give any indication, however, of the quality of the firms listed.
- *The Chambers & Partners' 1996–7 Directory of the Legal Profession*: a qualitative guide which lists the top lawyers in all fields (entry is by nomination from fellow lawyers and is based on merit). Lawyers are classified by the area they specialize in (with over 60 fields, from asset finance, environment and divorce to civil liberties, immigration and trusts), as well as by region. Try your local library; it's also available on CD-ROM.
- *The Legal 500* by John Pritchard, published by Legalease, serves the same purpose.
- The Law Society keeps a computerized list of all practising solicitors in specific areas of interest which you can search through free of charge.
- *The Bar Directory*: gives details of barristers and is available in public libraries.
- Although you can't approach a barrister without a solicitor there are exceptions, see **Solicitors**. Your solicitor will usually be able to recommend one, but you can choose a barrister yourself.

If you are applying for Legal Aid, you will be provided with a list of solicitors or law firms which you can then check using the directories above, or by contacting the Law Society. Organizations, such as Action for Victims of Medical Accidents, Age Concern, the Children's Legal Centre, the National Association for Mental Health (MIND), and the National Head Injuries Association (HEADWAY) among others, can advise on specialist lawyers related to their fields. Contact the organizations directly. The Law Society has also set up panels of specialist lawyers: contact them for more information.

COSTS

What you pay depends on where you live, the size of the law firm you consult and how high ranking your solicitor is. A partner in a central London firm will charge about £150 an hour plus VAT in a typical civil case (partners in the best London firms charge top rates of up to £350 an hour). Elsewhere, it would be nearer £100. *The Chambers & Partners' Directory of the Legal Profession* includes the hourly rates of some of the country's top lawyers. Often clients simply want a 'strong solicitor's letter' to state a point of view, but the letter and the visit to the solicitor's office beforehand can cost £75–£125 in London and £50–£75 elsewhere. Solicitors are not restricted to their hourly rates. They can, and often do, add a given percentage for what they call 'mark up', which is supposed to reflect any special features of the case. This is often simply an invented figure. Briefing a barrister, if you want representation in court, or seeking a counsel's opinion, will further add to the costs.

REPRESENTING YOURSELF

The Citizens' Advice Bureau is always available to give advice and help through the various stages of the legal process. To avoid high lawyers' fees, an increasing number of people choose to represent themselves. They are known as 'litigants in person' (LIPs). Most people going through small claims courts and tribunal proceedings represent themselves. However, it is also possible to represent yourself in the intimidating and often hostile environment of the High Court. In 1995, there were 14,000 inquiries to the Royal Court of Justice from people who wanted to represent themselves. Only about 10% of them succeed: the alarming but understandable failure rate suggests that they should be provided with more support. Representing yourself at this level shouldn't be taken on lightly, and you should always contact a CAB if you are planning to do so.

Your behaviour in court can make an enormous difference to the outcome. There are obvious advantages in being clear and calm in your presentation. In addition, the proceedings will run more quickly and cost less.

IN COURT
- The most important point to establish before going to court is whether or not the person you are fighting is in a position to pay. If they are not, you may waste a great deal of time, and money. Remember, if you lose, you will be liable for the defendant's costs as well as your own.
- Give yourself time to prepare. Assemble, in order, all the documents relating to the case, and make a list of all vital points you want to bring up. In the same way, make a list of questions you may want to ask, and try to anticipate questions you may be asked yourself. Be clear about what it is you want.
- If you will be calling witnesses, make sure they are aware of the court date, and will be available.
- If you cannot attend on the date set (due to illness or being abroad, for example), let the court know immediately so they can fix an alternative time.
- Go to bed early the night before even if you find difficulty sleeping.
- Dress in comfortable smart clothes.
- Arrive early and locate your courtroom.
- Keep calm, breathe deeply and don't be intimidated. The court is there to serve you.
- Form of address: although you will not be penalized for forgetting (and even lawyers often do), it is useful to know that magistrates and district judges are called 'sir' or 'madam', county court judges 'your honour' and high court judges 'my lord' or 'my lady'.
- Answer questions politely and clearly. Confine your answers to the question asked. Don't try to speak in 'legalese', it may confuse you and won't necessarily impress anyone else. Say what you mean – succinctly.
- Don't argue with the barrister or try to score points.
- Don't try to think on your feet.
- Don't baffle the court with technical knowledge, or use technical terms without explaining them.
- Don't react to another's evidence. You may find that upsetting or untrue things are being said, but the judge is there to act fairly, and exaggeration or lies are quickly detected. Calling out in protest will do you more harm than good. Wait until it's your turn to speak, then address what you believe to be untrue.
- Don't take a barrister's criticism personally.
- Don't lose your temper.
- Never interrupt. You will be told when it is your turn to speak, and when you can ask questions of witnesses.
- You can bring a friend or adviser with you, but you must inform the court beforehand.
- *The Directory of Expert Witnesses*, with more than 2,500 names from all disciplines, is published by the Law Society and FT Law & Tax. In it you will find guidelines for making your choice. All expert witnesses are required to adopt the code of practice outlined in the publication.

COMPLAINING ABOUT SOLICITORS' FEES
Solicitors' are notoriously expensive. The mystery surrounding solicitors' bills is exacerbated by the fact that solicitors are not required by their disciplinary body, the Law Society, to tell their clients at the outset of the likely cost of their work or their basis for charging; they are merely 'encouraged' to do so. Furthermore, the details of each case will always differ, so comparing bills will not always be revealing.

Each year around 19,000 dissatisfied people appeal to the Solicitors' Complaints Bureau (SCB) – a department of the Law Society. The majority of these complaints concern overcharging and are aimed at solicitors. However, after conducting its own research, the Law Society discovered that two thirds of those who complained were 'very dissatisfied' with the results. In response they have renamed their complaints department 'Office for the Supervision of Solicitors' (OSS), which many see as a purely superficial solution. The OSS is not an independent body; it is largely staffed and funded by the Law Society, although it is overseen by a board which includes non-solicitors.

If you are dissatisfied by the reaction of the OSS, you can approach the Legal Services Ombudsman, based in Manchester. Only around 10% of complaints are taken to the ombudsman, largely because people are not aware that it's an option. To have your case considered, you must first have complained to the solicitor in question, and then to the OSS.

AVOIDING OVERCHARGING

Always take precautions against being over-charged from the outset.

- On taking instructions, your solicitor should give you an indication of the likely cost of handling the case. S/he should also discuss with you how the costs may be met, which includes Legal Aid or insurance.
- If the solicitor doesn't agree a fee or provide an estimate from the outset, s/he should clearly explain how it will be calculated.
- The issue of costs should then be confirmed in writing, in as much detail as possible. If you feel the written confirmation is vague or ambiguous, ask for further clarity and get it in writing.
- You should ask to be informed of costs as they are incurred.
- Keep a record of all conversations you have with your lawyer and compare it with an itemized final bill.
- Your final bill may still exceed the estimate. You should first approach the solicitor involved.
- If you are very unhappy about your bill DO NOT PAY ANYTHING. By paying you will be disqualified from contesting it through the OSS.

ARE YOU BEING OVERCHARGED?

- Check to see whether you have been charged the rate of a highly qualified solicitor for legal research, photocopying and other work that could be carried out by a junior, and try to re-negotiate these figures at the junior rate.
- Check how much you have been charged for services such as phone and fax.
- Remember: solicitors may charge overtime for work done after hours, at weekends or if you contact them at their home numbers. Be wary of treating them as friends, or a shoulder to cry on (which can often happen in emotionally charged legal cases) – you may find you have to pay heavily for their sympathy.

REMUNERATION

- If your solicitor will not re-negotiate the bill, and providing it does not exceed £50,000 or involve court proceedings, you can ask for it to be sent to the OSS.
- In order to qualify, you must not have paid your bill. If you have given your solicitor permission to draw on funds held on account, the bill will be considered paid, and you will be ineligible.
- You must also apply within one month of receiving the bill, or of being informed of your right to ask for remuneration (this is often just printed on the bill). If you are not informed of your right to complain, you have three months after receiving the bill.
- Your solicitor will have to complete a form and send it, with your file, to the Law Society. The file will be examined by the OSS to decide whether you have been overcharged. They will then issue a 'remuneration certificate'. This is a free service.
- Note: at this stage your solicitor can ask for 50% of the bill, plus VAT and specific expenses.
- In 1995 the Law Society received nearly 1,800 applications, and of them, about 600 legal bills were reduced. The majority of clients were dissatisfied with the results.
- From application to decision generally takes about four months. Most of the applications concern bills of under £1,000.
- Be aware that asking for a remuneration certificate will more than likely damage any future relations you have with your solicitor.
- If your application fails, or you are unhappy about the results or the treatment you received, you can contact the Legal Services Ombudsman who can order compensation to be paid. This is also a free service. However, as the Ombudsman's

recommendations are not binding, you may have to take your case to court to see any results. There is a firm time-limit of three months within which you must act.

'TAXATION'

The alternative to the remuneration procedure is to have your solicitor's bill 'taxed'. 'Taxation' involves going to court where the solicitor must justify the charges. You will also be able to query any bills incurred in the court proceedings.

- If you apply to the court within one month of receiving the bill, the court will always order a 'taxation'.
- Between 1 and 12 months of receiving the bill: they may, but do not have to.
- After the bill has been paid, you will have to prove you had special reasons for applying. If 12 months have elapsed since paying, you will be ineligible.
- This is the only option for checking bills for cases that involved court proceedings.
- If the bill is reduced by less than 20%, you will be liable to pay not only your own costs but those of the solicitor as well. It is a risky business.

NEGLIGENCE

Negligence has a specific legal definition. If your solicitor's actions have caused you loss, s/he may have been negligent and the case may have to be resolved in court. First, discuss the matter with your solicitor. If you disagree, contact the OSS. The OSS cannot deal directly with cases of negligence: they are only concerned with 'inadequate professional service' and 'professional misconduct'. However, they can advise you on how to proceed.

- If the OSS decide that your solicitor's service was poor or inadequate rather than negligent, they may be able to resolve the matter for you directly. The main deciding factor is your potential financial loss: the maximum compensation paid out by the OSS is £1,000.
- If, on the other hand, the behaviour was seen to be negligent, you will be referred to the 'Negligence Panel'. Through it, independent solicitors are on hand to give one hour's free advice, although you may want to instruct a solicitor of your own.
- If you want to make a claim for negligence against your solicitor, you must inform him or her of your intention.
- The solicitor you're claiming from will then contact the Solicitors' Indemnity Fund (SIF), who will act on his or her behalf. SIF will review the case and decide whether or not to settle. If the decision is to settle, they will set the amount.
- If the decision is against settling, your only recourse will be to go to court.

CONSUMER LAW

Each time you buy a ticket on public transport, eat in a restaurant or have your hair done, you are entering into a contractual agreement, although you may not be aware of it. This 'contract' does not have to be a written document, but it will confer certain rights and duties on both the consumer and the trader. Consumer law is a relatively new branch of the English legal system.

Although Acts of Parliament outlining the relationship between the consumer and trader have been around for over 100 years, most of the finer points on which we now operate came into force as recently as the 1960s. The EU has also introduced new directives which are being reflected in the marketplace over here: many concern the contents and labelling of products, but others address health and safety – the banning of British beef being a case in point. Consumer law can involve both civil or criminal prosecutions, depending on the circumstances. In civil cases (for example, when the product is unfit or the service offered unsatisfactory), the buyer must take the seller to court. In criminal cases (for example, when the product is dangerous to the public, or the trader was misleading about the price), prosecutions are usually made by either the police or trading standards department. It pays to know your rights.

LEARN HOW TO COMPLAIN

- Often a firm and specific complaint (calmly delivered) will remedy a situation. Make it clear that you know your rights. If you do need help, the law can intervene.
- Always keep your receipt.
- Decide whether you want a refund, to exchange the item or have it repaired.
- Take the goods back as soon as possible. If it is awkward to return them, ring the vendor and explain your problem.
- Explain the problem clearly.
- Always follow up any complaint in writing if it is not resolved straight away.
- If you are unhappy with the response you receive, or if you receive no response at all, write to the head office.
- Alternatively, go to the local authority and complain to the trading standards department. If there is one, you could also try the relevant trade association which may have an arbitration scheme, or ombudsman.
- If all else fails, contact a Citizens' Advice Bureau, consumer advice or law centre. If you do decide to sue, find out whether you're eligible for Legal Aid.
- Don't underestimate the power of consumer organizations such as *Which?* magazine and television and radio programmes.
- *Which?* Personal Service, for £7.75 a quarter, offers consumers legal advice over the telephone about goods and services. They can also take on a case for a set case fee, from £50–£300.

CONTRACTS

This may take the simple form of a ticket or receipt, and it won't matter whether or not you have signed it.

Contracts are only legally binding between the parties directly involved. If you buy something which you give away as a present and it proves to be faulty, you are the one who has to complain. However, the trader may waive this formality and deal directly with the recipient. If the goods are dangerous, the recipient can complain directly to the shop under the Consumer Protection Act. If physically hurt as a result, the recipient can sue the manufacturer.

CONSUMER PROTECTION

English law supports 'freedom of contract', which essentially means that people can put whatever clauses they like into their contracts. These can either be accepted or rejected by the other party. However, there have been amendments made to protect the consumer against dishonest traders.

CREDIT REFERENCE AGENCIES

If a firm refuses you credit or you are unable to obtain a loan, you may be on a credit 'blacklist', which means that a 'judgment of debt' is held against you. The holding of personal information on computers has been regulated by the Department of Trade and Industry, and guidelines were published in 1993. It is possible to remedy the situation (provided you're no longer in debt), but the timing is vital.

- Ask for the name of the Credit Reference Agency from the shop refusing you credit within 28 days of their refusal. They must supply this information within seven days: failure to do so is a criminal offence.
- Contact the agency and request a copy of the records against you. You will have to pay a fee of £1. The agency must send you the file within seven days.
- If the records are inaccurate, you can have them changed or taken out.
- If you are unhappy with the agency's response, you have 28 days in which to supply them with a note of no more than 200 words outlining your objections. These must then be included in your file. If they refuse, you can appeal to the Director General of the Office of Fair Trading. Heavy fines are imposed on agencies acting unreasonably.
- You may find that you are blacklisted because a member of your family is a bad credit risk, but if you can prove that your finances are not linked to theirs, you will be given a clean record.

Further information is available in the booklet *No Credit*, available through the Office of Fair Trading. By contacting the Data Protection Registrar you can obtain information about all organizations which hold individuals' information on computer.

IMPLIED TERMS

Certain terms are automatically included.

- All goods should be of a merchantable quality and fit for their purpose.
- Goods should match the quality of the sample provided by the trader.

Equally, certain terms are automatically excluded. Under the Unfair Contract Terms Act, it is illegal to exclude liability for personal injury or death. Any breach can be taken up in the civil courts, although it may not be enforceable by criminal sanctions. Note: if you're buying for a business, not, in other words, as a 'consumer', the vendor is allowed to insert various exclusion clauses. Look carefully for these.

CRIMINAL SANCTIONS

The threat of being reported to trading standards officers may be enough for the trader to offer an informal settlement without the consumer taking the case further. If this doesn't work, you can take your case to the civil court.

THE SMALL PRINT

New EU regulations require that all terms are written in plain and intelligible language. 'Ancillary terms' (or the 'small print') are the real target. Even if you do get round to reading them, you may not understand the implications, which is often the intention. The trader will be in breach if these terms cause an 'imbalance in the party's rights . . . to the detriment of the consumer'.

- Note that these regulations don't apply when a contract has been individually negotiated.
- If the trader is found to have unfair 'small print', just the small print may be struck out leaving the rest of the contract binding. In other words, the main intelligible part of the contract, including the price, will generally remain the same.

DISCRIMINATION

- Anyone can refuse to serve a customer provided they are not discriminating unfairly.
- It is illegal for suppliers of goods or services to discriminate against you on grounds of race, disability (however, if a disability results in greater cost to the suppliers, they are permitted to charge more), sex or marital status. This extends to (among others) accommodation, banking, credit facilities, access to public places, entertainment and transport.
- You can sue anyone in breach through the civil courts.
- If the discrimination took place at work, you will have to resort to an industrial tribunal.
- Racial or sexual discrimination can be dealt with by the Commission for Racial Equality, or the Equal Opportunities Commission, respectively.

OBLIGATIONS OF THE SELLER

- The goods must be of satisfactory quality. If you buy 'shop-soiled' or 'imperfect' goods which are clearly labelled as such, you will not be able to return them as damaged products. However, if they are unsafe, you do have recourse.
- Inadequate instructions can make a product unsatisfactory.
- If a shop sells unsatisfactory goods, it will not be exempted by a 'No refunds, no returns' clause. If you buy goods in a sale you are entitled to return them for a working replacement or a full refund, regardless of the notice.
- If you tell the trader of specific needs before buying, and are then sold goods that fail to meet your requirement after being promised they would, the trader is in breach.
- If most consumers would be satisfied with the product, but you have a particular quirk that makes it unacceptable, you will not be in a position to complain, e.g. if you are allergic to a particular ingredient in the product which most people find acceptable, it would be your responsibility to have checked before buying. If you were misled, however, the trader is responsible.
- The goods must be described accurately. If you bought a jacket which was described as leather, and turned out to be plastic, you could take it back and demand an exchange or full refund.

IF YOU ARE THE SELLER

Do not let the buyer take the goods until you have received the full payment. If you are selling a car you should accompany any potential buyer on their test drive. A cheque supported with a false address will be no good if it bounces. Insist on payment by cash, bank draft or printed

building society cheque (not handwritten).

- *The Buyer's Guide* is available from the Office of Fair Trading and Marketing.

OBLIGATIONS OF THE BUYER

- Once you have agreed to buy, at the price stated, you cannot flippantly change your mind. Having found something you like better, or that costs less, will not dissolve your obligation.
- If you have paid a deposit and change your mind, the trader has the right to keep it, and may even be able to claim the balance.
- Goods must be used for their proper purpose. If you use a guaranteed bread knife for sawing wood, you will probably not be in a position to complain if it breaks.

ACCEPTING THE GOODS

You will have 'accepted the goods' in the legal sense if:

- you have kept them for a considerable length of time,
- you said that you accepted them,
- you alter them in some way (with a security mark, for example).
- You do not have to accept goods delivered to you if they are the wrong ones.
- Having accepted goods, you are no longer in a position to reject them, or the contract.
- If there is a breach in the terms of the contract, you are eligible for compensation.
- You can always claim damages for a defective product.
- The delivery firm may ask you to sign a delivery note: read it first. If it says 'goods received and in good condition' – replace 'good condition' with 'subject to inspection'.

STOLEN GOODS

If a trader has sold you stolen goods in good faith, and the rightful owner claims them back, the trader is liable to reimburse you. If you knew they were stolen, you were committing a criminal offence by buying them.

SIGNING

Never sign any contract without reading it. Once signed, you may be bound by it, even if you weren't aware of the details. If someone has misled you, you couldn't read it or you misunderstood it, you may have an argument for breaking the contract.

ENTIRE CONTRACT CLAUSE

Entire contract clauses often cover agreements for large items (cars, computer systems, etc.). They mean that the agreement signed is the whole contract and that the trader is not liable for any misrepresentation made before you signed it. You may lose your right to complain. However, if the clause is seen to be unfair, you may be able to appeal against it. Seek advice if in doubt.

BUYING IN YOUR HOME

If you buy anything over a certain value (about £35) in your own home, you have specific rights by law. Once you have agreed to pay, or have paid, for the goods, you have a seven-day 'cooling-off' period during which you can change your mind and ask for the return of your money.

- Call the vendor as soon as you change your mind.
- Make a note of the person you spoke to.
- Follow this up immediately in writing, stating that you no longer want the goods, and include the name of the person you spoke to. Keep a copy of your letter.
- Either fax this letter to the vendor, or send it by recorded post to prove you were within the seven-day time limit.

ORDERING BY PHONE

When ordering goods to be delivered, you may specify a date by which they must arrive. If they then fail to arrive within this time, you can refuse them. Companies have a legal obligation to deliver within a reasonable time (often 28 days) even if you don't specify a date. If they are very slow, you can write to the company specifying a time after which you will want your money back.

POSTAL SELLING

- The Unsolicited Goods and Services Act 1971 states that if goods are sent to you without you having ordered them, you may keep them and ignore the invoice.
- You can write to the sender, pointing out that

you did not order them, and suggest they collect them. If they fail to do so within 31 days, the goods will be yours.

- If you do nothing, and the goods aren't collected after six months, they will belong to you.
- Many ads offer a 'free-trial period' of 14 days. If you order the item, you are legally bound to pay for it if you fail to return it within the set period. If you do return it, make sure to get a proof of posting slip from the post office to prove you returned it within the time limit.

SELLING BY TELEPHONE

People who ring up and claim to be conducting market research but then try to sell you something are not acting illegally, however suspicious or irritating it might be. However, the Market Research Society does not approve of this method.

- Ask for the name of the company.
- You can then report them to the Market Research Society who will penalize any members involved in this practice.
- If you have been conned, you will not have any legal recourse.

PYRAMID SELLING

- Approach with trepidation: you may lose money through 'pyramid ventures'. Any advertising produced by these organizations must outline the risks involved. Even companies claiming not to be pyramid ventures may operate on the same lines.
- Contact the DTI's Consumer Affairs division for a free leaflet about them, and do not enter into any agreements before reading it.
- The companies are not allowed to take more than £75 from you in the first seven days.
- If you are unhappy about the arrangement you can return the goods within 14 days of signing and get all your money back.
- The contract must also contain a clear explanation of how to opt out at any stage.

GUARANTEES

The law sets out that all goods and services must meet certain standards and perform for a reasonable period. While guarantees can increase these obligations, they cannot decrease or retract them. Be wary of guarantees that make wild promises: they may simply indicate a company on the verge of taking off without fulfilling any obligations.

- If the goods have broken down while under guarantee, the manufacturer must, by law, put the situation right within 'reasonable time'. Unfortunately there are no real guide-lines to set out how long 'reasonable' can be.
- Check the small print of the guarantee.
- If you find the wait intolerable, contact the relevant trade association – they may suggest their own arbitration procedure which will not involve court.
- Contact a CAB or law centre.

HIRE PURCHASE

If you buy on credit, the goods belong to you immediately. If buying on hire purchase, on the other hand, the goods do not belong to you until you have made the final payment. It would therefore be illegal to sell them before this point. Read more about hire purchase and other credit agreements in the **Money** chapter.

SERVICES

There is a huge range of different services available and again the private consumer is given the greatest protection by the law. In all cases, a satisfactory job should be performed using 'reasonable care and skill'. Trade associations define 'reasonable', and so it is wise to use one of their members. (See **Home** chapter for more on choosing builders, etc.)

- The contractor is obliged to use the right quality materials for the job.
- The job performed must be the one you requested.
- The contractor must not damage your goods while performing the service.
- The job should be completed in 'reasonable time': before the work is begun, cover yourself by stating in writing when you want the job finished.
- You can claim damages should the contractor be in breach of any of the above.
- Broken appointments can cost money. If you fail

to turn up to meet someone supplying you with a service, they can charge you (e.g. missing a hairdresser's or dentist's appointment).

- The reverse applies too. If you have taken time off work to let someone into your house, for example, and they fail to turn up, or turn up hours later than they arranged, you can charge them a reasonable sum for your time. The most effective approach is to knock the sum off the bill with an explanation why. It's very unlikely the company will try to sue you for the difference if the reduction is reasonable.

CHARGES FOR SERVICES

- A price agreed in advance must be paid even if you discover that you have been ripped off. This works both ways: if you are quoted a particular price and the work takes longer than the service contractor imagined, that is their problem not yours.
- Quotes are binding. Estimates are only guidelines and may change.
- Always ask for quotes and estimates in writing.
- Make it clear before the work begins that you want to be told of any extra work that needs to be done.
- If extra work is necessary, and the cost is likely to be more than the estimate, set a figure which the contractor cannot exceed without your approval.

FORGOTTEN GOODS

- Companies should write and remind you of goods left with them for a long period of time. However, most cover themselves with a clause in the agreement warning that the item will be disposed of (usually sold) if not collected within a certain period.
- Let friends or family know where you are leaving very valuable property (e.g. jewellery or camera left for repair) – if anything were to happen to you at least they could track it down.

HIRING

- Generally the same rules apply when buying or hiring goods with the exception that hired goods have to be returned in the same condition you received them in – a charge may be deducted from your deposit if you have damaged them in any way.

- Do not accept clauses that refuse liability for personal injury: they are worthless. You should check the small print for unreasonable clauses and remove them before hiring.

INJURY OR DEATH

The Consumer Protection Act 1987 made the 'own brander', manufacturer or importer of a product liable for damages to personal property over a certain sum and for injury or death caused by defective goods. All service industries and goods are covered under this act including the electricity, gas and water companies.

SMALL CLAIMS

The small claims court was set up for people representing themselves. Technically there isn't anything called the small claims court; there is however a small claims procedure in the county court called Arbitration. Currently, a small claim is anything under £3,000 – a figure which many people feel should be reassessed annually. Claims over this amount may be considered, but the court has to agree to this beforehand. The small claims court will also hear personal injury cases of up to £3,000. The Lord Chancellor's department has produced a series of leaflets explaining the whole process, which are available free from your local county court. Most disputes over goods and services can be resolved by complaining to the company involved, but if you are unsatisfied by the results, you can take the case to the small claims court. It isn't a complicated procedure, you don't need a lawyer and it isn't expensive.

You can apply for 'actual' losses and 'consequential' losses. If, for example, your car broke down, the cost of the repair would be an 'actual' loss, while 'consequential' losses might include the cost of renting a replacement or taking taxis. You can also claim reasonable compensation for any inconvenience caused.

The small claims court is part of the county

court, but the procedures involved are relatively informal and less complicated. There are, however, limits set on the sums you can be awarded. Remember, winning the case is only the first stage – you then have to enforce the claim. Claims over £3,000 have to be dealt with in the county court. If you lose, you may be liable to pay not only your own costs, but also those of the other side.

SMALL CLAIMS COURT

- First complain to the person or company you have a grievance with in writing as soon as possible. If complaining or conversing by telephone, make a note of the date and time of the phone call, take the name and title of the person who spoke to you and write down what was said.
- Follow up the telephone call with a brief and concise letter reiterating your conversation, restating the problem and what you want done. Give a reasonable time limit (e.g. 14 days) within which you would like a reply and send it by recorded delivery. Always keep copies of any correspondence and store them in an orderly file.

LETTER BEFORE ACTION

If you receive no response, and you have decided to sue, you must first send a 'letter before action' explaining that you will take the company or individual to court if they do not settle the situation. If you have paid or have to pay anything for the return of your goods, make it clear that you are paying 'under protest'. This can be pointed out in correspondence, and written on the cheque.

CHECK THE DETAILS

- Check whether you are suing the right person. You need the full name and address of the individual or company you intend to sue.
- Check that the trader or firm you are dealing with is still in business. The trading standards department for their area can help.
- You may need supporting documentary evidence. Photographs of poor workmanship, estimates or engineers' reports to support your argument can all be important. Costs incurred in collating such evidence will generally be reimbursed, at least in part, should you win.

SUMMONSES

- Your local county court will be listed in the phone book under 'Courts'. From them you can obtain a 'summons form'. You need to fill this out (CAB and other legal centres can help you with this) stating your claim. A description of the problem, additional background information and how you want it remedied should be included.
- There are different forms for claiming either fixed amounts, or estimated figures which can include compensation for inconvenience.
- Take the completed form, and two copies, to the local county court. It will be checked to make sure you have completed it correctly, and then filed, for which you will have to pay a fee (about £80).
- The court will give you a case reference number and will post the summons to the defendant who is given 14 days within which to acknowledge, and a further 14 days within which to file a defence. If they fail to respond before either deadline, you can apply for a 'judgment in default' which results in an automatic judgment in your favour. To do this, ask the court for form N30.
- If the defendant does reply, you will receive a copy of their defence, and the 'automatic directions' which include the date set by the court for the hearing and the steps both sides should take.
- At least seven days before the hearing, you must exchange any documents you will be referring to at the hearing with the defendant, as well as supplying the names and addresses of any witnesses.
- The hearing will take place anything between 14 days and six months later.

PREPARE YOUR CASE

Make notes of all vital details of the case and go through your file of correspondence thoroughly. If you are concerned about presenting your case you can ask a friend or adviser to help, but notify the court of this beforehand (see **Representing yourself in court**).

THE HEARING

Hearings generally take place in private under informal conditions. Some judges will simply listen to both sides of the story, others will intervene to ask questions. The judge will give his/her decision immediately afterwards and it will be confirmed in writing a few days later.

THE OUTCOME
If you win, you can claim compensation and any expenses incurred. These include the court fee, reasonable travel expenses, (limited) loss of earnings for you and any witness you called, and up to about £150 for an expert's report. If you lose, you will not be reimbursed for the costs incurred in bringing the case to court and will have to pay the defendant's costs.

ENFORCING YOUR CLAIM
If the loser won't pay up, you can take formal action to enforce the judgment. Leaflets are available from your county court to advise you on procedure, but a lot will depend on the defendant's ('judgment debtor's') financial situation. Get help from your local CAB or neighbourhood law centre.

CRIMINAL LAW

You may feel socially or morally obliged to 'help the police with their inquiries', but you are under no legal obligation to do so. The police cannot insist you accompany them to the station without arresting you, and they can only arrest you under certain conditions. However, if you are seen as a vital witness and don't help the police you could be accused of 'obstruction'.

STOPPED AND QUESTIONED
You may be stopped by the police and asked basic questions such as your name and address. Equally, you can ask them why you are being questioned and they have to give you a good reason. Although you are not obliged to give your name and details, it is wise to do so. At the same time, you can also take down their details.
- Note the officer's number (displayed on the uniform) and ask which police station s/he is from.

Any reasonable officer will supply this information without hesitation, and it can have a salutary effect on officers who are behaving badly.
- Do not get into a debate.
- If the questioning continues you should remain silent.

STOPPED AND SEARCHED
There are detailed guide-lines on 'Stop and Search', many of which were introduced to curb police harassing young black men. Basically, a police officer can stop and search anyone reasonably suspected of carrying 'certain prohibited items'. These include
- protected plants, animals, birds, etc.
- illegal drugs
- firearms or other offensive weapons (razor, sharpened comb, knife, etc.)
- suspected terrorist devices
- stolen goods, or adjuncts to theft (including screwdrivers, bunches of car keys, etc.).
  Before a search, police officers not in uniform must identify themselves by showing a warrant (identity) card. You must be told
- the police officer's name and station
- the grounds for searching
- the object of the search
  You must also be informed that after a year you can ask for a copy of the record of the search.

SEARCHED IN PUBLIC
- You cannot be asked to remove more than your coat/jacket and gloves.
- If you are out of public view (i.e. in a police van or station) the police can conduct a strip search, as long as it is conducted by an officer of the same sex.
- An intimate body search (of the mouth, ear, nose, anus or vagina) must be authorized by a police superintendent on the grounds that the suspect is carrying Class A drugs (cocaine, heroin). Searches of this kind are usually carried out by a nurse or doctor on police or medical premises. Alarmingly, you do not have to be arrested before searches of this nature are carried out.
- After the search, you must either be arrested or allowed to leave. Under the 1984 Police and Criminal Evidence Act, you are not obliged to

give your name and address after a search. Only when arrested may reasonable force be used to search a suspect.

ARREST

The police must have the lawful authority to make an arrest, otherwise they are subject to being sued for false imprisonment and/or assault. However, they do not need a warrant for the majority of offences, and these range from the apparently trivial to the most serious.

An 'arrestable offence' is one that could lead to five years' (or more) imprisonment. Arrestable offences include (among others) actual bodily harm, grievous bodily harm, death by reckless driving, manslaughter, murder; rape, indecent assault and other serious sex offences; shoplifting, burglary, theft, stealing a car, armed assault, some firearm offences, arson; and living off immoral earnings.

You can be arrested without a warrant if you
- have committed, are in the act of committing, or are reasonably suspected to be committing any 'arrestable offence'
- are reasonably suspected of having committed an arrestable offence
- are reasonably suspected of being about to commit an arrestable offence
- are breaching the peace
- are drunk and incapable of looking after yourself
- refuse to give your name and address when you are legally obliged to (e.g. after a traffic accident)
- are soliciting
- refuse to take a breath test
- are driving while disqualified, or while drunk or on drugs
- are committing certain immigration offences
- are breaching rules laid out to control the sale of alcohol at sporting events
- fail to comply with directions issued by the police concerning conduct at demonstrations/marches seem likely to injure yourself or others

The police can also arrest if they have reasonable grounds to suspect the arrest will prevent
- any vulnerable person being harmed
- loss or damage to property
- an offence against public decency
- an obstruction of the highway

YOUR RIGHTS

As soon as you are detained you must be cautioned ('you do not have to say anything but it may harm your defence if you do not mention when questioned something which you later rely on in court. Anything you do say may be given in evidence.') and informed of your rights.
- Don't answer any questions (and never admit to having committed a crime) before your solicitor arrives.
- Don't swear or try to bribe the police. Remain calm and polite, don't bluster.

THE CRIMINAL LAW

A crime is defined as 'an act punishable by the law'. The British criminal legal system is based on several basic principles, and they are always applied. Whether the crime committed was shoplifting or first degree murder, it is taken that:
- The accused is innocent until proven guilty.
- The prosecution must show beyond reasonable doubt that the accused committed the offence.
- There is no obligation to help the police with their inquiries. This refusal to co-operate cannot be held against the accused in the trial.
- The suspect must be tried only on the facts relating to the case. Previous convictions may not be referred to during the trial as they could be seen to prejudice the jury. If the suspect is found to be guilty, however, previous offences may influence the sentence.
- Written evidence is generally inadmissible as the author cannot be cross-examined; criminal trials are based on the oral evidence of witnesses.
- The suspect is protected from any speculative reporting in the press which is treated as a contempt of court. But the press are allowed to record the evidence given in the trial.
- The police treatment of suspects is carefully regulated by specific guide-lines.

CRIME

Criminal law is designed to deal with the offender rather than the victim, but there are three main options available to you if you have been the victim of a crime.

1 The criminal can be ordered to pay you compensation (a 'criminal compensation order') through

the criminal court. This seems refreshingly fair, but there are drawbacks. 70% of magistrates' convictions are made in criminal damage cases. Although the maximum compensation is £5,000, most of the victims are awarded less than £50, and many of the defendants are unable to pay at all, or only in very small instalments.

2 You can sue the criminal in the civil courts. These claims are rare, mainly because victims are unaware of their right to sue. Often the offender simply isn't worth suing unless they are insured: household insurance may cover them. A motoring offence is an example of a case worth pursuing.

3 You can sue the police if you have been a victim of police brutality. These claims can be difficult to prove, but if you succeed, the awards can be substantial. In exceptional cases, you can even sue the police for failing to prevent the crime. If you suffered personal injury, you can claim from the Criminal Injuries Compensation Board (CICB), which is financed by the State (see below).

COMPENSATION

Applies if you have been injured as the result of
• a violent crime
• apprehending an offender or suspected offender
• an offence of trespass on a railway (this was introduced to compensate train drivers suffering distress as a result of 'traintrack suicides')
In 1990, the CICB received over 50,000 claims. In order to qualify your case must
• involve a claim of over £1,000
• involve bodily or psychological injury
• have been reported to the police 'without delay'
• be presented to the CICB within three years: this is waived in exceptional cases such as sexual abuse
• not have been provoked by you (e.g. if you were hurt as a result of starting a fight). 'Contributory negligence' can reduce the size of your claim.
The CICB has the right to refuse compensation to 'dubious characters', which is vague, and easily abused.
Each award is assessed individually. Since 1979 the victims of domestic violence have been eligible for compensation, providing
• the victim (if adult) was no longer living with the offender when the application was made, and does not intend to live with him/her again
• the offender was prosecuted (a conviction isn't necessary)
• the Board is convinced that the offender will not have access to the award.
The award must be seen to be made in the child's best interests in the case of a child victim.

MAKING A CLAIM

• Collect all information relevant to your case (medical reports, record of police report, proof of loss of earnings).
• Apply to the CICB for an application form – there is no fee.
• Fill in the form and return it as quickly as possible. The staff at the CICB can help should you need it.
• If the case is serious, you should get an independent medical report, and if possible, legal advice.
• Your case will be reviewed, and you will be told how much your award will be.
• If you are unsatisfied with the amount, you can appeal but you may want to supply additional medical information for the hearing. You can attend, and bring a lawyer or a friend with you.
• Unfortunately Legal Aid is not available, but you can get two hours of advice under the Green Form Scheme.
• Remember that your legal fees (should you receive an award) will have to be repaid from your compensation.
• Victim support schemes can also offer advice.

THE SIZE OF THE AWARD

The amount settled on will take into account
• pain and physical suffering
• psychological trauma: extreme in rape cases
• loss of earnings as a result of the injury (social security benefits are subtracted from this)
• future loss of earnings, and difficulty in obtaining work in the future may be reflected in a lump sum payment
• funeral expenses, and the financial effect of the victim's death on family/dependants.
Unfortunately, no allowance is made for bereavement.

POLITICS

The world of politics can leave us feeling angry or helpless, or both. It doesn't help that the current British political structure hasn't changed much since it was established centuries ago. We're saddled with a structure riddled with archaic traditions, bizarre rituals and some politicians who seem almost as old as the system itself. How is being part of Europe going to change things? What's a quango? And why do MPs need whips?

The trends throughout Europe suggest that women will be playing a much bigger role in politics in the future. In Norway 44% of the parliamentary seats are held by women, in Finland 40%, Sweden 38% and Britain 18%. Ireland, Britain and France have all had female leaders while Iceland – where the top three positions are all occupied by women – is run by a single mother who got in with 95% of the votes. The current Labour government has the highest number of female Cabinet Ministers in British political history. Things are beginning to change . . .

In this chapter you'll find a description of the roles of the various players, the way the system works and a breakdown of some of the major issues. A better understanding can lead to taking a more active involvement in the way this country is run, and to this end, you'll find tips on how to demonstrate, campaign and influence government beyond simply using your vote.

GOVERN- MENT

THE HOUSE OF COMMONS

Each member of the House of Commons is elected by people living in a particular geographical area of the UK, i.e. their constituency. There are 659 MPs, of whom 120 are women. General Elections, when every constituency is entitled to vote for a parliamentary candidate, must take place at least every five years. The majority of candidates in a General Election belong to and represent a major political party. The party whose members gain the most seats in the House of Commons is officially invited by the Monarch to form a Government and its leader has the dubious pleasure of becoming Prime Minister. As the Government, the elected party gains executive political power: the power to suggest and implement new laws through its ministries. It can pass these laws and follow through its policies more easily if it has an overall majority. If it does not have an overall majority, it has to be extremely tactical to ensure it gets its own way.

On becoming Prime Minister the leader of a newly elected Government appoints a Cabinet: around 18 senior MPs who become Secretaries of State or ministers over particular government departments – Health, Transport, Education, etc. Also includes the Chief Whip and the Lord Chancellor. As such they must work alongside state employees – civil servants – who advise and monitor on the public's behalf. Throughout his/her term as Prime Minister, the leader will periodically reshuffle Cabinet, sacking, promoting and moving ministers.

The political party that gains second most seats in a General Election is officially acknowledged as the Opposition and forms a Shadow Cabinet through which its senior MPs are set up as direct foils to ruling Cabinet members.

THE HOUSE OF LORDS

The House of Lords is made up of unelected members who are either hereditary or life peers. Life peerages are awarded to judges, politicians, industrialists, etc. for services to the state and their children do not inherit the right to sit in the Lords. Hereditary peers inherit their title from their family. There are 1178 members of the House of Lords and the majority are life peers. There are fewer than 100 women and almost all of them are life peers. The main function of the House of Lords is to debate and amend legislation that is not yet law. Life peers, or working peers as they are often known, are in the Lords to bring a level of expertise to debates. There is an ongoing argument about whether hereditary peerages should be phased out. Is it democratic that an unelected group of people, by privilege of birth, can affect Government policy which in turn affects us all? Contact the House of Lords Public Information Office for more info.

WHIPS

All political parties who gain representation in the House of Commons appoint Whips to keep their leaders informed of opinions amongst their members and to be responsible for ensuring that their own particular MPs attend and vote.

FROM BILL TO ACT

The party in power has a mandate to put into practice the proposals it made in its election manifesto, but before they become law they must be put forward as Bills in the Commons, pass through the Lords and then gain Royal Assent.
• Parliamentary legislation is introduced in the form of private or public Bills.
• Private Bills originate outside Parliament, e.g. from a local authority or an individual.
• Public Bills are sponsored by the Government or an individual member and may be introduced in either House (except a finance Bill which must originate in the Commons).
• After a first reading a Bill will be printed and debated in a second reading.
• It is then referred to a committee where it may be amended.
• The amendments are considered by the whole

House and the Bill then has its third reading.

- It is then sent to the other House where it goes through a similar procedure. (The Lords may not veto a finance Bill for longer than a month and may veto other Bills for only two successive sessions.)
- After passing through both Houses a Bill receives the Royal Assent and becomes an Act of Parliament and part of the law of the land.

LABOUR PARTY

The Labour Party originally grew out of the Trade Union movement. It represented the workers and promoted equality. In 1995, the Labour Party published a new statement of its aims and values. The Labour Party is a democratic socialist party. It believes in the strength of common endeavour and works for a dynamic economy, a just society, open democracy and healthy environment.

CONSERVATIVE PARTY

Conservatism believes that the role of the state should be kept to a minimum so that individuals can be free to attain their full potential. They believe in market forces rather than collective ownership as the best way of creating wealth. They stress conventional family values as a means of upholding social harmony. The Conservative Party is the oldest political party in Europe. It descends from the Tories from the 17th and 18th centuries. 'Tory' is originally an Irish word meaning 'predator'!

LIBERAL DEMOCRATS

Liberalism emphasizes the importance of freedom, choice and tolerance for the individual. It proposes minimum economic or political interference in the individual's decision-making. Three core concepts: freedom; equality (politically, in

law and in opportunity); tolerance (accepting the existence of the individual's natural rights means tolerating opposing viewpoints). The Liberal Democrats were established in 1988 when the Liberal Party formally merged with the Social Democratic Party (SDP).

HOW TO VOTE

Anyone who is a British subject and over 18 or a citizen of the Irish Republic or the Commonwealth is entitled to vote (there are a few exceptions, e.g. if you are insane). In order to vote, however, your name must be on the local authority's register of electors. It's simple enough: an X marked against the name of the desired candidate. Voters can also vote by post if they are housebound for any reason or if they have moved house. People who work outside Britain are allowed to nominate someone to vote for them (proxy).

WHAT DOES YOUR MP DO?

It is the job of an MP to act as a delegate on behalf of the constituency in parliament. Anyone has the right to contact his MP on any issue and s/he can be contacted in one of the following ways:
• By a letter/fax to the House of Commons.
• At a 'Surgery' session held within their local constituency: most MPs hold them on a weekly basis.
• Go direct to the House of Commons, fill in a green card and give it to the doorkeeper who will try and find your MP for you.
• If you want to contact another MP, ask yours if s/he will do this for you: this is a standard procedure.

MPS' WORK

In addition to their work in Westminster (Palace of Westminster is the official name of the Houses of Parliament), MPs have to be active in their constituency to maintain the support of party members and their electorate. For those MPs with constituencies far from London this can mean a lot of travelling each week. MPs normally spend Fridays in their constituencies. Many MPs have to work more than 70 hours per week when the House is sitting and the conditions can be difficult and very unglamorous. Traditionally the House only sits in the afternoon: this was to allow members to pursue their own private business interests in the morning. Debates often don't finish until late at night. Now, things are shifting slightly and debates are being held on Wednesday mornings, enabling an earlier finish on Thursday particularly so MPs can get back to their constituencies.

MPs are responsible only for matters over which Parliament or central government is responsible. Though their time is limited and they on average represent 68,000 constituents, there are a number of things your MP can do for you.

• MPs can take your issue up with the relevant department or minister.
• Your MP can also represent the problem to the Parliamentary Ombudsman who investigates complaints by members of the public about the way they have been treated by Government departments or various other public sector bodies. Complaints must be submitted via your MP and the results of the investigation are presented to a select committee of MPs. (Complaints can cover inappropriate advice, harassment, refusal of access to official information, unfairness or avoidable delay.)
• Raise an issue in the House of Commons at 'Question time'. Questions are ordered in advance and unless they are directed at an MP, they have to be aimed at a particular department.
• If your problem is common to others there is also the opportunity for the MP to introduce a 'Private Member's Bill'. These rarely go anywhere unless they involve a high-profile campaign.
• If you feel strongly about a certain issue you can organize a petition to the House of Commons that can be presented by your MP. Contact the Clerk of Public Petitions at the House of Commons for more information.
• Your MP could table an 'early day motion'. This is an MP's petition, and is a useful indication of parliamentary support for a particular position. A Standing order can be used by MPs to draw attention to a topical matter.

- Adjournment debate: the last 15 minutes of business each day in the House of Commons is an adjournment debate, in which detailed discussion about particularly pressing issues takes place.

Contact the all-party Public Information Service at the House of Commons for further information on the work of MPs.

PROPORTIONAL REPRESENTATION (PR)

PR is a form of electoral system in multi-party democracies. It provides a share of legislative seats for all political parties competing for power proportional to the votes received. It is designed to give a balanced image of public opinion. There are strong arguments for saying that it is a true reflection of public opinion, but those against it say that it leads to a fragmented government. New Zealand, Belgium and Finland operate this system. Our current electoral system is a 'first past the post': whoever gets the majority of the votes, wins. this is seen by many as not very democratic.The Liberal Democrats have led the demand for proportional representation.

WOMEN & WESTMINSTER

To date there has been concern that the number of women parliamentary candidates was very unrepresentative of the number of women in the population, although with Labour's landslide 1997 victory the number of women MPs tripled overnight. All three main parties claim that they are taking active steps to encourage the selection and election of more women. In terms of women's representation in the European Parliament, the UK's women MEPs total only 18%, alongside Greece, Portugal and Italy. To put it in a world-wide context, on 30 June 1994, only 23 parliaments of the 178 national parliaments had more than 20% women members.

Read the Hansard Society Commission report on *Women at the Top*.

VOTING TRENDS

Women make up just over 50% of the population and generally vote in larger numbers than men. Across all classes and national differences, women are more likely to vote Conservative than Labour. But women in the 18–34-year-old group are more likely to vote Labour than men of the same age. A poll by MORI suggested that young women in particular have a cynical attitude to political parties, believing that politics as it is currently organized fails to represent their concerns or priorities. For a full report on *The Gender Gap in Voting Patterns and Priorities* contact the Fawcett Society.

WOMEN'S PRIORITIES

In the report *Values & Visions: the What Women Want Social Survey* published by the Women's Communications Centre in 1996, women expressed deep concern about political issues and had a basic distrust of the system. In response to this, women have developed a 'parallel political culture'. They are more active in voluntary organizations, community groups and local campaigns. The traditional view is that women are more likely to focus on those issues that affect them or their families directly, while men are more likely to be concerned with more abstract problems such as the economy and foreign affairs.

The difference is a reflection on the differing daily existence of men and women. Women are more likely to come into direct contact with the education system, the health system and inflation. Women still have primary responsibility for child care, are more likely to be poor than men, less likely to be entitled to an adequate pension and so on. Given their tendency to use their vote, no political party can afford to ignore women and they all clearly need to address women's lack of faith in mainstream politics.

To get more information on the main parties' policies on women contact the Labour Party's HQ, the Conservative Women's Organization and read the Liberal Democrats' *Equal Citizens: Proposals to promote the equal treatment of women* available from Liberal Democrat publications.

THE 300 GROUP

Set up in 1980, with membership open to anyone aged over 15, it is a voluntary organization to encourage women to seek and hold public office. It works towards getting 300 women as MPs. The group provides training in skills necessary for political life, media skills, public speaking, debating, knowledge of networks, etc. It also runs conferences on topics such as 'Women and Europe', 'Increasing Opportunities for Women'.

EMILY'S LIST UK

In 1994 Emily's List (which stands for Early Money Is Like Yeast, i.e. it makes dough rise) was established. The idea behind it was to raise money to fund women MPs through the early expensive years of launching their careers. More than 53 women have benefited from the fund to date.

EUROPE

The UK joined what was then called the Common Market in 1973. There are currently 15 members, with more applications pending. Membership of the EU has made an impact on a number of domestic policies ranging from the length of the standard working week to the bend in our bananas. The EU has a political and an economic agenda and in the UK there is still intense debate centring around how much power is actually given up to the European Union by each member state.

THE MAASTRICHT TREATY

In 1992 the 12 Heads of State in what was then the European Community agreed on a Treaty to increase joint policy-making decisions, strengthen the European Parliament, timetable economic and monetary union and give weight to the Social Charter set up in 1989 (this is now known as the Social Chapter, see below). All member states signed the Treaty, though opt-out clauses were agreed with Denmark and the UK.

THE SOCIAL CHAPTER

Health, safety, a common minimum wage, agreed maximum working hours: these are examples of measures covered by the Social Chapter. The Labour Government has made a commitment to sign the Social Chapter.

THE ECU (EUROPEAN CURRENCY UNIT)

Economic and monetary union in the EU mean the planned disappearance of national currencies and the introduction of a single European currency, the ECU or Euro as it will be more commonly known after monetary union. It also means the setting up of a central European Bank with powers to set interest rates for the whole EU. The UK withdrew from the first stage of the process, the Exchange Rate Mechanism, in 1992. Simply, the ERM means that EU currency exchange rates can only fluctuate against one another within a narrow band and that they function as a currency block against other world currencies.

THE EUROPEAN SUPERSTATE

The current debate is whether the UK may be overpowered by a centralized Europe. The federal aspects of the European Union – or ways in which political power is centralized – are, essentially:

- When major policy decisions affecting the whole Union must be made, responsibility should be exercised at both EU and member state level. An example would be in the case of 'mad cow disease', where both the European and UK Parliaments had to make rulings to protect the health of EU citizens as a whole. The Superstate, by necessity, dictated the nature of the UK's policy decisions.
- When a dispute of law between the EU and a member state exists, the European Court of Justice has authority to rule.

Though the influence of the EU has increased, the balance of power is with the member states; the control of financial resources remains national (the EU budget making up 3% of total national budgets); the rights of EU citizenship are extremely limited.

GETTING INVOLVED

This could mean getting more involved with the activities of your favourite political party, putting yourself up as a councillor, representative, MP or even MEP.

STANDING AS AN MP

The number of people who seek to become candidates for local, national and European elections is very small. The question is, is it a representative cross section of the population? There are no particular educational qualifications required to become an MP and you can basically stand for Parliament as an independent candidate as many times as you like. General qualities include being able to present a case forcefully and persuasively in a debate, to the media and at a local level, which is why so many lawyers end up going into politics. Anyone over 21 can become an MP. The socio-economic background of MPs is predominantly white, male and middle class. This is a cause for concern to those who feel that the House of Commons should be a microcosm of society. The Conservatives tend to draw people from professions such as the Bar, banking and the business world. The Labour Party tends to have more lecturers and teachers and a broader spread of white-collar occupations. The Liberal Democrats have a large majority of MPs from the legal profession.

STANDING AS AN MEP

1979 saw the first direct elections to the European Parliament. These take place every five years. There are currently 87 seats for UK MPs. The electoral system is the same as that used for General Elections. MPs can stand as MEPs, and all political parties put forward candidates besides those making independent applications. MEPs have an important say in a wide range of community legislation made within the EU that has, and will have, an increasingly direct effect on you.

STANDING AS A COUNCILLOR

Anyone who is a UK citizen can stand for office as a councillor. The level of commitment required depends on whether candidates are standing at parish, district or county level. Parish councillors have little power and are rarely involved in party politics. For district and county council elections, independent candidates have to find friends and supporters to help launch their campaign. Candidates who stand on behalf of political parties are selected at a special selection meeting. At these selection meetings the candidate is interviewed thoroughly and then a vote is held. If support is agreed then the candidate can take advantage of the money and personnel of the political party. Being a councillor is unpaid and most councillors hold a full-time job. It can be a stepping stone to becoming an MP.

INFLUENCE GOVERNMENT

The communications business is booming but at the same time it could be said that the communications gap between the people and those who govern is widening. Usually the way we hear about new laws being passed is via an announcement in the media. Democracy is based on the right of the individual to be fairly represented by those s/he elected to govern and we have a duty to inform our representatives of our views.

WHAT CAN YOU DO?

'People power' can have an impact. Starting a campaign is one of the options open to you. Gathering people's opinions and focusing on influencing government is another approach.

PRESSURE GROUPS

Examples of pressure groups include Amnesty International, the Worldwide Fund for Nature and Greenpeace. Pressure groups range from ad hoc local groups to huge national organizations. There are thousands. They all want to influence political decisions. Some groups have become permanent institutions while others cease to exist once they have achieved their aim. By joining a pressure group people can express their strength of feeling about certain issues: it's a way for Josephine Public to take part in political activity between elections and a way of ensuring that views get heard by the decision-makers.

There are two main types of pressure group:

1 **Sectional groups:** these seek to represent the common interests of a particular part of society, e.g. the National Union of Teachers or the British Medical Association.

2 **Cause groups:** these pursue a particular set of objectives (a cause), for example CND whose cause is nuclear disarmament. There are three types of cause group although some cut across two categories of pressure group:

• **Sectional cause groups:** protecting the interests of a section of society, for example Shelter working on behalf of the homeless.

• **Attitude cause groups:** aim to change people's attitudes about a particular issue or policy like Friends of the Earth or Greenpeace.

• **Political cause groups:** aim to change the political system or process, for example Charter 88.

INFLUENCING POLICY

Ministers and civil servants are really the key people to approach when trying to influence the policy-making process. Backbench MPs (MPs who do not hold office in government or opposition) in committees can exert some influence over decisions. Pressure groups can approach these committees in the hope that they may adopt the issues themselves and present them to the Government. Ministers and civil servants are involved at all stages of the making of governmental policy. Some policies go through a consultation process; others are put forward as Bills straight away.

The key stages of the consultation process are:

• The Government produces what it calls a 'Green Paper', a consultative document setting out the policy options for discussion. This is when the civil servants invite pressure groups to comment.

• Following this they produce a 'White Paper' out-

lining proposals for legislation. The proposals will then be put into a Bill which will be debated in the Commons and House of Lords. Changes can even be made at various points, but once it's been passed by both Houses and received Royal Assent it becomes an Act of Parliament and enters law. The length of time from the Green Paper stage to an Act of Parliament can be extensive, sometimes ten years.

Contact the relevant Ministry to find out whether public consultation is possible on the policy you are concerned about.

If you wish to organize a mass lobby of the House of Commons on a particular issue, contact the Sergeant-at-Arms Department directly, well in advance of the lobby.

Approach a relevant quango (quasi autonomous non-governmental organization). Under the Tory Government, these unelected bodies grew. They are responsible for spending public funds – a role previously fulfilled by local authorities.

INFLUENCING LOCAL GOVERNMENT

Central government looks at the broader issues and makes the policies while local government deals with the nitty-gritty of the things that affect our daily lives: social services, education, welfare issues, carrying out government policy at a grass roots level, etc. within legislation created by Parliament. Local authorities are democratically elected. Anyone may stand for political office as a councillor. There are over 25,000 councillors in the UK. Most council meetings are open to the public and decisions reached within the meetings are implemented by officers who are full-time employees. Local government is democratically important to counterbalance the power of central government but in recent years the powers and responsibilities of local authorities have been gradually eroded. Many local government services have been privatized, rubbish collection for example, and this has not always led to improved services.

The Local Government Ombudsman – as for Parliament, there is also an ombudsman for complaints concerning local government services. Most of the lobbying techniques relevant to MPs also apply to local councillors, although the latter will undoubtedly be more sympathetic or responsive to local concerns. The Council Information Office will provide you with names and committees. Find out the times of council meetings which you are entitled to attend. Petitions are particularly effective with local government. A hundred names backing your campaign will ensure you catch someone's attention: every vote counts to a politician.

USING THE COURTS

Sometimes you can challenge and overturn a government decision in court. Legal actions are expensive and lengthy. The publicity surrounding a case may be more important than actually winning it.

PROFESSIONAL LOBBYISTS

Lobbyists act as intermediaries between pressure groups and Parliament. Most professional lobbyists focus on Parliament. Their job is to advise how best to organize and put the campaign's case across to decision makers.

HOW TO
CAMPAIGN

National and multi-national companies, privatized industries and health and education services have enormous power over our daily lives. Anyone can be a campaigner protecting interests and highlighting problems: anything from stopping a road through your back garden to initiating new projects. The simplest contribution can make a difference. There are more charities, community or voluntary organizations and pressure groups per head of population in Britain than in any other country.

To be an effective campaigner
- Be positive, seek to be 'for', rather than 'against', a proposal (i.e. *for* animal welfare as opposed to *against* fox-hunting). Constructive action is more appealing. If possible seek to embrace the positive achievements of councils or the bodies concerned within your strategy/campaign.
- Build a campaign to a scale that you can manage and keep standards of professionalism high. Delegation and management are skills that you should brush up on.
- Communicate with people in their own laguage; be realistic and reasonable in presenting your case.
- Tailor your campaigns for the broadest appeal.
- Use the press constructively: remember, they need you as much as you need them.
- Never resort to violence.

BEGINNING A CAMPAIGN

The first essential step is to determine your aims and objectives.
- What do you want to achieve and what part of the objective is actually achievable? Try and present the essentials on one page.
- Decide on a name for your campaign and a logo if it helps to communicate the aims behind it.
- Research the problem, become the expert, strengthen your case and help outline possible solutions. With research come knowledge, authority and, hopefully, success.
- Identify where the power lies, who makes the decisions which are affecting you. Is it a local authority, a ministry, commercial company, a school board, etc.? Make up a hit list of key people, their responsibilities and their positions. These are your campaign targets.
- Having identified the targets, look at what is most likely to influence them and the best way to get to them.
- With this information you can plan your strategy: how you will carry out the campaign, the timetable and the cost to you.
- Select your team and link up with like-minded groups to pool resources. This kind of coalition adds to your credibility. Allies might be other local conservation groups, environmental organizations, etc. or try approaching individuals and groups to put their names as sponsors of your campaign.
- Organize your team, delegate tasks and responsibilities: one person in charge of money, press etc.
- Research case histories of other similar projects

to learn from their experience.

- Undertake the legal work necessary if you register a company or make an application for charitable status.
- Approach your local councillor and Citizens' Advice Bureau to take their advice on your most effective course of action. Local councils also provide a useful resource in terms of identifying possible funds to tap, or sponsorship partnerships to make.
- Identify the various activities you can initiate and what objectives each of these has.
- Design is always underestimated when putting a campaign together. Try to find a designer who is sympathetic to your cause who will volunteer services to the campaign.
- Read *The Campaigning Handbook* by Mark Latimer, published by the Directory of Social Change.

PREVENTATIVE ACTION

- Always try to stop a project at the planning stage.
- Evaluate the project, find the weak links and contradictions and provide an alternative approach to the issue.
- Use the media to build public awareness, provide a constant stream of new ideas and angles that the press can write about. Keep the letters pages of newspapers alive with the debate. Journalists and photographers love cheeky photographic opportunities. This is a good way to attract attention.
- Create an independent communications network, dedicate an answering machine to the campaign and provide daily updates. Set up telephone trees where one person calls five others and they in turn call five more, to harness people as volunteers, building momentum behind the objection. Use Internet bulletin boards and create a web page.
- The authority concerned will obviously tend to play down the drawbacks and exaggerate the benefits, so demand a cost-benefit analysis or an economic evaluation of the project. Analyse it with the help of someone who is used to reading these kinds of documents: this will give you the basis for a judicial review (review in court). This is a lengthy process but can be effective. Look into

getting Legal Aid for this. See **Law** chapter for more information. If you feel the cost-benefit analysis is inaccurate you can inform the district or central government auditor, depending on whether it is a local or central government issue.

- If the project impacts on the environment it can be referred to the European Environment Commission. Again it is more effective to go through your local MP.

SUPPORT FOR CAMPAIGNS

Anyone can campaign to improve their environment within their community, for example creating children's facilities, traffic solutions, design improvements for amenities, involvement in the outcome of a building development. There are various organizations around that support and advise community initiatives and campaigns: the Civic Trust promotes community action; Friends of the Earth works on a wide range of local-based issues such as recycling waste; the Association of Community Technical Aid Centres represents national networks of professionals providing technical support to local groups; Community Matters provides information centres for community groups; the Development Trust Association; the New Economics Foundation promotes community visions; and the Environmental Information Service keeps a database on all environmental organizations – useful if you wish to gain support and advice for campaigns.

DEMONSTRATION/RALLY

- They should be non-violent.
- They should be imaginative and done with a sense of humour to encourage a broad-based appeal.
- They should involve local personalities where possible.
- Planning is crucial, e.g. in terms of banners, placards, inviting the relevant media correspondents.
- Consider the involvement of the police: sometimes they can add a sense of occasion (like bit actors in a drama).
- Maximize the opportunity of the event, have leaflets available, get on local radio, hold a press conference and open briefing session to set the

demonstration off.

- Ensure that there is minimum disruption to the public generally.
- Make sure it is legal and within the parameters of the 1990 Criminal Justice Act.

TIPS FOR EFFECTIVE LETTERS

They can be effective if they are written well, either to your MP, councillor, etc. Don't underestimate how difficult letter-writing is in reality.

- Grab the reader's attention in the first paragraph.
- Be precise about what you want from the reader and touch on their own public sentiments: articles that they have written, personal experience they have had.
- State what your organization does, who's involved and your aims and objectives. Make it brief, clear and concise.
- Use your Citizens' Advice Bureau to help with translations for ethnic groups.

HANDLING THE MEDIA

The newspapers, radio and television are businesses like any other and they depend on good stories or exclusives. Research all the relevant contacts and media outlets you wish to approach.

- Press releases: there are three basic principles to follow:

1 They need a professional approach; a clear, well-researched brief is essential.

2 A good press release will catch the attention of the journalist. Try to sum the whole issue up in one sentence so it reads like a headline. That will grab a journalist's instincts and imagination. It should include what is happening, who is doing it, when and where it is happening, and why it is happening. Give them a suitable quote and avoid giving an opinion. Keep it factual.

3 Give a contact name and number for further follow-up.

- Feature ideas: keeping a file of newspaper cuttings will give you a good idea about the different newspaper styles and journalists' angles, as well as providing a useful resource for the campaign. Always provide a reporter with an A4 page of researched facts and figures to back up the story.
- Remember the media need stories to make news.

TIPS FOR PUBLIC SPEAKING

A big part of raising support involves speaking at public meetings, to your own team, to the media, at rallies and so on. There are a few basic rules to follow but apart from that it is simple as long as you talk directly, factually, sincerely and briefly.

- Prepare an outline, organizing it under major headings, see **Presentation skills** in **Work** chapter.
- Most people go on for too long, so stick to the key issues and make it to the point.
- Don't get emotional, just be yourself. (If you're naturally over-emotional get someone else to do the talking.)

FUND-RAISING

Raising money is the hardest part of campaigning. Facilities, help and materials in kind may be easier to get so target people accordingly.

- Estimate how much money you will need and at what point you will need to use it. Break that down into manageable amounts and spread it out over a period of time.
- The first source of income must come from you.
- Try to get a donation from all the supporters when they join. Start a separate bank account and have two people as signatories to the account.
- Target the most sympathetic members of the public, the people who are also affected by the issues.
- Check with your local council about available funds or companies willing to sponsor.
- Look at nationwide charities and funds to which you can apply. Contact the Directory of Social Change for a variety of publications that list possible sources.
- Organize fund-raising events centred around fun.
- Try to link in to an educational campaign: this usually involves parents, more possible donors.

RESEARCH

- Supply factual weight to any arguments and campaigns. Many successful campaigns are launched on the back of good research.
- Before using research you must assess its credibility and the credibility of the organizations that produced it, its independence and its government

links. Any figures quoted should be accompanied by their source and method of calculation.

SOURCES OF INFORMATION

- **The press:** libraries keep back issues of newspapers and newspaper computer online services can be useful. Some newspapers have cuttings libraries that can sometimes help in searching for relevant articles. The British Library in Colindale has the most comprehensive newspaper library in the country and you can order photocopies through them.
- **Commercial Research Services:** the British Library's charged research services or the business information service.
- **Government:** the State publishes an enormous amount of information about itself, the country and the people. Her Majesty's Stationery Office (HMSO) is the UK Government's publisher as well as publisher to the EU, United Nations and the Council of Europe and produces 9,000 items of research a year. The most useful are documents published by them on behalf of the Central Statistical Office and the Office of Population.
- **Think tanks and academic bodies:** usually affiliated to a political party, they produce and publish research and are keen to disseminate it widely, e.g. Centre for Policy Studies, Institute for Public Policy Research and the Policy Studies Institute.
- **Market research:** there are a range of companies that publish market surveys on industry sectors, products and trends. The best are MINTEL, MSI (Marketing Strategies for Industry) and the Central Statistical Office.

SEX

DRUGS (& ROCK 'N' ROLL)

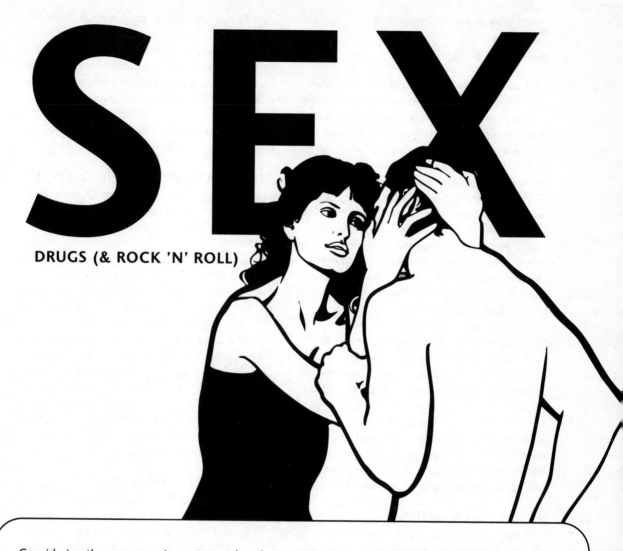

Considering the enormous importance placed on sex, most people know surprisingly little about it. An alarmingly low number of women in their twenties and thirties enjoy a regular and satisfying sex life. Many women never experience an orgasm at all and, on average, the male orgasm lasts only a few seconds and occurs just a few minutes after the man has become aroused.

Whether you're alone and want to improve your masturbation technique, on the prowl for a new lover, or have fallen into a stale routine in a long-term relationship, a real knowledge of sex is extremely empowering.

This chapter is about increasing your self-awareness whether to give pleasure or to protect yourself. It covers sexual technique; women should be able to climax in not just one, but several ways. Men are capable of reaching a stage where lovemaking can continue for hours. We also cover safe sex, contraception, sexually transmitted diseases and addictions, basic self-defence and rape. Whether alone, or with others, liberation begins in bed.

SEX

A lot of women subconsciously set up negative patterns of behaviour based on childhood experiences. Feeling unloved, suffering excessive criticism, rejection or lack of attention can reappear as a denial of your sexual needs. Patterns can emerge which feel impossible to break. Alternatively, women may be so anxious to please their partner that they don't really explore their own sexuality. Many women have their first orgasm through masturbation and only climax with a lover when they find someone mature enough to accommodate and encourage them. Men suffer too, particularly from the anxiety of 'not doing it right', which has the effect of cutting off or reducing their pleasure.

The way you behave in bed is extremely revealing of the preconceptions you hold about yourself. Many women feel that they simply don't deserve an orgasm. Fear, ignorance, embarrassment and low self-esteem can all have devastating effects in bed. The good news is that as soon as you are aware of the problems, you can start to redress them. This is a low-tech guide: all you need to reach intense pleasure is a knowledge of your own body, your lover's body, and determination.

KNOW YOUR BODY
The most effective way to gain a good knowledge of your anatomy is simply to sit in front of a mirror with your legs open.
The vagina is protected by the two soft lips of skin known as the labia. Pulling the lips apart reveals the inner labia, the opening of the vagina and the opening of the bladder, the urethra.

THE CLITORIS
The clitoris is the ridge positioned just above the point where the two inner labia meet.
• What is generally referred to as the clitoris is in fact the glans clitoridis. For practical purposes this is what we are referring to with the term 'clitoris'. It is extremely sensitive and, under normal conditions, is covered with a 'hood' of skin. Gently pulling back the hood will reveal it as pearl shaped, deep pink and shiny.
• When aroused, the clitoris swells to roughly twice its normal size and protrudes from under its hood. On nearing orgasm, it retracts back. The more it is stimulated, the more sensitive it becomes.
• There is no correlation between the size of the clitoris and the pleasure it generates.

THE ANATOMY OF THE G-SPOT
The G-spot was named after the German physician Ernst von Grafenberg. The G-spot is located on the roof of the vaginal canal, behind the pubic bone.
• Its location on the path taken by the nerves between the clitoris and the spinal column leads to its sensitivity. There is also a nerve connecting the G-spot to the bladder which, when pressed, can make you feel the need to urinate.
• The best time to search for your G-spot is after orgasm when it is enlarged and more sensitive.
• To find your G-spot: enter the vagina, keeping your finger close to the top of the opening. Slide your finger along the roof of the vaginal canal about four to five centimetres. The G-spot feels slightly ribbed or textured compared to the smooth walls of the vagina.

WHAT'S IN A NAME?
Some people find the cultural associations of the names given to sexual organs – 'cunt', 'pussy', 'prick', 'dick', 'willy' and 'cock' (among others) – constricting or embarrassing. It is revealing that they're all used as terms of abuse. If it makes you feel more comfortable, use private names with your lover.

PREPARATIONS FOR SEX
• Keep a good lubricant handy, an oil-based lubricant (a good massage oil, olive oil or Vaseline) is best for stimulating the clitoris or penis – one with a water base will dry up too quickly. However, when stimulating the G-spot (inside) a water-based lubricant (KY Jelly) is better as it won't block the natural vaginal secretions. (Note: oil-based lubricants can render condoms ineffective.)
• Keep a good supply of condoms handy.

- Smell is very evocative. Scented candles or bath oil can be arousing.
- Ensure that your fingernails are trimmed and smooth.
- Hygiene is important: pay particular attention to your genitals. A scented bath or shower can be sensual and relaxing, but avoid too many harsh chemical smells.
- The temperature of the room should be warm enough for you to feel comfortable without clothes.
- Lower the lighting.
- Have something to drink for long sessions.
- Empty your bladder.

GIVING AND RECEIVING PLEASURE

You may feel, as many women do, that you will never be able to teach your lover to give you as much pleasure as you can achieve alone. But provided you are both prepared to experiment, with patience and stamina, there is no reason why not. Equally, it makes sense to find out as much as you can about their body and sexual preferences. The biggest obstacle for most women is allowing themselves to feel they deserve to receive pleasure. Failure to do so can lead to self-consciousness which, in turn, makes it more difficult to orgasm.

- Both commit enough time to explore your bodies.
- Be systematic and, although it's easy to get lost in pleasure, keep contact. Avoid vague or general questions, be brief and specific: 'up/down?', 'more pressure, less pressure?', etc.
- Remember that while considerate lovers will feel a tremendous sense of achievement when they succeed, they may feel vulnerable too. Be encouraging, and observe a 'sexual etiquette' – guide them without being negative.
- Arousing you will be a very erotic experience for a sensitive partner. It builds deeper intimacy and there is also a great feeling of having mastered a skill.
- If your mind drifts to thinking of work or other obligations, exhale deeply and focus completely on your vagina and the sensations in your body.
- Don't begin with preconceived notions of what you feel should happen – relax and enjoy it. You will be taking responsibility for your sexuality while gaining a greater control of it.

STIMULATING THE CLITORIS

Foreplay: if someone is doing this for you, erotic foreplay beforehand is very important and makes it much easier to relax. Ask them to stroke your whole body very lightly before touching your genitals. A light touch and a real awareness of the other person is essential for good sex. Feathers, fur, silk and warm breath feel very erotic against naked skin.

HOW TO DO IT YOURSELF

- Give yourself at least an hour to an hour and a half to explore the clitoris.
- Stroke the neck, lips, nipples, underarm, belly, your inside thigh and feet.
- Concentrate on the erogenous zones. You may want to stroke your breasts and pelvic region throughout.
- Breathe slowly and deeply, focus on the sensations.
- Cover your fingers with lubricant.
- Lightly stroke the genitals. Put your hand over the whole area and vibrate.
- Spread the lips of the vagina and lightly play around the opening.
- Press the lips together and massage them from the outside.
- With only two or three fingers you can cover a wide variety of movements. Hold the shaft of the clitoris under the skin with your thumb and middle finger. Slowly massage in a circular motion.
- Use your forefinger to stimulate the still hooded clitoris.
- Slide one finger up and down and make small circular motions with the other.
- Lay your fingers flat over the whole genital area and vibrate, applying quite strong pressure.
- Use the thumb and middle finger to hold the base of the clitoris and, with your forefinger, gently massage the tip of the covered clitoris.
- You can directly stimulate the clitoris, but wait until you're strongly aroused and it stiffens and protrudes, otherwise you may find that you're too sensitive.
- Pull back the hood and rub it lightly and evenly, or hold the skin around it and slide the fingers up and down. Pulse the pressure or massage with a circular motion.
- Try to develop a rhythm you feel happy with, and keep it steady. When you reach the edge of orgasm, slow down if you want to prolong the sensation. When you're ready, increase the stimulation. You can continue this for some time, building the arousal in steps.
- When you do want to orgasm, try to relax rather than tensing. Increase the stimulation and pressure until you feel the release. If you have led up to this in the stages described, you should find it more powerful.
- You can try other forms of stimulation: spraying water directly onto the clitoris or using a vibrator (which you can buy fairly anonymously by post) are both effective. A vibrator can make the clitoris temporarily numb from over-stimulation if you use it for long periods.

- Contracting and releasing the pelvic floor muscles can add to the excitement, and by repeating this exercise you will gain much greater control of your vaginal muscles during intercourse. It is also a good exercise to get the vagina back into shape for those who have recently given birth.
- Massage of the genitals during masturbation can help heal and revitalize scar tissue around the vagina (such as that left after childbirth).
- Learning to masturbate allows you to get to know your body and what turns you on without the pressure of having to satisfy anybody else.

CUNNILINGUS

Oral sex is called cunnilingus when performed on a woman and fellatio when performed on a man. It should be intensely pleasurable for both involved. The high concentration of nerve endings in the tongue and lips makes them extremely sensitive – perfect for direct stimulation of the exposed clitoris.
- Saliva makes a very good, natural lubricant.
- Combine cunnilingus with hand movements and rhythmic massage.
- Flick the clitoris with the tip of the tongue.
- Cover the inner labia and clitoris with your mouth.
- Gently suck the clitoris and clitoral shaft while flicking and stroking with your tongue.
- Use the whole tongue. The tongue is rougher towards the back and gives a pleasant 'rasping' sensation.
- VERY DELICATELY hold the shaft of the clitoris between the teeth while flicking the exposed clitoris with the tip of the tongue.
- Roll the shaft of the clitoris lightly between the teeth and the tongue.
- Again, hygiene is very important. Wash carefully, but don't use strong soaps or deodorants which can be drying. Natural (clean) body smells are very erotic. You may want to play around with food. Ice cream or warm cream and honey feel surprising, are good lubricants and taste delicious.

SIGNS OF AROUSAL

Although there are fundamental differences between men and women, and sex underlies most of them, there are a lot of similarities too. The clitoris shares several properties with the penis. It is an erectile structure which is highly sensitive, and, like the penis, it is provided with a suspensory ligament and two small muscles. The G-spot, with its ability to generate deep, penetrating orgasms, can be compared to the prostate gland. The Glands of Bartholin, which lie on either side of the vaginal canal, are analogous to the Cowper's gland in the male. They are capable of releasing a fluid which can be propelled out by the contractions of the vaginal canal during orgasm in a 'female ejaculation'.

Women

the nipples become darker and erect
the clitoris becomes darker, stiffer and more visible
the vaginal opening becomes darker and larger
and produces natural lubricant

Men

the testicles contract towards the body
the penis gets very hard and the veins become
more pronounced
the head of the penis gets darker
clear fluid is released shortly before ejaculation

Both

the back arches
the breathing pattern changes: it may become
faster and more shallow, or slower and deeper
the pelvis is thrust forward
the muscles in the thighs, buttocks and abdomen
tense
the fingers and toes 'curl'

THE FEMALE ORGASM

Most women achieve orgasm through stimulation
of the clitoris, fewer through penetration (which
indirectly stimulates the clitoris), and fewer still
attain a deeper internal orgasm. Some women
become very still and quiet as the sensation rises;
some cry out, others may even burst into tears.
Orgasms vary widely.

There are several levels of orgasm. As you
approach climax you will feel a tingling or buzz
from deep inside you. Your breathing may
become shallow. The first level involves rhythmic
pulsing around the entry to the vagina. The
second is characterized by involuntary contractions felt deep inside, and is accompanied by
pulsing sensations in the clitoris and vagina. The
third is a more fluid, buzzing sensation which
spreads through the whole body and can last up
to half an hour. But the boundaries between them
aren't clearly defined. You may experience some
of these sensations or all in close succession.
After reaching orgasm your clitoris will be
extremely sensitive and can only be stimulated
very lightly. It might be uncomfortable for you to
touch it at all. You could assume that you can't

go on, but may be pleasantly surprised to find
that you can if you try. The body in its post-
orgasmic state is still highly excited and it
becomes much easier to arouse a series of 'mini-
orgasms' with relatively little stimulation.

Don't feel under pressure to orgasm: this creates
tension which itself can lead to disappointment;
just commit yourself to learning more about your
body and what makes you feel good.

THE G-SPOT AGAIN

Try to get someone to help you with this one – it
is awkward (until you know where to look) to
stimulate the G -spot yourself. It is essential to be
aroused first (see **Foreplay** and **Stimulating the
clitoris**). Start by following these guidelines.

• Place your free hand under the buttocks at the
base of the spine.
• You may want to raise the pelvis with a pillow.
• Allow your thumb to rest against the vaginal
opening while stimulating the clitoris.
• As excitement increases, the vaginal opening will
become darker (as it fills with blood), more lubricated, and the vaginal canal will open up. Your
thumb will naturally be pulled towards the
opening. In this position the thumb is very useful
for gauging sexual excitement.
• Ask before penetrating. Remove your thumb and,
with your palm upturned, slide your middle finger
or first two fingers into the vagina, following the
roof of the canal.
• Crooking the fingers, you should be able to feel a
pea-sized bump with a rougher texture – different
from that of the smooth vaginal walls. Press
firmly, getting feedback from your partner as you
do. You may have to penetrate quite deeply.
• Massage by moving your fingers from side to side
over the G-spot, by stroking up and down, or by
applying a pulsing pressure. Don't stay on the
spot for too long at first, and get continuous
feedback from your partner.
• Rocking the pelvis makes it easier to relax.
• With your free hand, apply pressure on the G-
spot from the outside by pushing down on the
lower abdomen. Run your hand over other
erogenous areas. As arousal increases, apply
more pressure, vibrating the spot with your
fingers.

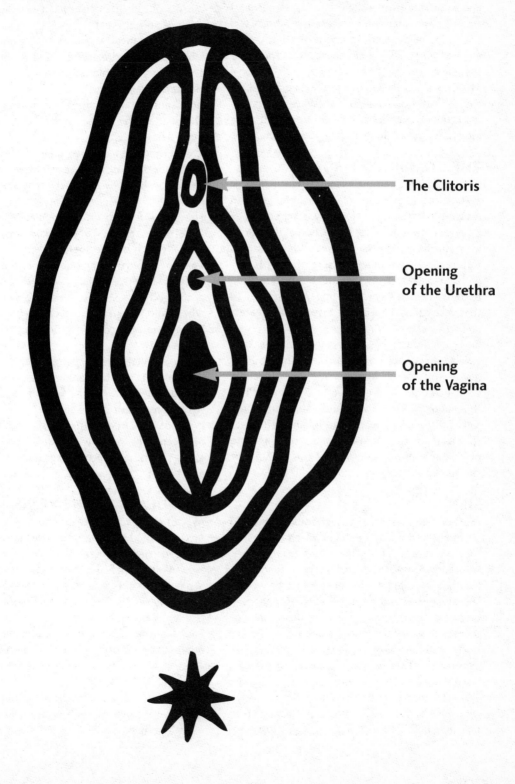

'IMPRESSION OF A VAGINA' (!)
For more accurate anatomical diagrams see *Our Bodies Ourselves* or *Gray's Anatomy*

The Clitoris

**Opening
of the Urethra**

**Opening
of the Vagina**

If your G-spot hasn't been stimulated before, your first experience may be unremarkable, uncomfortable (with a slight burning sensation – this will pass as tension is released), or it may feel great. You might feel a need to pee but, if you emptied your bladder beforehand, this is probably the effect of applying pressure on the nerve which connects the G-spot to the bladder. Take it easy at first, don't expect immediate results and relax. All women respond differently. It may require several attempts before you feel pleasure.

THE COMBINED ORGASM

By stimulating both the clitoris and the G-spot simultaneously you can achieve a prolonged and resonant orgasm. Again, foreplay is important.

- Experiment by alternating stimulation of the clitoris with stimulation of the G-spot. While concentrating on one, maintain pressure on the other.
- Work up to a regular rhythm, and begin stimulating both at once. Try synchronizing your strokes so that your hands are working together to create a unified sensation.
- Build up arousal in stages by nearly peaking, slowing the stimulation, and continuing. You can repeat this for as long as you like. The first combined orgasm can be pretty explosive. When this happens, keep your hands still, but in the same position, and (when ready) lightly stimulate to maintain the post-orgasmic tingling and pulsing sensations. Contracting the pelvic floor can spread the feelings through your body.

MEN

A lot of men feel under tremendous pressure to perform ('anxious performers') which can lessen their pleasure and, consequently, yours too. Their sexual organs are external, and many (unjustifiably) feel their penis to be inadequate. Most men would like to improve and extend their performance – premature ejaculation is just as frustrating for them as it is for their lover. By understanding the body and learning how to control it, the experience of sex can be enormously expanded. Lovemaking can last for hours before ejaculation. The male orgasm can become more powerful, with some of the subtler sensations lasting up to half an hour.

POINTS ABOUT THE PENIS

- The penis is mainly made up of spongy tissue.
- When aroused, it becomes filled with blood which makes it stiff or erect.
- Circumcision involves the surgical removal of the foreskin. Both circumcised and uncircumcised penises are capable of generating the same pleasure. An uncircumcised penis may feel slightly more sensitive under the foreskin when limp.
- The head of the penis is quite distinct from the shaft. The skin is finer and smoother. It may be several shades darker than the rest of the penis.
- The underside of the penis, where the shaft meets the head, is extremely sensitive (like the clitoris).
- The testes are two oval, glandular organs which secrete the semen. They are suspended in the scrotal pouch by the spermatic cords. The sacs, which hang outside the body, store the sperm at a slightly lower temperature than that of the rest of the body.
- When cold, or just before ejaculation, the skin around the sacs contracts, bringing them closer to the body.
- During ejaculation, the sperm travels through the vas deferens to the prostate gland, and out through the urethra. The prostate secretes the liquid constituent of the semen.
- It is possible to feel the prostate through the perineum. The prostate gland can be compared to the G-spot in women. The prostate is vulnerable to cancer – check-ups are important.

STIMULATING THE PENIS

- As with women, foreplay is important.
- Arouse the whole body by stroking, squeezing, licking or sucking. Tease him by circling the area around his genitals using light strokes.
- Slide your hands over his whole body, and let them linger on his penis and testicles.
- Use an oil-based lubricant.
- Stimulate the penis with one hand, and with the other stroke his body, circling his nipples.
- Press down on his lower abdomen. This puts pressure on the prostate.
- Experiment with different strokes: hold the base tightly with one hand while stroking up and down with the other.

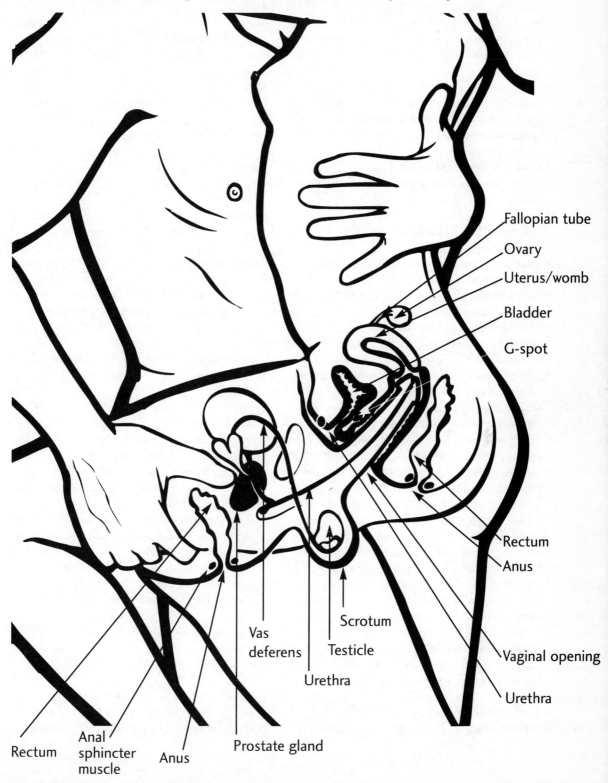

WHAT YOU DON'T SEE
For more accurate anatomical diagrams see *Our Bodies Ourselves* or *Gray's Anatomy*

Fallopian tube

Ovary

Uterus/womb

Bladder

G-spot

Rectum

Anus

Vas
deferens

Scrotum

Testicle

Vaginal opening

Urethra

Urethra

Rectum

Anal
sphincter
muscle

Anus

Prostate gland

- Rub the shaft between the palms of your hands.
- Spiral your hands around the shaft, caressing the head when you reach it.
- Tell him to focus on the sensations and to breathe deeply. By contracting and relaxing the muscles around the perineum, pleasure can be increased.
- Communicate: ask him to tell you what feels good, how much pressure you should apply, ask him to show you how he stimulates himself. Be systematic until you really know the effect of each approach.
- Keep eye contact: as well as being able to judge his reactions more accurately, it increases erotic intimacy.

TIPS FOR FELLATIO

- Hygiene is important.
- Make sure that your nose is clear and that you can breathe easily.
- Hold the penis firmly at the base and explore it with your tongue.
- With light flicking motions, move up and down the shaft, concentrating on the sensitive underside where the shaft meets the head.
- Take the whole head into your mouth, covering your teeth with your lips. While it's in your mouth, move the tip of your tongue from side to side over the point where the shaft meets the head.
- Very gently, and with a lot of saliva, use your teeth to lightly scrape the same area.
- Suck the head, and, if you're comfortable, slide the shaft into your mouth. If the penis goes too far into your throat, it may trigger a perfectly natural gagging reaction.
- While playing with the head, hold the base firmly with the thumb and forefinger of one hand and put pressure on it with the other. This will stimulate the prostate and help control ejaculation.
- Build up a steady rhythm. As he comes closer to climaxing, slow down, and encourage him to breathe deeply. Repeat this several times before allowing him to orgasm.
- The more you understand his body, and the more you are able to give him pleasure, the more exciting and erotic it should be for you.
- Some women like the man to ejaculate in their mouths; others don't. If you've had a bad experi-

ence, you may want to try it again.
- Different foods can affect the way the semen tastes.

CONTROLLING EJACULATION

Some men initially find it frustrating to withhold their orgasm, just as women may feel driven to climax when their clitoris is aroused. It is much more satisfying to make the control of the orgasm an integral and erotic part of lovemaking, one which focuses the energy back into the whole process. Once you are able to control your body, the sensations will be more varied and subtle, lovemaking can last much longer; potentially for hours, and the final orgasm will be much more intense.

- When the man has nearly reached the point of climax, put pressure on his perineum with your fingers while holding the base of the shaft.
- If you are stimulating the prostate internally, pressure from within will have the same effect. If he has gone too far, press the penis just below the head with the thumb and forefinger of both hands.
- Deep breathing will help to calm him and release tension. Repeat this several times before allowing ejaculation.

THE PROSTATE GLAND

For many men, the first experience of the prostate is an unpleasant and insensitive examination by a proctologist. As the prostate is so sensitive, men may find they get an erection even under these conditions which can make them feel acutely embarrassed. The conservative social attitudes surrounding anal sex can be difficult for many men to overcome. But potentially the prostate is a source of enormous pleasure. Good hygiene is vital in order for you both to enjoy the experience. If your partner has had medical difficulties in this area then he should check with a doctor before penetration of the anus.

EXTERNAL STIMULATION OF THE PROSTATE

- Foreplay is extremely important.

Using a massage oil or oil-based lubricant, massage his lower back, the tops of his thighs and his buttocks. Be vigorous, particularly with the buttocks. You should feel the tension leave before moving on.

- Ask him to breathe deeply.
- Either sit to the side of him, or between his legs – whichever is most comfortable.
- Arouse him (see **Stimulating the penis**). When the penis is very hard, begin to explore the perineum – the soft spongy area between the testicles and the anus. There will be hard and soft areas. Press where the tissue is softest. You should be able to push your fingers quite far. Ask him where it feels good. This is where you should apply pressure when you want to halt ejaculation.
- The man will be able to relax more easily by rhythmically contracting the muscles around the perineum. Make a fist and use your knuckles to massage and vibrate this area, concentrating on the places he pointed out. With your free hand, stroke the rest of his body.
- Put your hand beneath him supporting his sacrum (the lower back), leaving the heel of your hand over his perineum. Place your other hand over his lower abdomen so that you are holding his pelvis from above and below. Vibrate the whole area.
- Work up to stimulating the penis and prostate simultaneously. Or ask him to stroke his penis while you concentrate on the perineum.
- Build up a rhythm with both hands. Try various strokes. Bring him to the edge of orgasm, and slow down until he is ready to go on. Work up to an ejaculation.
- It doesn't matter if he loses his erection when you first begin exploring new areas. If he is comfortable and enjoying it, keep it up. If he isn't, take a break. It often takes time to get used to (and get pleasure from) new sensations.

STIMULATION OF THE PROSTATE

Many men are instinctively excited by the prospect of anal penetration, others can be frightened. Most negative reactions stem from cultural conditioning which can result in a fear of homosexuality and a horror of being penetrated. The idea that it's 'dirty and disgusting' may have been instilled in early childhood.

Once you get over this, you can have a lot of fun.

- Hygiene is important and if either of you worries about it, your enjoyment will be reduced. Your partner may want to try a simple enema (available in most chemists) with lukewarm water before beginning. Cleansing can heighten sensitivity and, with massage, keeps the prostate healthier, can soothe haemorrhoids and may reduce the risk of prostate cancer. The skin lining the anal passage is more delicate than that of the vagina and can be damaged more easily. It's very important to use a good, oil-based lubricant and trim and file your fingernails. A latex glove (or condom) will cover any rough skin and is also 'good, safe sex'.
- Foreplay: (as in **External stimulation**) take the time to really relax with a long sensuous bath or shower.
- Make sure that your partner is completely aroused, and bring him to the edge of orgasm at least once.
- Use a lot of oil. If this is the first time he has been penetrated he may be frightened as well as excited. Tension can be eased by rocking the pelvis back and forth, contracting and relaxing the muscles around the perineum and anus, and by breathing deeply.
- After bringing him close to climax, press your finger against his sphincter. He may tense.
- Ask whether he is ready. When he relaxes, gently push your finger inside him. If you meet resistance, stay still and wait. Don't force it.
- When you are inside, bend your finger and move

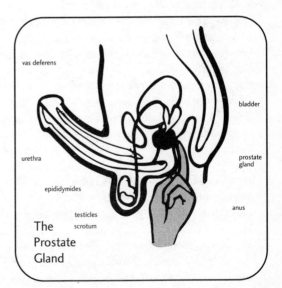

vas deferens

bladder

urethra

prostate gland

epididymides

anus

testicles
scrotum

The Prostate Gland

it around the rim of the sphincter muscle. Gentle vibrations can help. Circle slowly and find a rhythm that feels comfortable.

- Try to ease tension away. It may take a few trials before he really relaxes.
- When he's ready, push your finger further inside, curving it upwards towards his stomach. You should find a firm, convex pad of tissue, approximately the size and shape of a chestnut.
- While you are concentrating on the prostate, he can stimulate his penis.
- As with the G-spot, the first sensations may feel strange rather than pleasurable. Take your time. If it is painful, stop and try again later. The same basic strokes for stimulating the G-spot apply here.

COMBINED MALE ORGASM

- Work on building up a rhythm and stimulate the penis at the same time. Aim to synchronize the rhythm of stimulating the prostate and the penis. Put pressure on the prostate while moving the hand down the shaft, and vice versa, so that the hands are working together.
- To build towards a peak, increase pressure and speed. Have your partner tell you when he feels he's approaching orgasm, and slow down or stop stimulation. Put pressure on the prostate to prevent ejaculation. Deep breathing will help him spread the sensations through his body. When he is ready, begin again.
- With each peak, the sexual energy will increase and become more intense. He should begin to feel ripples of energy throughout his body. As you continue, it will take less stimulation to keep this sensation going.
- You can either bring him to ejaculation, or let the feelings dissipate. Combined orgasm, with stimulation of the prostate, is felt internally and more deeply. Women experience similar sensations with a G-spot orgasm.

ANAL SEX FOR A WOMAN

- Women don't have a prostate gland, but anal penetration can still give a satisfying feeling of fullness. The anus is not as elastic as the vagina and needs more lubrication. Remember not to use oil-based lubricants with a condom. The anus can be stimulated with the fingers, tongue, penis or any other slender object. Follow the same preparations as you would finding the prostate in a man. If you are going to try anal penetration, take things slowly. If it hurts or you don't want to go through with it, tell your partner to stop. Anal sex carries a greater risk of infection (HIV) through tissue damage. Anal bacteria can cause vaginal infections and cystitis, and stomach infections can be contracted by licking the edge of the anus.

- Avoid moving back and forth between the anus and the vagina to minimize the risk of infection. If you want vaginal sex after anal sex, your partner should clean himself or wear a fresh condom.

INTERCOURSE

You should be fully aroused and you may want to reach the edge of climax or full orgasm before you allow yourself to be penetrated. There are a huge number of positions to experiment with. The *Kama Sutra* is a good guide book. The shape of your clitoris, cervix and uterus will determine what feels best for you. New knowledge of yourself and your partner should contribute to a fuller sexual experience. Use the same techniques of bringing each other to the edge of orgasm, followed by a slowing up of the pace to prolong lovemaking. You can put pressure on your partner's perineum during intercourse to this end, and either of you can stimulate your clitoris throughout. To really appreciate being penetrated, let the head of his penis rest at the mouth of your vagina before allowing it to slide very slowly inside you. Keep eye contact to increase intimacy. Savour all sensations. Breathe deeply. Pelvic contractions can increase pleasure for both of you. Sex should be potent and intense. While it is important to extend your knowledge and improve your technique, sex shouldn't be treated so seriously that it becomes joyless. Be passionate, playful and sensuous. Explore your emotions as you explore each other's bodies. Instinct can take you a long way in understanding your lover.

If you're curious and want to develop your sexual skills, try a Tantric Sex training course (based on ancient Buddhism), to develop a more heightened spiritual experience of sex. Books can never take the place of 'the real thing'.

SEX IN A RELATIONSHIP

In a long-term relationship sex will go through different phases and as long as you are emotionally and physically aware of each other, this should not be a problem. You may go through periods of not being interested in sex at all. Circumstances, such as illness or pregnancy, may prevent you having sex at all. Whatever, however, whenever, as long as both partners are happy, you are having what can be considered a 'normal' sex life. If you're unhappy there are many options open to you, from one to one counselling, to self-help guides. See **Options for treatment** in **Health**.

SEX IN PREGNANCY

Some men can feel incredibly turned on by pregnancy, others feel terrified of violating the baby. Initially some women feel very tired and sick but then feel very sexy as the extra oestrogen and testosterone kick in. If you are into sex together it can be an amazing and inventive experience as your breasts and stomach increase and milk becomes a new bodily fluid.

SEX FOR OLDER WOMEN

Before contraception was widely available, menopause was when real sexual freedom began for women. Physically women will experience changes as they get older. The vagina can become quite dry and this can be helped by using a lubricant which can be bought in any chemist (KY Jelly). Masturbation can encourage more natural lubrication and will also help keep the vaginal muscles toned. Hormone replacement therapy (HRT) can increase sexual responsiveness in older women particularly those who may have had a hysterectomy. Older men may have more difficulty in achieving and maintaining erection and may need more encouragement. Some older couples find that this allows them to find other ways to sexually stimulate each other such as mutual masturbation or oral sex. Older men who ejaculate are still producing sperm that can make you pregnant, so if you are still able to conceive, and sexually active, keep using contraception. If you have not had a period for two years and are over the age of 50, you are probably unlikely to conceive again. However period loss can be caused by being ill or underweight, so it is best to have a talk with your GP.

ALTERNATIVE SEXUALITY

Acknowledging and acting upon our sexual desires is essential for our physical and emotional well-being. Everyone needs to love and be loved. It is a myth that everyone is innately heterosexual or conventional, but unfamiliar or unusual sexual habits can sometimes be disturbing to those with limited sexual experience. Even if only in fantasy many of us will experiment with someone of the same sex. If you're curious about some of the more obscure options read *The Encyclopedia of Unusual Sex Practices*.

HOMOSEXUALS

Homosexuals are men and women who are physically attracted to members of their own sex. Generally, homosexual women are referred to as 'lesbian' and men as being 'gay', although 'gay' has become pretty generic. While society is now a great deal more accepting, homosexuality is still misunderstood and even feared, leading to prejudice and both social and legal discrimination. Homosexuals are actively ostracized from many professions such as the armed forces.

HIV/Aids has tragic consequences for anyone who has been diagnosed with it or who has watched close friends suffer. Aids is obviously a threat to everyone who is sexually active regardless of gender or social background. However, the delicate tissue of the anal passage makes blood/semen contact more likely and therefore puts those practising unsafe anal sex with men more at risk. On a more positive note, the gay community has become much more united as it has fought to dispel the confusion and prejudice surrounding HIV/Aids and homosexuality in general.

LESBIANS

As lesbians share the same anatomy, there is an innate sexual understanding which can be very rewarding. Many women, young, old, married or single may find that they experience or enjoy a lesbian relationship at some stage and yet remain heterosexual. The number of celebrities who have recently 'come out' has enhanced the popular 'lesbian chic' revision that has been gaining momentum in the 90s. Lesbians can remain overtly feminine or might cultivate a more masculine appearance taking on 'butch/fem(inine)' roles within a relationship. Lesbian relationships can be as varied and satisfying (or unsatisfying) as heterosexual ones. Increasing numbers of lesbian couples are sucessfully having or adopting children, although a great deal depends on local policy (see **Adoption and Surrogacy** in **Babies** chapter). Contact Lesbian and Gay Fostering. If you want to explore, check local listings for details of lesbian and gay nightclubs, bars or events. Inner cities have a great deal more to offer and are far more accepting than the provinces. Call the Lesbian Information Service for more information and the other contacts listed in the Directory.

BISEXUALITY

Bisexuality is considered to be a sexuality in itself. Alternatively, many people go through a period of being bisexual and then settle with a single partner of either sex. Contact the London Bisexual Helpline for information.

TRANSGENDERED

Transgendered is a term that covers anyone who has a problem with their gender identity, as well as being used to describe those who live permanently as the opposite sex without resorting to surgery. There are a range of support groups and helplines available through which you can get advice, information, details of befriending schemes and meetings, as well as referral to trained counsellors or psychologists if you feel you need it.

TRANSVESTISM

Transvestites derive erotic pleasure from wearing

clothes of the opposite sex. Crossdressers who are not sexually aroused by it (which could include drag queens or female impersonators) are not transvestites. Crossdressers can be any age, race or from any social group. They can be gay or straight, male or female, but are generally heterosexual men. According to FTM (Female to Male network), there are nearly 3,000,000 transvestites and approximately 35,000 transexuals living in Britain. Contact FTM and Gender Trust helpline for more information.

TRANSSEXUALS

A transsexual has the physical characteristics of one sex, and the psychological characteristics of another. Many live as heterosexuals, but even if they marry and have children, many remain unhappy. They feel that they should have been born as the opposite sex and yet some transsexuals who go through with an actual sex change still feel their identity is confused, even after the operation. If you decide to have a sex change, it can be a lonely experience. You may face rejection from friends and family, and people who decide to have the treatment often end up moving away from their homes to try to start a new life. The law will not allow one's sex to be changed on birth certificates or passports, and you cannot marry or adopt children. Sex changes are accomplished by a mixture of hormones and surgery and should always be preceded by proper analysis and counselling. Make an appointment with your GP, and contact the Gender Identity Consultation Service.

COMING OUT

'Coming out' (revealing your sexual indentity) can be protracted or sudden depending on your personality and circumstances. Most people first 'come out' to themselves, then within the gay community, and finally with friends, family and colleagues. Telling family and friends can be very difficult. For most parents the discovery that their son or daughter is gay or bisexual can be an emotional experience. They will anticipate the prejudice and discrimination their child will face. If you come from a religious background the issues can be further complicated.

You should only come out if you feel sure you will benefit from it. Don't be pressurized by your partner or peer group. Only you can decide. Pick your time carefully and make sure you can answer the question 'are you sure'? with 'yes'. If you are unsure, whomever you are telling may think you are just 'going through a phase' and may ignore the issue without dealing with it or accepting it. Don't expect immediate acceptance: the process can take years and some may never come round, while others will respond positively. Ring Identity – a support group for those coming out.

BEING TOLD

If your child or parent tells you that they are gay:
Remember
- It takes a lot of courage.
- Think about all the issues as rationally as you can, accept that this is something that you cannot change and understand that you are not responsible.
- If you can, reassure your child or parent that you love them.
- If you need time, keep the discussion lines open and arrange to meet and talk as soon as you are ready.
- If they want to introduce you to their partner, try and be as open and as friendly as possible.

CONTRA-CEPTION

Advice on contraception is freely available from your GP, family-planning clinic or chemist. The Margaret Pyke Centre is the largest contraception centre in the UK. Doctors have the right to decline contraceptive procedures for children under the age of 16. Britain has one of the highest teenage pregnancy rates in Western Europe. Fear of being 'exposed' to their parents is one of the biggest blocks to young girls seeking advice on contraception. Each year approximately 160,000 women have abortions and many of these are under 18 years old. The British

Medical Association (BMA) emphasizes that it puts patient confidentiality at a premium, but this message is not getting through. We have a responsibility to educate young women about safe sex. Read *The Pill* by John Guilleband and *Your Guide to Contraception* published by the Family Planning Association for further information.

Family-planning clinics provide an information service on all aspects of contraception. See Chart overleaf.

ABORTION

This is not a form of contraception. Abortions are available on the NHS, but there is always a waiting list and the earlier the operation is performed the better, so most are done privately. Two doctors recommend you to a clinic where it costs at least £350. The NHS is free.

Abortion is defined as a termination of pregnancy within 24 weeks, although very few are carried out that late. If it becomes apparent after a 24-week period that the child will be born seriously handicapped, there is no time limit at all.

Abortions are granted on the understanding that: either a continued pregnancy will put at risk the patient's life, her physical or mental health, or that of her other children; or there is a substantial risk that a child will be born with a severe physical or mental handicap. In many 'abortion clinics' this is a formality, 'the patient's mental health' being a fairly flexible clause. A man cannot prevent a wife or girlfriend from having an abortion, neither can parents take out an injunction against a teenage daughter to the same end. Call the Brook Advisory Service for advice on unplanned pregnancy.

There are three legal methods

1 The suction or vacuum method: you need to be less than 12 weeks pregnant. The earlier it is done, the less painful, both emotionally and physically. You have to have both an assessment and counselling before the operation. The operation is done in a day with a local or general anaesthetic and a few days' rest at home afterwards.

2 The abortion pill (RU486) or non-surgical abortion: this involves 2–3 visits to a surgery or hospital. A miscarriage is brought on. This feels like strong period pains. Studies suggest that women find this method less psychologically and physically traumatic. For 5% of women this doesn't work and they will be referred to the vacuum method.

3 Late abortion: this may involve induced labour and is usually confined to problem pregnancies. The Marie Stopes Clinic is a registered charity providing pregnancy testing and advice if pregnancy is unplanned.

HIV AND AIDS

Sexual intercourse and certain other activities put you at risk of becoming infected with HIV (Human Immunodeficiency Virus) which causes AIDS (Acquired Immune Deficiency Syndrome).

At present there is no vaccine and no cure. It is estimated that in the UK 28,383 people have become infected since reporting began in 1984, though many of them could have protected themselves by following the safe sex guide-lines.

HIV can be transmitted by

- Having vaginal or anal sex without a condom with a partner who is HIV positive. You can be infected through vaginal fluid, semen and blood which can transmit HIV into another person's body. Oral sex is less risky but not 100% safe.
- Using needles or other drug-injecting equipment that is contaminated with infected blood.
- A woman with HIV to her baby. This can happen during pregnancy, birth or breastfeeding.
- Receiving unscreened blood in a blood transfusion.

HIV cannot be transmitted by

- Kissing/tears: unlike other bodily fluids, saliva and tears do not pass on the virus.
- Touching, shaking hands or any other form of

METHODS OF CONTRACEPTION

	WHAT IS IT?	HOW DOES IT WORK?	IS IT RELIABLE?	ADVANTAGES	DISADVANTAGES
Combined pill	A pill containing the hormones progestogen and oestrogen.	The pill stops ovulation so there is no egg for the sperm to fertilize.	25% of women use this method, fewer than 1 in 100 users get pregnant.	Easy and convenient to use, reduces bleeding during periods and PMS, may protect against cancer of the ovaries and womb.	Must be taken conscientiously, minor side-effects such as headaches and nausea, not suitable for smokers or breast-feeding women.
Progestogen-only pill (mini pill)	A pill containing the hormone progestogen.	If taken at the same time every day, it causes changes in the cervical mucus, making entry for the sperm difficult, and stops ovulation.	Statistics say fewer than 1 in 100 users get pregnant, but it is said to be less effective than the combined pill.	Easy and convenient, safer for women who are breast-feeding or who smoke.	May cause irregular periods, weight gain, headaches and/or nausea. It is essential that the pill is taken at the same time every day.
Contraceptive injection	An injection of progestogen given by a doctor every 2–3 months.	The same way as the combined pill, by stopping ovulation, but is not usually a first choice with doctors, unless it is the only option for you.	Fewer than 1 in 100 users get pregnant.	You only need one injection every 2–3 months and don't have the worry of forgetting to take your pill, but have to remember your appointment.	May miss periods, fertility may take a year to return, weight gain, cannot be reversed once taken and takes three months to wear off, i.e. if you have side-effects you will have them for three months.
Intra-uterine device (coil/IUD)	A small plastic or copper device inserted into the womb.	Prevents the sperm from meeting the egg or the fertilized egg from settling in the womb.	1 in 200 users get pregnant.	Can be used for five years – needs to be checked every six months.	Cramping periods may be heavier and more painful, complicated fitting procedure which a doctor has to carry out. It may impair fertility, which is why it is usually given to women who already have children.

Method	Description	How it works	Effectiveness	Advantages	Disadvantages
Intra-uterine system	A small plastic device which is put into the vagina and left there.	It releases the hormone progestogen, causing changes to the cervical mucus, making it difficult for the sperm to enter and pregnancy to establish.	Fewer than 1 in 1000 users get pregnant.	It lasts up to three years, periods shorter and lighter.	Possible side-effects such as breast tenderness and acne. It may affect fertility and increase the risk of pelvic inflammatory disease. Difficult to insert.
Female condom (femidom)	A polyurethane sheath.	It stops sperm from entering the vagina.	It is supposed to be as effective as a Durex, but the effect rate is poorly documented.	It theoretically protects you from sexually transmitted diseases.	Lack of spontaneity, expensive to buy every time.
Diaphragm/cap with spermicide	Soft rubber dome or cap which is inserted into the vagina.	It stops the sperm getting into the womb. The diaphragm must remain there for 6 hours after intercourse.	2–6 in 100 get pregnant	Can be inserted any time before intercourse, may protect against cancer of the cervix, cheap.	Allergy to rubber, itching. Cystitis can be a problem.
Persona in conjunction with the rhythm method (natural)	Persona measures your personal hormone levels.	A urine test tells you when you are safe to have sex.	It is suited to those with regular periods and is as effective as a male condom.	No side-effects.	It does not protect against HIV.
Female sterilization	Surgery.	The Fallopian tubes are cut or tied, preventing the sperm from meeting the egg.	3 in 1,000 get pregnant	Permanent, so more suited to people who have had all their kids.	Surgery, general anaesthetic and a stay in hospital. Generally irreversible.
Emergency or Morning-after pill (MAP)	An oestrogen-based pill.	It brings on a false period, emptying the womb. This works for up to three days (72 hours) after the mistake.	Not 100% foolproof, so see your GP if you don't get your period. Call the Emergency Contraception Helpline for advice.		

'dry' physical contact.
- Sneezing or coughing: the virus can't survive outside the body.
- Sharing swimming pools, toilets, food, cups, utensils, etc.
- Animal/insect bites.

SAFE SEX

- Make your partner wear a strong new condom with a new water-based lubricant and make him withdraw before the condom comes off.
- Make sure his condom carries the British Standards Kitemark or the new CE mark and check the sell-by date on the packet.
- Don't share syringes if you are an intravenous drug user. Better still, don't use drugs intravenously.
- If you are going to have your ears (or nipples?) pierced, get a tattoo or have electrolysis to remove that beard, make sure you go to reliable and registered practitioners who use sterilized equipment.

If you're travelling to Third World or Eastern European countries, MASTA (Medical Advisory Services for Travellers Abroad) can advise you on how to deal with a medical emergency that might require a blood transfusion for example.

AIDS TESTS

For the majority of people with HIV, their antibodies develop within three to six months after infection. The presence of the antibodies are a marker to the virus. You need to have had no risk of infection in the three months prior to taking the test to get an accurate reading. If you test positive, it may take many years for you to experience any symptoms. There is no cure at the moment. Contact the Aids Freephone Helpline, Terrence Higgins Trust, or Positively Women for information.

STDS
SEXUALLY TRANSMITTED DISEASES/GENITAL INFECTIONS

TREATMENTS (SEE CHART)

The consequences of sexually transmitted diseases can often be far more serious for women than men (other than with HIV). Left untreated, they can cause infertility, ectopic pregnancy (when the foetus forms outside the uterus) and genital cancers. Most can be cleared easily with antibiotics from your GP or local hospital genitourinary clinic. STDs can be transmitted from close body contact or oral sex as well as full penetrative sexual intercourse.

ALCOHOL

FACTS

- A unit is a standard pub measure of spirits, wine, or half a pint of lager.
- 11% of women drink more than the recommended 'sensible limit' of 14 units of alcohol a week.
- 1% of women are classified as 'very heavy drinkers' consuming more than 35 units a week.
- There are 25,000 alcohol-related deaths a year and 10,000 of those are women.
- Women need fewer drinks to get drunk than men. Their bodies contain less water than men's, so the alcohol is less diluted and has a greater impact.
- Women tend to feel the effects of alcohol more intensely just before or during their periods.
- Drinking alcohol increases the risk of liver disease, breast cancer, early menopause, osteoporosis and heart disease.

However, for most of us, alcohol is a way of relaxing and an important element of our social lives which in moderation won't do us a great deal of harm. For those occasions when we may overdo it, the following tips may assist in both prevention and cure of a hangover.

HANGOVERS

Symptoms

Headache, unquenchable thirst, monkey slept in your mouth, nausea?

Cause

Alcohol is a diuretic. It dehydrates the body by causing you to pee more liquid out than you are putting in. Dehydration gives you a headache and makes you feel thirsty.

Alcohol stimulates the production of insulin which lowers the blood sugar and makes us feel sick while craving something sweet.

Prevention

- Line your stomach before you go out by eating a meal and drinking a large glass of milk.
- Don't smoke. It makes you drink more. Alcohol is a vaso-dilator causing the veins and arteries to expand, while nicotine is a vaso-contractor, the opposite, which is why you always feel like a cigarette when you get drunk to balance the dilation.
- Stick to one type of drink. Remember the rule that the darker and sweeter the drink, the worse the hangover.
- Vodka and gin straight and undiluted will take longer to get you drunk – the stomach lining produces a protective mucus and closes the pyloric sphincter between the stomach and lower intestine, slowing down the passage of alcohol and delaying the effect.
- White wine topped up with still water is the least harmful thing to drink if you are trying to avoid a hangover.
- Fizzy alcoholic drinks get you drunk quicker as the alcohol reaches your bloodstream more quickly. Drink still water with alcohol.
- If you can't stick to just two glasses of anything, drink at least two pints of water before you go to bed.

Head from hell – for breakfast

- Take vitamins B and C plus 2–3gm of evening primrose oil.
- Mix up one sachet of Dioralyte (rehydrator available from chemist) with water and drink it to replace the minerals and other good things that you have destroyed.
- Take two Alka-Seltzer.
- Eat plenty of protein.

	What it is/does	Symptoms	Treatment	Prevention
CHLAMYDIA:	This is the most common of STDs, affecting 1 in 10 sexually active women. It can lead to pelvic inflammatory disease (PID), infertility or ectopic pregnancy. If you catch chlamydia when you are pregnant it can lead to pneumonia for the foetus.	Sometimes it has no symptoms, but it usually causes abdominal discomfort and thick discharge. Having a pee may be painful and sex uncomfortable.	A two-week course of antibiotics. Your partner will need to be treated too.	Condoms.
CYSTITIS:	This isn't necessarily sexually transmitted as it is caused by the germs from the anus entering the bladder through the urethra. This can happen if you wipe yourself in the wrong direction after going to the toilet – always wipe from the vagina towards the anus – or it can happen during sex, especially if mixing anal and vaginal penetration.	Stinging burning pain in the urethra when peeing, feeling that you need to pee all the time without being able to, a dragging ache in your lower abdomen, dark strong-smelling urine.	Lots of water to flush out the infection – at least four pints a day and a pint before bedtime. A spoonful of bicarbonate of soda dissolved in water neutralizes the acid. Avoid coffee, tea, juices (except cranberry), or alcohol. Take showers until it clears up, bubble bath and soap can aggravate it. Cystitis can require antibiotics if it is really bad.	Hygiene and drinking lots of water. Washing genitals after sex.
GENITAL HERPES:	This is a contagious and incurable condition which can lead to infertility in women. It can be seen in your smear test, but it can stay dormant for many years, meaning many men and women pass it on without even knowing that they have it	Burning, itching and blistering in genital area, and flu-like symptoms.	Anti-viral drugs can control outbreaks and avoiding stress can help.	Condoms, spermicide, avoid sex if partner displays symptoms. Wash genitals after sex.
GENITAL WARTS:	Mainly found in 16–25-year-olds. Caused by the human papilloma virus which is transmitted through close bodily contact. These warts can be linked to pre-cancerous cell changes in the cervix which may lead to cervical cancer.	Soft gritty lumps of flesh around or inside the cervix, vagina or anus.	Ointments, freezing or surgical removal.	Condoms.

SEXUALLY TRANSMITTED DISEASES

SYPHILIS:
Rare. When not treated it attacks the internal organs and can cause death. If passed to unborn children it can cause still-births or neurological and cardiovascular diseases.

Painful sores and rashes in or around the mouth, vagina, anus; body rashes, hair loss, difficulties in speaking.

Antibiotics.

Condoms.

GONORRHOEA:
Can cause blindness in the foetus of an infected pregnant women and can lead to PID.

Similar to chlamydia, as well as swollen lymph glands, abdominal pain.

Antibiotics.

Condoms.

THRUSH:
Thrush is very common and comes from a yeast fungus called candida albicans. Many women develop thrush after taking antibiotics, or it can be a result of too many late nights, alcohol and an unbalanced diet. It can also be sexually transmitted.

Itching inside and outside of the vagina, stinging sensation when you pee, discharge.

Canesten cream and pessaries are available over the counter in your local chemist and if you go to the doctor this is probably what they will prescribe. Eat live natural yoghurt and smear it on your vagina to relieve itching and soreness.

HEPATITIS B:
It is a virus affecting the liver that is transmitted through sexual contact and dirty needles (through drug injection). It is extremely infectious. (Not just a sexual disease.)

Generally unwell and jaundiced.

It can be detected through a blood test. There is a vaccine called Hep B, available through any drug service, or your local GP. Recovery can be 100% but for some they can remain carriers of Hepatitis B.

Condoms and Hep B.

ADDIC-TIONS

An addict is someone who is devoted to a habit, i.e. s/he is probably dependent on a specific drug and is unable to do without it. It is often impossible for them to give up without adverse effects. The most addictive drugs are those that affect one's mood. Usually used socially, people enjoy their effect and use them to overcome feelings of inadequacy or to make a difficult situation more bearable. People can be addicted to anything – chocolate, co-dependence, drugs, exercise, food, cigarettes, gambling, hygiene, flashing, pornography, marriage, sex, sugar, shoplifting, work, violence. Get help if you have a compulsive and dependent pattern of usage with anything which is detrimentally affecting the quality of your life, work and relationships.

MOST COMMONLY USED ADDICTIVE SUBSTANCES

Alcohol: see above. Active ingredients are ethyl alcohol or ethanol – beers, wines, spirits, liqueurs, Vodka is the purest. It is legal for anyone over the age of 18 but can be drunk at home by anyone over the age of five. It makes users feel relaxed and uninhibited. It can lead to double vision, loss of balance and decreased sexual performance, also known as brewer's droop. Excess of alcohol can lead to dependency, liver damage and eventual death. Alcohol is a major factor in 65% of suicide attempts, 40% of domestic violence, 75% of stabbings, 40% of child abuse cases and 65% of murders. Alcohol-related problems cost the NHS £150 million a year. Women have a lower tolerance for alcohol, especially just before their period is due. Recent research now vindicates what most women have known for years, that a glass of wine a day during pregnancy does no harm at all; however women who do drink excessive amounts of alcohol during pregnancy can severely damage their unborn child. 3 units a week should be the the absolute maximum and no more than 2 units at a time. Contact the Women's Alcohol Centre and DAWN.

Amphetamine is a synthetic drug and is available in a variety of forms: capsules, powder and tablets. It costs about £10 a gm. It increases the heart rate and blood pressure, generally speeds body processes and makes people feel confident and energetic for a couple of hours. These feelings can change to depression, exhaustion and irritability when the drug wears off. Physical symptoms include loss of appetite and weight. Next to cannabis this is the most commonly used drug.

Amyl nitrates: more commonly known as poppers; used in medicine as an antidote to cyanide poisoning. It is a pharmacy medicine but is sold over the counter mainly in sex shops. It gives a head rush when sniffed that makes the user feel light-headed and can enhance sexual pleasure if used during orgasm. It also causes headaches, vomiting and dermatitis and can lower oxygen levels in the blood which can leave you unconscious. Tolerance to it develops quickly.

Anabolic steroids: derived from the hormone testosterone and used medically to restore weakened muscles. Prescription only, they are considered Class C if misused. Usually used by body builders or sportsmen/women, they are believed to increase strength and athletic performance. The available research shows that they increase the risk of liver and kidney malfunction and decrease fertility in men. Women can develop an enlarged clitoris, which might sound like a bonus but unfortunately it is associated with more hair on your face and body, a deeper voice and smaller breasts.

Cannabis: comes in two forms – 'hash' which is the brown solidified resin/oil of the cannabis plant and 'grass' which is made from the dried leaves. It is smoked mixed with tobacco in roll-ups, called joints or spliffs. It can also be eaten in food, e.g. hash cakes. It's an illegal Class B drug and possession carries a maximum sentence of five years, but first-time offenders are often just cautioned. Cannabis has been successfully prescribed by doctors to alleviate pain for some patients and there is a debate now as to whether it should be used to help other sufferers. Indeed many people feel that cannabis should be legalized completely. It is relatively mild but can have a range of effects. It can make you feel relaxed, spaced out, paranoid or simply send you to sleep. It can also give you the munchies. Newer types of cannabis are now being grown in much stronger strains, known as skunk weed. They are much more powerful and can be almost hallucinogenic.

Cocaine/crack: a Class A drug, derived from the leaves of the Andean coca shrub, cocaine is a white powder that can be snorted, injected, smoked in nugget form as crack, or rubbed on the gums. Coke increases self-confidence and energy but the effects wear off quite quickly. It is widely used and considered more socially acceptable than other drugs, such as heroin. Side-effects include paranoia, depression, heart palpitations and a sudden rise in blood pressure. Repeated snorting can erode the lining of your nose and, although it is not supposed to be addictive, tolerance to the effects build up with continued use, meaning serious users gradually increase the amount they take to get the same high. Crack is much more addictive, and psychological dependence can develop with both.

Downers: benzodiazepines, tranquillizers that include Valium, Ativan and Librium. Used medically to relieve anxiety and induce sleep, they are on prescription only. Without a prescription they are considered Class C. They are swallowed as pills or prepared for injection. They make users feel calm, relieve anxiety and are often taken to offset the effects of amphetamines (uppers). After two weeks of regular use these drugs become ineffectual as sleeping tablets and after four months they don't have any effect on anxiety at all. Withdrawal symptoms can include

insomnia, perceptual hypersensitivity, tremors, nausea and, with higher doses, mental confusion and convulsions. If injected, the gel in the capsules can solidify in the veins, causing gangrene and abscesses.

Ecstasy or E: a Class A drug, it contains MDMA and is swallowed in tablet or capsule form, costing between £8 and £15. In the UK approximately 500,000 young people take Ecstasy every weekend, but there are growing concerns about the safety of the drug. Since 1988, 50 young people have died from using Ecstasy, though no one has been able to say exactly why. The drug induces feelings of heightened perception, energy and friendliness. Users are advised to stagger regular fluid intake throughout the evening and not consume large volumes of liquid in one go, as evidence suggests that Ecstasy inhibits the performance of the kidneys. High doses over a long period of time can cause psychosis. Current advice for Ecstasy users is: drink one pint of fluid (fruit juice and water) each hour, take regular rests from dancing and eat salty foods.

LSD: or acid, is a white powder which is absorbed into tiny squares of paper (tabs), sugar cubes or sheets of gelatin. Illegal Class A drug, possession carries a maximum seven-year sentence. A trip costs about £2 and the effects last for many hours. Users experience auditory and visual hallucination – trips can be good or bad. On a bad trip the user can become paranoid and suffer hours of extreme anxiety. Tolerance develops very rapidly, so that after three or four days the effects are negligible, although flashbacks can occur years later.

Magic mushrooms: Liberty Cap mushrooms can be picked wild in the UK in the autumn and dried. They are illegal if prepared for consumption as the drug they contain, psilocin, is considered to be Class A. They can be eaten raw, cooked in food or made into tea, which can cause hallucinations, tripping and fits of the giggles. The greatest danger with mushrooms is that you might pick and eat a poisonous one, but unless you experience a 'bad trip' there are no known serious side-effects.

Opiates: heroin, smack or horse, is derived from the poppy family, can be dissolved in water and injected under the skin, swallowed, heated and inhaled through a straw or snorted. Heroin is a Class A drug. Methadone, a synthetic opiate, is legally prescribed to help addicts treat their dependence. Highly addictive, heroin gives feelings of pleasure, security and self-confidence. Users often share needles with others, and run the risk of catching HIV and hepatitis. They may also need more and more to generate the same effect and end up overdosing. Opium, also Class A, is less refined than heroin. It is a dark sticky resin and is smoked.

Solvents and gases: glue, lighter fuel, cleaning fluid, aerosols are inhaled as vapours. They cost about £1.30 and induce hallucination and euphoria. They are cheap and accessible for children intent on experimentation. Breathing and heart-rate become depressed and cause disorientation and loss of control which can lead to accidents. Long-term use leads to brain damage.

Tobacco: it contains tar, nicotine and other additives; and is legal for anyone over the age of 16. Smoked as cigarettes, cigars, or in a pipe, chewed or sniffed. Gives users the impression that they look relaxed or cool but the sight of 14-year-old schoolboys lighting up on their way home often has exactly the opposite effect. Smoking increases the risk of lung cancer, chronic bronchitis, heart disease, blood clots, cancer of the mouth and throat and emphysema. Every year over 100,000 die from smoking-related illness in the UK. Babies of women who smoke are more likely to be underweight, premature or miscarried.

EMERGENCIES
If you find a friend drowsy or unconscious after taking drugs or alcohol
- Make sure they have plenty of fresh air.
- Turn them onto their side and don't leave them alone (they could suffocate on their vomit).

- Stop them falling unconscious, keep them awake.
- Call 999, ask for an ambulance.
- Collect anything that seems to have been used in the drug taking and give it to the ambulance crew. This could be tablets, silver paper, solvents, powders, needles, etc.

If they lose consciousness
- Keep them warm but not hot, loosen tight clothing. Check breathing. Give mouth-to-mouth resuscitation if you can.

If they are tense and panicky from a bad trip
- Talk quietly. Calm them down with assurances that the feelings will go.
- Keep them away from loud noises and bright lights.
- Help them to breathe slowly with counting: hyperventilating can lead to sickness.
- If they overheat, move them to a cool area, splash them with cold water, call an ambulance.

DETECTING DRUG ABUSE
You may notice
- mood changes
- bad temper, aggression, telling lies, secretiveness
- loss of appetite, gets sleepy
- stops hobbies, schoolwork or seeing friends
- money and possessions disappear
- powders, tablets, tin foil, needles
- strange smells and staining, looks sloppy, can't be bothered with appearance
- saying one thing, doing another

If you use drugs recreationally, doing it openly and passing the joint to your kids will not bond you more closely. All it's saying is, 'It's allowed'.

GETTING HELP
If you are worried, want to come off, need advice or can't cope, or just want to know more, call National Drugs Free Helpline; Release, a 24-hour confidential helpline and drugs-in-school helpline; Adfam for families and friends of drug users; Coda for drug treatment and care.

DRUGS AND THE LAW
- The Medicines Act controls the way medicines are made and supplied.
- The Misuse of Drugs Act places banned drugs in

different classes.

- Class A drugs carry the highest penalty, Class C, the lowest. Any classified drugs are illegal to have, sell or give away.
- First offenders, possessing drugs for their own use, will be fined or cautioned and have a criminal record.
- Regular offenders, drug dealers/sellers, can be sentenced to life imprisonment for trafficking.
- In England and Wales, children (ages 10–16) are dealt with by a juvenile court and can be sent to detention (not prison), and their parents fined.

SMOKING
AND HOW TO STOP

Fewer women than men manage to give up smoking and more young women than men take up the habit. 11.9 million people in the UK are ex-smokers. 10 million have stopped and stayed stopped. The vast majority of them failed the first time they tried to quit.

WHAT HAPPENS

Eight hours after your last cigarette, the oxygen levels in your blood return to normal. Within 48 hours the nicotine has been cleared from your body and after about six weeks your lungs will see a 70% improvement.

HOW TO QUIT

- Don't be hard on yourself: there are several fronts on which you will battle with this and you might want to tackle them one at a time.
- Nicotine patches can help for the first few days.
- Vitamin C helps your body to get rid of nicotine more quickly. The key to success is really wanting to stop.
- Opt for a clean break, take up a physical activity and change your routine so that you avoid the things that you enjoyed a fag with, i.e. avoid the pub, coffee breaks etc. for a while. Chew gum or carry worry beads to hand so that you have something to do with your hands.

- Quitting in the middle of the menstrual cycle means less discomfort and withdrawal. Keep at it. Quitline and Action on Smoking and Health (ASH) offer support and advice.
- It is a myth that you will gain weight if you quit smoking.
- Look at replacing old habits with new ones, see **Alternative treatments** in **Health** chapter. Giving up smoking makes you richer, and healthier.

SELF-DEFENCE

There are certain ways to minimize the risk of attack or assault, e.g. avoid hitch-hiking or wandering around by yourself late at night. If you are attacked, the number-one strategy is to avoid violence and get the hell out of there as fast as you can. The majority of crimes are committed against property and if you are at risk you are better off letting the mugger take your purse and cutting your losses. Most physical attacks happen on the street between mid-evening and early morning and are usually very quick.

ON THE STREET

Plan ahead, take common-sense precautions:
- Carry the number of a reputable taxi company.
- Keep some money separate from your other cash to pay for taxis and telephones.
- Carry a chargecard or mobile phone.
- Cover up things that look expensive (jewellery or phones).
- Look confident, walk purposefully, keep your head up high but avoid eye contact.
- Carry an alarm or whistle to deter potential attackers.
- If possible, don't go out alone, get a friend to escort you.
- If walking alone, carry something in your hand that could temporarily injure your attacker. If you scratch them with your keys the marks can make identification easier for the police.

- When on your own in a car, don't stop for anyone, however innocent it might appear, and lock all the doors at all times.

AT HOME
- Never let a stranger into your home.
- Always look for credentials before allowing anyone in. If you are unsure, e.g. you were not expecting a health visitor or a plumber, leave them outside and shut the door while you phone and check them out.
- Fit a viewer or a peephole so you can see the person.
- Fit an outside light for night-time viewing.
- Consider a panic button as part of an alarm system.
- Door chains must be strong enough to resist a hard kicking.
- If you are alone, give the impression you have company, shout out to your imaginary friend.
- Never put 'Miss' in front of your name on the door entry.
- Don't put your full name in the telephone directory, use anonymous initials that can't be identified as female.
- At night always lock all accessible doors and windows.
- If you hear anything, call the police, it is better to be safe than sorry.
- If you disturb a thief, don't block his exit path – you may get hurt in the process.

TELEPHONE NUISANCE
- Being ex-directory is a good preventative measure.
- Keep a loud whistle by the phone.
- Never give your name and number on your machine, some people just dial random numbers.
- If you suffer from persistent calls, tell the police, it is possible for them to monitor them.
- Dial 1471 on the telephone to have the last caller's number identified.
- Get an answerphone and screen your calls.

DEFENDING YOURSELF
Violence breeds violence. Be wary of hitting out at someone who has a clear physical advantage over you or who might be carrying a dangerous weapon. You need to develop some way to defend yourself. Simply being fitter will increase your confidence and will allow you to escape from the situation more quickly. Self-defence and martial arts courses are widely available, but attending a few sessions may give you a false feeling of security. Courses must be taken seriously to achieve real results.

THE LEGAL SITUATION
You may only do what is 'reasonably necessary' (in the words of the Law) to defend yourself from an attacker. Basically, the action you take must not be excessive. The Law expects you to run from violent situations, but this is not always possible. Disabling sprays are illegal.

SENSITIVE BODY PARTS
- Eyes are very sensitive and if you can cause temporary blindness and confusion it may allow you enough time to escape from the situation. Spray water or perfume to disable your attacker, drop the bottle and run.
- Nose: hitting from beneath the nose causes the eyes to water and stuns the attacker.
- Throat: the throat is a particularly vulnerable area and if you strike them there they may have difficulty breathing.
- Stomach: a blow to the stomach may leave the attacker winded, giving you time to get away.
- Groin: a well-aimed squeeze, kick or punch in the goolies is always a good bet.
- Knee: the knee joint is very sensitive and a well-aimed kick can immobilize your attacker.
- Kidneys: a blow to the kidneys from behind is very painful and can cause breathlessness.

RAPE

The shock and trauma of rape or sexual assault is very difficult to get over; some women never do. Many victims feel discouraged from reporting rape because of the ordeal that may follow and consequently, the number of women who have suffered is higher than that suggested by police figures. Rape is disturbingly common. 86% of reported rapes have been partially or wholly planned; the majority (60%) take place inside a building and 31% in the woman's home (a double violation). The rapist is rarely, as is popularly believed, some kind of sex maniac on the loose, but is usually a young, inexperienced and sexually unsatisfied man. In over 50% of cases the rapist is known to the victim and 16% of women are raped by a male friend, lover or relative which can make the decision to report the crime even more difficult. Since 1991, marriage no longer defends a husband from the charge of raping his wife although the sentence, if the charge is proven, is generally less severe. Not all rape victims are women; men can also be the victims of male rape, and sexual assault can be (technically, at least) committed by members of either sex.

All rape victims need someone to talk to who understands their fear and sense of violation. This may be a friend, someone who has had a similar experience, or a professional counsellor. It is equally important to talk to someone who can provide sympathetic medical and legal advice. The Internet is a good place to get help. Most of the sites are based in the US, but you can have on-line conversations with other rape victims, go through case histories and apply for programmes to help you cope after the event. Studies have shown that those who have not been able to discuss their experience suffer more, and often have difficulties in their relationships with men.

What to do if you are raped or sexually assaulted

- If the man is violent or has a weapon, try not to struggle. Generally when brutal physical force is used, strong resistance provokes higher degrees of violence. It is advisable not to fight if there is any danger the violence will escalate.
- Try to memorize the rapist's appearance.
- Call your family, a close friend or neighbour immediately for moral support. They can also confirm your distress if evidence is required. If this is not an option, you can contact a counsellor through the Rape Crisis Centre (which is unfortunately suffering from severe cutbacks) or the Samaritans.

- If the rapist is a friend, lover, husband or relative, the anonymity of the Rape Crisis Centre or Samaritans can be a good immediate option before you decide your next step. Most importantly, you should not isolate yourself.

If you contact the police:

- Don't bathe until you have been examined by a doctor. DNA evidence is very effectively used in tracking rapists. Ask for a female doctor if you don't want to be examined by a man. A record of any physical injuries will be important evidence.
- If you are too distressed to go out, try to get a female police officer to come to your home. If you have to go to the station, it helps to take a friend with you. Don't feel you have to answer questions. You're not the accused – you can go home at any time.
- As soon as you feel able, make detailed notes – you may want a friend to help you with this – they can be used as evidence in court.
- It may seem absurdly obvious, but it is an important legal point to register that you told the rapist before the experience that you did not consent to having sex.
- Remember that you may be eligible for criminal compensation (see **Law** chapter).

THE LEGAL PROCESS

Beyond the physical and mental trauma of the event itself, a lot of obstacles facing a victim of rape remain. The accused rapist still has the legal option of representing himself in court and cross-examining the victim. In the wake of recent widely publicized cases which highlighted the trauma caused by this arrangement, a scheme was proposed to address this in March 1997. Legislation should emerge in the near future to close this barbaric legal loophole. When this new power is exercised (which will be at the discretion of the courts), cross-examination by defendants representing themselves will have to be conducted through a legal representative. This power will apply in all cases which involve a vulnerable victim. If you are taking your case to court, you should seek legal advice from a lawyer who specializes in rape cases (see **Law** chapter).

COURT

Unfair preconceptions or prejudice still surround rape and these can be reflected in court questioning. Remember, it is the duty of the lawyers representing accused rapists to try to clear their clients. The methods by which this is achieved may seem unfair or hurtful to the victim. Despite the changes resulting from the Sexual Offences (Amendment) Act, a woman's past experience and behaviour can still be brought up in court.

TRAUMA

Women who have been raped will usually go through a 'rape trauma syndrome'.

- An acute phase of unacceptance: feeling dirty, worthless or permanently physically changed.
- Feeling guilty, ashamed, helpless, angry, vengeful, humiliated and overwhelmingly anxious about her physical safety and finding it very difficult to be alone.
- If the rape occurred at home, it may be difficult or impossible to remain there.
- This is often followed by a period during which the woman tries to block the experience.
- An integration stage generally follows when the woman will try to assimilate the experience into her own life. This process can be greatly aided or hampered by the reactions of those she has come into contact with, i.e. the police, courts, friends and family, etc.
- There are ways of using sex itself as a method for healing the trauma of rape.

Rape is a traumatic experience for all women and is never something for the victim to be ashamed of.

RELATION-SHIPS

It is difficult to define exactly when an 'acquaintance' or 'love affair' becomes a 'relationship'. Relationships – and the codes which govern the feelings between two people – are almost always extremely complex and subtle. In order for a relationship to last and continue evolving, it helps to know what you want. The same rules of 'mutual respect' apply as much to platonic friendships as they do to sexual affairs.

Marriage is the traditional way of formalizing a heterosexual relationship. Where marriage used to be an institution which involved a wide circle of family and friends, and often had economic motives, it is now more focused on the direct personal needs of the couple involved. Expectations vary widely, and the clash between dreams of unparalleled devotion and harsh reality largely explains the fact that four out of every ten marriages end in divorce. The remaining six survive either through understanding, hard work and compromise, or fear of the unknown.

According to surveys, the vast majority of people want a secure relationship of some sort – to love and be loved. This chapter doesn't venture into the labyrinthine territory surrounding 'love', but it does cover the practicalities of dating, marriage – and divorce should it all go wrong.

DATING

Sadly there is no great recipe for finding Mr (Ms?) Right or even Mr OK. Most of us meet our partners in college, at work or through friends, so getting out and about (evening classes, DIY, football matches?) has got to be the key. However, most of us eventually find the person we are looking for – when we are not looking. Although initially most people would say they are attracted to each other because of looks, having compatible personalities and shared interests is more important in the long run. Feeling relaxed and having a laugh together could well be better than multiple orgasm on the first night.

THE INTERNET

They're never going to find you if you're slumped in front of the TV every night, though the small screen might just help you find them via the Internet. The Internet offers many opportunities for finding a date. Using a search engine, type in words like dating, personals or friendship and you will get lists of home pages that will allow you to reply to existing ads and place your own message. Many people feel less inhibited as the interaction happens in the privacy of your own home – it seems less calculated/desperate than joining a dating agency. But there is no vetting procedure . . . you are warned.

DATING AGENCIES

Call a variety of them and make comparisons on price, service and whether you like the sound of them. Before signing up for anything, check their authenticity by calling one of their regulating bodies and ask questions:

- Does the agency keep up personal contact after you pay your fee?
- What kind of people do they keep on their books?
- Male/female ratio?
- Does the agency offer a maximum / minimum number of introductions?
- What are the fees and what do you get for them?
- Is there a proper written contract with guarantees? (Never send a cheque first.)
- What security/confidentiality measures do they take?
- The Society of Marriage Bureaus or Association of British Introduction Agencies are good reputable starting points. *The Directory to Dating Agencies* by Henry Goldburg is a good book to start with.

ADVERTISING

- Classified ads which tell the truth get the biggest response.
- Lonely hearts: most national papers and weekly magazines have columns.
- Talking hearts: the telephone version of Lonely Hearts
- The Internet: try www.match.com or www.swoon.com and take it from there.
- Don't mention sex, it's asking for trouble.
- Never give your address or phone number.
- Request a photo.
- Only respond to people you feel are genuine.
- Never agree to meet someone you have not spoken to.
- If you decide to meet someone you don't know, it is always advisable to follow some precautions.

SAFETY TIPS

- Never give your address to anyone before you get to know them.
- Always arrange to meet in a public place and tell someone you know who it is you are meeting, where and when.
- Only agree to a drink on a first date.
- Don't go home with him the first night: if there is anything there, it's worth waiting for.
- Always trust your instinct: there is never a time you can't say NO.

TIPS

No one can tell you how to have a relationship and live happily ever after, but there are some common-sense tips for avoiding conflict which can offer a basic guide-line.

Flexibility: is one of the most important qualities for long-term relationship success. Couples who can adapt to change will be better equipped to deal with life together. A couple need to be able to adjust their relationship to accommodate the arrival of children, illness, unemployment or disability, the onset of old age, anything that life throws at them.

Controlling arguments: find a way of having disagreements that allows both of you to have your say but does not damage your relationship. There are two types of argument. A circular row is when you and your partner argue about the same issue time and time again without ever resolving anything. This type of argument is very damaging and can only be sorted out when both of you take responsibility and stop being defensive. An explosive or verbal row is one where your intense argument is followed by a period of reflection where you both examine what has been said and find a resolution. This type of argument can actually lead to a more positive relationship. If you need help, get in touch with RELATE, or read their guide to a better relationship.

Making decisions together: consult each other on issues that are relevant to both of you, for example if the cost of your new outfit puts a strain on the finances, then it is your partner's business.

Communicating: talk openly about everything – no matter how difficult. Being able to discuss everything with each other is also a key. Couples should be able to talk through everything, no matter how embarrassing or difficult the subject. Being able to tolerate hearing things that you don't want to hear works both ways and is a way of showing complete commitment to one another.

Avoiding financial conflict: if you have two incomes, have three bank accounts – one personal account each and one house account where you deposit set amounts to cover your joint costs of living. This avoids potential financial conflict. In households with only one salary the unemployed partner should receive some personal cash that is not related to housekeeping.

An active sex life: maintain your sex life. Sex is central to a good partnership – keep it active, stimulating, experimental and loving. Sex is when you are closest to each other, an uninhibited mutual sharing of physical pleasure. Couples who have been married for a few years may find that they develop their own individual patterns for having sex. If you and your partner are happy with your marital arrangements then the fact that you don't do it as often or in the same way as other couples does not matter. Couples may also have periods where one or the other partner might not feel like sex at all. If this happens, discuss it openly and don't let it become a big issue. If you are patient something should trigger your physical relationship again and if it becomes a problem you can get help through counselling. Often just getting things out in the open and refraining from pressurizing your partner will help enormously. Don't let children ruin your sex life. Try to find times when you are both awake to have some physical adventures together, even if it means taking a hotel room or meeting in your lunchbreak. Read *How to make love to the same person for the rest of your life* by Dagmar O'Connor.

Stay in touch with your friends: don't isolate yourselves as a couple. It's important for both of you.

MARRIAGE

51% of marriages are held in a register office and 49% in a church. 99% of all marriages cause anxiety, stress and family arguments before the big day and nearly 50% of them end in divorce. The key to a successful marriage is to keep the stress levels to a minimum.

PLANS
Organizing a wedding, whether it is large or small, requires planning. You and your partner should decide what you would really like and then stick

to it. The average wedding plus honeymoon now costs about £10,550, so draw up a realistic budget and discuss it with whoever is paying the bill. Traditionally, the bride's family paid for the wedding and the bridegroom paid for the honeymoon, cars and any expenses centred around his best man and ushers. However, this is now changing and you may want to contribute yourselves or have both families split the bill down the middle. Once you have agreed a budget, try to find your venue. This must be first on your 'to do' list as popular places can require 18 months' advance booking for a summer wedding. Then delegate tasks to reliable relatives and get on with it. Read *The Good Marriage Guide*.

CHECKLIST
- venue for wedding
- venue for reception
- caterers
- photographer, video etc.
- florist
- entertainment
- wedding cars and transportation
- honeymoon

HOW
There are two ways:
Civil marriages
- These are often held in register offices or premises approved by the local authority (hotels, stately homes).
- You will need to contact the registrar of the district where you wish to marry. You may marry at any register office premises, although you will need to give a formal notice of your marriage to the superintendent registrar of the district where you live.

Legal formalities
You and/or your partner must visit the register office for the district where you live and give 'notice' of your marriage.
Notice can be given in two ways:
1 **By certificate:** both of you must have lived in a registration district in England or Wales for at least seven days prior to giving notice. If you both live in the same district you only need one individual notice. You must then wait for 21 days

before the marriage can take place.
2 **By licence:** known as a 'special licence' and more expensive; you need to have lived in a registration district in England or Wales for at least 15 days before giving notice. You must wait one full day before the marriage can take place. All necessary licences or certificates must be given to the registrating official before the civil marriage can take place. For further information contact your local register office.

Licensed venues
There are 1,500 specially licensed places (for example Chelsea Football Club, London Zoo, Brighton Pavilion) other than register offices where you can get married. Local lists are available from your local register office and a national list from the Office of National Statistics (ONS). A civil ceremony in a licensed venue will cost between £100 and £300 depending on the venue.

Religious ceremony
- If you wish to be married in the Church of England or Wales, generally you will only be able to do so if you or your partner live in the parish. Speak to your local vicar for more information. The marriage is also registered by the vicar. Some pre-marital counselling will be offered.
- If you wish to marry in other places of religious worship you should arrange to see the person in charge. It will also be necessary to give formal notice of your marriage to the superintendent registrar of the district(s) where you live.

OUT OF THIS COUNTRY
You can organize your own marriage abroad without all the fuss of a big family event. It can be cheaper and less hassle. You may be asked to take blood tests locally and you will need to bring your birth certificates with you.

- The Caribbean is the most popular. You must be resident in the country for 2–3 days before the marriage can take place.
- Barbados requires only one day of residency.
- French Martinique requires one month's residency.
- Depending on the hotel, a Caribbean wedding plus honeymoon costs around £2,500.

- If you are pregnant or have divorced in the last ten months, you may not be allowed to marry in some religious countries.
- In some Mexican villages you may be told that you cannot marry, but if you keep asking them they may change their mind for no apparent reason.
- In Las Vegas you can do it with no residency for the princely sum of $35.
- The Maldives only accept Muslims.
- If marrying abroad, check that the ceremony will be recognized in Britain, and find out how easy it is to get a replacement certificate if yours gets lost.
- Wedding holidays are available from most holiday companies. They combine the marriage ceremony with the honeymoon. You can get married during a double bungee jump in New Zealand, on safari in Africa, or in Disney World with Mickey, Minnie and a cast of cartoon characters in attendance.

LEGAL ISSUES
- You cannot marry anyone who is closely related to you. This covers blood relatives though first cousins are allowed to marry. You cannot marry your brother even if he was adopted and is not your blood relative.
- Marriage can only be between two people 'of the opposite sex'.
- Homosexual/lesbian marriages are not legally valid.
- If you marry someone who has had a sex-change, the marriage is considered invalid regardless of whether or not you knew before the ceremony.
- A man can be prosecuted for raping his wife but not vice versa.

LEGAL IMPLICATIONS
- A wife doesn't have to take her husband's name or nationality and a husband can take his wife's name.
- If a woman decides to take her husband's name, she can continue using it even after divorce and remarriage, or after his death.
- A woman can have a new passport after marrying, and can even be issued with one before the marriage for a foreign honeymoon.
- A British woman can keep her citizenship after marrying, or depending on the law of the other country involved, claim dual nationality. Not all countries accept this and in order to claim citizenship of her spouse's country, she may have to give up her own.
- Once you marry you should make a new will as marriage automatically revokes a will.
- Marital confidences are respected by the law. It is assumed that secrets are shared between man and wife.

MARRIAGE CONTRACTS
- Pre-nuptial agreements are usually made before marriage but they can also be made during marriage.
- Pre-nuptial and marriage contracts are generally entered into by those who have a lot to protect.
- Their use is much more widespread in the USA.
- Divorcees who don't want to repeat the possibility of a drawn out court battle if they divorce again, often desire a marriage agreement.
- Marriage contracts are generally used to avoid dealing with a court.
- However, the court is under no legal duty to uphold marriage contracts and they may simply be treated as an outline of the couple's intentions.

Things to include:
- Ownership of income and assets acquired before, during and after marriage.
- Whether assets are to be owned jointly, and if so, in what proportions.
- Whether assets below a certain value are to be excluded.
- Treatment of gifts or inheritances.
- Ownership of personal items, e.g. jewellery.
- Liability for tax and debts.
- Provisions relating to duration, variation and review of the contract.
- Which country's law will govern the agreement.
- Liabilities for costs and expenses in relation to drawing up the agreement and any ancillary documentation.
- Methods of resolution of any disputes arising from the document.

TAX AND FINANCE
- Property transferred between husband and wife is exempt from tax.
- Husbands and wives are taxed separately.

- There is a married couple's allowance with which the tax bill of one can be reduced depending on income.
- A wife may be eligible for her own state pension if she has paid enough National Insurance contributions.
- Otherwise she can claim, based on the contributions made by her husband.
- A wife can claim widow's allowance, widow's pension and widowed mother's allowance.
- Spouses can insure against each other's death.
- A husband is accountable for his wife's domestic debts and vice versa.
- If either partner dies without leaving a will, everything goes automatically to the living spouse.
- If a will has been made, which excludes the surviving spouse, an appeal can be made and the courts can determine the award.

ABUSIVE
RELATIONSHIPS

Violence can be found in any home, anywhere. People who suffer domestic violence can be female or male, young or old, rich or more or less socially privileged. 30,000 women and children resort to refuges each year and about 100,000 calls for help are taken. On average a woman is assaulted 35 times in a relationship before seeking help. Some women might not recognize that they have been suffering domestic violence until they share their experiences. If you are being abused and need help, contact the Women's Aid Federation, the Celestial Fund for battered women and children, or for immediate assistance call the emergency services.

DOMESTIC VIOLENCE – THE LAW
- A court order can be obtained by a woman to exclude a violent partner from their home regardless of whether her name appears on the rent book or title deeds.
- A court order is necessary to end a marriage, and divorce is not an option in the first year of marriage, although there are exceptions.

HOW TO LEAVE
If you are in a violent permanent relationship with or without kids:
- Call the emergency centres, listen to their advice and act on it straight away.
- Talk to others, don't keep it to yourself.
- If you are in urgent need of temporary housing, local refuges may be able to put you up.
- See **Renting and letting** in the **Home** chapter.
- Contact the various helplines for more information and advice (see **Directory**).
- Read *All My Fault: Why Women Don't Leave Abusive Men* by Dee Dee Grant.

DIVORCE

KEY STATISTICS
- 160,000 couples divorce each year.
- This is the highest rate in the EU.
- 1 in 10 marriages lasts less than two years.
- The rate of marriage has declined by half in the last 20 years.
- Currently, 36% of marriages are remarriages.
- Second marriages are twice as likely to end in divorce, third marriages, three times more likely.
- Couples who live together prior to marriage are more likely to divorce.
- 72% of divorces are filed by women.
  Contact the Family Mediators Association or the National Association of Family Mediation and Conciliation Service for advice.

IRRETRIEVABLE BREAKDOWN
- You can ONLY file for a divorce if you have been married for at least a year.
- After that time the marriage must be seen to be beyond repair: this is called 'irretrievable breakdown'.
- There are five grounds: adultery, unreasonable behaviour, desertion, two years' separation if the respondent consents to divorce; five years' or more if they don't.
- Irretrievable breakdown is a blanket cover for divorce where nobody is shown as being at fault or solely responsible for the breakdown of the marriage.

- It is hoped that making procedure simpler will mean fewer acrimonious divorces.
- There is no time restriction for separation.
- Alternatively, you can opt for a two or five year separation period at the end of which the divorce is granted.
- In the current climate, mediation is actively encouraged in the process of divorce. RELATE (marriage guidance) can provide counselling whether you stay together or not. There is usually a waiting list. See **Directory** for other contacts.
- Contact Both Parents Forever or the National Council for the Divorced and Separated for advice on how to handle the children.

THE COST

You can now divorce without using a solicitor, reducing costs considerably. DIY divorce can be risky if a case is being defended and there are children or financial settlements involved. In these instances it is worth investing in a recommended family solicitor. But remember, the more the lawyer gets, the less the family has to share between them, even when your spouse is paying for your costs. Try to keep things simple.

Understanding how the legal system operates, what it costs and how lawyers charge, can free you from unnecessary worry. It is now more difficult to get Legal Aid (see the **Law** chapter).

- Read *How to do your own Divorce* by Jeremy Rosenblatt.
- Most straightforward divorces cost between £450 and £2,000, depending on the circumstances.

PROCEDURE

- You can save about £300 by requesting the paperwork by post or collecting it in person from your County Court counter.
- It is wise for both parties to seek legal advice.
- Fill in a Petition for Divorce. This costs £40 from the court and is free if you're on family credit or benefit.
- File a Certificate of Reconciliation at the court along with the divorce petition – this shows that reconciliation was sought.
- Hand them in with the marriage certificate and a statement of arrangement for any children, as agreed with the respondent.
- The court must have proof that the respondent has a copy of the petition: either you (or the court) can give him a duplicate document.
- He must then reply to the court within seven days and inform them whether or not he intends to defend the case.
- If you can both agree to an undefended case, a divorce can be quick, cheap and relatively simple.
- If one of you decides to defend the case, call your solicitor and start counting: court cases mean time, money and are often emotionally fraught.
- The court supplies the petitioners' applications, affidavits and any requested or relevant corroborative evidence to the district judge who gives directions for the trial, if there is to be one.
- The judge will then consider the evidence and, if satisfied, will fix the decree's (divorce proceedings) pronouncement day in court.
- Neither of you has to attend.
- The judge grants the divorce and the court issues a Decree Nisi.
- Six weeks after the decree nisi is granted, you can apply for a decree absolute by lodging notice with the district judge (via a form and a fee).
- The divorce registry or court provides you with the certificate.
- Once the decree nisi is made absolute, both parties are free to remarry.

CHILDREN

Your children should be your first consideration. However you handle your divorce, your children are going to be affected, so make it as amicable as you possibly can. The Children Act 1989 has radically changed the approach to the arrangements in divorce for the custody, caring and sharing of the children. Courts now encourage parents to work out the arrangements rather than dictating conditions, though they will help to enforce the court's welfare service and any conciliatory recommendations. The Act also states that the court's decisions must put the good of the children first, allowing for their wishes to be heard, not just the welfare and social services reports. Contact the Child Support Agency, Parent Line, or National Council for One Parent Families.

SEPARA-TION

There are alternatives to divorce. Four of these involve different approaches to separation, which essentially means that although the couple are no longer obliged to live together, they are still considered married for legal purposes. Unsurprisingly then, neither can remarry. Many couples have a 'trial' period of separation before the more final decision to divorce. These periods can also have the effect of cooling down what might otherwise explode acrimoniously.

Informal separation
- This, as its name suggests, is a decision made by the husband and wife without seeking legal advice.
- A correspondence between them outlining their intentions may be treated as legally binding, but the courts generally do not approve of documents entered into without legal advice.

Formal separation
- A formal separation will involve a written agreement signed by both parties, each having had legal advice.
- The agreement generally covers issues such as the matrimonial home, maintenance payments, other assets and children (if any).
- It may also remove the obligation to cohabit, meaning that should there be a divorce, desertion can no longer be used as grounds for the petition.

- The court will still have the power to change the details of the deed, and will generally do so if one of the couple has been misleading (e.g. about their assets).
- The wife should always make sure that she is entitled to maintenance, even if she does not need it at the time.
- This is easily done by including a nominal but specific payment (as little as 10p a year) which can always be increased by the courts at a later date if necessary.
- It is also advisable to indicate any circumstances which would end the agreement.

By magistrate's court order
If there is the threat of violence to either the wife or children, the court can issue a personal protection or exclusion order which would result in a legally enforced separation.

Judicial separation
- This is rarely used – it is generally sought by those with religious objections to divorce. The majority of applications are made by women.
- It isn't necessary to wait a year before applying. The spouse making the application must use one of the same five grounds as those used when seeking divorce (see **Irretrievable breakdown** above), but it doesn't have to be proved that the marriage has 'irretrievably broken down'.
- The couple are no longer bound to live together, but they are not free to remarry.
- After five years' separation, the other spouse is able to get a divorce in spite of any opposition.

HEALTH

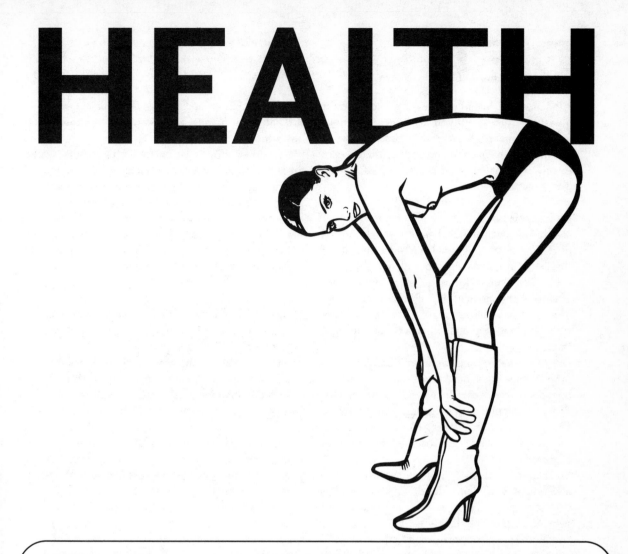

Although there is a general movement to bring women's medical concerns into the mainstream of general health issues, a bias towards men is built into the health system. A vast range of activities including research, testing, funding, treatment and the analysis of medical data use male bodies as the standard. Many women also feel uneasy about the prevailing perception within the profession of menstruation, pregnancy and menopause as 'medical problems' rather than naturally occurring 'events'.

Active campaigning for change, and the increase in the number of female doctors, have meant that the situation is improving, but a great deal still remains to be done. Preventing problems is always better than having to cure them, and the more aware you are of your body and its needs, the better equipped you'll be. Simple dietary changes and regular exercise can mean vast improvement.

In this chapter you'll find all you need to know for setting up your own holistic approach to eating, exercise and healthcare. Remember, if you take care of yourself now, you can look forward to becoming a wild old woman, sprinting past hordes of youths and raving until dawn.

DIET

Food is nourishment and eating should be a pleasure, something you can enjoy without feeling tyrannized. Most people have an instinctive idea of what's good and bad for them. Learn to rely on your common sense, but back it up with a few facts.

DIETING

Nearly every woman puts herself through the hell of 'dieting' at least once in her lifetime, in spite of the fact that quick weight-loss plans hardly ever work. There are a lot of different approaches around at the moment, but if you're on a long-term, well-thought-out 'regime' that particularly suits you, you're probably already on the right track.

- **Fad diets:** eating one food and abandoning all others, using 'liquid meal replacements' or eating only once a day, generally has short-term results. You may simply be mistreating your body. In addition, when normal eating habits are resumed, the weight usually comes back – and you may gain more.
- **Starvation diets** lower your metabolism, which means that you'll 'burn' food more slowly after the diet than you did before, leading to weight gain. You'll probably feel lethargic, suffer mood swings and your body may not be in a position to properly absorb vitamins and minerals. Starving yourself shows up negatively, and pretty quickly, in your skin and can make you lose your hair. Rapid gain and sudden losses of weight can also lead to stretch marks and a loss in skin elasticity.
- **Slimming and dieting products** usually claim to increase metabolic rate so that the body burns off excess calories which would otherwise be stored as fat. But the effect is mainly psychological and people just tend to eat less on them. Products containing amphetamines (which really do suppress hunger) are normally only available by prescription and should be handled with care; while they can help you lose weight they take their toll on your health.
- **Natural or herbal appetite suppressors** and dieting aids are generally harmless and may give you the psychological boost you need to set up new habits.

Sadly, persuasive media images lead many women to hate their bodies, and dieting is often treated as a form of punishment rather than a desire to be healthier. Why do we fall for it? It's essential to really examine your approach. Anorexia and bulimia are illnesses that take obsessions with thinness to the extreme (see **Eating Disorders**). However, too many women are on a daily treadmill of calorie counting, dieting, guilt and unhappiness and think far more about food than they really need to. If you're in the trap, try to get out.

TIPS

- Stop stepping on the scales. Using scales daily can easily turn weight into an obsession. If you must have a weighing scale, use it only when you feel positive about the way your body looks. You may be surprised to find that you weigh more than your abstract 'ideal weight' – your real ideal weight is a healthy one which you feel comfortable with.
- Avoid irregular dieting. Instead, aim to set up a good general programme. Before making radical changes detox your system for a couple of days.
- When you begin exercising you may find that you're getting smaller but your weight increases. Remember – muscle weighs more than fat.
- If you want to monitor yourself while trying a new exercise routine, try measuring rather than weighing yourself and use the way your clothes fit as a guide.
- Give yourself time and set realistic goals. Although you can feel the effects of exercise the following day (you'll find muscles you forgot you had), aim to settle into a balanced routine for life and a real awareness of your body.
- The best way to decide whether or not you need to lose weight is by standing in front of a mirror and making a really honest appraisal.
- If you have no image of yourself – if just the idea of looking at yourself naked in a mirror makes you feel miserable – or you don't know whether you are overweight or not, your GP should be able to help you.

- You can have a 'fitness test' or assessment at your local gym (see **Exercise**).
- If you feel that you or someone you know has an eating disorder, there are ways of dealing with it (see **Eating Disorders**).

Don't be ashamed of your body – be pragmatic and take control. You'll find it enjoyable and liberating.

FOOD

Most of us are aware that eating the right food can boost energy, make us look better and feel healthier. According to recent research, eating the wrong foods may cause up to 50% of all cancers and be as much of a risk as smoking.

Try and buy organic fruit and vegetables when you can. Many of the large supermarkets now stock organic produce. It may be a little more expensive but it can also taste much better.

You can join a box scheme and have fresh organic vegetables delivered to your door. Contact the Soil Association for details and general information. The Nutrition Society can help with dietary and health information.

SHOPPING LIST
- Any kind of unpolished rice.
- Variety of cereals.
- Beans, lentils and other pulses.
- Any kind of pasta including the Japanese varieties made with buckwheat.
- Crispbread: rye, sesame or mixed seed.
- A range of herbal teas and infusions, green tea and caffeine-free coffee if you're a big coffee drinker.
- Soy sauce, tamari, fresh garlic and ginger for seasoning.
- Herbs: fresh and dried, basil, marjoram, thyme, sage, rosemary, dill, parsley, coriander and mint. You can grow many of them in a window-box if you don't have a garden.
- Good quality, cold-pressed, extra virgin olive oil; sesame, walnut and other nut oils can add enormous flavour to salad dressings.
- Tofu and other soya bean products are extremely high in protein and have virtually no fat. You can use them in a stir fry, add them to soup or crumble them in a salad.
- Fresh meat and fowl, preferably organic; fish and shellfish.
- Fresh fruit: keep fruit that has been washed and snack on it during the day. It's not only good for you but it looks beautiful as well. The high sugar content in many fruits will satisfy the yearning for a chocolate bar. Frozen or baked bananas make a delicious sweet snack.
- Yoghurt which contains live bacteria; goat and sheep milk yoghurt are delicious and are particularly good if you have a lactose intolerance.
- Fresh spreads: hummous, guacamole, roasted aubergine (baba ganoush) are delicious on thin sesame crackers and make a high protein snack.
- Freerange eggs.

TIPS FOR HEALTHY EATING

- Eat breakfast and give yourself time to enjoy it, even if it's only something like fruit and yoghurt. It sets you up for the day.
- You should try to eat at least two servings of carbohydrate a day: root vegetables, rice, cereals and pulses, wholemeal bread.
- One serving of protein a day: meat, fish, tofu, beans and rice, cheese, eggs.
- Eat slowly and try to drink at least eight glasses of water a day.
- Steam, grill, stir-fry, stew or bake foods: use their natural juices rather than a lot of fat.
- Avoid highly refined foods, cut down on salt and learn to look at labels to avoid products that have excessive additives and preservatives.
- If you're trying to set up new eating habits, a light detox is a good way to make the transition and may also be the time to clear out your kitchen. Get rid of all the half-finished packets of unhealthy food you no longer need, and replace them with the right staples for a new approach. The whole process can be extremely cathartic. Invest in a really good health cookbook and get advice on a good detox diet from your health food store.

BASIC DE-TOX

The idea of de-toxing your system is to give it a break; to cut out all potentially irritating toxins, to cleanse your system by eating high fibre fruit and vegetables, and by drinking a great deal of water to flush out the impurities. Toxins are released with sweat through the skin so you'll be speeding up the process if you can exercise during a de-tox.

Choose a quiet two days: cut out caffeine, alcohol, all dairy products except live goat or sheep milk yoghurt, smoking – if you can, or at least cut down.

- Breakfast: Fruit, herbal teas.
- Midmorning: Vegetable juices in juicer/blender.
- Lunch: Vegetable salads – with olive oil and lime or olive oil, tamari and garlic.
- Afternoon Snack: Avocado with a drizzle of olive oil, or half a cup of almonds or sunflower seeds. Warm mineral water with juice of half a lime.
- Supper: Hot beetroot and vegetable juices, steamed vegetables in miso soup with fresh ginger and lemon juice. An hour after supper have a small bowl of live goat or sheep milk yoghurt, sweetened with honey.
- Drink between 2.5–5 litres of still mineral water a day at room temperature.
- Combine your de-tox with physical and mental pampering. Take long, luxurious baths scented with oils of lemon and juniper, for their purifying and de-toxifying effect. Avoid television, replace it with soothing music and reading or meditation.
- Because you are expelling toxins you may find you get a headache. If it's severe you might need to cut out caffeine gradually. You'll feel amazingly refreshed after a couple of days.

FOOD SUPPLEMENTS

By eating a wide variety of foods from each group we should get all the vitamins and minerals we need. However, the unavoidable hazards of daily life – such as chemical pollutants, petrol fumes, UV rays and VDR screens, smoking, drinking, and poor eating habits – all take their toll. On top of this, natural nutrient sources are depleted through food processing, storage and cooking techniques. Research in both Britain and America has shown that most people are deficient in at least one nutrient (according to recommended levels), and usually more. So it's generally agreed that food supplements are a good idea (spending on supplements has reached £250 million a year in the UK alone), but which ones? How are we supposed to choose? The baffling rows of vitamins, herbal supplements, antioxidants and amino acids in chemists and health food stores can be enough to make you despair. How are we supposed to react when faced with Ginkgo Biloba, Acetyl-L-Carnatine, Devil's Claw and advanced Proanthocyanidin Complex? A lot of the larger companies produce information packs on their products: you can ring their helplines for detailed advice.

Vitamins
- Vitamins are complex organic substances necessary for the normal growth and metabolism of the body. They're called 'vitamins' from 'vita'

(meaning life) and 'amin' from amino, under the mistaken idea that they all contained amino acids. Now we know better, but we're still stuck with the old name.

- Some vitamins are ineffective without their complements, such as A and E for example.
- The antioxidants A, E, C and selenium are very important in combating dangerous free oxygen radicals which cause damage to cells and DNA in the body. Unstable oxygen molecules fix onto other cells in their attempt to become stable. In the process they damage cells, including the genetic coding, or DNA, in the cells. Once the process of oxidation begins, it can be hard to stop and the consequences can range from heart disease and high blood pressure to arthritis and birth defects. Antioxidants are substances that help neutralize the damage of oxidation in the body.

Minerals
- Minerals are inorganic substances which occur naturally in the earth such as calcium, magnesium, iron and zinc. They move up the food chain and occur in both meat and vegetables as well as coming in pill form.
- They act as catalysts for many biological reactions, are constituents of the bones, teeth, nerve cells, soft tissue, blood and muscles, and are important for hormone production.

Amino acids
- Amino acids are the building blocks of protein and fall into two classes – 'essential' and 'non-essential'.
- The 'essential' can't be manufactured by the body and must be supplied through the food we eat.
- The 'non-essential' the body can manufacture itself. However, despite these names, we need both.

WHAT TO TAKE AND WHEN

You have to take vitamins and minerals regularly in order for them to be effective. Aim to take your supplements during your first meal of the day or within 15 minutes before or after eating. Unfortunately in this field, more expensive does usually mean better and more easily absorbed.

Remember – you won't feel the effects immediately – allow at least a month. It's difficult to overdose, but not impossible so it's best to remain within the dosage suggested on the product, and if in doubt ask your doctor or nutritionist.

- **If you're eating an inadequate/unbalanced diet** with fewer than 1,000 calories a day, are restricted by allergies or you're a strict vegan or vegetarian, it is essential to take a good multivitamin and mineral supplement to supply the vitamins and amino acids found only in meat.
- **If you're menstruating and have heavy periods** you may need extra iron and vitamins, especially C and E, to help regulate normal bodily functions such as the menstrual cycle, blood clotting, and blood pressure. If you're on the pill take extra A and E.
- **If you're suffering from fatigue** a poor diet may be one of the reasons. A combination of Bs can help enormously. For an energy boost try chromium polynicotinate, ginseng or guarana. Guarana is similar in effect to caffeine without the destructive side-effects.
- **If you smoke** take extra vitamin C or a good antioxidant formula. Smoking interferes with the body's ability to absorb vitamin C.
- **If you drink**, have a hangover or are planning to get one, remember that alcohol depletes the body of B vitamins and zinc.
- **If you're planning a pregnancy** or are pregnant/breastfeeding, see **Diet** in **Babies** chapter.
- **If you take a lot of aspirin** you may find you need to supplement your iron intake.
- **If you're on prescription drugs** you may need to take supplements to replenish the nutrients in the body that are destroyed by some medications.
- **If you're finishing a course of antibiotics** always take live yoghurts which contain L. acidophilus and B. bifidum to replace the 'good' bacteria that were destroyed along with the bad. For 'yeast' infections yoghurt can be taken orally or applied locally.
- **If you're over the age of 45**, you should take precautions against osteoporosis, particularly if your family has a history of it. Supplement your diet with calcium, magnesium, vitamin D, and boron. You should be able to find a single supplement that combines these for you. Absorption of

Supplements Chart

Vitamins/minerals	Natural sources	What do they do?
A and Beta carotene	fruit and vegetables, dairy products, fish oils, liver, eggs	for eyes, skin, hair, nails, bones and teeth. Taken with C and E as an antioxidant, they fight damage from unstable oxygen molecules/free radicals
Vitamin B-complex (1, 2, 3, 5, 6, 12)	brewer's yeast, whole wheat, liver, kidneys, heart, nuts, cheese, milk, green vegetables, beans, soya products, brown rice	necessary for healthy nervous system and red blood cells, breaks down carbohydrates into energy, aids appetite, healthy skin and hair
Vitamin C	citrus fruits, berries, green vegetables, brassicas, peppers	antioxidant: protects against infection, aids wound healing, bones, teeth, capillary walls, builds collagen
Vitamin D	sunshine, fish liver oils, dairy products, salmon	metabolizes calcium and phosphorus for strong bones and teeth
Vitamin E	wheat germ and oil, whole grains, green leafy vegetables, vegetable oils, meat, eggs, avocados	antioxidant and anticoagulant: increases blood's available oxygen, helps prevent hardening of arteries
Copper	fish, seafood, lentils, seeds, nuts, fruits, calf and beef liver	needed for red blood cell formation, helps keep skin elastic
Zinc	red meat, whole grains, wheat germ, brewer's yeast, pumpkin seeds	essential for the synthesis of protein and the action of many enzymes
Calcium	milk, dairy products, cheese, fish, nuts, dried figs	builds and maintains bones and teeth, prevents osteoporosis, helps blood to clot, aids regular heart rhythm
Magnesium	milk, whole grains, wheat bran, leafy green vegetables, nuts, beans, bananas, apricots	regulates calcium uptake by cells, helps prevent calcium deposits/kidney and gall stones
Potassium	citrus fruits, watercress, all green leafy vegetables, sunflower seeds, bananas, potatoes	necessary for normal muscle tone, nerve, heart and enzyme reactions
Iron	liver, dried apricots, wheat germ, tofu	prevents anaemia, keeps red blood cell count up, helps food metabolism

vitamins C, D and the B-complex can diminish as you get older. Vitamin E can take some of the sting out of the menopause, is good for your skin and can also boost your sex life.

ALLERGIES/CRAVINGS

Up to 25% of the population could have food allergies, although those suffering from other forms of allergy (such as hay fever, asthma, or eczema) are generally more prone. Ironically, and annoyingly, a craving for a particular type of food can indicate an allergy to it. Anaphylaxis is a state of altered immunity which can lead to an extreme allergic reaction. This is very rare but can be fatal as the sufferer's respiratory system can shut down. However, even mild forms can cause a great deal of discomfort. The symptoms can include one or more of the following: mood swings, depression, migraine headaches, weight gain, fatigue and sluggishness, water retention, and those associated with Irritable Bowel Syndrome (constipation, flatulence and bloating). The most common triggers are wheat, dairy products (especially cows' milk), chocolate, eggs, caffeine, nuts, fish and shellfish.

If you feel you may be suffering from a food intolerance, the usual approach is to remove all potentially offending foods from the diet, and replace them individually to identify which is causing the problems. You can also have a blood test to pinpoint the culprit. Call the Society for the Promotion of Nutritional Therapy for a register of qualified therapists and expect to pay between £25 and £45 for a session. The British Allergy Foundation can help by providing leaflets and advice. Your doctor can refer you to an allergy specialist through the BSCI. Have a look at *The Complete Guide to Food Allergy and Intolerance* by Dr Jonathan Brostoff and Linda Gamlin.

KNOW YOUR FOOD
Labelling

Reading labels is almost an art. Trying to read between the lines to figure out what we want to know rather than what they want us to believe takes practice. Look out for misleading descriptions, wild claims and over-the-top adjectives. A basic rule of thumb is that the labels which take the least time to read indicate products which contain the least rubbish.

Additives

Britain allows the use of more chemical additives than any other Western country. On average we consume 8–10lb of additives a year, and of the nearly 4,000 in use only 350 are regulated. Additives are used for the following purposes: to change the physical characteristics of food by aerating, emulsifying or thickening it. They can also alter its flavour, colour, texture, acidity and nutritional status as well as increasing its storage life. They're a boon to the manufacturers, but not to our health. For more information read the fact sheets available from the Soil Association.

EATING DISORDERS

Over 90% of those suffering from eating disorders are female, and of those one in ten are estimated to have serious problems. Every year more than 6,000 new cases are reported in Britain. Eating disorders describe a range of behaviour where food and body size are used to express an underlying emotional conflict. For many women, peer pressure and emotion play a large part in shaping eating patterns. We may eat to make ourselves feel good, to calm our nerves, because we feel bored, to put off something that needs to be done, or to relieve feelings of guilt.

Many factors can contribute to eating disorders. The most common include
• An early traumatic experience: sexual abuse, having been excessively controlled as a child or put under severe pressure to achieve.
• Extreme self-denial, repression of anger/conflict.
• A desire to remain childlike in body shape: a fear of growing up, which can be sexually related.
• A feeling of having no control over anything except the body.

ANOREXIA NERVOSA

Anorexia is severe and deliberate self-starvation which in extreme cases (10–20%) can be fatal. Women with anorexia see their body as being much larger than it actually is. The sufferer may be hungry and think about food all the time, but eats very little or nothing at all. The side-effects can be alarming, and are often not considered by the sufferer. Constipation, broken sleep, hair loss, loss of periods, brittle bones which break easily, depression and difficulty in concentration are some of the consequences. However, 75–90% of those treated early recover completely. Any treatment needs to address both physical and psychological problems and can include family therapy, psychotherapy or behavioural therapy. Contact the Eating Disorders Association.

BULIMIA

Bulimia affects three in every hundred women and those in their twenties and thirties make up the majority of sufferers. Bulimia is a cycle of 'bingeing' or 'gorging' – eating far more (of often very fattening food) than you need, usually in secret – followed by 'purging' – vomiting or taking large quantities of laxatives. Vomiting can cause injury to intestines, oesophagus and throat, and tooth decay (the stomach acids dissolve the enamel). It can also upset the balance of fluid in the body, leading to kidney damage, heart failure and epilepsy. Swollen salivary glands can lead to a puffy face. Laxatives can cause persistent stomach ache, swollen fingers and damage to the bowel muscles which can mean long-term constipation. Many different treatments are used, often in combination. They include cognitive-behavioural eating programmes, the use of food diaries and self-esteem enhancement.

COMPULSIVE EATING

This is far more common than anorexia or bulimia. Sufferers think about weight obsessively and their frequent binges, usually done in secret, are often followed by strenuous dieting. Food is used as a way of 'stuffing down' and avoiding feelings such as anxiety, anger, loneliness, etc.

For any eating disorder it is important to get help as soon as possible. The hardest part may be accepting that you have a problem. You can contact an organization directly, or your doctor can refer you for counselling or other treatments. Contact Overeaters Anonymous.

See also the **Stress, Anxiety and Depression** section for other types of treatments.

EXERCISE

Exercise is not about sporting excellence, it's about keeping our bodies fit enough to cope with the demands of everyday life. So why is it that exercise itself usually feels like one of the biggest demands of all? Of those who make the noble decision to shape up and work out on a regular basis, 80% drop out after six months – the majority simply through boredom. The key to remaining one of those enviable 20% is variety, or cross-training. If you get bored, take up a different form of exercise or develop a programme that includes several different kinds. Not only is this approach more entertaining, it has other benefits: variety means that you exercise a wider range of muscles in the body; and with fewer repetitions the smaller as well as the larger muscles are developed, leaving you with a more streamlined shape, a stronger body and fewer injuries.

TIPS

- Before you begin an exercise programme have a fitness assessment at your gym or have your GP check your blood pressure, and confirm that your heart, lungs and joints are all healthy.
- 'Feel-good' chemicals called 'endorphins' are released to the brain during exercise. Endorphins are also natural painkillers.
- Moderate exercise raises the metabolism which helps burn fat.
- Exercise increases blood flow to the skin, giving you a healthy glow.
- Exercise releases more oxygen to the heart, lungs, working muscles, cells and brain.
- Exercise makes muscles stronger, bones denser, decreases tension and ultimately gives you more energy.
- The positive effects of exercise can be felt for up

to two hours afterwards.

- Don't exercise if you have a cold or are not feeling well.

HOW FIT ARE YOU?

If you don't take regular exercise you can give yourself a basic fitness test by climbing three flights of stairs. If you can do it quickly and easily then you're probably in pretty good shape; if you feel breathless and sweaty it's time to do something about it. Test your strength by doing situps. About 20 to 25 per minute is average for anyone under 50.

TWO TYPES OF EXERCISE

- **Aerobic (with oxygen):** the best way to improve general fitness as it increases the efficiency of your heart and lungs – running, swimming, dance, step, cycling, anything that raises the pulse and gets your heart and lungs pumping (cardiovascular).
- **Anaerobic (without oxygen):** consists of short sharp bursts of intense muscle activity which can be used to isolate specific areas that need toning – Dynabands, weights, Pilates.

HOW MUCH?

- To burn fat you need 20 minutes of aerobic exercise three times a week in combination with strength and endurance or anaerobic work twice a week.
- When beginning a programme of exercise don't dive in at the deep end. If you make things too difficult, or too boring, you probably won't stick at it.
- Begin with gentle exercise, enough to raise the heart-rate. Gradually build up time spent and intensity as you become fitter. Everyone, regardless of their age, can and should make exercise an integral part of their daily life.
- You should be able to walk at least two miles very briskly before attempting to go jogging. Fast walking is just as beneficial as jogging, and you are less likely to damage your knee and ankle joints. If you must jog begin by doing alternate walking and jogging for three-minute periods and build up.
- Infrequent bouts of intense exercise can do more harm than good. Aim to be consistent.
- If you join a gym, find a trainer to help you develop an exercise programme and monitor your initial fitness levels.
- Allocate specific times in the week for your visits to the gym, write them in your diary, and stick to them – don't let other people, or work, intrude on this time.

A–Z
OF EXERCISE OPTIONS

Check local papers and listings magazines for details of unusual ways to exercise near you. Double up with a friend if you feel weak-willed – you can each inspire the other. Check the notice boards of local gyms and fitness centres. If there's a performing arts centre in your area, you may be able to attend dance classes and workshops with the professionals. Don't enter at a level beyond your ability – it's discouraging, and you could hurt yourself. Equally, if you have been very active in the past and have taken a break, work up to your old standard gently. Take a bottle of mineral water with you whichever exercise you choose.

The following list is by no means exhaustive, only exhausting.

- **Aqua fitness:** by reducing the effects of gravity, the strain on knee and ankle joints that can arise through running or aerobics is lowered, making this a gentle option. It's particularly suitable for overweight or pregnant women, anyone suffering from arthritis or injury, the disabled and mermaids. But although water resistance slows down movement, the pressure uses up a surprising amount of energy. You don't need to be able to swim – check your local swimming pool for classes, or contact the National Organization for Water Fitness (NOWFIT).
- **Aerobics – or exercise to music:** having tortured many of us through the 80s, these classes are now often disguised under names like 'cardio

circuit'. They do provide a good all-round work-out. Make sure that you have a good sports bra and invest in a good pair of running shoes. Check that your trainer is RSA qualified. It helps if you share the same taste in music.

- **Alexander technique:** designed to help you realign your body and correct your posture. It's particularly good if you suffer from back pain and can also literally add inches to your height. Usually one-to-one, it's more expensive. Shares similarities with Pilates.

- **Astanga vinasa ('dynamic yoga'):** provides the benefits of a cardiovascular routine through the techniques of yoga. The aim is to tone the whole body inside and out, as different postures put pressure on different organs.

- **Badminton:** can be one of the fastest and most ruthless of racket sports. Unlike tennis or squash, beginners can pick it up almost immediately and the lightweight racket and shuttlecock mean that you don't need great strength to play – and win! Develops speed, skill, flexibility and co-ordination.

- **Boxing training:** it's a great way to get fitter while letting off steam. Training sessions involve punchbag, speedball and pads, as well as skipping and light weights. Check your local gym for details.

- **Clubbing/raving:** wild dancing for several consecutive hours is an excellent cardio-vascular work-out and a great way to get in shape.

- **Cycling:** there are shamefully few provisions for cyclists in inner cities, but this is still a great way to get in shape and get around. Wear a mask, keep your eyes open and stick to parks and Sundays for peace of mind.

- **Dance:** you can choose from ballet, ballroom, the Brazilian capoeira, Latin American, flamenco, jazz, tap, belly or rave and you can dress up in wild clothes to take part. Dance builds endurance, co-ordination and flexibility.

- **Deep-sea diving:** reveals a whole new under-water world, which is great if you're in the Caribbean, less great if you're in a slurry pit in the north of England which is how a lot of people get their diving certificates. You can also qualify by training in a swimming pool though you will have to do some real dives.

- **Feldenkreis method:** by increasing awareness of how the body works, this elaborate collection of exercises aims to organize the body into moving with maximum efficiency and minimum energy, releasing tension and improving flexibility. It's particularly good for people involved in sport or the performing arts.

- **Frisbee:** no longer the strung-out hippy-chick pastime it used to be, it's now organized into local clubs under the Ultimate Frisbee Federation. Playing in teams of seven, it's a non-contact sport which will give you a tough cardio-vascular work-out, while building stamina, control and friendships.

- **High diving:** depending on how far you develop it, this can be thrilling and invigorating exercise. Contact the Crystal Palace National Sports Centre which runs an 11-week course for all abilities.

- **Horse riding:** an excellent aerobic sport which exercises the entire body, strengthens the legs and improves co-ordination. You can also establish an interesting relationship with the horse – providing you can stay on its back. If you haven't ridden before, try a couple of sessions before investing in any expensive equipment. You'll need clothes which fit well but are not excessively tight, a hard (undamaged) riding hat and boots which allow you to easily remove your foot from the stirrup. Contact the British Horse Society, who publish *Where to Ride* which has details of your nearest approved riding school or livery stable.

- **Martial arts:** there are several different martial arts disciplines, from aikido, ju-jitsu, qigong and tai chi to karate and kickboxing. Most are based on ancient disciplines which focus on the relationship between mind and body where true well-being is seen as a balance or centring of mental and physical energy. Techniques vary from the controlled breathing exercises, warm-up, stretching, confidence building and relaxation techniques of quindo to the more physically energetic kickboxing.

- **Medau:** a technique developed in Germany in the 20s based on flowing movements using balls, hoops, clubs and flags. Aims to develop co-ordination and a sense of rhythm, but in the process you'll also improve muscle tone and stamina. Contact the Medau Society.

- **Pilates:** usually one-to-one training to work with,

rather than against, the body to build, lengthen and strengthen muscles, correct body alignment and posture. The effects of gravity are reduced by performing most exercises lying down. The aim is to create an awareness of the body, and to encourage a sense of calmness and concentration.

- **Rollerblading:** fast, groovy and, judging by the number of people trying to ban it in public parks, extremely obnoxious. Try renting a pair of blades before investing. Contact the British In-Line Skating Association for details of blading etiquette (the streetwise *Code of Conduct*) and information on where you can do it in the face of least hostility. Ice skating is a good alternative and, like blading, it's a great way to tone the lower body while improving balance, co-ordination and flexibility.

- **Sex:** a fabulous way to work out, which is as good an excuse as any.

- **Snowboarding:** like skate boarding on snow, this is apparently much easier to pick up than skiing. It's invigorating and glamorously hip as well as giving you an excellent all-body work-out. It's more fun to travel in a group.

- **Swimming:** as with aqua fitness, the density of water reduces the effects of gravity which (providing you stay in your lane) makes the swimming pool an impact-free zone. Invest in a good pair of goggles, cover your hair with a protective conditioner and wear a well-fitting cap if you plan to swim regularly. You may also want to investigate an underwater Walkman and even synchronized swimming which is now an Olympic sport.

- **Trampolining:** an exhilarating way to develop strength, co-ordination and your nerve. Check your local sports centre for trampolining clubs. There are strict safety codes which require the presence of a qualified coach.

- **Work-out videos and books:** you may find yourself wondering why you ever allowed these freaks of physical perfection into your home. On the other hand, work-out videos and handbooks can act as a good incentive to exercising in private, and save you time and money in the long run. You can go at your own speed and target your particular problems. Their image is improving – new 'street cred' tapes are emerging with decent music (from street funk to salsa) by the original recording artists. Remember – celebrities are no guarantee of quality. Look out for the Exercise Association of England (EXA) sticker of approval.

- **Yoga:** there are several different forms of this ancient technique which aims to achieve physical, mental and spiritual harmony, based on the principle that a calm body will contribute to a calm mind. Of those available in this country, 'Hatha' is the most common and combines body postures and breathing exercises. 'Mana' involves meditation as well as energy balancing, and 'Iyengar' promotes a strict adherence to technique. Yoga can greatly improve concentration and focus, as well as developing suppleness, flexibility and balance. It's extremely good for pregnant women, keeps the body toned and can make childbirth easier. Contact the British Wheel of Yoga to find your nearest class.

- **Zero balancing:** using pressure and stretching exercises, this technique relieves stress and tension to return you to 'zero balance' – a state of energized calm.

Don't forget to relax. Treat yourself to long baths and a massage. Track down your nearest sauna, steam bath or flotation tank for real escape.

PERSONAL TRAINERS

- A trainer will help motivate where self-motivation isn't doing the trick and ensure that exercise is safe and effective.

- A personal trainer can come to your home, gym or workplace and will tailor a programme to your personal requirements.

- Your trainer should be trained in first aid, CPR (cardio-pulmonary, respiratory), have public liability insurance and be prepared to supply references.

- Most teachers will update their qualifications by attending regular courses and workshops. However, having a list of qualifications is not necessarily a guarantee that your instructor is committed and able to communicate.

- Sessions can vary in cost from £25 to £75 an hour. They're generally arranged in blocks where some trainers will offer a slight reduction. Alternatively you may want to share the sessions, and the cost, with a friend.

- For more information on trainers contact the National Register of Personal Trainers. Or you could send an SAE with a letter telling the Exercise Association of England what you're looking for.

WOMEN'S HEALTH

Our ability to reproduce is what fundamentally, or at least physically, distinguishes us from men and so the reproductive system – our breasts, ovaries, uterus and cervix – is the focus of women's health. There are a variety of different health concerns and issues. As soon as you begin even thinking about sex you should be aware of contraception and sexually transmitted diseases (STDs). As you get older you may be more interested in how to become pregnant than how to avoid it, while in later life – liberated from the fear of conceiving when you don't want to – you may need to know how to deal with aspects of the menopause.

One of the keys to long-term health is caution. Regular screening will detect disease (should there be any) early, allowing the most effective treatment. There are several main issues and essential tests, and while we can give you a brief rundown this is something you really should follow up for yourself. If you haven't been screened recently, set up an appointment. Keep a record of when you go and make a note in your diary to remind you to book the next date – it's very easy to forget. Ring the Health Information Service Freephone for details of clinics, tests and what's involved.

GENERAL GUIDE-LINES

- Understand your body: a woman's body, particularly the reproductive system, is far more complicated than a man's. Be sure you understand the basic physiology of menstruation, pregnancy and childbirth, and the menopause. An excellent and comprehensive guide to these subjects is *The New Our Bodies, Ourselves* (Penguin) – written by women, for women.

- If you are sexually active, practise safe sex.
- Purchase high quality condoms, and make sure your partner uses them correctly. (You might try putting them on him: some men find it erotic!) Safe sex is not only preventing Aids and STDs, but also unwanted pregnancies: learn about the available contraception and choose a method that is effective for you. Remember that depending on your age and other factors, the pill is not always the best option. (See **Contraception** in **Sex** chapter.)
- Get a good GP. There is a tremendous range in quality, but every woman has the right to a well-trained, sympathetic, and communicative doctor. Don't ever be afraid to ask questions or even be a pest – sometimes being persistent and assertive is the only way to hear about all your options and receive good treatment.
- Learn about the women's health screening programmes (especially breast and cervical cancer screening, see below). Keep up to date and make sure any results out of the ordinary are clearly explained to you by your GP. Learn and practise regular monthly self-examination of your breasts.
- Keep track of your periods. Many women's health problems are manifested by changes in the menstrual cycle (or abnormal bleeding). Doctors will always ask about your 'last menstrual period'. (Obviously relevant if pregnancy is suspected!) If your periods aren't regular, keep a note in your diary. When seeing a doctor be sure to know the brand name of any contraceptive pill you use, and mention any other drugs you might be taking.
- Lead a healthy lifestyle: it's boring but true that drinking sensibly, quitting smoking, eating a healthy diet and getting regular exercise does wonders for your general health, mood, emotional and mental state – not to mention your looks and sex life.
- Stay informed: medical science, and especially reproductive health, contraception, cancer screening and treatment, abortion and AIDS are all changing rapidly, not only in the medical arena but with regard to legislation and openness. Follow these matters in a quality newspaper or good women's magazine, and be sure to ask your GP if there are new advances that might affect you.

WOMEN AND CANCER

Cancer is a general term for a multi-faceted disease that develops in a variety of forms, but basically characterized by a malignant growth of cells that invade and destroy body tissue, forming a tumour, lump or swelling. Cancers can affect any organ of the body.

Everyone is terrified of cancer, and understandably so. These days, however, treatment options for most cancers are better than ever. Every cancer is most readily treated when detected early on, so be sure to keep up with screening programmes and report any unusual symptom (such as nipple changes or discharges, or any unexpected vaginal bleeding) immediately to your GP. Any breast lump must be investigated (remember that most are in fact non-cancerous). If you feel your GP isn't acting on your concerns, ask to see another doctor.

If cancer is detected insist on referral to and expert treatment by an oncologist (cancer specialist), who will know far more about modern treatments than the average GP, however well-intentioned the latter is. At the same time educate yourself about the condition. There are excellent support groups for every type of cancer. These are essential sources of information (sometimes more up to date and knowledgeable than your GP!) and also provide crucial emotional support. (If you have Internet access, a multitude of cancer support groups and information websites can be found online. The easiest way to find one is to go to the Yahoo! directory at www.yahoo.com and look in the health listings.)

The good news is that screening methods and treatments are continually improving. Recent advances in genetic engineering mean that genes causing some cancers can now be identified (if there is a family history of cancer). New drugs mean better chemotherapy and hormone therapy with fewer side effects. The rise in the number of female doctors means that women patients are often being treated with more sympathy and courtesy than under the old, sometimes quite chauvinistic, medical system. These same women doctors (and more vocal patient groups) are leading the drive to increase funding for research into female cancers and other women-only diseases.

The main female cancers are naturally enough those dealing with the reproductive organs: breast, ovaries, uterus and cervix. (For many years breast cancer was the leading cancer of woman; now, reflecting increased smoking rates among women, lung cancer has that dubious honour.)

BREAST CANCER

- Affects around 1 in 12 women.
- Early detection and treatment is the key.
- Many breast lumps are benign (non-cancerous) but every one must be investigated.
- Benign breast lumps are common in all ages. They can be fatty deposits, benign tumours of breast tissue, cysts, and other types. Some women are more prone to these than others.
- Breast cancer (malignancy) has many forms. Some behave aggressively; others respond well to treatment and have a better prognosis.
- Women with a family history of breast cancer (mothers, sisters, aunts) must be especially vigilant, as they may carry the breast cancer gene.
- Other women considered at higher risk are those with late first pregnancies (or childless women), women who menstruate early, post-menopausal women and those with high-fat diets.

EXAMINATION, SCREENING AND TREATMENT

- Breast self-examination is essential. Learn from a nurse, good book or video, and do it once a month. Use soapy fingers, this makes it slightly easier. Report any lumps in the breast or armpit.
- Contact the BCC (Breast Care Campaign) for leaflets on breast pain, lumps and risk factors.
- Mammography (X-rays of the breast) is advised for women 50 years and over, on a regular basis. Screening programmes vary by region: in many the age has come down to 40. Consult your GP.
- Treatment should be based on the type, location and severity of the disease. Surgery, radiotherapy (destruction of cancer cells by radiation) and chemotherapy (anti-cancer drugs) are among the treatments used.

- Every woman dreads mastectomy (removal of the entire breast). There is still a great deal of controversy over mastectomy versus lumpectomy (removing the lump only), and as doctors and surgeons differ widely over this, it is essential to get several opinions before agreeing on any treatment.
- Be forceful and direct with your surgeon. Have the risks and possible outcome of any procedure explained in advance. As with any operation or procedure, when you are asked to consent in writing, ask exactly what the possibilities are. This is a big problem in hospitals, partly because the medical staff are rushed and don't have time to explain things. This puts the burden on the patient – before signing the 'Informed Consent' document make sure all your questions have been answered.
- Some doctors are uncomfortable when discussing the implications of cancer with patients and their families. Write all your questions down; bring a family member or close friend along for support and to make sure all your questions are answered.

CERVICAL CANCER

- Cervical cancer is malignancy of the cervix – the entrance to the uterus.
- It is more common in women with multiple partners, smokers and those exposed to a certain sexually transmitted virus called HPV (human papilloma virus, a type of wart).
- Most cancers begin as localized dysplasia in the cervix. You may hear this term from doctors or on smear results; it is simply unnatural cell growth. Smokers are much more likely to have dysplasia – another excellent reason to stop smoking!
- If dysplasia goes unchecked, it turns into 'Carcinoma in situ', another phrase you may hear. This is further along the road to cancer, but the cells are still confined to one specific region.
- The cervical smear test involves a nurse or doctor gently scraping a sample of cells from the cervix for microscopic examination with special stains to detect unusual or cancerous cells.
- All sexually active women should have a smear test when they reach 20, and regularly thereafter. Most good GP practices now have computerized systems to contact you when it's time for another

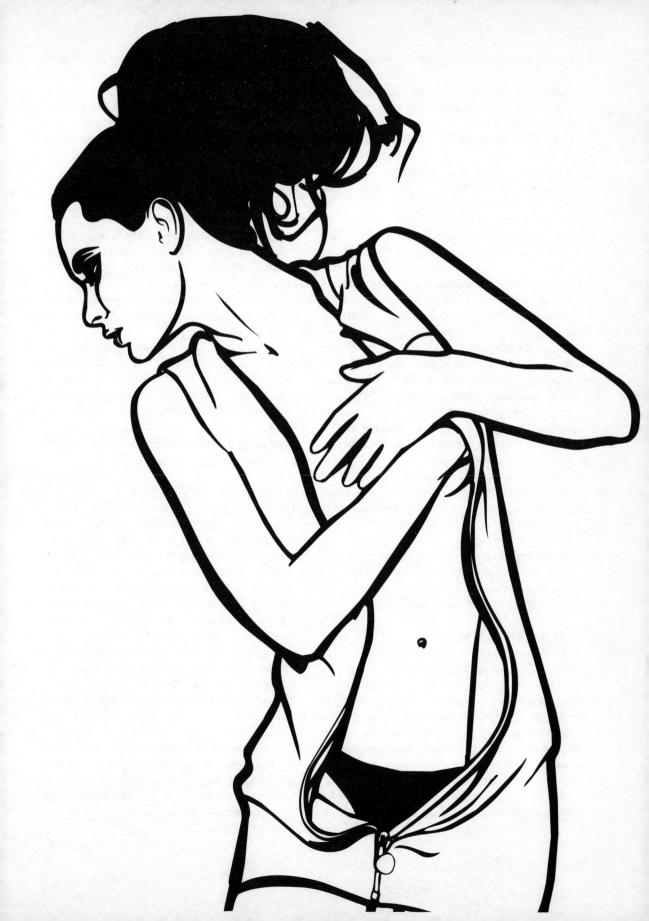

smear test (approximately every three years).

- As with any medical procedure, be sure to ask questions if you aren't sure what's going on.
- This is a very intimate procedure, and you have a right to basic privacy. In some hospitals medical students may be present; if you don't want to be on show, politely ask them to leave. (This holds true for any gynaecological exam or procedure. Students need their education and practice, but you have a right to privacy.)
- You will get the smear results in a few weeks. (The actual duration depends on the region.) Insist on a full explanation of any abnormal findings from your GP.
- If suspicious pre-cancerous or obvious cancerous cells are found on the smear test, a colposcopy will probably be organized. This involves examination of the cervix by a trained gynaecologist using a special microscope. Further samples may be taken and treatment initiated at this session.
- If the cells appear cancerous, the doctor may cut them away, freeze them (cryotherapy) or use a laser to destroy them. If all goes well, the entire cancer is removed at this time. You will need a follow-up and you will be considered at higher risk of cancer in the future.
- If the cancer has spread up the cervix into the uterus or into the area surrounding the cervix (a so-called invasive cancer), more extensive surgery is required. This can be a reason for hysterectomy (removal of the uterus).
- As with breast cancer, early detection is thus the key to successful treatment of cervical cancer. If you haven't had a smear, or haven't had your scheduled one, book one immediately.

OVARIAN CANCER

- Unlike breast cancer and cervical cancer, there is no good screening programme.
- Ovarian cancer has a high death rate because of its silent nature – often it remains symptomless until it has spread outside the ovaries and becomes impossible to remove surgically.
- It tends to appear in older, post-menopausal women. There is a strong hereditary component, so women whose mothers or other female relatives have had ovarian cancer are at special risk.
- Pregnancy, breast feeding, and the Pill appear to reduce the risk of ovarian cancer. Fatty diets (and obesity) and a history of other cancers increase the risk.
- Because the ovaries lie deep within the body, tumours can develop without symptoms for months and years. See your doctor if you experience unexpected swelling or pain around the abdominal region.
- Special investigations include ultrasound of the ovaries, X-rays and CT scans.
- Treatment will involve exploration of the ovaries and the region to see if there is any spread outside the ovary itself. Typically both ovaries will be removed along with the uterus and any other tissue affected.
- If there is evidence of spread, chemotherapy is usually attempted. Radiotherapy may also be advised.
- Ovarian cancer is a true oncological speciality, and it is best to get advice from a doctor who specializes in this serious, often deadly, cancer. Discuss the different types of chemotherapy treatments and learn about possible side-effects.
- As with all cancers, a patient support group will be of invaluable assistance, as will the Internet patient groups if you can get online.

UTERINE CANCER

- This is usually a disease of post-menopausal women, although it can affect pre-menopausal women. Those who are overweight, diabetic or have high oestrogen levels are at higher risk.
- The most common symptom is unexplained vaginal bleeding in a post-menopausal woman, or bleeding between periods in pre-menopausal ones. Any abnormal bleeding from the vagina must be investigated, whatever your age.
- Investigations will include a biopsy of the lining of the uterus or a dilation and curettage (D&C), or scraping away of the uterine lining.
- If cancer is detected, a hysterectomy is almost always performed. If the cancer has not spread outside the uterus, it is a curative operation.
- If spread outside the uterus is detected, radiotherapy, chemotherapy and additional surgery may be performed.
- Generally the outlook is very favourable if the cancer is detected early enough.

OTHER DISEASES OF THE REPRODUCTIVE ORGANS

With the complicated structures involved, plus the various hormonal fluctuations and the actual process of pregnancy and childbirth, it's not surprising that there are a number of other disorders of the female reproductive tract. Once again, we recommend a book like *Our Bodies, Ourselves* as an essential manual. The most common diseases include the following.

ENDOMETRIOSIS

Endometriosis occurs when some of the tissue that lines the uterus (endometrium) is found growing in other sites in the body – usually the pelvic area. These 'growths, nodules or lesions' are not cancerous. The condition can affect women of any age, not (as many wrongly believe) just 'career women who don't want children' – these women may be more likely to be tested and therefore diagnosed, but it's certainly not exclusive to them.

Some women can suffer a great deal of pain, and others none at all. Symptoms can include painful intercourse, bowel movements, ovulation and menstruation, as well as diarrhoea, constipation, backache, infertility and recurrent miscarriage. The symptoms are usually relieved by pregnancy – breast feeding will lengthen this period of relief. If unable to conceive because of endometriosis – try fertility treatments, alternative treatment (or both), or the conventional prescribed drugs.

TREATMENT
- If mild and wishing to conceive, none.
- Hormone treatments: the active ingredients are similar to testosterone and have side-effects.
- Severe cases may require removal of the growths.
- 'Radical' surgery: removal of the uterus (hysterectomy) should be treated very warily. Unless the ovaries are also removed (which causes instant menopause) the symptoms may continue after the operation.
- Alternative treatments: include nutritional, homoeopathic or herbal treatments. Contact the National Endometriosis Society for details.

OSTEOPOROSIS

Each year more women die indirectly (through broken bones and related complications) from osteoporosis than from ovarian, uterine and cervical cancer. There is no routine screening for osteoporosis so if you think it may be affecting you ask your GP for a referral to a Metabolic Bone Disease Unit. There are no early symptoms. The results can be moderate to severe back pain, dowager's hump, minimal trauma bone fractures and breakage from minor falls and from picking up heavy objects.

WHO'S AT RISK?
- Women who don't exercise, and have a poor nutritional record.
- Women who smoke excessively.
- Menopausal women with low oestrogen levels.
- Athletes of any age.
- Anorexics.
- It has also been linked to multiple sclerosis and other diseases where there is no mobility or bone-building activity.
- Over-active thyroid.
- Women who are taking corticosteroids in tablet form, long term or high dosage.

TREATMENT
- Preventative measures are extremely important; dietary supplements containing calcium, magnesium, boron and zinc; multi-vitamin supplement with A, D, C, E and the Bs.
- Take as much weight-bearing exercise as possible and any physiotherapy or targeted exercises that are necessary. HRT for menopausal women can slow down, and sometimes halt, further bone loss.
- Contact the Osteoporosis Screening Centre.

OVARIAN CYSTS

Any menstruating woman can develop ovarian cysts; they're quite common.

They may not cause any symptoms, but a disturbed menstrual cycle, painful sexual intercourse and abdominal swelling could indicate a problem. Diagnosis is determined through routine pelvic examination.

TREATMENT

- Most ovarian cysts disappear without treatment.
- Some need draining or surgical removal (though not the ovary – seek a second opinion if this is advised for a benign cyst).
- Improving your diet (see **Tips for healthy eating**), cutting out caffeine (which has been linked to fibroid and cyst formation), and reducing stress can help prevent cysts forming.

PELVIC INFLAMMATORY DISEASE (PID)

PID is a general term covering infection of the pelvic organs. The Fallopian tubes are the usual site of infection. There are four classes of PID which range in severity and occurrence. It is difficult to diagnose as it shares many of the same symptoms as endometriosis, and a lot of GPs are not well informed about it. It can become serious if left untreated for years, and cause extreme discomfort. Testing at your local genito-urinary clinic (usually in hospitals) rather than with your GP is the best bet.

The cause is unknown, but if you have recently had a miscarriage, an abortion, gynaecological operations, IUD insertion, sex without barrier methods, or follow anal intercourse with vaginal intercourse, you may be at risk.

Symptoms: dull ache in the lower abdomen on one side, swelling or excessive pain, painful urination, nausea, depression, fatigue, painful periods and intercourse, abnormal discharge, back or leg pain.

TREATMENT

Effective treatment depends on accurate diagnosis as early as possible, to prevent the infection spreading. Early treatment with antibiotics should clear it up for good.

- If you have been diagnosed – have your partner checked out.
- Contact the PID Support Group.

FIBROIDS OF THE UTERUS

Fibroids are tumours which are usually solid, benign and slow growing. They're usually discovered in routine pelvic examination, and then monitored. If they haven't increased in size after six months, you'll be monitored once a year.

- By the age of 35, about 20% of women will develop them.
- Smaller fibroids usually have no symptoms. Larger, or numerous fibroids, can change the size and shape of the uterus, cause abdominal and back pain, urinary problems and heavy periods. They can also interfere with conceiving or bearing a child.
- Menopausal women may find that fibroids naturally shrink as their oestrogen levels fall.

TREATMENT

May not be necessary.

- Fibroids can be removed through (major) surgery if they are causing severe problems. The operation is called a myomectomy, and it should be noted that there are more complications associated with this operation than with hysterectomies.
- Alternative treatment includes yoga which can relieve some of the uncomfortable symptoms, and visualization techniques.

MENSTRUATION

'Periods', 'the curse', 'that time of the month' are euphemisms for menstruation. Our bodies become sexually mature some time between the ages of nine and 17. Whatever our age, our bodies are preparing us for pregnancy. If we don't get pregnant, the vascular lining of the womb is shed and menstruation begins – a light to heavy flow of blood that can last between three and seven days within our (usually) 28-day cycle.

ABSENT PERIODS (Amenorrhoea)

If menstruation doesn't occur – there is a reason.

- This happens naturally post menopause, when pregnant or breast feeding.
- It can also occur as a result of strenuous athletic training, eating disorders (anorexia nervosa), starvation, the contraceptive pill, stress and emotional factors, cysts and tumours, hormone imbalance, severe anaemia and being 15–20% below your normal weight.

Note: this is not a form of contraception; you can still get pregnant even though you are not getting your period. Always have it checked out.

PAINFUL PERIODS (Dysmenorrhoea)

There are many ways to alleviate painful stomach cramps and lower back pain. You don't have to just take an aspirin, hot water bottle and go to bed. Changing your eating habits (see **Premenstrual syndrome**), exercise, relaxation techniques and attitude can help a lot.

- Mucus-producing food (dairy products and red meat) makes it harder for the uterus to clean itself and it becomes strained cleaning out excess toxins (alcohol, sugar, tobacco, processed foods).
- Caffeine (Coke, coffee, tea, chocolate) increases muscle tension and sensitivity.
- Exercise will assist with the flow of oxygen through the muscles while toning them up (lack of oxygen in the muscles makes contractions painful during menstruation).
- If dysmenorrhoea is caused by endometriosis, fibroids or pelvic inflammatory disease, treatment should be sought by a qualified medical practitioner. If caused by an intra-uterine device (an IUD – contraceptive coil), have it removed and try a different method.

PREMENSTRUAL SYNDROME (PMS)

PMS occurs between ovulation and the next menstrual period because of changing hormonal levels and is a common problem.

The symptoms include bloatedness, fatigue, headaches, irritability, nausea, spots, swollen and tender breasts. Some are the result of increased water retention in the tissues because of higher levels of oestrogen and aldosterone hormones and lowered progesterone levels. Many women simply take extra progesterone at this time. To alleviate symptoms try:

- A change of diet: try to avoid sugar; complex carbohydrates (fresh fruit, vegetables, grains, nuts) will release natural sugar into the blood.
- Take evening primrose oil and vitamin B6 for overall symptoms.
- Stress and anxiety can be treated with camomile and vervain teas and oats (daily helping of porridge, oat bran or oat cakes).
- Couch grass and dandelion tea three times a day during the PMS period and natural diuretics such as pineapple juice, parsley and strawberries will help reduce bloating, as will essential oils of geranium or rosemary in a warm bath.
- Regular gentle exercise (yoga, swimming, cycling, walking) and meditation can also help.
- Contact a qualified practitioner if no changes occur after a couple of months.
- See the **Directory** for good reading suggestions.

MENOPAUSE

The menopause is the natural end of menstruation and the fertile years of a woman's life and happens usually between the ages of 45 and 56. Consult your doctor if things happen earlier or later.

- Physically, the menopause is the end of ovulation due to a decline in hormone levels.
- Oestrogen is no longer produced by the ovaries and its absence causes a thinning of the vaginal walls.
- About a quarter of post-menopausal women find a reduction in lubricating secretions. This can be uncomfortable during sexual intercourse but is easily compensated for either by using lubricating jelly (vitamin E oil or KY Jelly) or by going onto a treatment of hormone replacement therapy (HRT).
- HRT: your doctor can prescribe oestrogen only (for women who have had hysterectomies) or a balance of oestrogen with progestogen (for pre- and ongoing menopause). This does make menstruation return, but offers protection against heart and arterial diseases and can also deal effectively with some of the other side-effects of the menopause such as osteoporosis (brittle bones).
- There is no solid proof that taking HRT actually stops the feelings or symptoms that a quarter of menopausal women suffer, such as hot flushes, night sweats, insomnia, palpitations, sore eyes, headaches, emotional outbursts or irritability.
- It will not be prescribed to women with a history of thrombosis or high blood pressure, liver, pancreatic or gall bladder disease, or those who have been treated for cancer or are high cancer risks. Endometriosis or fibroid problems need to be considered if HRT is being sought.
- The 'effects' of menopause can often be as much to do with emotional as with physiological

changes. Children leaving home, lack of self-worth, an inability to see one's place or purpose in the world and an end of any chance of reproduction can all take their toll, and it's important to try to fill gaps left in your life.

- The bonus side of the menopause can be a relaxed attitude to sex with no fear of pregnancy (once two years with no bleeding have passed), the end of PMS each month and the boring practicalities of menstruating, tampons, sanitary towels and contraception.
- Eat food rich in hormone-like substances: ripe bananas, carrots, apples, bee pollen, royal jelly, seeds and whole grains; avoid excess salt, sugar, alcohol or any coffee.
- Taking a supplement of wheat germ, kelp or vitamin B complex and calcium carbonate supplements whilst avoiding sugar, will help to keep your skin supple, prevent weight gain, relieve depression and increase vitality.
- Herbal teas based on vervain, sage, wild yam and lavender will help with the other symptoms.
- See reading ideas in the **Directory**.

NHS

GENERAL PRACTITIONERS

Everyone has the right to be registered with a GP although most will only accept you if you live locally. You must be registered in order to be seen, which you may be able to do on the spot. Get a list of all local doctors in your area from your local health authority.

CHANGING YOUR DOCTOR

You can change your GP at any time without explaining why. However, it's wise to first find a replacement to take you on. If you have difficulty in finding a GP, write to your local health authority explaining that you want to change. This works both ways – you can also be struck off a GP's list without explanation.

REFERRAL TO HOSPITAL
Questions to ask
- Try to establish the reputation of the hospital.

- Ask your GP and check with your local Community Health Council.
- If your condition is anything unusual ask to be referred to a teaching hospital. You will be seen by doctors who are up to date with current research and have access to specialists.
- Find out how long the waiting list is. An NHS helpline will connect you to your local health authority's Information Service where they can tell you the waiting times for key operations in your area.
- Ask if you can go on standby in case of cancellation.
- Ask for a copy of the Patient's Charter which clarifies patients' rights. All patients, for example, have the right to a clear explanation of treatments.
- If you are on a long waiting list for NHS treatment you may want to look into private options.
- See **Private Health Insurance** in **Money** chapter.

MEDICAL NEGLIGENCE

Medical professionals are liable for negligence. As with other professionals, they must exercise a 'reasonable degree' of skill in their work. The powers of the General Medical Council concerning the discipline of doctors have recently been increased. Their targets include underperformance (poor examination of patients, or sloppy record-keeping) as well as general misconduct. However, it can be extremely difficult to establish cause and effect.

Cases of medical negligence can be based on the doctor's failure to
- provide the patient with adequate information about the operation
- obtain the patient's consent before the operation
- check the patient's medical history before prescribing treatment
- supply adequate details of the patient's medical history to those treating the patient

MEDICAL LAW

Doctors are protected by the Medical Defence Union and the Medical Protection Society. They generally advise on settling out of court if it seems likely the doctor will lose. You have three years in which to act if you are making a claim, but the process is notoriously slow so if you feel you have a case you should act quickly.

The relevant health authority or hospital trust is responsible for accidents caused by any staff working under the NHS – from student nurse to consultant. The employers are responsible for the working conditions and excessive working hours, and are therefore liable to pay compensation should accidents result.

IN A CASE OF NEGLIGENCE
- Call your local Community Health Council, Action for Victims of Medical Accidents, NHS helpline or the Patients' Association for more information and advice on the steps to take.
- It is unwise to pursue a claim for medical (whether conventional or alternative) negligence without first taking legal advice from a solicitor who specializes in this field (see **How to find a solicitor** in the **Law** chapter). Your solicitor will ask for your medical records which will be assessed by an independent specialist. The specialist will also examine you to help determine whether or not you have a case worth pursuing.
- The private patient must sue the doctor concerned. Doctors in private practice should have special accident insurance cover. If the accident was caused by an employee of a private hospital, the hospital is responsible.

STRESS
ANXIETY AND DEPRESSION

Certain circumstances in our lives are so threatening and upsetting that the anxiety and stress they generate remain long after the event. Rape, muggings, fires, car crashes can all have this effect. An estimated six million people every year consult their doctors because they feel depressed, anxious or unable to handle the stress in their daily lives, and the numbers are increasing. This is not necessarily because more people are suffering, but simply reflects greater awareness among the public and medical profession. Tolerance to stress varies from person to person. It's impossible to avoid it altogether and while too much can be destructive, a little can be positive, even necessary to raise adrenalin and keep us going.

CAUSES
- New job or change of career, overwork, retirement, redundancy or getting the sack.
- Family problems, death, marriage, sex, divorce, children, pregnancy and moving house.
- Money causes an enormous amount of anxiety and stress: debt problems, escalating debt and an inability to face the facts and do anything about it; the fear and panic that a letter from a bailiff can cause; large mortgage; and extreme change in your finances.
- Serious personal injury or illness.
- Changes in any regular patterns of behaviour.

SYMPTOMS
- Symptoms can be physical as well as mental: irritability, sweating, muscular tension, dizziness, inability to concentrate, difficulty in eating and sleeping, panic attacks, high blood pressure, digestive problems, diarrhoea, premature ejaculation for men, menstrual disorders for women.
- Hyperventilation can cause heart palpitations. This frightening feeling can be mistaken for a heart attack and increase the stress even more. However if there is pain with the palpitations a doctor should be consulted immediately.
- Continued stress and anxiety can weaken your immune system making you more vulnerable to a variety of diseases. It can be particularly damaging in long-term diseases such as cancer where a positive attitude is absolutely necessary.

DEPRESSION
Most people periodically feel stressed, anxious or depressed when things go wrong. That is very different from a depressive illness, which can be long lasting, severe or completely paralysing and from which the sufferer may be unable to recover without professional help. There are no laboratory tests for depression, so doctors can only diagnose it through discussion with the patient and by monitoring their behaviour. Depression can be mild at first and slowly escalate and it can

occur at any age. Women tend to be more affected by it than men.

CAUSES
- Genetic predisposition, chemical imbalance and poor diet.
- Unconscious childhood experiences.
- Living with painful illness: depression can result when you are very low physically.
- Side-effects of medication.
- Excessive drinking: alcohol is a depressant which depletes the body of B vitamins.
- Any addictions; drugs, gambling.
- Living with someone who is an alcoholic or takes drugs.
- Social factors: unemployment, bereavement, taking care of elderly parents or disabled children, social isolation.

SYMPTOMS
- Feeling hopeless, worthless and helpless; unable to face anyone, even those who want to help.
- Unable to get out of bed, lying with face turned to the wall, unable to see anyone, or answer the telephone.
- Loss of energy, apathy and disconnection from the world around you. Loss of a sense of time.
- Guilt and fear.
- Brooding, melancholy, insomnia.
- Morbid, desperate, despondent and suicidal.
- Self-hatred, self-destructive, self-mutilation.

OTHER FORMS OF DEPRESSION
- **Manic depression:** characterized by extreme fluctuations in mood and behaviour with highs of incredible energy and lows which can be paralysing. Contact the Manic Depression Fellowship.
- **Seasonal affective disorder:** due to lack of sufficient sunlight and can be treated with light therapy. Contact SAD Association for information.

Stress, anxiety and depression often overlap and can appear and disappear according to the circumstances of our lives. If you have difficulty in handling any of these conditions, if they become overwhelming and self-help no longer works, SEEK OTHERS' HELP quickly. It is out there.

Don't wait until you've reached rock bottom, it may be too late then.

OPTIONS FOR TREATMENT
There are many different approaches for selecting the right treatment. Have a good friend help you to take the initial steps. Find out what qualified help is available and who you can see to try and identify the root problems. Never dismiss it – actively deal with it.

DOCTOR/GP
Consult your GP first. This is important as your symptoms may be side-effects of medication you are taking. Be wary of GPs who lightly prescribe drugs without trying to investigate the reasons why you feel the way you do. It's always better to treat the cause rather than alleviate the symptoms.

There are over 50 drugs described as tranquillizers or antidepressants so it's best to go to someone who is familiar with the range of drugs and their side-effects. Thoroughly investigate any drugs that are prescribed and find out what the possible reactions and side-effects could be. Even the tranquillizers that are considered minor, like Valium or Ativan, can be seriously addictive.

SELF-HELP
- Debt is a major cause of stress. Try to plough through unopened letters and bills regularly. Don't let them pile up. Don't approach them with dread and fear. It may not be as bad as you think. If you contact the debtors, they may be helpful.
- Nutrition: check your eating habits. Stress, anxiety and depression can deplete your system of vitamins and minerals (see **Healthy eating** section).
- Dietary supplements can help, as can frequent injections of B vitamins. Contact your GP.
- Physical exercise releases endorphins that induce a sense of well-being and make it easier to handle stress. Vigorous aerobic exercise can tire you so that you sleep more soundly.
- Yoga which concentrates on breathing and slow, gentle stretching, is excellent for the relief of tension. See the **A–Z of Exercise Options.**
- Discover the things that help you relax and

pursue them: music, massage, a lazy bath containing soothing oils, seeing good friends, going to a movie or watching a feel-good video at home.

- Meditation: clinical trials show that regular meditation does reduce stress. Try a class to learn the different ways to meditate.
- Assertive training classes can help by making you proactive in the management of your life and to help you to avoid stressful situations. Your local authority may run courses. Contact them for details.
- If you have a practical problem – debt, ill health, housing – look at individual sections in this book.
- Go to your local Citizens' Advice Bureau for help and advice. MIND has an information line for all aspects of mental distress.

COUNSELLING

- Counselling guides people, either individually or in groups, to make decisions and solve personal problems by giving advice, information and psychological tests.
- Counselling services are often specialized: marriage, family, bereavement, vocation, etc., and can cover the same ground as psychotherapy or various branches of applied psychology.
- Counsellors can often be volunteers who have completed a specialized training course. Ask about their training references.
- The British Association of Counsellors has lists of counsellors and organizations offering counselling nationally.

PSYCHIATRY

Psychiatry specializes in all mental illness. Psychiatrists are qualified doctors with a general medical training, which enables them to prescribe drugs, unlike psychologists or psychotherapists (unless they are also qualified physicians).
While some psychiatrists accept other psychotherapeutic techniques, the treatment is more likely to be physical, using drug therapy.

PSYCHOANALYSIS

Originally Freudian only, his theories have subsequently been applied to many different methods which still retain an emphasis on the unconscious, free association, transference and interpretation by the analyst.

- The psychoanalyst must have received full training at a recognized institute of psycho-analysis and five or six years of analysis.
- This treatment requires a considerable, long-term commitment on the part of the patient. Every aspect of the patient's early life is examined to see how it may have affected or caused current problems.
- In sessions, usually lasting an hour, the analyst will interpret the patient's conversation to try and guide her/him into an understanding of the destructive behaviour patterns which are blocking the patient's ability to function properly.
- NHS treatment is rarely an option.

PSYCHOTHERAPY

- Psychotherapy covers all forms of treatment for emotional and psychological disturbances by psychological rather than physical (drugs etc.) methods.
- Some psychotherapists are trained in clinical psychology or have a background in counselling but there is no legal requirement to have any particular training at all.
- There are many different types of psychotherapy: analytical, behavioural and cognitive are three of the main approaches. Most offer treatment based on conversation in a controlled, confidential environment.

SPECIALIZED AREAS

- **Family therapy:** family members are encouraged to examine their behaviour towards each other and work out a mutually agreeable way forward.
- **Group therapy:** sharing past experiences within a small group to learn from their experiences.
- **Sex therapy** can help couples overcome sexual difficulties without sexual contact until they are able to communicate and trust each other.
- **Nurses and health visitors:** few have specific mental health training but can be helpful in contacting specialized help groups.
- **Social workers** can provide counselling and practical help in solving problems that cause stress. Available through hospitals or local social services.

- **Community workers** can be contacted through community centres and are a good source of information on help groups in your area.
- **Dance and art therapy:** communicating through creative activity for people who have difficulty discussing their feelings. Contact the Institute for Arts in Therapy and Education.

COPING WITH A DEPRESSIVE

It is important that those close to you – family, friends, etc. – understand your illness and treatment so that they can give you the right support and avoid taking things personally. There are many help groups to turn to for advice.

TERMINOLOGY

Common terms used by social workers, counsellors and psychologists are listed below. They are technical terms used to help show us how our minds work and how we react to certain situations.

- **Conversion:** deep, hidden fears may be repressed and manifest as physical symptoms.
- **Denial:** convincing oneself that there is nothing wrong when there is; things that make us uncomfortable are disguised and avoided.
- **Dissociation:** to become unconnected or separated from people/situations.
- **Fixation:** obsession, dependency or concentration on a single person or idea.
- **Identification:** conscious or unconscious modelling of oneself on another person; this can have positive or negative implications.
- **Introjection:** turning feelings and attitudes towards others inwards.
- **Inversion:** the exaggeration of tendencies opposite to those which are repressed. Being a prude may be an inversion of repressed sexual desire.
- **Projection**: personal inadequacies are projected onto others or other things.
- **Rationalization:** a form of self-deception whereby socially acceptable reasons are found for conduct with less worthy motives.
- **Regression:** going back to earlier childhood behaviour, which could include childish temper tantrums.
- **Repression:** an unconscious pushing aside of ideas and impulses which do not fit with what the individual regards as correct.

- **Transference:** directing emotions towards one person which are derived from experience with another, for example angry feelings previously felt with a parent may be reproduced with someone else in authority.
- **Withdrawal:** withdrawing physically and emotionally from a stressful situation.

ALTERN-ATIVE TREATMENTS

Alternative treatments (either in conjunction with, or independent of, conventional medicine) are recognized as a valuable addition to health-care, and are becoming much more widely available.

FINDING AN ALTERNATIVE PRACTITIONER

- Go by recommendation wherever possible.
- There is no legal requirement for them to be registered (in fact, many are registered under their own organizations who set a level of competence – check whether your practitioner is registered).
- Phone to talk to the practitioner before making an appointment.
- Check where they trained and how long they have been practising.
- Ask what experience they have had (if relevant) in treating your particular complaint.
- Ask how they ideally like to work, what's involved and make sure you feel comfortable with the prospect.

PRACTITIONERS – THE LAW

The general rules of negligence also apply to alternative practitioners. However, it is important to remember the following:

- They are not required to be trained to the same level as qualified doctors.
- They have no legal duty to take insurance cover (although most responsible practitioners do).

OPTIONS

Here is a list of available treatments (see **Directory** for contact numbers):

- **Acupressure/acupuncture:** restores the flow of energy through needle puncture, heat, laser electricity or pressured massage.
- **Alexander technique:** retraining to rediscover natural body movement, reduces physical and mental tension, improves neuromuscular co-ordination, backache, depression and headaches.
- **Aromatherapy:** uses concentrated essential oils extracted from plants to treat diagnosed illness; a form of herbal medicine.
- **Bach flower remedies:** use of floral extracts to balance excessive or poor emotional states related to temperament or personality; available from chemists.
- **Bates therapy:** a series of eye exercises to keep eyes healthy; *Perfect Sight without Glasses* by Dr William Bates (1860–1931) is still in print. Therapists teach his methods.
- **Bioelectrotherapy:** low-energy electric current submitted to the body through a pad to activate the body's natural pain relief or healing process. Used for addiction treatment and childbirth.
- **Biofeedback:** self-controlled machine, lowers blood pressure (pulse meters), treats stress-related disorders (electric encephalograms) by producing alpha brain waves.
- **Cellular regeneration:** a technique of regenerating, self-healing and balancing the body through meditation, breathing, diet and visualization.
- **Chiropractic:** physical manipulation of the spine and pelvis to realign muscular and skeletal dysfunction; now the most common way of treating back, bone and muscle-related injuries.
- **Colonic irrigation:** pumping water through a tube placed in the anus, up into the colon to clean and detoxify the body; used for pre-bowel surgery and to improve hair and skin condition.
- **Cranial osteopathy:** relieves pressure that causes headaches, migraine, whiplash or crying/sleepless/unhappy babies, by gentle manipulation of the skull.
- **Flotation therapy:** total relaxation floating in a tank full of Epsom-salted water in a dark and sound-proofed environment rids the body of

harmful toxins at the same time re-energizing it.

- **Herbal medicine:** use of herbs for their health-giving properties and for treating illness; a third of all pharmaceutical drugs are herbal derivatives.
- **Homoeopathy:** based on the theory 'like cures like', treating illness with an extremely small quantity of a drug capable of producing symptoms of that disease in a healthy person. Homoeopathy is a holistic treatment.
- **Ionizers:** combat the effects of pollution and electrical appliances that destroy the negative ions in the atmosphere. Good for depression, respiratory problems, hay fever and insomnia.
- **Iridology (ophthalmic somatology):** the study of the iris, the only visible part of the nervous system, showing disorders and physical tendencies. Good for detecting allergies.
- **Light therapy:** a light box/bulb which stimulates our bodily reaction to produce vitamin D and boost our immune system. Good for depression, insomnia, premenstrual tension and skin problems.
- **Magnetic healing:** people are exposed to low frequency magnetic radiation (called Delta waves) which can have a healing effect.
- **Meditation:** a technique of deep relaxation of all muscles, total passivity and utter tranquillity, the only awareness being of calm and breathing. Connected to many religions as a route to finding spiritual enlightenment; antidote to stress.
- **Megavitamin therapy:** for people unable to assimilate vitamins unless given huge quantities to combat a deficiency; used successfully in hyperactive children, depressives, schizophrenics and cancer sufferers. Should only be taken when prescribed.
- **Naturopathy:** holistic approach to curing the body of illness, through diet, osteopathy, hydrotherapy, exercise, relaxation, breathing and yoga. Patients are made responsible for their illness so that the power of the body to heal itself is released.
- **Reflexology:** by pressing on particular parts of the foot, which represent areas of the rest of the body, it clears the body's blockages.
- **Reiki:** healing by channelling the body's energy through the hands.
- **Shiatsu:** a form of finger-point massage applied to the acupuncture points to release the body's energy; other connected curative measures may include dietary and lifestyle changes.
- **Sound therapy (cymatics):** high density sound as a healing device; targeting particular diseased areas of tissue with sound waves can promote healthy ones to attack diseased cells. Used in breaking up kidney/gall stones, arthritis, fibrosis, gout, myalgia, muscle and bone problems.
- **Thalassotherapy/hydrotherapy:** using the healing powers of water (fresh or sea), the skin absorbs the trace elements and minerals. Buoyancy of sea water allows exercise of stiff joints; being massaged by water jets is a relaxant.
- **TCM (traditional Chinese medicine):** includes diagnoses through pulse and tongue and treatment through acupuncture, aromatherapy, reflexology, shiatsu and herbal medicine.
- **Voice therapy/work:** vocal and breathing techniques that enable the pupil to express their emotions and find their full vocal range; for sufferers of anxiety, depression or physical disability.
- **Yoga:** in Sanskrit it means 'unity with life and the divine'. Yoga is a way of life and of caring for your spiritual, physical and emotional development within a state of harmony which encourages a healthy way of being; benefits stress-related problems.

BEAUTY

Today beauty is a billion-pound industry and the more complicated and mysterious the corporations make it seem, the more money we end up spending. We're bombarded with hundreds of different fad diets, exercise programmes and fashion 'essentials', not to mention the thousands of 'miracle' cosmetics. When these fail, plastic surgeons are waiting in the wings with their knives sharpened. But how do we choose and why should we care?

Attitudes to beauty have come a long way. Most of us want to look 'good', but no longer accept being dictated to. This is the age of the individual and personal style. Now we can manipulate our own images to convey whatever messages we want. We can enjoy all the glamour, frivolity, fantasy and total self-indulgence the beauty industry can offer, but at the same time can laugh at it when it gets absurd.

Health and beauty are inseparable. The way you feel depends on the condition of both your mind and body, and if you feel good – you'll look good. We suggest you read this chapter in conjunction with the **Health** chapter.

SKIN

Beauty, as we've all been told endlessly (usually by our mothers), isn't skin deep. However, the skin does mirror the health of the whole body. The condition of the skin isn't only determined by what we put on it, or how we cleanse it, but also reveals the state of our diet, how much we exercise, drink and smoke, and our state of mind.

Skin is the largest organ in the body, and has three layers – the epidermis, the dermis and the subcutaneous tissue. The epidermis, the protective layer, contains no blood vessels, but has many small nerve endings. The outer scale-like layer of skin is continually shed and replaced. Overlapping cells are covered by a thin layer of oil making the skin almost waterproof. The mid-layers allow light through tiny transparent cells to the deepest layer which contains melanin or skin pigment. The dermis has two layers: the first contains elastic tissue, while the second, deeper layer contains blood and lymph vessels, fat cells, oil and sweat glands and hair follicles. The subcutaneous tissue is a fatty layer below the dermis.

TIPS FOR HEALTHY SKIN

- Drink plenty of fluids: water, fruit and vegetable juices. Water cleanses and purifies.
- Avoid processed and fried foods, animal fats and junk food (soft drinks, refined sugar, chocolate, crisps and chips).
- Excess sun damages skin causing dryness and premature wrinkling. It can also lead to sunspots and skin cancer.
- Stop smoking. It leads to wrinkling around the mouth (each time we take a puff), and around the eyes (as we squint to avoid smoke). Smoking causes dryness and constricts the capillaries, leading to a 'grey' complexion.
- Get plenty of sleep, allow your body/skin to rest and regenerate.
- Always cleanse your face before bedtime, whether or not you wear make-up.
- Regular exercise makes a big difference to the skin as well as the body, increasing circulation which brings oxygen to the cells. This makes them grow more quickly and absorb nutrients more efficiently. Sweating cleanses the skin from within, and speeds up the expulsion of toxins.

CARING FOR YOUR SKIN

- Always begin with clean hands.
- Cleansing removes old make-up, dirt and grime from your skin. Depending on your skin type, you can use a mild facial or glycerine-based soap (most companies produce soaps especially for the face – ordinary soap is often too harsh), foaming creams and gels, cream or milk cleansers, petroleum jelly or vegetable oils (avoid mineral oils which may be carcinogenic and aren't absorbed by the skin), light moisturizers which work perfectly well as cleansers (the reverse isn't necessarily the case).
- Apply your cleanser with fingertips (use middle and ring fingers, not your index fingers – they're much stronger than the others and can drag at delicate skin). Using a circular motion, massage it in – not forgetting your hairline and around your nose. The cleanser can be removed with moist cotton wool, a damp washcloth or muslin or by rinsing with water. Rose and orange waters make luxurious alternatives for rinsing and are cheap and easy to find in chemists or Indian food shops.
- After cleansing, your skin should feel clean and supple, not dry and tight.

TONERS AND ASTRINGENTS

Toners and astringents are two different products – both remove dead skin cells from the skin surface, but astringents contain alcohol and should only be used on oily skin or on the T-zone of combination skin. If you're unsure whether or not the product contains alcohol, ask at the counter. A mild skin toner is usually perfect for most skin types. If your skin is very dry or sensitive, use rose or orange flower water instead, as these leave the skin's natural oils behind. Apply using an upward motion, using cotton wool. Avoid the eye area.

MOISTURIZERS

Again the type of moisturizer you use depends on your skin type. If you find you need excessive moisturizing, your cleansing routine may be too harsh. Some women may need to rehydrate skin before bed, others may not. Unless your skin is very oily, moisturize before applying make-up to give foundation an even base. This also prevents your skin from 'eating' your foundation.

EXFOLIANTS/SKIN SCRUBS

Exfoliants are generally abrasive particles suspended in a cream, milk or gel base. The particle size varies and the coarser the particle, the more abrasive the effect. Don't use body scrubs on the face. Try to choose a scrub with water-soluble granules as these generally cause the least irritation. A washcloth or muslin soaked in warm water can be equally effective. Exfoliation can help remove blackheads, and makes open pores appear smaller. Dead surface cells are removed and circulation is increased giving your skin a healthy glow.

Do not exfoliate more than once a week. Be gentle. A tendency to over-scrub can do more harm than good.

ACNE

Too much oil in the skin prevents the natural shedding of the dead skin cells which means that hair follicles become clogged, then infected and can cause spots. If the condition is severe this is known as acne. Spots seem to appear magically when we least want them to, and can cause real distraction and distress. 70% of teenage girls suffer from acne, as do 30% of women in their late 20s and early 30s. Several factors can contribute including diet, hormone activity (a lot of us develop a carbuncle just before our period) or stress.

- Try vitamin and mineral supplements, particularly vitamins E, A and D. Sometimes skin problems are diet related.
- Over-the-counter treatments containing benzoyl peroxide or salicylic acid help unblock pores and regulate the oil in the skin.
- If the problem is making you feel very self-conscious, you may want to see a dermatologist. Your GP should be able to supply you with names.

- Avoid picking at spots: as you probably know, it makes them worse by spreading the infection. If you must, cover nails with clean tissue and cleanse with witch hazel.
- If your skin is excessively oily, go for products which are labelled 'non-comedogenic' which essentially means oil-free.
- Don't overwash your skin: you may dry it out and increase its sensitivity.
- If your skin has been scarred or pitted because of acne, you may be able to do something about it.
- See 'Retin-A' in **Terminology**, and check non-surgical treatments in **Cosmetic surgery**.

CELLULITE

What is it? It is fat normally found on the bottom and around the back of the upper thighs. Its texture resembles that of orange peel. No one really knows what it is; one theory is that it relates to the changing hormone levels in our body. As the skin grows thinner with age the cellulite becomes more visible.

What contributes to cellulite?

- Diet, excess sugary and fatty foods, lack of fresh fruit, vegetables, water, too much animal fat, artificial additives.
- Stress and smoking.
- Food allergies and slimming pills.
- Lack of exercise.

How to treat it

Nothing can make cellulite disappear but regular, healthy diet and exercise can improve it.
Some tips:
- Detoxing the body.
- Drink one or two litres per day of still pure water.
- Have regular meals of an average size. Eat high fibre food, fresh fruit and vegetables and buy organic products where possible.
- Stretching and toning excercises.
- Stimulating the skin's surface with a body brush or massage glove (brushing needs to be in an upward motion towards the heart). Try massaging skin with aromatherapy oils.
- Reduce stress (see **Stress** in **Health** chapter).

BEAUTY
PRODUCTS DEMYSTIFIED

When choosing products, more expensive does not always mean better. You're often simply paying for the packaging, brand name and marketing campaign, not necessarily the contents. Many of the more expensive brands manufacture the cheaper creams and make-up for M&S, Miss Selfridge and Bourgeois. Skin creams have radically changed and visiting the cosmetics counter has become an increasingly intimidating experience. Instead of the simple, old-fashioned moisturizer, there are 'complexes', 'gels', 'face-lifts', 'therapies', 'serums' and 'time capsules', containing, in various combinations, antioxidants, ceramides, enzymes, AHAs, SPFs and UVAs. They don't look, feel, and certainly don't sound, the way they used to. The main advance came with the discovery that many substances when put on to the skin don't just sit on the surface – they penetrate to lower levels.

Cosmeceuticals, the media term for new high-tech creams on the market, are clearly divided between drugs and cosmetics according to the US Food and Drugs Administration (FDA). This depends on their level of skin penetration, and whether or not they affect cell activity.

According to the Cosmetic, Toiletry and Perfumery Association (CTPA), there are no real guidelines setting out who can manufacture cosmetics in the UK. Cosmetics are monitored by the Department of Trade, and must meet government and EU standards which concern safety rather than efficiency. Drugs, on the other hand, are licensed by the Department of Health's Medicines Control Agency (MCA) and need a licence. If cosmetic companies make too many medicinal claims in their advertising, the MCA can ask them for proof and demand they apply for an expensive medical licence – very few have.

- However, it does signal that the pharmaceutical companies are moving into the lucrative beauty industry, and could mean that your GP may have to prescribe your beauty treatments in the future.

BEAUTY WITHOUT CRUELTY

Cruelty-free products are much more readily available, although testing ingredients and products on animals still continues. It is advisable to check for 'Not tested on animals' on the back of the product. The British Union for the Abolition of Vivisection publishes a product guide called *The Approved Product Guide to Cosmetics and Household Products*.

THINGS TO CONSIDER

- Most product lines are designed to work in conjunction with the rest of the line, but if you find that brand A's cleanser with brand Z's moisturizer works for you then stick with it.
- The beauty industry thrives by making us feel we must have products we don't necessarily need. Just as there are trends within every other branch of the beauty industry, cosmetics follow fashions. Don't be fooled, and if what you're using works, continue with it.
- *The Beauty Bible* by Sarah Stacey and Josephine Fairley gives tested opinions on named products. From the end of 1997 manufacturers will have to provide a full list of ingredients for all personal care products from sunscreen to toothpaste, for all potential allergy sufferers.

TERMINOLOGY

- Alpha-hydroxy acids (AHAs), glycolic acid, citric acids and fruit acids: mild acids derived from natural extracts remove the dead surface layer of cells, revealing the younger, fresher skin underneath and allowing other ingredients to penetrate to lower levels of the skin. Don't overdose on AHAs. If you are going to use them, stick to one AHA product only, follow the instructions, and remember more is not better in this case. If you have sensitive skin, or your skin becomes irritated, stop using them. Not all AHA creams contain moisturizer (oily skins may not need moisturizer). Remember, while your skin may look brighter within a few days, it can take up to a month for any results in fighting fine lines. AHA products make good foot creams and can help with the removal of callouses.
- Ampoules (sealed glass phials) administer the correct 'doses' of concentrated, and often very

expensive, products, as do capsules, pipettes (measure drops) and metered dispensers.

- Antioxidants: beta carotene and vitamins C and E combat the effects of pollution, the sun and cigarette smoke.
- Beta-hydroxy acids: also derived from natural ingredients such as willow bark, these work in much the same way as AHAs.
- Cerebosides and ceramides: plant lipids which are similar to the intracellular 'glue' of our skin, and can help retain moisture which is useful for dry or more mature skins.
- Collagen fibre: the substance in the skin which gives it its suppleness. As we age we produce less of it, leading to a loss of elasticity and smoothness. Whether applying it superficially will actually halt the process is debatable.
- Desquamation: another term for skin peeling through the use of mild hydroxy acids, such as Retinova. Reveals a smoother and younger looking layer of fresh skin underneath, but can cause irritation and sun sensitivity.
- Elastin: the foundation protein that contributes to the 'springiness' of the skin (see collagen).
- Emollients: the moisturizing ingredients in creams, natural moisturizing factors (NMFs).
- Enzymes: generally derived from fruit (usually papaya and pineapple), they work on the same principles as AHAs to strip back the surface cellular layer, but aren't damaging or irritating.
- Humectants: containing ingredients such as sorbitol, glycerine and urea, they fix airborne moisture to the skin, improving the effectiveness of moisturizers for dry skins.
- Liposomes penetrate to lower skin levels allowing deep, thorough and visible moisturizing.
- Moisturizers: containing 'emollients' or 'hydrators', moisture can temporarily 'plump up' the surface layers of the skin.
- pH indicates acid/alkaline balance. Stick to products which come closest to your normal level of pH 4.5–5.5. The lower the number, the more acidic the product. Avoid anything at either extreme. Soap is very alkaline and can disturb your natural balance.
- Pro-vitamin B5/Panthenol: a conditioning ingredient of both skin and hair products, which can 'plump up' the skin in the short term.

- Retin-A was originally formulated as a treatment for acne and associated scarring. A side-effect was the reduction of fine lines which led to the claim that it has anti-ageing effects. It's more concentrated than Retinova.
- Retinova (0.05% tretinoin): a 'retinoid' or vitamin-A derivative, it's a milder version of Retin-A. It's only available by prescription (not available on the NHS) and is to be used under the supervision of a GP or dermatologist. It is used to treat acne.
- SPF (sun protection factor): a rating to indicate how effectively a product will protect you from the effects of the sun (ageing, skin cancers). The higher the factor, the more protection given.
- Tretinoin: active ingredient of Retin-A and Retinova, its anti-ageing properties were discovered as the side-effect of treating acne. In addition, it fades patchy pigmentation and can regenerate collagen. It has been in use in clinics for over 30 years.
- UV (ultraviolet) protection: titanium dioxides are the most common ingredient used to block UV rays from the sun, slowing ageing and reducing carcinogenic risk.

For more information read *The Cosmetic Ingredients Decoder* which you should be able to find in, or order from, a good health food shop.

MAKE-UP

A flawless finish can only be achieved in good light. The general rule is less is more. Enhance positive features rather than trying to disguise points you're unhappy about. Blending is everything – avoid harsh lines. A natural look using neutral tones is an easy option for daytime. When making up for the evening, you can go for something more dramatic, but emphasizing everything can be overpowering. Strong eyes and more subtle lips or vice versa balance well. If you are going for striking eyeshadow and lips then play down the blusher. Carefully check your final make-up in an honest light to avoid unpleasant surprises, then check it in a flattering mirror under dishonest light for a confidence boost.

FOUNDATION
- Finding the right foundation for you can take time. The key is to pick a base that matches your skin tone and type.
- It comes in several forms: liquid, cream, sticks and combinations of creams and powders in a compact.
- It can either be water- or oil-based and should be chosen according to your skin type: water-based for oily skin, oil-based for dry.
- Liquid and cream foundations need to be 'set' with powder.
- 'Combination foundations', 'all-in-ones' can be applied with a damp or dry sponge. A damp sponge gives lighter coverage. A time-saver.
- 'Matte' gives a flat, powdery coverage which works best with oily skins. It should be used carefully to avoid looking overdone. Needs blusher to bring back colour.
- 'Semi-, demi-matte, or satin finish' has the coverage of matte, without the heaviness. Allows a more natural look.
- 'Light diffusing' contains light reflecting particles which can disguise fine lines.
- 'Pan-sticks' are coming back into fashion after their popularity in the 60s. They give a very opaque finish although they can be used more sparingly for the day – almost like a concealer.
- Tinted moisturizer/sheer foundation is a combination of moisturizer and transparent colour which works best for unblemished, even skin. It will not cover blemishes or dark circles.
- 'Non-comedogenic' means 'oil-free'.

CONCEALER
- To cover thread veins, blemishes and dark circles. You may find that a good concealer, sparingly applied, can replace foundation particularly for day use.
- A shade lighter than skin colour usually works.
- Mixing concealer with a small amount of foundation can create a much better match for your skin.
- Apply only to the blemish – blend in with a brush or cotton bud. Blotting with fingertip gives a more natural finish.
- Several thin layers are better than one thick one.
- Fix final application with powder: concealer on top of powder can look 'cakey'.
- For dark circles a creamy product works best: a

stick can drag, and a liquid can 'gather', emphasizing tiny lines.
- Apply concealer after foundation: foundation may give the coverage you need.

POWDER
- Powder is used to 'finish' foundation and concealer, and remove shine. It comes in loose and pressed forms.
- Use loose to fix foundation, and pressed for touch ups.
- Apply loose powder with a brush, or roll on to skin with a puff.
- Powder should never be rubbed into the skin.
- Excess powder can be lifted off with a damp puff.
- Loose powder can be messy – put in a shaker (improvise with salt or sugar shakers).
- Powder can also be fixed with a store bought water mister. Use mineral water in a spray bottle.

EYES
You can use eyeshadows, eyeliners and mascara in any combination to create a very wide range of effects. Once you've established your basic eye make-up, this is an area where you can really experiment and have fun. Colours go in and out of fashion – a basic neutral palette of earth tones (greys and browns) works for any skin colouring and any occasion.

EYE MAKE-UP
- Light shades bring features forward, while dark shades make them recede. Eyes set far apart can be cheated inwards by darker shading on inside corners of the eyes, blending upwards towards the eyebrows. The reverse is true for eyes set too close: emphasize the outer corners.
- A lighter colour applied above the pupil, close to the lash line, brings attention to the eyes.
- Wetting the applicator darkens colours for a more dramatic (or evening) effect.
- A layer of loose powder across the cheeks can catch 'stray' eyeshadow and can be brushed away afterwards without disturbing foundation.
- Foundation applied on the eyelid can even tone and fix your eyeshadow.
- Eyeliner applied all the way round the eye makes the eye appear smaller.

- Applying liquid eyeliner takes practice: to steady a shaky hand, support your elbows on a firm surface.
- A dusting of eyeshadow will fix pencil liner.
- Avoid leaving a space between lash line and liner.
- Frosted eyeshadows can be dramatic, but take care because they also emphasize wrinkles.
- Eyepencils should be soft, but firm. Always keep them sharp – very soft pencils can be firmed up in the fridge before sharpening.
- A matte white liner applied to the inside lower rim opens up the eye.

EYELASHES
- Replace mascara every 3–6 months: the container is a breeding ground for bacteria which can cause eye irritation. For the same reason avoid pumping mascara applicator in and out of the tube.
- Blondes look more subtle in dark brown or grey mascara rather than black.
- An eyebrow comb or old toothbrush can be used for separating eyelashes if they get stuck in clumps.
- If you tend to get mascara smudges beneath the lower lashes, avoid it and use a shadow instead.
- If you use an eyelash curler, invest in a good one and keep clean: cheap curlers can damage lashes.
- Curling lashes makes them appear longer and 'opens up' the eyes.
- Use curler before applying mascara: afterwards the lashes can stick to the curler and be pulled out.
- Applying false eyelashes can be tricky. A full or partial strip can be used, cut to size before application. A small strip, or individual lashes, can be applied towards the outside of the eye for a more natural look. You may find it helpful to use tweezers. Aim to keep them right on the lash line, fill in any gaps with eyeliner and use mascara for an integrated look.

EYEBROWS
Eyebrows frame your eyes and shape your face.
- Choose a matte powder or pencil matching your eyebrow colour, or a shade lighter – don't go darker.
- Use a pencil to create tiny strokes throughout eyebrow rather than one continuous line.
- Mascara, hairspray or gel can be used to keep stray hairs in line. Apply using a toothbrush or eyebrow comb.

BLUSHER

Blusher comes in several forms – powders, creams and gels – and adds warmth to the face.

- Apply blusher over foundation and under powder for staying power. A soft, rounded, natural hair-brush is the best applicator.
- Apply to the 'apple' (when you smile, this is the full part of your cheek), blending across the bone.
- Blusher can emphasize cheekbones – face contouring needs great care, but can be achieved using a soft brown powder a little darker than your natural skin tone. It's generally better to enhance the features you like, rather than minimizing those you don't.
- Too much blusher can be corrected by softening with powder.
- Gels: for a fresh, healthy look apply gel blusher where the sun would naturally strike the face – forehead and across cheeks.
- Beige, tawny and pink tones should be used for fair skins, warm brown and copper for almond and yellow skins, deeper shades of plum, fuchsia and auburn for dark skins. Orange tones work for redheads and tanned skins.

LIPSTICK, LINERS

- Prepare the lips by letting a lip balm sink in before applying lip colour.
- When necessary, exfoliate dry skin from chapped lips by applying Vaseline or lip balm and buffing with a soft toothbrush.
- Lip liner 'contains' the lipstick, and helps prevent lipstick bleeding into lines around the mouth. Bleeding can also be reduced by applying a clear 'fixative' over your lip colour.
- You can also reduce 'bleeding', and maximize staying power by putting on a coat of lipstick, blotting, dusting with powder and applying a second coat.
- Liners can enhance lip shape but shouldn't be used to make radical alterations: the goal with lip liner is to achieve a balance. Thin lips can be made to look fuller by lining just outside the natural lip line, and vice versa.
- Avoid lip liner darker than your lipstick. You don't need a lip liner to match every shade of lipstick – one neutral lip liner a couple of shades darker than your natural lip colour will work for all lipsticks except the very pale.
- Dark lipstick makes lips appear smaller, whereas the reverse is true for light lip colours.

- Mixing the colours you have will vastly increase your range.
- Tinted lip glosses can have a natural sheer effect if you feel uncomfortable with full lipstick.
- Lipgloss or Vaseline can be worn over lip colour for extra shine.

FAKING IT

If you don't like the 'pale and interesting look', a light bottled tan can make a good, year-round alternative to wearing foundation. It is now accepted that the sun speeds up ageing and can lead to skin cancer, and tanning beds do exactly the same. Carotene-based pills are considered a little old fashioned and are too unpredictable often with day-glo orange results. Fake tans now come in liquids, creams, lotions and foams. Choose whichever you feel is easiest to apply evenly. They are far more sophisticated than they used to be: streaky, strong smelling products are a thing of the past. They're certainly an easier, safer and cheaper alternative to a week in the Caribbean. Self tanners contain a tanning agent dihydroxyacetane (DHA) considered safe by dermatologists. A chemical reaction occurs in the epidermis to form a new chemical colour and it doesn't affect melanin.

- The key lies in choosing the right product and applying it properly.
- Experimentation is really the only way to find the right colour and shade. Before investing (and some are expensive) test as many as you can. Cover at least a couple of inches of unobtrusive flesh, and remember which product is which! Most take at least four hours to 'develop'.
- You can use preparations for the face on your body, but it's wise not to reverse this. Body preparations are generally a little harsher.
- Exfoliate the whole body and remove the hair from your legs in advance. Pay special attention to dry areas of skin (elbows, knees and heels) which can absorb more of the product and end up darker.
- Protect fair eyebrows with Vaseline.
- Spread on and massage in evenly.
- Wash your hands immediately afterwards.
- Until the preparation has set (45 minutes to an hour) watch clothes and furniture as these can 'tan' too.
- If things go wrong, you can always scrub the offending area with a loofah or bleach with lemon juice.

SKIN COLOUR CORRECTORS

Skins with colour imbalances can be corrected by applying their complementary colour. They are generally creams or fluids that can either be used on their own, over moisturizer and under foundation, or mixed with a foundation before applying.

- For covering broken veins, scars and bruises apply correcting colour to affected area only using a small brush or cotton bud.
- Some correctors contain aromatherapy oils aimed at the cause of the colour imbalance. They are calming and soothing for skin that looks flushed, and revitalizing for 'tired' looking skins.
- White used on pale skin can highlight, cover circles or make a porcelain or opaque base.
- Yellow: counterbalances red or purple tones.
- Lilac: counterbalances grey, sallow or tired looking skin. Brightens skin.
- Green (pistachio for lighter and olive for darker skin) used on florid skin, neutralizes warm tones and controls redness.

CAMOUFLAGE

- For covering scars, birthmarks ('port wine stains'), burns or tattoos. The same rules for concealer application apply, but you may need to cover larger surfaces. See also **Skin colour correctors**.
- Many camouflage products are available on prescription. Ask about them in a well-stocked chemist and then go to your doctor.
- Your doctor can refer you for a consultation with the British Red Cross who have developed a cosmetic camouflage programme. Local Red Cross centres have a beauty care officer who can supply more information
  The Doreen Savage Trust offers advice and information on covering birthmarks.

NATURAL BEAUTY

As so many of the most expensive cosmetic products today rely on natural ingredients for their most beneficial effects, it makes sense to turn to the original natural source. 'Fruit acids' have taken over the beauty market and salons now charge fortunes for the same simple ingredients available from your local greengrocer. Keep in mind that as these natural products don't contain preservatives, they will have a limited life. Store in the fridge and use within a few days. Oils and waters will last for several months.

SCRUBS
- Table salt (rather than the large crystals) makes a great body scrub. Follow with an application of olive or avocado oil.
- Oatmeal moistened with a little peach or papaya juice and honey makes a good face and body scrub.

EXFOLIANTS AND TONERS
- Papaya (for its proteolytic enzymes) is the magic ingredient of many new products, and the effects *are* remarkable and rapid. Cleanse your face. Swab the whole area with a small slice of papaya. Lightly massage the juice into your skin and allow to dry (the colour of the fruit alone gives a 'fresh faced' appearance). Leave overnight if possible, and rinse off the following morning. The enzymes speed up cell growth and renewal leaving the face smooth and soothed. Fine lines are reduced. Dry patches, small spots and irritated skin also respond well. Keep the papaya in the fridge and slice off fresh pieces when necessary. As you are exfoliating, don't do this more than once or twice a week unless you're targeting a particular problem.
- Pineapple has the same properties, but is more astringent, and so is suited to oilier skins.
- Make your own skin toners by bottling flower petals or fresh herbs in distilled water.

Alternatively, swab oilier skins with a cut grape, or a slice of fresh cantaloupe or watermelon.
- Mashed peach makes a good compress for irritated skin.
- Cold rosemary water makes a good hair rinse for dark hair, while camomile suits blondes.
- Cucumber or melon slices and chilled herbal tea bags make soothing and toning eye packs.

MOISTURIZERS AND MASKS
- Olive oil (scent it by putting orange and lemon peel into the bottle) and avocado oil are very rich moisturizers: add to your bath, but towel dry yourself carefully to avoid 'salad dressing' your clothes.
- Drops of cooled sweet almond, grapeseed or walnut oils soften the skin and make good day moisturizers.
- Dried cows' milk (scented with a few drops of rose oil) added as you run the hot water is a good 20th-century alternative to an asses' milk bath.
- Fresh avocado flesh makes a very enriching face mask, best suited to those with dry skin.
- A yoghurt and honey face mask is both refreshing and moisturizing. Yoghurts (particularly live ones) can irritate certain skins so test a patch first.
- Lanolin (or sheep's wool oil), a main ingredient of many lipsticks and glosses, can be bought very cheaply from most chemists. In its pure form, it restores chapped lips in a few hours. It can be used overnight for intensive moisturizing. Steam your face over a bowl of boiling water for it to really sink in. 'Hydrous lanolin' contains water.

HAIR HEALTH

The scalp is a continuation of the skin and therefore subject to some of the problems that beset the skin in general. Hair grows at an average of half an inch (13 mm) each month, which speeds up in warmer weather. The hair itself grows out of 120,000 hair follicles in the scalp. Although it is dead, its condition still depends on nutrition and a poor diet shows up very quickly and can even lead to hair loss. We lose 100 hairs on average a day.

TIPS FOR HEALTHY HAIR

It's possible to get your hair and scalp in good condition relatively quickly.

- Try to avoid washing hair every day if your hair is below your shoulders as it dries it out and strips the natural oils.
- Avoid hair dryers that overprocess or overheat as they can severely damage the hair.
- Stick to a balanced diet, reduce stress, get plenty of sleep, take food supplements (see **Health** chapter).
- Dab conditioner onto the ends of the hair before drying to prevent splitting.
- Look for B5 in shampoo ingredients as it is practically the only vitamin that the hair strand will absorb.

HOW TO DEAL WITH DANDRUFF

Dandruff is the most common problem for hair. The white scales are the dead skin cells shed by the scalp. Massage a dry scalp with coconut oil or use cleansing dandruff solution. Beware of strong dandruff treatments as they tend to strip the scalp and the dandruff will return.

DYING HAIR – THE OPTIONS

- Chemical dyes contain ammonia and peroxide which penetrate the hair shaft. They are semi-permanent and can last from 8 to 20 shampoos.
- Vegetable dyes coat the outer layer of hair with colour and are semi-permanent.

- Henna gives a permanent metallic stain; you have to wait for it to grow out.

HEADING FOR CHANGE

- You should always have a consultation before making any changes to your hair, particularly if they're radical ones. If you're satisfied with the consultation, book an appointment.
- Give the stylist a clear idea of who you are, and what you do.
- Dress to reflect your personality rather than wearing work clothes.
- Work out beforehand how much time you want to spend on your hair.
- Give the stylist an idea of whether you want a low or high maintenance style.
- Photographs are generally more effective at describing a style than words. Bring one with you if you've seen something you like.
- Always speak up if there's anything you're unhappy about.
- Speak up if you don't understand the salon jargon.
- Once you've found a stylist you like, stick with them for consistency.
- If you like the finish, ask the stylist to show you how to style your hair yourself, and about the products used.

HAIR REMOVAL

Bodily hair – outside the realm of religious edicts – is really a matter of personal taste. You may decide to tweeze your eyebrows or wax your moustache into an elaborate pretzel shape – the choice is yours.

BLEACHING

- A good solution if you only want to disguise rather than remove your hair.
- It can be done at home or professionally: contact your local hair or beauty salon.
- It usually needs touching up after two to four weeks.

- It takes time and can be messy. Stick to restricted areas such as upper lip or forearms.
- Sensitive skin can react badly: timing is important. Follow the instructions carefully if you're doing it yourself and try an inconspicuous test patch first.
- Always rinse with cool water.
- Fresh lemon juice in strong sun is a natural alternative: it works best for genuine blondes.

LOW TECH SOLUTIONS

Shaving
- It can be done quickly at home.
- Regrowth (as any man can tell you) begins pretty quickly: shave shortly before going out, or when you want to appear your 'smoothest'.
- It's good for the underarms and legs.
- You don't need to change the blade every time you shave (six shaves is a guide) – but you should be able to feel when it's time for a change.
- Shaving in the bath or shower will mean that the hairs soften: you're more likely to get a smooth shave and less likely to cut yourself. Using hair conditioner, bath oils or body cream will condition your skin while you shave.
- Don't share razors (particularly with a lover you met the night before!): any blood-to-blood contact can allow the spread of Aids.

Waxing
- This can be done at home or professionally: both hot and cold methods are available.
- Fine regrowth begins after a couple of weeks, heavier regrowth after a month.
- Generally used to target hair on the upper lip, legs and bikini line: the underarm requires a very high pain threshold!
- Prepared strips (less messy than the spread-on and gauze kinds) are available from most chemists.
- It hurts! Try a test patch before committing yourself to being covered with wax. Over time, it does become less painful. Pull the skin taut before removing the strip.
- Between half and a whole centimetre is the ideal hair length: this makes the whole process gentler and quicker. Trim hair if longer.
- Tweezing is a time-consuming (but very accurate) alternative, and can be used to tidy up stray hairs.

Sugaring
- It can be done at home or professionally.
- It is based on the same principles as waxing and has been in use since Cleopatra did her bikini line for Antony. A sugar-based paste sticks to the hair (rather than the skin *and* hair) which many find less painful than waxing.

Hair removal creams
- This is painless, but usually messy, time-consuming and the chemicals in the preparations often have an unpleasant smell.
- Regrowth usually occurs after about two weeks.
- After continued use, hair may be sparser.

PERMANENT SOLUTIONS

Both electrolysis and galvanic tweezer hair removal can only be done professionally. An electric charge is delivered to the root of the hair (in electrolysis via a needle inserted under the skin and by the tweezer method via a 'gel electrode solution') which is destroyed, preventing regrowth. As each hair follicle is treated individually, both methods are expensive and time-consuming. Several sessions may be necessary, and the tweezer method relies on the hair being removed at the right time in its growth cycle for its effectiveness. With electrolysis, it's extremely important to ensure that needles are sterilized (any needle can be an Aids risk). Go to a reputable salon and check on this beforehand.

TATTOOS
AND BODY PIERCING

Permanent tattoos involve injecting pigment under the surface of the skin. It will be swollen and scabbed for some time. Test first for allergies and always use a reputable salon. This also applies to body piercing. Tattoos can be permanent or semi-permanent. Permanent tattoos can now be removed by laser. If you are getting your loved one's name tattooed remember the tattoo might last longer than the relationship. Henna 'tattoos' or body decorating use natural henna pigment to dye the skin and can last for weeks.

TEETH

On reaching their late twenties and early thirties, the majority of the population suffers from some form of gum disease, the major cause of tooth loss. An alarming number of very young people are losing their teeth unnecessarily. Your gums shouldn't bleed when you brush – if they do, you may be suffering from a mild form. Some people are more susceptible than others. It's easily avoided and treated, but shouldn't be ignored.

- You should have your teeth professionally cleaned at least twice a year, more often if you smoke or have gum disease.
- Flossing before you brush is extremely important. It's more effective and less likely to cause damage or pain than toothpicks or dental sticks. Try to get under the gum line and up and down the sides of the tooth.
- Brush your teeth properly (most people don't). It's better to clean your teeth really thoroughly once a day, than several times ineffectively. Hold a medium soft brush at a 45-degree angle to the teeth and gums. A small circular motion should get the bristles under the gum line, removing the plaque that does the most damage. First brush the areas which are most difficult to reach. The brush should be in contact with both the teeth and gums. Massaging the gums improves circulation and therefore their general condition. Use a brush with a head small enough for comfort. Brushing too hard horizontally can lead to gum recession.
- Use bicarbonate of soda on a damp brush to whiten teeth.
- Avoid abrasive smokers' toothpastes and check tooth polishes for abrasive ingredients – with repeated use they can wear down the enamel on your teeth.
- Bad breath, can be caused by excessive bacteria in the mouth, food caught between teeth, digestive or dental problems. Good oral hygiene, brushing and flossing can help. If it persists see a dentist. Mouthwashes last about 15 minutes and mints don't really help at all. Test: Lick inner side of wrist with back of tongue and smell.

- If you're using natural toothpastes, it's a good idea to choose those which contain fluoride.
- Sea salt in hot water makes a good rinse after dental work, or for infected or inflamed gums, as does Golden Seal Powder (available from health food shops).

With the NHS you pay 80% of the cost of your treatment. Outside the NHS, prices and service vary widely. Beware of an unknown dentist. It's best to go to the dental department of a large teaching hospital. They have the facilities and are aware of all the latest advances and treatments in dentistry. If you're in a hurry, check to see how long it will take to get an appointment (sometimes the waiting list is over a year), then decide whether or not you can wait. Some of the hospital consultants have private practices. If you want to take this route, discreetly enquire among the students to get opinions on reputations. Contact the British Dental Association for more information. You may want to consider dental insurance to cover treatment.

COSMETIC DENTISTRY

- Crowns: dentists are now working with 'porcelain' which is so hard that metal reinforcement is unnecessary. As a result, they look much better.
- Plastic and ceramic fillings are replacing amalgam. They're strong and much better looking than a mouth full of metal.
- Bonding and veneers: a thin veneer is bonded to the tooth to cover discoloured or misshapen teeth.
- Implants are an alternative to removable bridges or false teeth. Where there is insufficient bone for a titanium screw implant, surgeons can now graft bone from another part of the body into the jaw to support the implant.
- Orthodontics: wearing braces is no longer the exclusive hallmark of the teenager. More and more adults are turning to corrective treatment. Ceramic technology means that braces can be very unobtrusive. This is a longer term commitment, but the effects can make a major difference to both bite and appearance.
- If you are having cosmetic treatment done, ask for a cast of your teeth and mouth to illustrate the effect of the planned work.

MAKE THE MOST OF YOURSELF

Dressing well is about understanding your body and developing a personal style. The key is preparation and confidence with what you wear. Understanding fashion but not necessarily being a slave to it; knowing how to be selective.

STYLE

Look at yourself naked and pick out the parts of your body you like, for example a long lean neck, slim ankles, good cleavage, olive skin, thick hair; everybody has at least one really exceptional feature. Make a mental note of what people compliment you on and ask your friends. You may have a great feature that you have underestimated. Once you understand the best things about your body you can begin to shop with focus which ultimately saves time, energy and money.

HOW TO TAKE ADVANTAGE

- Slim neck: emphasize with long hair pulled back or very short hair, a lower neck line, plunging V-necks, scoop tops or high, tight polos. Large and long earrings (huge hoops especially), shimmering moisturizer on the bones around shoulders to highlight outline.
- Cleavage: aim to either hint at what's underneath with a tailored shirt over a coloured or padded uplift bra, for example, or go for the overt display.
- Corsets or a very fitted dress or top will automatically push the bosom upwards and enhance the cleavage (even the most minimal can work). Emphasize the shadow between breasts with carefully applied blusher – any blemishes should be covered with concealer. Sheer/transparent tops work well for smaller breasts.
- Long lean arms: so often in social situations the body is hidden from the waist down underneath a table, so the arms can be a provocative feature. Always make sure that they are well moisturized especially around the elbow. Dry skin can look unattractive. Long, tight sleeves slightly over the wrists also add emphasis.
- Narrow waist: thick belts, jewellery chain, pierced belly button and generally fitted clothes can emphasize the waist area. Especially good when balanced with wide skirt or wide pants to emphasize narrowness.
- Hips: two schools of thought here. A lot of women hate their round hips while many find them really attractive. Narrow hips tend to look more athletic and good in trousers. Marilyn had size 14-16 hips and used them to devastating effect in a calf-length pencil skirt. If you want to minimize, buy a long skirt with two box pleats running from the hipbone vertically down. Use darker colours around the hips.
- Legs: naturally long lean legs are a gift and can take experimentation with dressing and hosiery (patterns, colours). Draw attention from the waist to the foot: high-waisted garments and heels will increase the line. The truth is that with endless legs, you can really get away with anything.
- Feet: summer is the perfect season to draw attention to them with strappy sandals, delicate anklets and painted toenails. Give yourself a luxurious pedicure before venturing out.
- Backs are as much about good posture and clear skin as they are about length. Generally women who can get away without a bra benefit most from low-backed tops and dresses.

LINGERIE

- The line between under- and outer-wear has never been more blurred. Slips, corsets and what look like big, schoolgirl knickers have been trailing up and down the catwalk for some time now. But not only do bras, underpants and hosiery affect your overall finish, they can make you feel sexy and make a difference to the outline of your shape.
- Get yourself measured properly. Most people wear the wrong bra size, or ignore the fact that it may change over the years. You may also find that your size fluctuates during your monthly cycle: don't get measured up just before your period.
- Most good lingerie departments offer advice.

- If you're investing in an expensive set of lingerie, buy two pairs of knickers whenever possible: they wear out more quickly than bras.
- Consider how the colour of your lingerie relates to what you are wearing, particularly if you want to reveal it.
- It's always useful to have a basic black, white, and nude set to build from, with (if you wear them) suspenders in each colour. It can be helpful to store pale and dark coloured lingerie separately.
- Don't use body powder if you're planning on wearing hold-up stockings: they lose their grip (which can make you lose yours).
- Consider how heavily structured underwear will affect the profile of clothes you plan to wear over them, and if you plan to wear see-through clothes keep the design/outline of the underwear in mind.

Your posture, or how you carry yourself, can totally transform your presence and add a couple of inches to your height. Exercises developed through the Alexander technique or Pilates can help (see the **A–Z of exercise options** in **Health** chapter).

DRESSING 10LB SLIMMER

Forget the diet, a sensible approach to clothing can knock 10lb off your weight.

DOS
dark colours
vertical stripes
heeled shoes
tailored clothes
a single colour
a long-line slim jacket
detailing down the centre
corsets and support tights

DON'TS
light colours, white, cream etc.
horizontal stripes
flat shoes
voluminous square shapes
a variety of colours
short boxy jackets
detail on the edge

SHOPPING

The general principles are that you do get what you pay for in terms of quality and cut. The rule of thumb is to spend more money on a few good basics that suit you (coats, jackets, trousers and a good skirt) and mix and match anything else you want to last. Train your eyes with designer clothes, even if you can't afford them – yet! The trend in high street stores of ripping off designer styles and selling them at a fraction of the price means that you can update your wardrobe with details which will only be fashionable for a season. Many of these stores hire young designers and fashion editors to help them with their ranges, and the turn-around is unbelievably quick. Once you know the 'must have' items of the season it's easy to track them down. Contact the press offices of high street stores to find out who's designing and where the ranges are available.

SECOND-HAND SHOPPING

Some designers get their inspiration from exciting finds in antique stores, junk shops and street markets, so why not go straight to the source and save a few hundred pounds in the process? One big advantage is that they'll be completely unique. Look for the 'three Cs': colour, cut and cloth. When faced with an overwhelming quantity, let the colour (or pattern of the fabric) draw your attention, check the cut and judge whether it would suit you and then feel the material for quality. Remember, older clothes were often made of far finer fabrics and with better detailing than today. Check for holes and stains. If it's too small, throw it back. If it's too big you can spend a little money on altering it and get something that looks tailor made. Most good dry cleaners will have a tailor on hand and the cost shouldn't be more than £10–£20. If they're really good you could lure them into doing a little moonlighting and design your own collection.

SALES AND SAMPLE SHOPPING

Find out when designer sample sales are taking place, or where the factory outlets are. You can contact magazines or get in touch directly with the designers. Information is more forthcoming than you may think. Also check on sales of final year fashion students: they often use cutting-edge fabrics and will (or should) have put a lot of time into their clothes. If you make the effort you should be able to get something unique for a tenth of the price.

TRAVEL

TIPS FOR FLYING

- A general rule is to reserve a seat ahead of checking in. This is not always possible but is worth a try, particularly if you have special needs.
- Check on which seats have the most room: aisle seats, seats near the emergency exit and the bulkhead seats on long haul flights are generally a little more comfortable.
- Phone before you leave home (or check Ceefax) to make sure your flight is leaving on time.
- Plane cabins are dry and can affect the condition of your skin, so always carry a moisturizer. Spray water onto your face to keep it moisturized.
- Drink a lot of water before/during the flight and avoid alcohol: dehydration is a major contributor to jet lag. (Hot water and lemon is also good.)
- Set your watch to the time zone of your destination and try to get into the new routine as soon as possible. Eat at the right times.
- Pressurized cabins can make your eyes puffy, so use eye gel to treat them.
- Neck pillows make sleeping more comfortable.
- Take vitamin C (1gm) frequently to stop water retention.
- Avoid tea, coffee and gassy drinks as they further dehydrate the body – if gas goes in it has to get out!
- Take frequent walks in the aisle to keep your circulation going.
- The body swells during flight so wear loose, comfortable clothing and especially soft shoes.
- Use airline socks during the flight.

DEALING WITH JET LAG

70% of those travelling long distances experience jet lag. Rapid travel over time zones can disrupt the natural rhythms of the body and can result in tiredness, disrupted sleep patterns, erratic eating habits, reduced concentration, etc.

- Try aromatherapy and homoeopathy: lavender oil, arnica (6c every six hours during a long flight and the following day) or cocculus (before the flight and every four hours during).
- Flying westbound has the effect of lengthening your day so avoid naps during the flight as these will prevent you from falling asleep later (vice versa for eastbound flights).

COSMETIC SURGERY

Cosmetic surgery is no longer a taboo subject nor is it the preserve of the rich and famous or women. Appearance is important: first impressions are made in 30 seconds and confidence is always compelling. Last year over 65,000 people in the UK had cosmetic surgery operations. Many have had excellent results but other operations have gone horribly wrong.

The costs have come down but as most of it is done in the private sector, it can be very expensive. The methods are more refined, and the average age of those seeking corrective surgery has fallen. Not everyone wants a 'major overhaul', some people simply want to correct specific flaws. Remember, cosmetic surgery is a business and wherever there is money to be made there are bound to be unscrupulous people: people who could leave you scarred for life. Contact the British Association of Plastic Surgeons.

Examine your reasons, your expectations, the success rate and cost of your procedure.

Don't
- Think that cosmetic surgery will fix a crisis in your personal/working life.
- Consider surgery because others want it or after an emotional upset when you are vulnerable.

Do ask yourself
- If other people notice your flaw, or is it just you?
- If it causes you pain, affects your health (large breasts leading to back pain, varicose veins, breathing or posture problems).

Region	Problem	Solution
Eyes	Bags or fatty pouches under eyes. Hooded eyes causing obscured vision or tired appearance.	Surgeon makes fine cuts along upper or lower eyelid crease and removes excess skin and fat.
Nose (Rhinoplasty) *Most common operation*	Big, broken or misshapen nose. Difficulty breathing, nostrils too narrow/wide. Unsatisfactory previous rhinoplasty. Too much cocaine can destroy the soft inside of the nose.	Realignment of broken nose. Resculpture of profile or tip. Reduction in size.
Breast enlargement *After Rhinoplasty breast surgery is the most popular operation*	Breasts that are too small causing psychological distress. Replacing a missing breast after a mastectomy.	A small cut is made in the armpit, around the aureole (the pigmented area around the nipple) or under the breast. Implants (saline-filled or, the controversial silicone gel) are inserted, either behind or in front of the chest muscle.
Breast reduction	Breasts are too large causing physical or psychological distress.	Part of the breast is removed and the nipple is repositioned.
Liposuction Body contouring	Persistent areas of fat under the chin, lower abdomen, outer thighs (saddle bags) and hips (love handles).	Fat is removed by suction, laser.
Lips	Thin lips, or older lips. Lips can become narrower with age.	Collagen can be injected. Fat taken from the buttocks or abdomen can be injected into the lips Removing a thin strip of skin from the rim of the lip causes the lip to 'roll out' as the wound heals and contracts.

COSMETIC SURGERY

Risks	Cost	Recovery time
Inability to close eyes causing dryness. Watering eyes. Undesirable change in eye shape. 'Eye droop' (untreatable).	About £2,000 for upper and lower lids done under general anaesthetic.	In ten days swelling and bruising should subside. Eyes should look normal in three months.
A temporary runny nose. Unsatisfactory new appearance.	£3,000	Three weeks. Two weeks in plaster or splint. Possibly several months before all the swelling disappears.
Asymmetry. Loss of sensation, particularly in the nipples. Loss of nipples. Ruptured implant. Hardening of breasts.	£3,500	Two weeks
Infection, loss of sensation in skin and nipple, asymmetry.	£3,500	Two to three weeks
If too much fat is removed the skin can sag irreversibly.	£1,000–£4,500	Seven days. Bruising takes four weeks to fade.
Allergy to bovine collagen if used but no reaction from your own fat. As it comes from the body, it won't be rejected. Results last up to one year.	£680–£750 for the upper lip only, £1,300 for both. Collagen injections are absorbed after three to six months and so have to be repeated which can be expensive.	Recovery time: the lips will be tender for up to two weeks.

SURGERY OPTIONS

- It is important to learn all the risks associated with the procedures. Don't pick a surgeon from the *Yellow Pages* or from newspaper advertisements. Ask your plastic surgeon the same questions that you would ask for any operation.
- Computers can be used to simulate the 'before and after' effects, but they can't predict your skin's reaction. Most plastic surgeons who do cosmetic work are members of the British Association of Aesthetic Plastic Surgeons. They will send you details of specific operations and their list of members.

Key questions

- How many operations does s/he do each week and does s/he specialize or do a range? (Specialists are a better bet.)
- Is a hospital stay required and is everything included? If not what are extras?
- Are before and after computer-simulated photos available?
- What are the side-effects?
- What happens if/when things go wrong? Can they be corrected? Will I be charged for a remedial operation?

OTHER OPTIONS

- Skin resurfacing: for superficial wrinkles, fine lines, acne scars, poor skin texture and brown spots.
Methods
- Dermabrasion, lasers, chemical peeling.
- Botox involves injecting a toxin into the skin, temporarily paralysing muscles and so preventing wrinkles.
- Sclerotherapy is used for varicose veins.

Don't have any of this done at the local beauty salon. It must be done by a dermatologist, a cosmeto-dermatologist or aesthetic plastic surgeon.

HOME

'A house is not a home', but it's a pretty good start. There are few things more disturbing than not having anywhere to live, and moving house is one of the highest causes of stress there is. On the other hand, finding a place you love and decorating it yourself can be one of the most satisfying things you can do with your time – and after all, it is where you'll be spending a great deal of it. Cost is usually the determining factor when it comes to looking for a home, but even taking financial restraints into account there are several options to choose between. Is it better to rent or buy? What's the difference between wet and dry rot? And how *do* you change a fuse?

The housing market changes constantly. It's affected not only by government policy and the state of the economy, but also by fashion. It pays to do your homework. This chapter covers renting, buying and selling. It outlines what's involved whether you're a tenant or a landlord and how the new laws affect your rights. You'll also find sections on everything that lurks under your roof from the electrics, plumbing and the faults that require major repairs, to designing, painting and decorating. With a little help, 'home' really can be 'sweet home'.

RENTING & LETTING

RENTING (short leases)

Renting may be more flexible than buying, but bear in mind that the law currently favours landlords. Renting covers everything from bedsits to flatshares (where you're less protected) to professional arrangements involving tenancy agreements. You need to be fully aware of all the legal implications before entering into any agreement.

FINDING A SUITABLE PROPERTY

Begin with letting agents or the property sections of newspapers. Most letting agents are instructed by the owner to whom the fee is usually 10% of the rent for the initial letting period. If the agent is a member of the Association of Residential Letting Agents (ARLA) you'll only be charged for the preparation of the tenancy agreement and administration costs. The letting agent is legally obliged to ensure that you're offered correct professional advice. If you retain an agent to find a property there'll usually be a fee to be agreed before you start. Try scouring newspapers and free papers for housing options.

You'll need:

- A minimum of a month's rent in advance.
- A deposit to be held as security for non-payment of rent or damage to the property.
- References from your bank, building society, your employer or previous landlords showing your previous address.

CONTRACTS

The contract/tenancy agreement should include:

- The length of tenancy: ensure that the term for renewal is written into the contract. (Include a 'get-out' clause which will allow you to leave without penalty for certain specified reasons, say for instance you have to move because of your job.)
- The amount of rent: this must be at a reasonable market rate. If you want to check it, call in the Rent Assessment Officer. Each local council has one available for this; however, recent changes have meant that you can only have your rent assessed when your lease comes up for renewal. An appeal body can investigate further if you are dissatisfied with the outcome (contact the Rent Assessment Committee).
- Your rights and responsibilities and those of the landlord: in addition to the rent, tenants are usually responsible for paying utilities, phone, council tax and television licence. Read the small print of your tenancy agreement. Landlords' responsibilities include major repairs of the property, maintenance of the appliances and central heating. If the landlord can prove the faults were due to the tenant's negligence you'll be expected to pay.
- A full inventory (a list of everything in the property from furniture, fixtures and fittings down to the last teaspoon). Make this at the beginning of your tenancy, documenting the state of carpets, upholstery, etc. so there is little chance of dispute when the tenancy is up and you want your deposit back in full.
- The terms, if any, of repossession, and the procedure for it.
- Before parting with any money, make sure that the landlord actually owns the property they're renting by checking all the documents are in their name.

Breaches of obligations

If the landlord is in breach of their obligation to you there are a number of options but bear in mind you could still be evicted even if you are successful with a claim.

- Sue the landlord through the small claims court under 'specific performance' which compels the landlord to carry out specified repairs. (See **Law** chapter.)
- Notice can be given to the landlord under the 'self-help scheme', with reasonable time in which to carry out repairs. Under this scheme the tenant can also have the work done and deduct it from the rent due. It's advisable to get three quotes for the work. Submit them to the landlord

with notice of your intentions should they fail to make the repairs themselves. Make sure it's absolutely clear that the repairs are the responsibility of the landlord and that the landlord is clearly in breach before taking this route, otherwise you could be sued by the landlord for possession, on the grounds of rent arrears.

- You can get help from your local authority under sections 79–82 of the Environmental Protection Act 1990. This is designed to prevent what's termed 'statutory nuisance', i.e. if the state of disrepair could cause illness or injury from, for example, damp, condensation, defective plaster work or electrical installations.

HOUSING ASSOCIATIONS

Housing associations are the country's major providers of new homes for rent. They're non-profit-making bodies established to provide affordable accommodation. 75% of people are nominated to a housing association by their local authority (which means that the local authority has accepted responsibility for rehousing them in temporary accommodation, see section on **Local authority** below). Lists of housing associations are available from most local authorities and housing advice centres. Contact the Housing Corporation, the National Housing Federation, as well as Citizens' Advice Bureaux.

The Housing Corporation, the government body responsible for funding housing associations, has over 2,300 housing associations registered and also produces leaflets outlining what's involved in renting through housing associations. The National Housing Federation is a body which represents around 1,600 housing associations throughout England. There are similar organizations for Wales, Scotland and Northern Ireland. SHAC, the London Housing Aid Centre, offers help and advice with any type of housing problem. Unfortunately, the demand for housing association accommodation is greater than the supply. If you want to get on a housing list you must be persistent, assertive and, above all, patient. If you have been accepted on to a waiting list either by the council or a housing association, be prepared to wait.

LOCAL AUTHORITY

The Housing Act 1996 gives a homeless person the right to temporary accommodation for up to two years. After two years the case is reviewed and if the circumstances remain the same the period can be extended. To qualify for temporary housing you must be in 'priority need' and not intentionally homeless, i.e. you can't have contributed to your homelessness by not paying your rent. To obtain permanent housing you must be on the waiting list. The local authority decides who gets housing, giving priority to

- people living in insanitary or overcrowded housing
- people in temporary accommodation
- families with dependent children under 16
- the elderly
- households which include someone with real medical or welfare needs
- households whose social or economic circumstances are such that they have difficulty getting secure accommodation.

TEMPORARY HOUSING

Any woman suffering from domestic violence who needs somewhere to turn to should contact the local authority or a women's refuge. Addresses are kept secret in order to protect the women living in them. Social services and the police can give numbers of local refuges directly to the woman in need. For immediate help call Shelter. More information is available from the National Women's Aid Federation.

RIGHTS AS A SITTING TENANT

If you pay rent weekly or monthly you may be a sitting tenant under the Rent Act 1977. You have no right to buy the freehold but you can be in a good negotiating position if the landlord is keen to sell with vacant possession. You can either negotiate to buy, or get them to pay you compensation to leave. It is an imprisonable offence for them to attempt to evict you if you are a sitting tenant. If you're having trouble get in touch with the Lands Tribunal for Arbitration.

LETTING

You can let your property either furnished or unfurnished, but the choice you make will affect your terms and conditions. Read the *Which? Guide to Renting and Letting*.

THINGS TO CONSIDER

- If your property is mortgaged, get your lender's permission before seeking tenants. Lenders may wish to approve the tenants as well as the type of tenancy. Many lenders add 0.5% to mortgage rates if the property is let. See **Renting your property** in **Money** chapter for more information and check your tax situation.
- If letting to a company, a company search is advisable and evidence of previous payment records is essential.
- Signed inventories held by both parties at the beginning and end of tenancy are crucial and protect both of you. They should be as detailed as possible, for example, note the cracks in the furniture and the extent of wear and tear on carpets.
- Remember to cover your contents with household insurance in addition to your normal building insurance.
- If it's furnished, the upholstery, fillings and covers of furniture must comply with fire and safety regulations.
- Gas and electricity meters should be read both at the beginning and end of a tenancy. All gas appliances need to have certification confirming their reliability and safety: it's illegal to ignore this.
- Tenants must take out household insurance for their own possessions.

TENANCY AGREEMENTS

Consult a solicitor for advice on the best approach for your situation. You may want to consider using a managing agent.

Tenancy agreements fall into two categories: 'assured tenancies' or 'assured shorthold tenancies'. The Housing Act 1996 also gives the landlord more powers than before and scraps the need for written tenancy agreements which affect the rights of a tenant.

- **Assured shorthold tenancy:** fixed term of tenancy for a minimum of six months with no security of tenure. Under this form of 'assured' tenancy, the tenant has virtually no protection at all. It's designed specifically with the landlord in mind. S/he is offered a guaranteed right to repossess the property provided the correct procedure is followed.

The grounds for rent assessment have changed: where previously you could apply to have your rent assessed at any time if you felt it was unfair, based on the condition of the property itself, now you can only raise the issue of rent with the Rent Assessment Committee on expiry of your shorthold lease. It must be comparable to other rents in the area.

- **Assured tenancies:** the tenant has several rights over and above the landlord and has some security of tenure. The tenant has the right to stay on as long as the landlord cannot establish a valid reason to require possession. The property has to be the tenant's principal home.

IMPLIED COVENANT

Both the landlord and tenant are bound by law to observe certain duties. These duties are considered so important that they are binding whether or not they appear in the contract and are known as 'implied terms'.

To be observed by the landlord
- Fitness of premises: the property must be fit for habitation. The landlord is required to keep the premises in good order.
- The landlord cannot recover his/her costs through service charges.
- Safety regulations: the fitting of gas and electrical appliances (not the appliances themselves).
- If it is furnished, the upholstery and covers of all furniture, as well as curtains, must comply with fire and safety standards.
- Covenant for 'quiet enjoyment': the tenant is entitled to live free from disturbance by the landlord.
- If the landlord fails to honour his/her duties so that the property can be classified as a health hazard, the local authority has a duty to apply pressure until the situation is remedied. In practice this can be an arduous affair. The local magistrates can also order the work to be done. Failing this, appeal to your MP, and get advice from the CAB.

To be observed by the tenant

- The rent must be paid according to the terms of the lease/tenancy agreement.
- The landlord must be given access having provided written notice 24 hours in advance.
- The tenant must ask the landlord for permission to make any improvements. Since 1994, once this is granted (and it can't be unreasonably withheld), the tenant must be reimbursed for improvements on leaving the tenancy.

RIGHT TO BUY

If you are a council tenant or housing association tenant you may be eligible to buy, at a discount, the property you live in. Not all properties are available and the majority of schemes are extremely complicated. If you are interested you must ask your landlord or local council for details.

BUYING A HOME

YOUR REQUIREMENTS

- The area: check out the property during the week, weekends and at night. How far are you from local amenities, public transport and schools? Check whether surrounding land is being considered for development. You can get this information from the local council planning department. Talk to the neighbours – you don't want the Addams family as neighbours (or perhaps you do).
- Space requirements: space layout is a main consideration. Can you separate common and private space? Measure your existing furniture: will it fit, is the layout awkward? How wide are the stairs? Can you move the furniture around easily? Is the storage adequate? Does the property get plenty of natural light?
- Energy efficiency: insulation of the walls, roof and floors will keep costs down substantially. Large north-facing windows push up heating bills, as do front doors leading straight into living rooms. Ask about maintenance for the heating: poorly

maintained systems are usually more costly to run. If it's a flat, heating bills for the upper floors should be cheaper as heat rises.

- Security: check the access to the windows, balconies, doors and the back of the property. Is there street lighting? Make sure the property is secure.
- **Freehold** or **Leasehold:** see below.

The laws governing the ownership of property are among the oldest in the country. To make a legal mistake while negotiating the terms of contract for your home can have traumatic consequences. It's essential to get advice if there is anything at all you're unclear about and free advice is available. Be sure to speak to someone who specializes in property law. Contact the Law Society for help in finding a specialist (see **Law** chapter).

LEASE OR FREEHOLD?
Leasehold

- There are at least two parties involved in the agreement: the landlord and the tenant. The tenant is granted exclusive use of the property (under certain conditions and for a specific time) by the landlord.
- All leases contain 'covenants': these are the duties and obligations of the landlord and the tenant. Some may be implied by law and these cannot be removed by either party. But others can be inserted by the landlord and specific to the property. It is essential to read the lease in its entirety (including sub-clauses) before signing.
- All leaseholds have time boundaries which can range from a week to 999 years. The longer the lease, the firmer the ownership. However, regardless of the length of the lease, the covenants must always be observed by both the landlord and the tenant.
- The property reverts back to the landlord once the lease has expired. However, the tenant is fairly well protected by the law, and may not have to leave. Since 1993, it has been possible (under certain terms and circumstances) for a 'long leaseholder' to buy the freehold (see the Leasehold Reform Housing and Urban Development Act 1993).
- The landlord can also sell the freehold to a third party but under the Landlord and Tenant Act

1987 they have to give the tenants first refusal.
- A 'long leaseholder' can sell the 'remainder of the term' should s/he want to leave. The new tenant must abide by the covenants laid out in the original lease. The landlord can object to the new tenant, but only on reasonable grounds (e.g. if it was clear that they would not abide by the covenants).
- Contact the Leasehold Enfranchisement Advisory Service (LEAS) for more information.
- Things to be aware of with leasehold properties: service, ground rent and maintenance charges by the freeholder of the property can vary enormously. You do have the right (under the 1996 Housing Act) to challenge them when they are proposed if you believe they are excessive or results are of poor quality.

Freehold

- The property only involves one party: the owner.
- You do not have to pay rent.
- There are no time limits on the ownership.

A guide is available from the Department of the Environment (DoE can give advice generally, but not on individual cases).

FINDING A HOME

Investigate the areas where you'd like to live and check the local newspapers for homes for sale. Identify favourable streets and draw up a hit list. The value of an area can vary from street to street. Whether the property is at the end of a terrace, on the top floor or in the basement can also affect the price.

YOUR OPTIONS

- **Estate agents:** most are members of national associations: the National Association of Estate Agents, the Incorporated Society of Valuers and Auctioneers and the Royal Institution of Chartered Surveyors. Choose the area you want, and get on local agents' mailing lists.
- **Auction:** usually different from ordinary sales as these can be repossessed homes or properties sold by the executors after the death of the owner. By the day of the auction you must have carried out all the usual preparation work: had a valuation, raised a mortgage and done the

conveyancing. If your price is accepted you will be expected to exchange there and then and pay at least 10% of the purchase price.

- **Homelink on the Internet:** several companies act as property matchmakers on the Internet using a database of properties from all over the country (you can also find properties in other countries this way). The National Association of Estate Agents operates a scheme through member firms called Homelink which puts buyers and sellers in touch.
- **Housing Associations:** shared ownership schemes. A scheme whereby you jointly own a property with a housing association on a part-buy, part-rent basis. It is necessary to be on the local authority's or the housing association's lists but anyone can apply. See the **Right to buy** section above.
- Contact the National Housing Federation and the Housing Corporation for more information. You may also find properties from the Property Sales Register or Link Up Properties.
- **Institutions:** by digging around you can come up with some interesting and exotic options.
- **Breweries.**
- **Church Commissioners:** the Church of England is, after the Crown, the wealthiest landowner in the country, with property ranging from redundant churches to basic residential housing. Look in local phone directories for the relevant numbers.
- **British Rail, water boards, etc.**
- **Save Britain's Heritage** for historic properties around the UK.

DIY SURVEY
(before you bring in the official survey)
- Check the orientation of the property. North-facing properties tend to be darker and colder. South-facing buildings are brighter and lighter.
- Look for flaking brickwork, cracks or crumbling on the exterior.
- Look for the damp-proof course at ground level.
- Look for damp patches on ceilings and walls: it might indicate bad pointing in brickwork or a leaking roof.
- Lighter wallpaper around skirting boards at ground level could mean rising damp.

- Timber defects: check the floors, are they springy? If so, they could be rotten.
- Dry and wet rot: if the property is old ask about timber treatments or damp courses. Find out when they were done and if they're guaranteed. Check for spongy fungus and mushroom smells.
- Subsidence is a common problem: look for diagonal cracks in the main supporting walls. Tops of doors that aren't level can be another indication.
- If possible, ask the neighbours if there are recurring problems with the adjoining or party walls.
- Look at the roof structure, both through the loft and from the outside. Inside, check the eaves for woodworm; damp patches indicate leaks. Outside, check for loose tiles and crooked gutters which might indicate a poor level of roof repair.
- Get things switched on to check they all work, i.e. heating, cooker, etc.
- If it's an older/period property talk with English Heritage about the availability of grants for restoration.

THINGS TO CONSIDER
- Why is the seller selling?
- How long has the property been on the market?
- How many people have already seen the property?
- Have there been other offers? If so, what happened to them?
- Has a structural survey already been carried out on the property?
- Are fixtures and fittings included?
- Council tax: how much is it?
- Ask about the heating costs and the age and service history of the heating system.
- Check the loft insulation and find out whether or not the cavity walls have been insulated.
- Water supplies: check both hot and cold taps run clean. Discoloration could indicate a rusting storage tank and pipework. Older properties may still have lead pipes and any water supplied by them shouldn't be used for drinking.
- Electricity: how old is the wiring? Anything older than 20 years will probably need replacing.
- Drainage: check whether the property is connected to mains drainage or has a septic tank.
- Check on any possible building and planning activities in the immediate area through the planning officer at the local authority.

THE BUYING PROCESS

Financing

You will find it useful to refer to the **Mortgage** section in the **Money** chapter. For most people a mortgage will be their biggest financial commitment. Shop around and get a loan agreed in principle.

Cost assessment

Check your costs: in addition to the mortgage it is crucial that you are aware of the overall expense of buying. This will keep you in control and ensure there are no nasty surprises, see below.

Budget checklist

This checklist will help you assess the total outgoings of buying, selling (if you have a property to sell) and moving.

Cost considerations when selling a property

Estate agents' fees
Legal fees
Removal costs

Cost considerations when buying a property

The deposit
Valuation fee
Independent surveys fee
Stamp duty (see **Stamp Duty** in **Money** chapter)
Legal costs
Connection of services
Necessary structural costs
Necessary alterations, repairs and redecoration
New appliances

Cost considerations when making an ongoing assessment of expenses (approximate)

Monthly mortgage repayment
Insurance
Bills
Council tax
Ground rent and service charge (if leasehold)
10% contingency

Total cost to you = £???

SOLICITOR/CONVEYANCER

• Find a solicitor/licensed conveyancer (see **Law** chapter): paperwork and legal checks are done by a solicitor or licensed conveyancer – someone specifically licensed to perform property transfer (conveyancing work). Contact the Society of Licensed Conveyancers or the Council for Licensed Conveyancers for more information and a list of members' names. Make sure that the work isn't done by an unqualified clerk. If you have problems, or are unsatisfied with their work, contact their council or society direct. If that fails, approach the Legal Services Ombudsman.

The role of a solicitor/conveyancer is to:

• Explain the details of the mortgage deed.
• Check the legal title or the deed of ownership attached to the property.
• Check for restrictions on property use.
• Check that there are no planned developments locally that might adversely affect the property value.
• Arrange local land searches to check the exact restrictions affecting the property.
• Arrange exchange of contracts.
• Arrange the completion and ensure that the balance of money is paid to the seller.
• If you're buying a leasehold property (usually applies to flats) the clauses of the lease need thorough examination as they are more complicated.

MAKING AN OFFER

• You need to establish the cost of similar properties in the local area, deduct from the price the cost of fundamental repairs (if any are needed) and weigh that up against what you can afford. Take into account the mortgage company's likely valuation, then put in an offer.
• Are you in a bargaining position?
• What's your ceiling figure?
• Have you sold your existing property?
• Confirm your offer in writing subject to contract, survey and (if relevant) completion of any other work the seller has agreed to.

THE RIGHT SURVEY

There are three types of survey:

1 Valuation

If you're taking on a mortgage your lender will require a 'Valuation survey'. This is really only a basic check on the likely market value of the property to assess the security on the loan. It may not note all the structural defects, and neither does it always give you the approximate costs of essential building work. Some mortgage companies offer free valuations or refund the cost of valuation if the sale of the property goes through.

If your offer is accepted, it might be wise to have a full structural survey done, particularly for older properties. You can get the lender's surveyor to do the structural survey.

2 Home buyers' survey and valuation (HBSV)

This is a combination of valuation and survey. It should identify major faults with the property and things that will need work and ongoing maintenance. It is not comprehensive and it is not recommended for older properties that require a more detailed analysis.

3 Building survey

A full building survey should give you an accurate account of the state of the property. It is the most comprehensive survey you can get. It will also consider work you may want to have done, extensions or major alterations. It doesn't include a valuation but you can save money by combining the two. Get the surveyor to make a detailed list of work that needs to be done, with estimates of the costs involved. An inspection can last several hours and it is important to give specific written instructions for the particular areas you want them to concentrate on.

FINDING A SURVEYOR

As a general rule it is better to get a local surveyor as they will be savvy about local conditions and peculiarities.

- Personal recommendations are the best route.
- Go through the Royal Institution of Chartered Surveyors (RICS). There is no scale of fees for structural surveys: the cost will depend on the size and age of the property.
- The RICS and the Incorporated Society of Valuers and Auctioneers now offer the Home Buyer's Survey and Valuation. RICS have a leaflet available explaining the options in more detail. They also offer an arbitration service which is useful if there is a dispute down the line.
- Contact the Architects and Surveyors Institute.

FAILED SURVEYS

If a lender turns down your mortgage application after the valuation survey, it means that the sale value of your property doesn't cover the amount you need to borrow. Most building societies or banks should tell you why and send you their report. (The lender is usually conservative when estimating the value of the property because they have to consider protecting their own interests in the worst scenario.) Go back to the seller and negotiate. While the valuation is normally conservative, their calculation of remedial work to be done is usually high. Very occasionally a surveyor will miss a defect, in which case they are liable to compensate you for the full amount of correcting it (covered by their professional indemnity insurance).

IF THINGS GO WRONG

If unexpected problems surface that you suspect should have been detected in the initial survey you may be able to claim compensation. It is very hard as you'll have to prove that the problems existed when the survey was done.

- A second survey may be necessary to determine exactly what the problem is. You should ask the new surveyor to assess whether it should have been picked up in the initial survey. Keep all bills and use it to build your case.
- Photograph the problem, if you can, or record it.
- Write to the surveyor and/or mortgage lender with your conclusions.

If this doesn't produce results go to:
- Arbitration, independent assessment of the situation (depending on whether the surveyor is a member of an organization that has an arbitration service).
- The Banking or Buildings Societies Ombudsman

service (if it was a surveyor recommended by the mortgage lender).
- Court action is the final option (see **Law** chapter).

POST–COMPLETION DUTIES
- Insurance: it is necessary to take out life and buildings insurance as soon as you have exchanged contracts as part of the terms of the mortgage. (See **Buildings Insurance** and **Life Insurance** in **Money** chapter.)
- Make sure your solicitor applies to the Land Registry to have you registered as the new owner. The Land Registry fee is on a sliding scale depending on the cost of the property.

SELLING A HOME

The price and time of year are key factors in selling your home. All estate agents agree that good decorative order and central heating help sell, as do original features in older properties such as fireplaces and beams. Prices can vary widely from street to street. January to July is generally the best time for selling whether privately or at auction. The autumn and winter months are usually slower.

PREPARING
- Fix any decoration problems: peeling wallpaper, broken tiles, etc.
- Remove clutter: this makes the home seem bigger. Hide eccentric relatives while prospective buyers are viewing.
- Make sure that the kitchen and bathrooms are clean.
- Create an ambience in the home: coffee brewing on the stove or fresh flowers are old standards that seem to make a difference.

HOW
Estate agents
- They usually charge a fee of about 1–3% of the selling price, plus VAT.

- Check that the agents are members of a professional body, either the National Association of Estate Agents, the Incorporated Society of Valuers and Auctioneers or the Royal Institution of Chartered Surveyors. They all have a code of conduct and practice, and a grievance procedure for dissatisfied customers.
- Choose one that offers a realistic approach to price and ask them to justify their valuation.
- The fees are usually lower if they are the sole agent. Give an agent a period of sole agency (say three months) and if nothing has happened within this period, advise them that you may wish to bring in others. Agents act in competition: whoever sells gets paid.
- All instructions to the agent must be in writing with agreed viewing procedures, i.e. who keeps the keys, etc.

DIY selling
- Why pay an estate agent when you can sell it yourself? 5% of homes in the UK are sold this way but it does take more effort.
- Put the house details together, gather a few estate agents' examples for reference.
- To set the price compare with similar properties on the market, same square footage, etc. For about £150 you could get a professional valuer to give you a valuation through the Incorporated Society of Valuers and Auctioneers or the Royal Institution of Chartered Surveyors.
- Put a board up for the benefit of passers-by. It should cost you about £50. If you put up your own signs check with the local authorities about the size allowed.
- Advertise either through *Loot* or *Exchange & Mart*. There are a number of property magazines which advertise homes for a nominal fee. Once you've found a buyer let your solicitor deal with all the legal formalities.

TIPS FOR NEGOTIATION
- Skilful negotiation can make all the difference in how much you get for your property. Preparation is essential. Try to gauge whether or not the buyer is serious. If you have an agent, avoid negotiating directly with the buyer. Always go through the agent.

- Is buying your home dependent on them selling theirs? If so, what stage has that reached? Are there other properties involved in the chain? Are they close to completion? All these things can hold up the actual sale of your property considerably.
- Will the buyer need a mortgage? If so, how much will they be borrowing?
- What is the buyer's time scale, and how well does it match your own?
- Exactly what does the buyer expect to be included in the purchase price?
- Will the offer be subject to certain conditions?
- Before you negotiate your own sale obtain a few examples of properties similar to yours and study their particulars. Use these as evidence to justify the price of your own home and ask the prospective buyer how they arrived at their offer.

LEGAL PROCEDURE
- Contact your solicitor before you put your property on the market, ask what paperwork might be required in the event of selling and put it all together so you are ready to go when the time comes (this may include details of your own mortgage, deeds to the property, etc.).
- If you accept an offer, subject to contract and subject to survey, then instruct a solicitor/licensed conveyancer to prepare and forward the necessary paperwork to the buyer's solicitor.
- When the conditions are all satisfied, you then proceed to 'Exchange of Contracts' which commits you to sell to them.
- They'll be required to pay a deposit at this time (usually 10% of the total price), which may be forfeited if they pull out. Once the deposit is paid and contracts exchanged, a time for the completion of the sale is set, usually 30 days from that point.
- 'Completion' is when all the transactions are finalized, the balance of money is paid, you vacate the property and hand over the keys.

MOVING

Approximately 1.2 million households are likely to move each year. Moving is near the top of the list of causes of stress. How can you make it as painless as possible?

HOUSEHOLD REMOVAL
- Most removal companies base their price on volume, cubic capacity and distance. The final bill can be higher if there is special packing involved or extra hassle such as three flights of stairs.

They'll visit your home and assess the volume. Remember to show them cellars, lofts and anything else that might affect them.

- There are two main trade bodies that can supply a list of members: the British Association of Removers (BAR) and the Guild of Removers and Storers.
- Get three quotes; they can vary widely.
- Get a written quote and check the small print for liability for breakages etc.
- Ask for a quote for packing: the amount may be a small percentage of the removal cost and can dramatically cut down on stress.
- Household contents insurance: make sure your policy covers you for accidental loss or damage during household removal. Insurance premiums for a move are between 10 and 15% of the total cost of the removal (may not include some valuables). If your insurance does not cover it, check that the removers are covered for your property while it's in their care.
- Tradition has it that you pay the full costs of the removal up-front. This is not to your advantage so try to negotiate a deposit and pay up in full on completion.
- As you pack, label boxes with details of their contents and the room they're destined for.

STORAGE

Removal firms can offer storage as well, but this can be expensive and you might need to take out extra insurance. Containerized storage (huge wooden boxes stacked in a warehouse) can cost from £3.50 to £20 a week. Try and inspect the warehouse before signing the contract as some are old and damp with little security. Also check the inventory of possessions stored and any restrictions on viewing your belongings.

DESIGN YOUR HOME

WHAT DO YOU WANT?

It's important to get used to the place and really live with the shapes and spaces of your new home before making any dramatic changes. The quality of space has nothing to do with room size.

- Assess where it succeeds or fails to meet your everyday uses.
- What rooms do you use as the focus of your life? The bedroom, bathroom or kitchen, for example.
- What are each room's good features and how can you highlight them?
- Assess what areas are to be used as private and public space.

SPACE AND LIGHT

Space and light can define a building and understanding them is the first step towards transforming your home. Don't make any changes before you really get to know it. Watch how the natural light falls and changes throughout the day. Make decisions about what is worth preserving or accentuating.

TIPS FOR LIGHTING

Good lighting works on two levels, the practical and the emotional. Both can be used to modify space and alter mood. Background lighting is responsible for making a space either cosy and relaxing or cold and clinical.

- It saves time, money and effort to plan a lighting system at the outset of building work.
- Background (overall diffused or indirect) lighting is the first step to lighting a room, and brings out the character of a space. This can be done with wall or ceiling lights, table lamps, floor lights or even task lights angled to reflect light off the ceiling. Dimmer switches make background lighting more flexible.

- Direct lighting focuses on particular activities. Make a list of the activities in a room, and then the lights needed, e.g. desk lights, reading lights, working lights in kitchens, etc. Think about glare, position and the surrounding surfaces and colour. Task lights should be manipulable.
- If you're stuck with an existing lighting system, think about new fittings and shades, install dimmer switches or use lower watt bulbs where bright light isn't required.

MANIPULATING SPACE

Work out where you spend most time. Make a list of priorities and use this as a basis to organize space. Make the most of natural light. Small spaces can be made to seem larger by aligning doorways and windows to create long views. Take advantage of external views. Lowering a ceiling in a hallway can make other rooms seem tall and airy by comparison. High doorways can also make a space seem greater. If there's sufficient ceiling height it may be possible to make a galleried area. In open living space raised floor platforms can help define a sleeping or kitchen area.

Colour and Texture

Colour and texture are the elements that help to create the emotional tone of a room. Think of a house or flat as a whole rather than designing rooms in isolation. Paint is the cheapest way to introduce colour, but use strong colours with caution – we tend to underestimate the psychological effects they produce. It may be safer to start with neutral or subdued colours as a background and then add strong colour in small areas. Or invest in a range of sunglasses with different coloured lenses.

Manipulating space with paint

Create optical illusions of greater or smaller spaces by using paint creatively. Warm colours (red, yellow, orange) can make a space seem smaller and cool colours (blue, green, lilac) bigger. Experimenting with small pot samples of paint on an expanse of wall is a cheap and reliable way of determining what you want, especially as the colours on the postage-stamp-sized swatches never look the same on the wall.

PAINT

There are two main types of house paint: water based and solvent based (usually oil based).

1 Water-based paints include emulsion, acrylic and water-based gloss. These are used for walls and interior woodwork
2 Solvent-based paints include traditional eggshell, gloss, satinwood specialist lacquers or paints for metals. Solvent paints are usually used for hard-wearing interior and exterior woodwork.
- Names for finishes are always changing. You will find emulsion in matt, silk, soft or semi-sheen. There are now one-coat emulsions: more expensive but with very good cover. Oil paint can be gloss, eggshell or satin finish.
- Some paints have added ingredients such as vinyl, polyurethane or Teflon to make them extra durable. Every surface needs an appropriate primer to bind the paint to the surface.

For more information about eco-friendly alternatives in paint call the Women's Environmental Network Directory of Information or the Paint Research Association.

Natural paints

Natural paints breathe. The walls of a house can get clogged up with the fungicides and acrylics used to bind emulsion paints. Go for milk, water, plant or mineral-based paints which rely on natural raw materials for their ingredients. Contact Auro Organic Paint Supplies or BioFa Natural Paints for more information.

TIPS FOR STORAGE
- The key to a tidy or at least ordered home is well-planned storage. Most of us vastly underestimate what is required.
- Begin by making an inventory of what you have to store and estimate how much space is needed to accommodate it.
- Think about access, what you use frequently and what (like suitcases or ski gear) can be stored out of reach.
- Exploit dead space: under stairs, in the slope of an attic roof, in corridors, under beds, etc.
- Built-in storage is more space-efficient than free-standing wardrobes or chests of drawers. MDF (medium-density fibreboard), chipboard or

plywood are usually the cheapest DIY shelving and building materials.

- Industrial or shopfitting systems are economical for an industrial look. Or improvise with things like second-hand office cupboards which can be resprayed in any colour.
- Hallways or corridors can be lined with cupboards or bookshelves.
- Consider making a small room or cupboard into a utility room for laundry, boilers, tools, etc.

Useful sources for design ideas
- Any good bookshop or library has countless books on design, styles etc. It's down to personal preference.
- Video shops for films with acclaimed set design: good source of ideas for colours and styles and the more extreme design ideas.
- *Wallpaper* and *Elle Decoration* magazines; weekend supplements also have home style sections.
- Art books for ideas on colour schemes.
- See **Directory** for further ideas and contacts.

PROPERTY VALUE

Good design and decoration can add value to a property. If increasing resale value is the objective then check with estate agents to see what really sells before investing in major alterations.

BUILDING WORK

Building can be dangerous as well as costly. You should get professional advice, although it's useful to know a little about the processes involved and who's responsible for what.

PLANNING PERMISSION

Planning issues are subject to the Town and Country Planning Act 1990. If your proposal requires planning approval you will send your application to the local authority's planning department where a democratic process allows local neighbours to air their support or objec-

tions. The planning department will consider the impact of the development, taking into account factors such as suitability and compatibility with surrounding buildings. It's a good idea to talk to the planning department about your possible application before submitting full plans. Your application will need to be accompanied by accurate drawings describing the scheme. Read the DoE's (Department of Environment) booklet *Planning Permission: a Guide for Householders*, available from the publications division.

PLANNERS

Define the parameters. Try and meet or telephone your case officer at the planning department; a specific person will be in charge of your street. Planners don't judge proposals on aesthetic criteria (this may be beginning to change) unless they're in sensitive locations. Try to develop positive discussions with them right up to the point where they'll give their recommendation to the committee deciding on your scheme. It can take up to 12 weeks from the submission of an application. If your planning application is refused, find out exactly why. Ask if they have any recommendations that could improve your chances of having it accepted at appeal. Look for successful examples of similar projects and reproduce them for presentation to your building planner.

What you need planning permission for
- Extensions on your home (although you are allowed to add either 15% of the size of the original house, or less than 70 cubic metres with certain conditions: the full details are set out in the Town and County Planning General Development Orders).
- Change of use.
- External changes: windows, walls, etc.
- Permanent structures, sheds (depending on size), garages etc. Granted planning permission is valid for up to five years from time of approval.

BUILDING REGULATIONS

Planning permission is not required for internal changes but proposals will have to conform to building regulations and will need the approval of the buildings control officer.

- If you're a leaseholder check the terms of your lease on building work: you may need permission from your freeholder.

GRANTS

If you live in a conservation area or housing action area you may be eligible, either from local or central government sources, for a grant for repairs and improvements. The publications division of the DoE produces a booklet called *Home Renovations Grants, and A Guide to Grants* is available from English Heritage.

- Improvement grants (discretionary): available to bring a property up to a reasonable standard.
- Intermediate grants: available to pay for any missing standard sanitary amenities.
- Repair grants (discretionary): local authorities award grants to housing action areas or general improvement areas. They're usually awarded to properties that have suffered major neglect.
- Historic buildings grants: English Heritage is responsible for awarding grants for repairs to buildings of outstanding historic or architectural interest. The amount can be up to 50% of the total cost.

ARCHITECTS/ BUILDING SURVEYORS

Architects can come up with creative solutions to building or space problems. During the briefing process it's important to set out clear parameters for the architect to work within. Points to raise: the budget, the intended uses of the property, and perhaps your views on energy efficiency. You should also make your aesthetic preferences very clear. Reference to images can help. A sound working relationship between client and architect can contribute significantly to the success of the project. Work on the property may involve obtaining planning permission and co-ordinating teams of builders. The agreement between client and architect may be an exchange of letters for simple projects but for anything more complex it's best to go by the standard form of appointment. Read the booklet available from the RIBA (Royal Institute of British Architects) bookshop called *Architect's Appointment, the Standard*

Form of Agreement for the Appointment of an Architect (SFA/92) or for smaller work *Conditions of Engagement* (SE95). Ring the RIBA's advice line to talk through your requirements. For smaller building works consider using a building surveyor, see below.

- **Step 1:** the architect will need to draw up plans and, if necessary, apply to the local planning office for the relevant permissions.
- **Step 2:** the building works will involve detailed drawings which may incorporate the structural engineer's and builders' drawings. The architect makes a 'specification' which is a detailed list of all the work involved. The builders then quote on the specification. Following this, a schedule of work will set out the timing of each stage, in the correct order to efficiently control the building work. These are all agreed and fixed in a 'contract', see below.
- **Step 3:** the architect will supervise the builders on site. They also oversee site visits of the district surveyor who checks the quality of the work and ensures that it all adheres to the building regulations.

It may be possible to use an architect for one rather than all of these steps.

CHOOSING ONE

Make sure your architect belongs to the Royal Institute of British Architects, the Association of Chartered Architects, and most importantly, the Architects' Registration Council the United Kingdom. The building surveyor should belong to the Royal Institute of Chartered Surveyors (RICS). Local knowledge, experience, as well as connections with the local planning department, are important criteria to consider. Check out what they have designed before. All architects should have indemnity insurance which means they have continued liability for buildings they have designed.

FEES

You can choose to impose a lump sum fixed fee for the work. Fees usually amount to 6–15% of the total cost depending on the size and nature of the project. If they insist on a percentage of the total work, try and limit it to that. Always get a written agreement of the fee structure from the architect, and the stages at which you will pay. For more detailed information read *Engaging an Architect: Guidelines for Clients* available from the RIBA bookshop.

SURVEYORS

The Royal Institution of Chartered Surveyors is the largest professional body representing surveyors. There are three types of surveyor:

1 **Building surveyors:** appoint one on the same basis as you would an architect. Building surveyors are concerned with the technical side of building and could be used for site supervision.
2 **Quantity surveyor:** it may be useful to appoint a quantity surveyor who will itemize each part of the work and calculate costs accurately. This allows the client and the architect to monitor costs carefully.
3 **General practice surveyors:** carry out measured structural surveys and schedules of condition (a report on the condition of the building). (See **Home Buyer's Survey and Valuation.**)

RICS publishes a practice note, *Mortgages, Valuations or Survey*, which outlines what each entails.

CHOOSING TRADESPEOPLE

Each year the Office of Fair Trading receives about 100,000 complaints about builders, so it's a gamble at the best of times. Consult your local authority works department – usually they know of reputable builders. There are a number of trade associations covering the building industry, but beware: membership is no assurance of quality workmanship. The Federation of Master Builders operates schemes which guarantee the work undertaken for a cost of 1% of the total price of the job. Check that the builder has membership for this.

- Electrical work: it is in your interest to use someone who is approved by the National Inspection Council for Electrical Installation Contracting whose members conform to the regulations of the Institution of Electrical Engineers.
- Plumbers: the Institute of Plumbing maintains a register of plumbers. Otherwise try the National Association of Plumbing, Heating and Mechanical Services. Make sure they are CORGI registered.
- For a list of other specialist tradespeople try the Citizens' Advice Bureau, the local Office of Fair Trading or your local authority.

QUOTES

- Specifications are either provided by the architect or you can write your own: it is a complete list of everything that needs to be done and it is the basis for the quotation.
- In order to be accurate and realistic the quote needs to be based on a detailed specification of the work which enables the builder to calculate materials needed, labour and time. An architect will itemize a detailed schedule together with a package of drawings on which to base an accurate price. Alternatively, a good builder can produce one with guidance from you concerning the level of detail. You can negotiate with the builder once you understand the way the quote breaks down.
- Budget estimates are not precise enough. They are a useful initial indication but don't give a bottom-line figure.
- A schedule of works outlines the sequence and timing of the work. Once you've agreed the timescale, ask the builder to produce a programme in the first week. This way s/he's committed to finishing by the completion date. A forfeit known as 'liquidated damages' (a pre-agreed sum for each week over the agreed completion date) is payable should s/he fail to finish on time.

TIPS FOR CONTRACTS

- Never pay a builder up-front, only when stages of the work are completed as agreed. This way you always have leverage if you are unhappy with the work carried out. You may pay a deposit for materials or pay the supplier direct.
- Respond to the written quotation with a letter stating all the agreed points including the completion dates, the final price for the job. Keep a copy of all documents and amendments: it's very important to keep control.
- If there are any extras, they all need to be added to the quote in writing, and approved by you. This control helps prevent any nasty surprises.

- It's general practice to retain 2.5% of the whole contract cost (you must agree this amount in advance) at the end of the job to act as an incentive for the builder to return after six months to attend to small details which might need repair.
- It's crucial to get advice on the type of contract suitable for your job; there are many. Two common agreements available from any law stationers are the *Joint Contracts Tribunal (JCT)* and the *Agreement for Minor Building Works*.
- List all the subcontractors used (including electrician, plumber, etc.), at what point they are used and the extent of their responsibilities.
- Check how busy the builder is and whether or not they have a job conflict. This is extremely important as you don't want to be left with half the builders absent on other jobs while your own schedule is delayed. Confirm that they will be able to complete in the time agreed at the beginning.
- Ask for a copy of the builder's insurance to make sure there is adequate coverage for the work and workers while it's going on. It's wise to speak to your solicitor about this whole area as it's both an important and complex one.
- Once the building work is completed and the architect has issued a final certificate the responsibility for insurance passes from the builder to you.

GREENER MATERIALS

The world-wide demand for natural resources is increasing with devastating effect on the environment. As individuals we can help reduce this problem through our choice and use of materials. You can make your position known when making enquiries or selecting materials for building or renovation purposes. *Greener Buildings: Products and Services Directory* published by the Association for Environment Conscious Building lists architects and builders who work with the environment in mind. It also lists eco-friendly alternatives for some materials. The DoE may be able to give you more information.

TAKING LEGAL ACTION

Under the Defective Premises Act 1972 all tradesmen have a duty to see that work is done in a professional manner with the proper materials. If you buy a property that develops problems which you can prove were due to incorrect installation, negligence, etc. you can sue (see **Small claims** in **Law** chapter).

ELECTRICS

THE ELECTRICITY MARKET

OFFER, the Office of Electricity Regulation, supervises the whole industry and can give you the names of various suppliers. Substantial savings can be made by really looking around.

THE BASICS

Electricity is supplied via a cable which ends in a sealed fuse-box usually located near the front door, under stairs or in a cellar. Near this you should find a meter and a household fuse-box. The fuses connect to circuits which serve electricity to different areas of the house and, depending on what it's supplying electricity to, each circuit will have individual fuses which may have different amperage. Each circuit is protected by a circuit breaker and when there's an overload on one circuit, the circuit breaker cuts in. This is when the house goes black, you can't remember where the fuse-box is and you force someone else to go out to buy the candles. The master switch can disconnect the whole system and should always be turned off when doing any major electrical DIY repairs.

Tip: on the household fuse-box mark which fuse/circuit breaker applies to each area or appliance. Make a note of the different fuses they use in case you need to replace them later. Keep a torch near by.

Electricity flows in a circuit – the incoming flow is carried through the red-coated wire, the return flow through the black and the earth connection is either green or green and yellow (the earth connection allows the electricity to escape if something goes wrong). A basic circuit is where electricity runs through a wire from the main source to the appliance (for example) then back to the same source through a different wire. This is a complete circuit. If a circuit is broken for any reason the appliance will stop working. You break the circuit by switching off on a plug socket. The Regulations for Electrical Installations published by the Institution of Electrical Engineers lay down the law for wiring in all buildings. The meter located near the household fuse-box is there to remind you just how much electricity you've wasted, to the delight of the electricity board who read it when preparing your bills. Bills may also be estimated, and if they're really unreasonable, you can delay payment by demanding to have them come and check the meter.

JARGON

- **Voltage (V):** this is the measure of pressure behind the supply of electricity which drives it to the various outlets.
- **Amperage, amps (A):** a measure of the amount of electricity flowing through a circuit to produce the required wattage for an appliance. Fuses are rated in amps. You'll probably find several circuits of different amperage in your house.
- **Wattage, watts (W):** the amount of electricity

consumed by an appliance when working. The wattage of an electrical appliance should be marked on its casing. Greater pressure in the wires (voltage) causes increased flow of electricity (amps) and results in more work done (watts).

ELECTRICAL OUTLETS

- 13-amp power points (sockets) are the most common form of outlet.
- Switched outlets are used for immersion heaters and central heating boilers. Their switches are often neon lit to show when they're on.
- Cooker controls have a switch to isolate them.

ELECTROSTRESS

This isn't the angst of trying to DIY the wiring in your house. Research suggests that electromagnetic fields (EMFs) from electrical sockets, cables and ordinary appliances such as TVs can lead to stress, headaches, depression, allergies, etc. If this disturbs you, turn off the power at the socket, or investigate supply-demand switches where the electricity is only there when you need it.

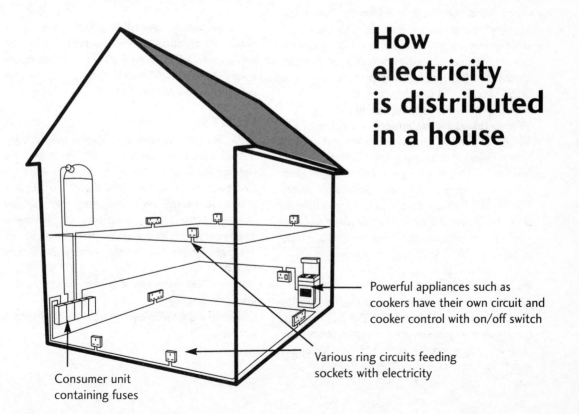

How electricity is distributed in a house

Powerful appliances such as cookers have their own circuit and cooker control with on/off switch

Various ring circuits feeding sockets with electricity

Consumer unit containing fuses

PLANNING YOUR SYSTEM

Unless you're very experienced it's probably wise to get a professional in, but you can reduce time and costs by knowing exactly what you want and how to go about it, including the placing of all fittings, sockets and the exact positions of switches. Get a written quotation before you give the go-ahead and insist on exact costs of all materials to be used. If you give a detailed specification that you've developed with the electrician, the quotation will be precise and leave no room for misunderstanding (see **Tradespeople** later on). Some things to bear in mind: individual lighting circuits for each floor, 2/3 way switches for lights in passage ways and lights on dimmers.

BASIC MAINTENANCE

(Where applicable turn off the electricity at the mains.)

Replacing a fuse in a fuse-box

- Check the home fuse-box and circuit breakers. A switch or button will be flipped indicating the circuit affected.
- Check the cause of the fuse blowing. Too many, or faulty, appliances can overload a circuit.
- Identify the correct amp for the fuse. Turn off the electricity at the mains before attempting to remove the fuse, and then replace (if the fuse keeps blowing, call the electrician).

5 amp (white) for lighting circuits
15 amp (blue) for an immersion heater
30–45 amp (red) for main sockets and cooker

- New fuse-boxes look like a row of light switches and are far simpler to maintain than in the past. When a circuit is overloaded, the switch simply flips off. It'll be the odd one out. All you have to do is flip it back having found the point of overload. (These switches often flip when a light bulb blows.)

Wiring a plug

- Plugs are generally fitted with a 13-amp fuse to cover appliances between 720 and 3000 watts, but check that you are using an appropriate fuse (the amperage will be indicated on the appliance). In some cases you'll only need a 3-amp fuse.

- Unscrew the cover of the plug with a screwdriver.
- Prise out the fuse if it's in the way of one of the terminals.
- Insert the appliance's flexible cable under the bar (the bar should clamp the sheathed cable not the bare wires).
- If necessary strip some of the insulation off the cable to expose more of the wires and do the same to the last centimetre of these wires.
- Connect the wires to the correct terminals: they should take the most direct route to their terminals and lie easily in the channels within the plug.

Brown to the terminal marked L (Live)
Blue to the terminal N (Neutral)
Green or green/yellow to the terminal E (Earth)

- If you are using two-core cables leave the Earth channel empty.
- Wind the tip of the wire clockwise around terminal post and tighten screw.
- Replace the fuse, checking that you've got the right amp.
- Tighten the bar to hold the cable in place.
- Replace the cover and screw down.

Electrical wiring, new circuits and ceiling lights should all be done by professionals – it can be dangerous to DIY. Check out *How to do* handbooks published by Reader's Digest or Collins for more detailed information.

LIGHTS

Regardless of the kind of bulb you use, its light output will be measured in watts. The higher the wattage the brighter the light.

- Compact fluorescent light bulbs, otherwise known as 'energy saving' or 'long life', use one quarter of the energy used by ordinary bulbs. They're more expensive in the short term but last ten times longer. They're not suitable for dimmer switches.
- Halogen light bulbs give a brighter whiter light: good for task lighting.
- Coloured light bulbs can change an atmosphere entirely.

PLUMBING

THE BASICS

1 There are two plumbing systems:

Direct; common in older properties. The mains pipe takes cold water straight to all the taps and WCs in the home, hot water goes via the cold water tank and the hot water cylinder.

2 Indirect; most homes have this system. The mains pipe takes the water straight to the cold water tank (usually located in the attic), and pipes branch down from there to supply all the taps and WCs. Hot water comes via the cold water tank and the hot water cylinder. This system is often combined with heating. Supply pipes bring fresh water to the taps and drainpipes take waste water away and if you live in a city it goes straight to the city sewer system, if in the country waste water may go to a separate septic tank.

A water meter and mains shut-off tap are usually located near the point where the mains supply enters the building. Internal stop taps control the separate supplies such as to the water tank and kitchen tap. The supply pipe delivers to a cold water tank, which feeds the toilet cistern and most taps in the house. Ball valves floating on the surface of the water control supply to the cold water tank and cistern. Pipes are usually copper or plastic, although in old buildings lead pipes may still be found. Check to see how your drinking water reaches you. If it's stored in a filthy tank, or the supply pipes are lead, you could get ill. Replace them if possible. Waste pipes are usually plastic and have 'traps': a loop of pipe filled with water which prevents smells returning.

- If you have a complaint about water quality, first go through the supplier's complaints procedure then contact the Office of Water Services (OFWAT) for further help.

How plumbing works in a house

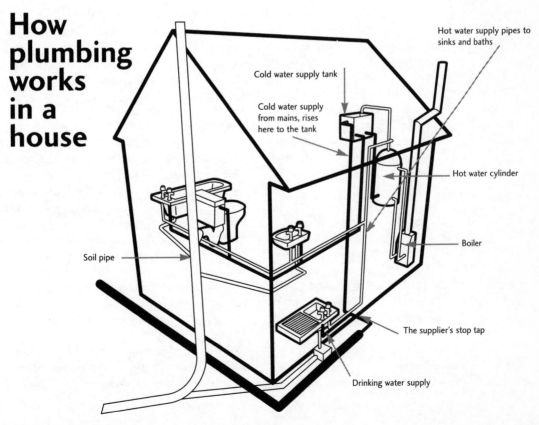

Hot water supply pipes to sinks and baths

Cold water supply tank

Cold water supply from mains, rises here to the tank

Hot water cylinder

Boiler

Soil pipe

The supplier's stop tap

Drinking water supply

- A water meter can mean quite a financial saving per year, although the charge for fitting one varies depending on your location: in some areas you'll be charged nothing, while in others it may cost up to £240.

HOT WATER

Domestic hot water and heating are supplied by a boiler which can either be free standing or wall mounted. After the water has been heated it's stored in the hot cylinder which you might find in an airing cupboard. Various fuels can be used to power the boiler and an immersion heater can be fitted to the hot water cylinder as a standby if the boiler fails. Some water heaters are gas powered or electric and they only heat the water when you turn them on which can be more economical but the flow of hot water can suffer. See **Heating.**

MAINTENANCE TIPS

- In order to deal swiftly with emergencies, or carry out simple maintenance jobs, you need to know where the mains and internal stop taps are located.
- Every bath/sink will have a valve that will close off supply of water.
- It's important to cover exposed pipes with lagging to prevent them from freezing and bursting in extreme weather. Keep the heating on at a minimum level in the winter even if you are going away for a short visit.
- Try and establish where water pipes (and wiring) are before doing any DIY in your home.
- Contact the Institute of Plumbing or the National Association of Plumbing, Heating and Mechanical Services Contractors for lists of numbers.

Leaky taps

If the tap is dripping from the spout, the leak is probably due to a worn washer (buy these from hardware stores and keep a supply at home). Using the stop tap, turn off the water supply to the tap. Drain the system before you start work by turning on all the taps and letting them drain dry. Use a spanner to dismantle the tap and then replace the washer.

Dirty, discoloured water

If dirty water flows from the tap investigate imme-diately. If the affected taps are supplied by the cold water tank, lift the lid to the water tank, check for silt, dirt or a faulty ball valve. Try moving the ball valve around, by bending its arm. If the dirty water is coming from taps connected directly to the mains, the kitchen tap, for example, then the fault lies with the mains supplier and you should report it.

Loose loo lever

If it feels completely loose and there is no flush, the hook that connects it to the flush might be broken. Take off the lid and make a new hook by bending some strong wire into shape.

Air locks

If water spurts from the tap or there are creaks and groans coming from the system, you've probably got an airlock.
1 Identify which part of the pipes the noise is coming from.
2 Connect the dodgy tap and the kitchen tap (or another cold water tap on a direct system) with rubber tubing or hose pipe.
3 Turn on both taps to drive out the air.
4 Repeat the process, if necessary, until the water runs freely. If you've had to use a long hose it'll contain a lot of water, so make sure you drain it all into the sink before removing.

Blocked sink waste trap

1 The U bend underneath the sink is usually called a bottle-trap nowadays. Place a large bucket beneath the pipe to catch the water and debris. Wearing gloves, unscrew the bottom of the tap.
2 Put a plunger over the outlet, pumping the handle up and down. You should force the water down the drain clearing the blockage.
3 If this doesn't work, poke a wire down the drain and then try the plunger again.
4 You can also try caustic soda. Take care when pouring as the fumes are poisonous and skin contact can be painful (it can burn your skin).

Blocked lavatory

Use a lavatory plunger (different from the standard plunger), which you may be able to hire from a hardware or tool supply shop.

WATER QUALITY

The trouble with tap water is that we don't know where it's been. However, what we do know (and wish we didn't) is that before it gets to us it's already been through several human bodies en route. It contains additives such as chlorine and aluminium nitrate to kill bacteria and settle contaminants, and whatever else it picked up from the pipes. If you do drink a lot of tap water only use mains supply through a filtering system (filter jugs are the simplest). Choose one that targets the particular pollutants in your local supply.

HEATING

THE MARKET PLACE

Fuel prices are increasingly competitive and vary across the country. Gas is generally the cheapest. Contact the government's independent watchdog OFGAS (Office of Gas Supply) or OFFER (Office of Electricity Regulations) for lists of companies offering services: there's a vast range available and it is worth investigating. Any cowboy can call themselves a plumber for heating and ventilation, but using a member of one of the trade associations does offer some protection.

There are two main types of central heating systems: 'wet' or radiator systems and 'dry' or warm air systems. Before deciding which type of heating you want, check the pros and cons of the different systems available, the various fuels (see below) and different methods of distribution.

'Wet' heating systems: which use hot water. Water is supplied via the cold water storage tank. The hot water cylinder is heated by the boiler, which pumps hot water through to radiators or heaters and then returns to the boiler. The flow is maintained by a pump and controlled by valves. It can be linked to a hot water system and run on any type of fuel: gas, electricity or solid

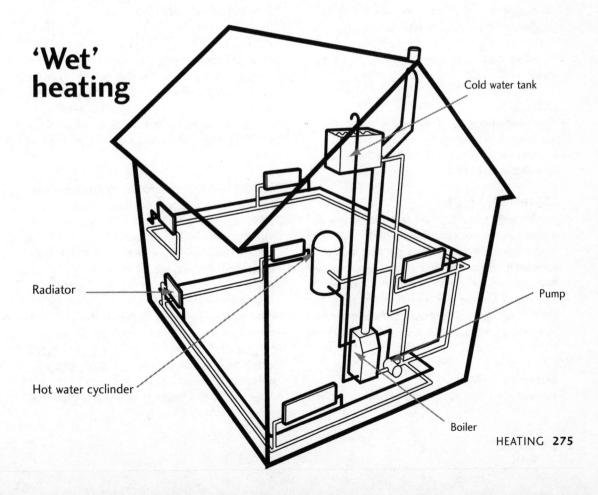

'Wet' heating

Cold water tank

Radiator

Pump

Hot water cyclinder

Boiler

fuels which require a chimney flue. The size of boiler will reflect the size of the property and the number of radiators required. All boilers should be approved by the relevant organizations.

'Dry' warm-air systems: air is heated and blown by fan through ducts in the floors which are controlled by shutters. Remember though that while you can linger over the air-ducts looking like Marilyn Monroe, they can't be used for heating water, and controlling room temperatures is difficult.

OTHER HEATING OPTIONS

• Electric storage radiators: each radiator is a self-contained heat source. This system doesn't allow a great deal of control over room temperature, but benefits from cheap-rate electricity.
• Boilers: old gas, oil and solid fuel boilers are floor standing and need a flue (like a chimney flue) to remove waste gases. Modern wall-mounted gas boilers have a balanced flue, they don't need a chimney and can be fitted to outside walls. A condensing boiler is compact and energy efficient, but expensive at the outset. Call the Confederation for the Registration of Gas Installers (CORGI) for advice.

JARGON

• The programmer: central control which determines when heating works and where.
• Thermostat: switch which controls the temperature of the water from the boiler.

MAINTENANCE

Regular annual servicing will keep gas boilers and oil-fired installations running efficiently. The work involved is quite complex, so it's wise to have a contract for regular servicing. Most gas companies have contract schemes for boilers. Contact the National Association of Plumbing, Heating and Mechanical Services Contractors, the Heating and Ventilating Contractors Association or the Home Heating Linkline for lists of registered plumbers.

Bleeding a radiator

Trapped air stops circulation of the water and prevents the radiator from heating up properly. This is a common problem, but releasing the air is simple. Each radiator has a bleed valve on its top corner. You'll need a key for opening it and if you didn't get one when the system was installed you can buy one from a DIY shop. (If the valve has been blocked with paint, clear it with wire.) Turn the key anti-clockwise about a quarter of a turn and the air will escape (a hissing sound). When a dribble of water appears close the valve again.

FUELS FOR CENTRAL HEATING

• **Gas:** the cheapest fuel for heating, especially if you install a condensing boiler. Always use a member of the Confederation for the Registration of Gas Installers (CORGI).
• **Electricity:** clean and easy to install, but expensive for heating.
• **Oil:** most commonly found in blocks of flats. Contact OFTEC (Oil Firing Technical Association for the Petroleum Industry).
• **Solid fuel:** boiler heats both water for taps and radiators, but requires high maintenance. Contact the Solid Fuel Advisory Service for information.

ENERGY EFFICIENCY

Hot water and heating use about 60% of the energy in the home. Small saving measures can be a big help to the environment. Burning fossil fuels (oil, coal, gas and petrol) releases carbon dioxide into the atmosphere. Over a quarter of the CO_2 produced in the UK comes from energy used in the home.

Reducing heat loss contributes to an energy efficient home. Of the heat you lose, approximately 35% is lost through walls, 15% in draughts, 10% through windows, 15% through floors and 25% through the roof. There are 33 Local Energy Advice centres set up nationwide to advise people on how to save energy, and grants are available under the Department of Environment's Home Energy Efficiency Scheme (HEES). The grants can cover better loft insulation and draughtproofing, for example. Discretionary minor works' grants are also available from your local council. House renovation grants cover part of the cost of insulating your house and putting in new heating systems, but this is discretionary.

- Get an assessment on how energy efficient your home is. Contact the Energy Saving Trust (EST) for a free survey and advice. The National Energy Service also offer a service. Contact the Energy Efficiency Office for booklets, and local Energy Advice Centres offer a free help service.

SAVING ENERGY

- Fit a programmer and thermostat to your heating system. You may need to take a degree to learn how to use them but they will control your heating precisely.
- Turn the heating down a degree or two.
- Insulation: increase the depth of loft insulation to at least 6 inches (150mm). Insulate walls externally and internally. Contact the Draughtproofing Advisory Association for more advice. Insulating your hot water tank and pipes can lower bills.
- Consider double glazing (expensive) or buy a clear film from DIY shops which can be stretched across window frames (preferably of rooms you don't often use because it looks pretty tacky) keeping heat in and reducing condensation.
- Lighting: change to energy-saving light bulbs.
- Use the 40°C cycle on the washing machine.
- Put foil behind radiators to reflect heat back into the room.
- Thermostatic radiator valves help control precise room temperatures.
- Appliances: choose energy efficient appliances by looking at labels for energy ratings.
- Don't leave appliances on standby: they can use up to a third of the power they normally need.

SOLAR POWER

The sun shines more on the UK than most people imagine. Each year we receive about 60% as much solar radiation as at the equator. Using the sun's power means cutting down on the use of fossil fuels and minimizing the detrimental effects on the environment. There are between 40,000–50,000 domestic solar water heating systems in the UK and about 1,800 new ones are installed each year. Systems can cost thousands of pounds, but savings are made in the long term.

There are three main types:

1 Solar panels, which use the sun's energy to provide domestic hot water.
2 Photovoltaic cells, which convert light energy to electricity.
3 Passive solar power, which involves the overall design and orientation of the building to make the best use of the sun's energy.

Many solar power companies belong to the Solar Trade Association which has its own code of practice. The UK Solar Energy Society also provides information on alternative systems. For information, publications and courses contact the Centre for Alternative Technology.

MAINTEN-ANCE

CLEANING TIPS

Our passion for cleaning has serious environmental repercussions though most cleaning products biodegrade within a couple of weeks. Read the packet carefully and opt where possible for eco-friendly products. There is general confusion about which chemicals are dangerous and which are not. Although it's impossible to avoid chemicals altogether, you can reduce your exposure by opting for simple, non-toxic alternatives. **Call the Women's Environmental Network Directory of Information for advice on the latest eco-friendly products.**

- Avoid buying cleaning products in aerosol cans.
- Avoid air fresheners: some irritate the mucous lining of the nasal passages. Use natural air fresheners such as scented candles.
- Bicarbonate of soda serves as a great cleaning agent, a scouring powder and a cleaning solution.
- To clean brass: use lemon juice or white vinegar mixed with bicarbonate of soda.
- Carpet cleaning: use white vinegar in boiling water for stubborn stains.

- Descaling kettles: fill with 1 part water to 1 part vinegar and bring to the boil.
- Dishwashing powder: make your own using 1 part borax with 1 part bicarbonate of soda.
- Drains: use washing soda crystals dissolved in boiling water.
- Dry cleaning: many chemicals are used, the two most common are too long to mention. Try washing by hand with mild soapflakes – most clothes can be cleaned this way.
- Floor polish: for wooden floors use wax polish.
- Glasses: use stewed tea leaves and boiling water. This solution can also be used for cleaning glass and furniture.
- Oven cleaners: use a paste made from bicarbonate of soda, water, washing up liquid and borax.
- Pans: soak in salt water overnight and bring to the boil next day.
- Rust: usually shifts if you use lemon juice and salt.
- Silver: soak articles in a saucepan containing hot water, a small piece of aluminium foil and a tablespoon of washing soda.
- Toilets: use borax and vinegar-based products to clean loos.
- Windows: use a mixture of vinegar and water and polish with newspaper.
- Washing-up liquid: use as little as possible and top up with a couple of tablespoons of distilled white vinegar to cut grease.

GUIDE TO STAIN REMOVAL

Always test a hidden area of the fabric for colour-fastness. Some fabrics react better to stain removal than others. Wool, for example, is absorbent so stains can be difficult to remove, while polyester is relatively stain resistant.
- Ball-point ink: methylated spirits or alcohol.
- Blood: a solution of one part borax to eight parts water will deal with a multitude of stains including blood, coffee and mud.
- Chewing gum: rub with an ice cube and crumble off. Try peanut butter on chewing gum in hair.
- Chocolate: turpentine or alcohol.
- Coffee and tea: methylated spirits followed by usual soap powders.
- Fruit: methylated spirits.
- Gravy and make-up (foundation): use a pre-wash/pre-soak powder then wash as normal.

- Lipstick: turpentine or alcohol.
- Oil-paint: turpentine then soap powder.
- Oil: smear in starch and then brush off after a while.
- Perspiration: dab with a solution of three teaspoons of white vinegar to half a pint of water and leave for five minutes. Soak in biological detergent then wash normally.
- Wax: put kitchen paper towels over the candle wax and iron. Paper will absorb the wax. Never apply the iron directly to the wax.
- Wine: try first with salt and soda water, then try borax and soap, finally wash.

LAUNDRY TIPS
- Put stockings, tights and lingerie in an old pillowcase to prevent them from tangling or snagging in the washing machine.
- Avoid leaving damp items in a linen basket for more than 24 hours or mildew stains may form and they're impossible to remove.
- Give dusty bedspreads and curtains a pre-wash soak to loosen dirt.
- Turn knitted fabrics, corduroys and vintage denims inside out before washing.
- If whites turn grey, rewash using 1 more cup of detergent, or soak fabrics in a colour-run remover.
- If your clothes have a yellow taint, rewash with a whitener product.
- Hard towels, stiff fabric: soak in water softener solution, rinse and rewash using fabric softener.
- White streaks or residue on fabrics: soak in water softener solution and rewash using fabric softener with detergent.

BACK OF THE PACKET
- Green washing products usually do not contain phosphates, optical brighteners or perfume.
- Biological: contains enzymes to loosen stains, can cause skin reactions.
- Non-biological: does not contain enzymes, can be less effective at removing stains.
- Biodegradable: the detergent breaks down naturally when you rinse it away.
- Phosphates: soften the water to improve cleaning.
- Perborate bleach/sodium percarbonate bleach: helps remove food stains and is not harmful to the environment.

For further advice and information contact Dylon International who have a consumer helpline. The Home Laundry Consultative Council offers advice on laundering, while the Fabric Care Research Association give advice on dry cleaning.

ALLERGIES IN THE HOME

One in ten children suffers from asthma. Doctors believe that 80% of allergic asthma is irritated by house-dust mites. These microscopic creatures live on the dead skin cells that make up 80% of household dust. They thrive in carpets, upholstery and curtains and, even worse, 90% of them live in beds and bedding.

- Clinical studies suggest that encasing the mattress and pillow on the bed with a special microporous cover helps reduce the presence of house-dust mites.
- Ensure thorough vacuuming on curtains, upholstery and carpets. There are special anti-allergic vacuum cleaners available.
- Dust mites cannot survive extreme cold. Believe it or not, people have treated their bedlinen with liquid nitrogen which has a temperature of −196°C, and this has proved to be very effective.
- Choose synthetic-filled pillows and duvets or cotton blankets that can be washed at more than 58°C (hot enough to kill).
- Use a damp cloth when dusting, it keeps airborne dust to a minimum.
- Choose machine-washable soft toys and wash regularly; put them in the deep freeze overnight.
- Asthma sufferers may be exempt from paying VAT on some products.

Contact the National Asthma Campaign or the British Allergy Foundation for more information.

RECYCLING

An average individual in the UK throws away one tonne of rubbish each year including plastics, metals, glass, paper, textiles and food wastes. Recycling should save energy and reduce water consumption and resources. Most local councils have recycling facilities. Check what range of facilities is available.

- Cans of soft drinks and beer make up 9% of the average household rubbish. Half are made from tin-plated steel and half from aluminium.

Recycling them can save vast amounts of energy that is required to produce the metal.

- Plastic waste makes up between 7% and 11% of domestic rubbish. Plastic takes centuries to decompose and it is difficult to recycle. Wherever possible, try to use refillable containers, and avoid products that come with lots of plastic packaging.
- Bottles: 28% of glass bottles/containers are recycled. They are relatively easy to recycle. Supermarkets tend to provide facilities for this.
- Paper: a large proportion of waste paper could be recycled. It saves trees and reduces energy consumption.

TIPS FOR RECYCLING

- Separate your rubbish; contact your local council to find out when different rubbish is collected.
- Cut down on packaging at shops: after you've bought something hand the extra packaging (e.g. carrier bag) back to the store. This is completely legal, and can be quite entertaining.

DOMESTIC APPLIANCES

Domestic appliances account for a large proportion of your energy bills. Choosing energy-efficient appliances/products can save a considerable amount of money. Look for an energy consumption rating label; the performance rating is also included on the label (EU legislation). Ratings range between A and G, A being the most economical for energy use. Not all appliances/products have these labels yet. When it comes to choosing, the Consumer Association publishes a series of magazines called *Which?* in which they make detailed comparisons of appliances and machines. You will find *Which?* in your local library. Also try the Women's Environmental Network Directory which has a large database on eco-friendly products.

If you pay by credit card for an appliance or item that costs more than £100 the Consumer Credit Card Act 1974 makes a credit card company jointly liable with a trader for a faulty item, so you can claim your money back from either one of them. Try the shop first and be persistent, reminding them of their legal obligation. This does not include American Express, Connect and Switch.

GUARANTEES/WARRANTIES

Electrical products should be getting more reliable, but in fact, millions of electrical appliances are dumped each year due to the hassle or expense associated with repairing them. We take out five million extended warranties each year. As a consumer under the Sale of Goods Act 1994 you are protected when buying goods that don't perform as they should: 'satisfactory quality' is the term they use. Most new appliances come with a 12-month guarantee and you can also take out extended cover (warranty). See **Law** chapter for more advice on consumer law.

To get the best deal for your money

- Check that the warranty is backed by an insurance company.
- Shop around for the best place to buy. Sometimes small independents offer better warranty deals.
- Check with the manufacturers (who usually offer the best deals): they may offer an extended warranty.
- Make sure you're not paying for cover twice. Some retailers add extra cover which you may already be paying for under your house contents insurance. However, accidental damage insurance might be useful.
- Use the warranty to bargain. Ask them for the price without a warranty or ask the price of the warranty itself and do the maths for them. Salespeople get an average of 30–40% commission on warranties.

CALLING OUT ENGINEERS

- Time is charged in slots. A complicated job done by the manufacturer's service engineer may end up costing more than if you had used a local engineer.
- Nationwide service companies (Bosch, Siemens,

Neff, Curry's) have their own service fleet for each region. Check how many brands the company services: it's important that they carry the right parts for your machine.

RENTING

If you don't want the hassle of repairs consider renting appliances. Insurance against accidental damage, and payment protection in case of illness and unemployment may be thrown in as part of the package.

BREAKDOWNS

The first things to check when an appliance stops working are loss of electricity from the power supply or a blown fuse. Have manuals handy to check the position of various parts. Most often the cause of breakdown can be traced to worn parts or blocked pipes. If dealing with electrics, always make sure the equipment is disconnected from the mains before you touch it. If the fault is not immediately apparent, call an engineer.

TRADES-PEOPLE

Everyone has a horror story to tell you about shoddy workmanship, delays and escalating costs. Anybody can set up as a builder or trades-person without qualifications or legal restriction (except where safety is a factor). There are prop-erly skilled people around, but the trick is to find them, remain in control and keep costs down. Ensuring that tradespeople are associated with the relevant trade bodies will give you some protection if things go wrong. Ring up the orga-nization and double-check their credentials. You should also ask about the trade association's code of practice and whether or not they have a conciliation service. Cover does vary, but they should give you some recourse if things go wrong.

Most of the major things that need repair and treatment like subsidence, damp, etc. need professional advice. A little knowledge about what the causes are and the treatment will help you feel a little more in control of the process.

DAMP

15% of homes are affected by damp. If you want to assess the damp problem precisely you can buy a battery-operated damp meter from a DIY store.

Common damp problems
- Damp through walls: if damp is detected coming through the walls, it means that they are not sufficiently watertight. The main reasons are:
- Exterior rendering: check that the finish on the walls is sound. Solid walls are more likely to be affected than cavity walls. In dry weather you can apply a damp-proofing liquid to the exterior.
- Leaking or blocked gutters and pipes.
- Window-sills without a drip channel underneath that stops water running down the walls.
- Cracked mortar between bricks which needs removing and replacing.
- Damp from the ground (rising damp): a damp-proof course is the first and really only defence against rising damp. Every wall should have one at ground level to prevent moisture from the ground rising. One sign of damp is a change of colour caused by the salts carried in the moisture that rises up the wall near ground level. Older houses are more susceptible to it.
- Condensation: cooking, washing and many other regular domestic chores release an average of five gallons of moisture per day into the atmosphere. If not controlled this can lead to mould and damp. Condensation occurs when there's an imbalance between humidity, ventilation and temperature. To determine whether damp is caused by condensation, dry the damp patch with a hairdryer, put a piece of tinfoil on to it and leave for a week. If there is moisture on the back it's rising damp, if it's on the front it's condensation.

TIPS
- Make sure that the walls are well insulated. If only a small patch is affected, try painting the wall with anti-condensation paint which has insulating particles.

- Check that the loft space is well insulated. Every surface should be covered. The cold water tank will need special attention if above this insulation to prevent it freezing.
- Keep the temperature of the house even.
- Keep moisture production to a minimum.
- Improve ventilation around the home. Each space should have an air change every three hours; bathrooms should have extractors and the kitchen, a cooker hood.
- You can use a dehumidifier to extract moisture from the air (particularly in damp cellars), but they're operated by electricity and can be expensive to run.

SUBSIDENCE

When the foundations of the house sink into the ground as a result of soil type, changed weather conditions or tree roots sucking moisture from the soil, it's known as subsidence. Cracks will appear on the inside and outside of the house which may begin to look like a jigsaw puzzle. You may also see bulging brickwork. To test whether or not the house is still settling, get a testing kit from Avongard which will show if the crack continues to shift. This may happen over a period of several months. (Not all cracks are due to subsidence.) The standard way of combating subsidence is to underpin the foundations, creating a sub-foundation, but it does involve excavating beneath the existing foundations and is very expensive. Once all is secure the superficial problems can be resolved. See **Buildings Insurance** in **Money** chapter.

ROT

- **Dry rot** is a fungus which feeds off damp and poorly ventilated timber and can travel through masonry. Look under stairs and floors, in cellars, under floorboards and behind skirting boards. It looks like cotton wool, and produces dust and bad smells. Early signs are cracked paintwork by windows and skirting boards. If the wood crumbles you know you have problems. All dry rot must be removed and timbers and masonry treated to prevent spreading. Contact the British Wood Preserving and Damp Proofing Association.
- **Wet rot** attacks damp wood. It's a fungal

infection and fans out rapidly. It usually attacks exterior timber exposed to the elements. Regular decorating and timber treatment with preservative can prevent it.

FINDING A TRADESPERSON

- Make a list of exactly what you want done.
- Ask relevant trade associations or friends to give you recommendations and check the quality of previous work wherever possible or relevant particularly if you're getting specialist work done.
- By knowing what you're talking about you'll remain in control, so do your homework before reaching for the phone.

TIPS

- Ring up the relevant trade bodies. Try to describe the job and, where possible, establish a rough time-span and cost before booking someone.
- Get a written quote with detailed job descriptions and all materials and labour.
- If it's a small job a letter of agreement may be OK.
- Insist on a schedule of works, no matter how small the job is. Establish how long it'll take, the materials needed for each task, and the cost of labour for each task.
- It pays to play a little dumb. Compare their explanation of what they plan to do with what you know needs to be done – it could be revealing.
- Ask for the telephone number of a previous employer (only if relevant to their trade) to check the standard of work.
- Never hand over money before work starts.
- Don't accept a daily rate; pay them for the job.
- Be wary of being charged for skilled labour while the contractor is paying for cheap labour.
- If the repair people don't turn up for an appointment and you have informed them that you're taking a day off work to be there, you can claim back in compensation any pay lost.
- Be wary of being charged extras that haven't been discussed and agreed in writing after the main quote. In some cases you can refuse to pay up.
- Don't be conned by being told that you will save VAT if you pay in cash. It may mean that they're not a registered member of the relevant trade association.
- Check guarantees, make sure all work and materi-

als are covered by guarantees, and be wary if no guarantee is provided.

- Keep a record of all financial transactions.
- In emergencies cut your losses, settle with a cancellation fee and get someone else in.
- Jobs that take up part of a day are more expensive and you will be charged for the whole day.
- Pay the bills in stages; use any retained payment as leverage to ensure that defects discovered after completion are put right.

INSURANCE

When having any kind of work done it's important that the company you've hired has insurance which will protect you and your property whatever the size of the job. It's less likely that an odd-job person will have the necessary insurance and so you should check that your own insurance covers the work undertaken. It's important to check and see proof of their insurance before you go ahead. There are various sorts of insurance, but these are two that may concern you:

1 **Public liability insurance:** protects the public and the property damaged by the contractor or his/her workforce.

2 **All risks insurance:** protects the premises, materials, machinery, and covers against theft or any damage done. Some insurance companies offer helplines where you can get specific advice.

TELEPHONE HELPLINES

There are telephone helplines for choosing a tradesperson. Helplines are available through membership of certain organizations or as an additional benefit arranged through a credit card company. Helplines claim to vet the tradespeople used and check up on customer satisfaction.

AN UNSATISFACTORY JOB

- If there's a problem with work you've had done try to resolve it with the firm yourself. Produce all the paperwork and talk them through it all calmly and methodically and be patient.
- If that fails try the relevant trade association's conciliation service although not all trade bodies offer one. This is a free and informal process.
- Arbitration involves sending written details and all documentation to an independent arbitrator, but

conveniently, not all trade associations offer this service either.

- An alternative is to take the contractor to court. You can use the small claims procedure if the amount you're claiming is not over £3,000. Your local Citizens' Advice Bureau can help, and see **Law** chapter.

THE LAW

The Goods and Services Act 1982 covers the law on consumers' rights and traders' obligations (but not in Scotland).

- **Goods:** this relates to the goods supplied as part of a service, for example, light fittings installed by an electrician. If they fail to work and are not safe you can claim a partial or full refund.
- **Services:** this relates to the quality of service provided by the contractor in your home. It states what you should expect from a service for which you are charged. For example, work must be done within a reasonable time and for a reasonable charge and to a proper standard of workmanship.

The Office of Fair Trading has a free consumers' guide called *Home Improvements*.

HOME SECURITY

The average burglary in the UK takes place in daylight between 2pm and 4pm and takes three minutes. On average each homeowner will be burgled twice.

How burglars break in

- Front door 25%, rear side door 23%, rear or side window 43%.
- Ground floor and basement properties are the most vulnerable, as well as houses set back and screened from the road by hedges.
- Building work in progress makes properties vulnerable, especially if scaffolding is erected.
- The Association of British Insurers offers guidelines on security, and which locks to use.

- Most insurance companies require five-lever mortice locks to front, side and rear doors as well as locks on any window that is easy to reach.

PROTECTION

Burglars will be aware of the street's potential, looking out for expensive cars, manicured lawns and well-stocked flower-beds, alarms and warnings of dogs, milk on steps, uncut grass, no lights and an absence of cars in the driveway. Extra locks can either make a burglar keener – assuming that extra locks mean more to protect – or will discourage them – too much hard work.

Nine preventative measures

1 Install window locks.
2 Install locks and bolts to the front and back doors. Check that the frames of the doors are in good condition (stout deadlocks or concealed mortice bolts can ward off efforts to force entry).
3 Install alarm systems (NACOSS approved) and make sure they're visible.
4 Join Neighbourhood Watch – it's a great deterrent.
5 Mark valuables with a code using an ultraviolet pen, or by engraving.
6 Install a safe. They begin at about £50.
7 If you're going away, cancel milk and newspaper deliveries and let the police know.
8 Install automatic lighting: it can be on a timer, activated by breaking a beam or by infrared sensor. Focus outdoor lights on windows and doors.
9 Plants act as deterrents. A prickly bush of thorns, a cactus garden or hedge of 15-foot spiky firethorn pyracantha will not only deter, but probably frighten any budding burglar (and your neighbours, friends and family too, for that matter).

The Home Office has a free booklet, *Your Practical Guide to Crime Prevention*, and the crime prevention officer at your local police station can come and advise you about security. For advice and recommendations for locksmiths contact the Master Locksmith Association.

LOCKS, ALARMS AND TIMERS

- **Door locks:** check for the British Standard Kitemark. There are many types but the most secure are those with several levers. The keys are difficult to duplicate and the lock harder to pick.
- When choosing a lock ask how many key permutations there are for the make and type, and choose the lock with the most. Top quality locks have only one key combination and keys can only be duplicated on written request. Always fit a deadlock on an external door. Their bolts lock into an extended position and can only be opened with a key. Always have a thick front door and position the letterbox 15 inches (40cm) away from the locks. Fit three locks and combine types.
- Mortice locks are sunk into the door and are drill proof. Rim locks are designed for surface mounting, the screws are vulnerable. Go for one with as many extras as possible. Rack bolts can be used on all doors and wooden-framed windows and are hard to detect. Locking the door while you're at home is recommended. When answering the door use a chain, and check who's there before fully opening the door. Banham Lock keys can only be duplicated by designated key cutters.
- **Window locks:** over 60% of homes still don't have window locks, and most burglars enter through windows. It's wise to fit locks on all windows. Most use a simple screw mechanism. Grilles and translucent curtains prevent easy viewing.
- **Alarm systems:** some insurance companies offer discounts on premiums if an alarm is installed, but investigate carefully and choose the right one for you and your home. Expect to pay about £400+ for the installation, excluding maintenance. The sight alone of one may be enough of a deterrent. Most alarm systems share similar features, and panic buttons can be incorporated into most.
- **Time controls:** handy as a deterrent if you are away for long periods of time. There are different types: light switch timers are connected to the lighting circuit; socket timers plug into sockets while the appliance plugs into it. They activate the appliance (lamps or radios, for example) at intervals, and can be set to various cycles.

See **Insurance claims** in **Money** chapter.

BABIES

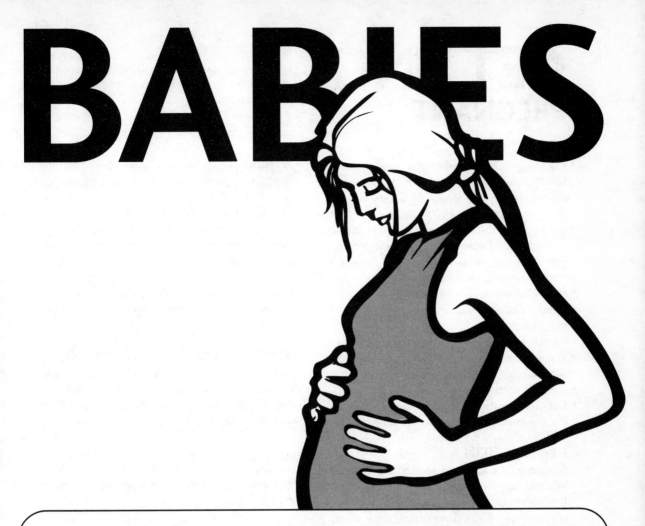

Pregnancy is an extraordinary and unique experience for all women. There are many powerful reasons for wanting a child. The discomfort, compromises and enormous changes in lifestyle are usually more than compensated for by the anticipation and overwhelming emotion of seeing your own baby for the first time. On the other hand, at the wrong time, or under the wrong circumstances, there are strong arguments against conceiving or going ahead with a pregnancy. It is an enormous decision, and shouldn't be made lightly. As a species, humans are not especially fertile. A couple has a 20–25% chance of conceiving each month if they are trying. Having carefully decided to go ahead, many women can suffer enormous frustration and difficulty getting pregnant. One in six couples needs medical help to have a child. Sophisticated monitoring methods have made it much safer for older women to have babies, and in vitro fertilization has given hope and happiness to many.

Although circumstances are rarely ever 'perfect' – there is no 'right time' to have a baby – the chances are, if you feel great about the prospect of becoming a mother, then you've got it right. Only you can decide when you're ready to have a child – no one else should ever make this decision for you.

Whether planned or unplanned (and unplanned doesn't necessarily mean unwanted), ideally, you should allow yourself time to really enjoy the experience. This chapter covers natural and artificial methods of conceiving, the stages of pregnancy, the practicalities of giving birth, surrogacy and adoption.

GETTING
PREGNANT

TOP TIPS

- Have regular sex between the twelfth and six-teenth day after the first day of your last period (ovulation).
- Stop smoking: you and your partner.
- Limit your alcohol consumption to less than two small glasses of wine or its equivalent per day.
- Talk to your doctor about any prescribed medication that you take regularly.
- Have a full check-up with your GP.
- Check your diet: eat a good balance of fresh nutritious food.
- Keep healthy, take regular exercise.
- You are less likely to conceive if you are under-weight.
- Have the right attitude: relax.
- Cut out recreational drugs completely.
- Read as much as you can on the subject.

CONCEPTION

Every month a ripe egg (or sometimes two) is released by the ovaries and travels into the Fallopian tube. In one ejaculation a man can release about 300 million sperm, some of which find their way into the Fallopian tubes where one penetrates the egg and fertilizes it. This is the moment of conception. The fertilized egg then travels down and implants itself in the wall of the womb where it begins to grow into a foetus.

WHEN IS THE BEST TIME?

To become pregnant, you should have sex one day before ovulating, or shortly after. Most women's cycles are about 28 days long, so ovulation takes place roughly 15 days before your next period. If you have regular sex between 12 and 16 days after the first day of your last period you dramatically increase your chances of conceiving. Sperm can live for several days inside a woman's body so if you have sex before ovulation they have time to travel up the Fallopian tubes and will be waiting for the egg to be released.

BEST POSITION?

- Lie on your back, knees up, with a pillow beneath your bottom and have full, deep, penetrative intercourse.
- If you have an orgasm (not essential) your con-tractions may assist the sperm on its journey to the egg.
- Withdraw the penis only when it is limp and remain on your back for half an hour afterwards.

HOW WILL YOU KNOW?

The most reliable sign that you are pregnant is a missed period though sometimes women who are pregnant have a very light period. Some women lose their periods if they have been dieting or are underweight. You can still get pregnant even if you have not been having regular periods. See **Testing** below.

SYMPTOMS OF EARLY PREGNANCY

- You may feel nauseous and tired. Unfortunately, morning sickness is not confined to mornings.
- Your breasts may become larger and feel tender and your nipples may become darker and stand out.
- You may feel constipated, have an increased vagi-nal discharge, get a strange metallic taste in your mouth, become more sensitive to smell and go off certain foods.

TESTING

Testing can be done by your GP, at a local clinic or at home with a kit bought at a chemist. This will give you an instant result even before you have missed a period. Kits cost between £8 and £12 and usually provide two tests so you can make doubly sure. If your test reads positive make an appointment to see your GP immedi-ately. Home tests are very reliable. A positive result means you are pregnant and the doctor will usually double check the result. However, a nega-tive result does not necessarily mean you are not pregnant. If you have a period yet experience other symptoms a re-test is advisable.

Contact the Maternity Alliance, the National Childbirth Trust and LIFE for more information.

ASSISTED
CONCEPTION

If you are having regular sex at the right times of the month, are following the correct guide-lines and are still unsuccessful, you may need to get some medical help. See your GP and discuss your situation with them. They will advise you on how best to proceed. Read the *Fertility Handbook* and contact CHILD and the National Fertility Association for support and information.

CONCEPTION

- One in six couples has difficulty conceiving.
- It takes the average couple six months to a year to conceive.
- Factors that make it more difficult include stress, being underweight or ill, having irregular ovulation, damaged Fallopian tubes, inflammation of the uterus or if you have a sexually transmitted disease such as herpes.
- Factors that make it more difficult for your partner include undescended or damaged testicles, the production of insufficient or abnormal sperm, inadequate sperm penetration, impotence or premature ejaculation.

TREATMENTS FOR WOMEN

The Human Fertilization and Embryology Authority are responsible for inspecting and licensing all clinics, both NHS and private. Ring them and ask for a free patient's guide to all the clinics in the UK (which includes their success rates), and their leaflets on the various treatments.

- **Hormone treatments:** stimulate ovulation and aid conception but can cause mood swings, pain and blurred vision. There is a 50% pregnancy rate after the use of clomiphene with gonadotrophins but the risk of multiple pregnancy, see **Multiple Births**. There are no national guide-lines and the treatment does not have to take place in a licensed clinic. Treatment should be carefully monitored as the level of dosage is crucial. In larger doses it can actually prevent conception.

- **In vitro fertilization (IVF):** this enables women who can produce eggs, but cannot conceive naturally, to fertilize their eggs outside the body ('in vitro' means 'in glass' hence 'test-tube baby'). The egg is taken from the woman, fertilized by the male sperm and then implanted in the womb allowing for normal gestation and birth. The overall live-birth rate per treatment is currently approximately 17.3% for under-25s falling to 5.4% for those over 40.
- **Egg donation:** eggs are supplied by a donor, fertilized outside the womb, often by sperm supplied by the husband of the infertile woman, and the fertilized eggs are then implanted in the womb for an otherwise normal pregnancy.
- **Donor insemination (DI):** sperm from screened donors is inserted into the woman during ovulation. 60% of DI can be DIY at home. The pregnancy rate is about 10% per cycle.
- **Artificial insemination by husband (AIH):** the woman's partner's sperm is used (does not require screened donors).

SURROGACY

Surrogacy is a variation of DI where the artificially inseminated genetic mother (i.e. her own egg) is not intended to be the eventual mother of the child after birth. Provided there is no exchange of money, or it is kept within the family i.e. between sisters or mother and daughter, there are no real legal difficulties. However, any commercial motives may lead to the courts being involved. No surrogacy arrangement can currently be enforced in the courts. A mother cannot be forced to give up her child, nor can the couple who 'commissioned' it be forced to accept it. The surrogate remains the lawful mother until the child is either adopted or the couple obtain a 'parental order'. These options are only open to married couples, and a parental order is only available if the child is genetically related to at least one of the parents.

AGE OF RECIPIENT

There is currently no legal limit to the age of women seeking fertility treatment but some local authorities have a cut-off age of 35. The Human Fertilization and Embryology Authority doesn't forbid treatment for women over the age of menopause, but equally, it does not encourage it. When refused in Britain, a 58-year-old woman travelled to Italy where she received treatment.

WHO IS ELIGIBLE?

The guide-lines for those hoping to qualify vary from clinic to clinic across the country: some women will need to prove they have been in a stable relationship for up to four years, while others may proceed from the outset intending to be single mothers. It is not necessary to be married in order to qualify. Each case is treated individually, and the outcome will simply depend upon the ability of the applicant to bring up a child well. The law is against discrimination, which in principle includes discrimination against lesbians, although this may differ in reality.

THE LAW

- The baby of a married woman who has had treatment with her husband's consent is treated as the legitimate child of that marriage. The husband, not the donor, is considered to be the legal father of the child.
- The Human Fertilization and Embryology Authority is responsible for licensing and inspecting all clinics that provide fertility treatments, both NHS and private. It also monitors all clinics that store or carry out research on embryos.
- Free treatment is available on the NHS, but it has been estimated that of all IVF assisted births in the UK, only 10% have been carried out on the NHS.
- NHS clinics are banned from allowing the parents to choose the sex of their child unless there is a risk of an inherited disease that is gender-specific.
- Private clinics however can offer you this option with a 70% success rate at an extra cost of £500.
- The National Fertility Association offers a great deal of help and information.

THE LEGAL RIGHTS OF THE UNBORN CHILD

- A child has no separate legal existence – and therefore rights – until it is born. If a pregnant woman is attacked, or involved in an accident, and her unborn child is stillborn as a result, the child cannot be said to have been 'murdered', as by law it was not yet 'alive'.

- No woman can be ordered to behave in a way that no harm comes to the foetus inside her. However, a court can take into account the behaviour of the mother before the baby was born, after its birth.
- A child can sue for damage caused while it was still in the womb through someone else's negligence including its mother's.

MISCAR-RIAGE

KEY POINTS

- Between one in four and one in five pregnancies ends in miscarriage.
- Most miscarriages occur within the first four months of pregnancy.
- 50% of miscarriages occur because of an abnormality of the foetus. Other causes are hormonal imbalance, fibroids, abnormalities of the womb, a weak or damaged cervix (neck of the womb), infections such as high fever, German measles or listeria, damage to the placenta or ectopic pregnancy (where the fertilized egg implants itself outside the cavity of the womb, usually in the Fallopian tubes). Most, if not all, of these conditions can be treated. Get medical help if you are experiencing difficulties in order to ensure a healthy pregnancy.
- Many miscarriages occur in first pregnancies and are more likely to occur at the time of your period.
- Statistics have shown that having a miscarriage doesn't mean that you won't be able to conceive again and go on to have a healthy baby.
- The Miscarriage Association specializes in helping women to get over miscarriage and LIFE can also give advice and information.

WHAT IS MISCARRIAGE?

When a woman miscarries a baby her body rejects the new foetus and delivers it before it is ready to survive alone. After a miscarriage many women need to have a small operation to remove anything left in the womb to prevent possible infection. This is done under general anaesthetic and does not require any cutting or stitching. After a miscarriage you will bleed for anything up to two weeks with the bleeding becoming progressively lighter during that time. If you experience severe pain, increased blood loss, a high temperature or an unpleasant discharge, contact your doctor as you may be experiencing complications. Use sanitary towels rather than tampons during this time and don't have sex until the bleeding stops to avoid infection. You can bathe or shower as usual but avoid public pools where you could pick up infections.

If you have had a miscarriage later in pregnancy you may feel your breasts leaking milk that was intended for your baby. Alleviate any discomfort by wearing a support bra. Take a mild painkiller if your breasts are painful. A miscarriage is very upsetting. Apart from the emotional trauma of expecting and then losing a baby, your body has to make many hormonal changes to adapt to the sudden loss of the baby it was preparing to nurture. Many people find it difficult to sympathize properly with a woman who has had a miscarriage, mistakenly attempting to comfort you by saying all the wrong things or even by pretending it didn't happen. People should accept that you and your partner need time to grieve.

Many women who miscarry will feel some of the following: grief, anger, bereavement, sadness, loss of interest in daily life, jealousy or pain at the sight of other mothers and babies, isolation, a constant desire to talk about it or a complete inability to do so, depression, loss of concentration, tiredness, feelings of guilt and failure, sleeping constantly or not at all, loss of interest in sex. These are natural reactions. Give yourself time to work through them. Share your feelings with a close friend or your partner, or with others who have had a similar experience and felt as desolated as you do about it.

REMEMBERING YOUR BABY

- See if you can obtain copies of your ultrasound scans.
- If it is a late miscarriage you may be able to have a photo taken.
- Have the hospital identify the sex of your baby.
- Name the baby.
  Note that after 24 weeks of pregnancy all miscarriages must be officially registered as stillbirth or death.

TRYING AGAIN

- Wait until you have had at least one period.
- Make sure you and your partner have recovered and are emotionally ready.
- Take good care of yourself with a healthy diet, plenty of rest and some regular exercise.
- Try not to be anxious: believe that this time it will all be OK.

PREG-NANCY

A normal pregnancy lasts between 37 and 42 weeks from the first day of your last period. If you don't know when you conceived, your ultrasound scan will give doctors a good indication of your baby's expected due date. You will be entitled to free healthcare (no prescription charges) and dental care during your pregnancy and for the first year of your baby's life. There are many good books on pregnancy, but before splashing out look at the Health Education Authority publications which are extremely thorough and free to all new mothers.

THE DEVELOPING BABY

A brief outline of the major stages

At twelve weeks

- The fertilized egg will have grown into a fully formed foetus with all its organs, muscles, limbs and bones.

At nineteen weeks

- The foetus will have developed its sex organs so you can find out whether you are expecting a boy or a girl, if you want to.
- You should have your first and most detailed hospital appointment where you will be weighed and offered tests for any potential risks.
- You may need to undergo further testing if you are over the age of 35 or in a high-risk category.

At twenty-eight weeks

- Your foetus has become a perfectly formed baby.
- It measures about 24 centimetres long.
- It responds to noise.
- It moves about vigorously inside you.
- The baby may still need some assistance with breathing and feeding if born now.
- Your pregnancy is less easy to disguise.

By thirty-five weeks

- Your baby is putting on weight and its wrinkled skin is becoming smoother.
- The baby positions itself with its head down ready for delivery.
- Some time before the birth its head will move down into the pelvis when it is said to be 'engaged'.
- Your baby will be ready to breathe alone on delivery. It will have developed suck and swallow reflexes which will allow it to feed.

DISCOMFORTS IN PREGNANCY

- **Nausea:** this can be helped by nibbling at dry biscuits. Eat smaller meals more frequently. Ginger is a natural anti-nausea remedy: add it to your diet.
- **Constantly urinating:** cut down on diuretics (coffee, tea, alcohol, pineapple juice). Lessen the pressure of your womb on your bladder by rocking back and forward while you are on the toilet; this helps you to empty your bladder more completely so that you don't need to pass water quite so often.
- **Stretch marks:** although there is no proven treatment for stretch marks, rubbing vitamin-E-based oils into your skin may help. Check with a pharmacist before using certain essential oils as many are unsuitable during pregnancy. Almond oil is excellent with no risks involved.

- **Constipation:** increase the amount of fibre in your diet (wholemeal bread, whole grain cereals, fruit, vegetables, beans, lentils), take regular, gentle exercise, drink lots of water and avoid iron tablets. These may have been prescribed by your GP but you can increase the amount of iron in your diet by eating the right foods.
- **Indigestion:** eat smaller meals more often. Eat more slowly and sit up straight to take pressure off your stomach. Squeeze a lemon over any salad. Drink peppermint tea after eating to help digestion. Avoid onions and fried or spicy foods.
- **Heartburn:** drink milk and keep a glass by your bed. Don't eat or drink for a few hours before you go to bed and if it persists get some medical advice. Check before taking over-the-counter remedies.
- **Backache:** improve posture, avoid heavy lifting and wear flat shoes. If you are still working, make sure you are sitting up straight at your desk. Stretch out your spine by kneeling down on all fours and arching your back up as far as is comfortable. Then curve your back inwards in the opposite direction as far as you can. Repeat these movements to release tension. At night, lie on your side with a pillow under your back and one between your knees.
- **Cramps:** can be relieved by massage and prevented by regularly exercising your legs and ankles. If you get foot cramp try wearing socks in bed, increase your calcium intake, and salt intake if it is very low.
- **Shortness of breath:** slow yourself down. Sleep propped up with pillows so that your uterus no longer presses against your lungs. Call your doctor if it gets worse.
- **Piles:** increase the amount of fibre in your diet, avoid standing for long periods and drink lots of water. Piles are swollen veins that protrude from your anus and can be painful, itchy and may also bleed a little. Your GP can give you pessaries or ointment to help if they become very uncomfortable. An ice pack can be soothing.
- **Swollen ankles and feet:** rest with your feet up, wear comfy shoes, do foot exercises and avoid standing for long periods. A little swelling at the end of the day (called oedema) or in hot weather is usually nothing to worry about, but excessive swelling could indicate the onset of pre-eclampsia and you should see your doctor. Approximately 75% of pregnant women experience oedema at some time during their pregnancy.

DIET
- Don't eat for two.
- Eat a balanced diet, fill up on vegetables, pasta, rice, beans, pulses and fruit.
- Avoid eating soft cheeses, paté, liver and liver products.
- Make sure all foods are thoroughly cooked, especially eggs and meat which should never be taken raw or rare in pregnancy.
- Don't drink unpasteurized milk, and limit your alcohol intake.
- Make sure that all foods you eat are clean.
- Always wash your hands before eating.
- For more help and advice contact the Centre for Pregnancy Nutrition Helpline, or Eating for Pregnancy Helpline.

TESTS DURING PREGNANCY
Not all tests are routinely available and no test provides 100% perfect screening. The availability of some will depend on your local health authority policy and whether they have the funds. The advisability of some tests depends on your age and past history.

All women are routinely given the following tests:
- urine: to test for the presence of protein or sugar
- blood: to check blood type, blood count, iron level, immunity to rubella, and to test for syphilis and hepatitis B
- blood pressure
- foetal heartbeat

97% of all births in the UK are normal. Some women need extra tests, particularly those aged 35 and over who are having their first child or who may have a hereditary disease or genetic disorder. The other main tests available are listed in the chart on the following page.

Other Pregnancy Tests

Description	Timing	Pros	Cons	NHS availability
Nuchal Test Measurement of fluid-filled space behind the neck of the foetus for Down's syndrome.	10–14 weeks	Immediate results. Non-invasive	Provides a (rough) estimate of risk Inconclusive results	Mostly available in south-east – may have to be paid for privately
Chorionic villus sampling (CVS) Sample taken from the chorionic villi tissue surrounding embedded embryo, detects some handicaps	11 weeks+	Results available within 10 days, so early decision to terminate is less traumatic	Risk of miscarriage is 1 in 100 tests	Usually offered to women over 35 as early alternative to amniocentesis
Alpha-foetoprotein test (AFP) Checks level of protein from the baby in your blood. High may indicate spina bifida, low Down's syndrome	c.16 weeks	No risk of miscarriage. Results in up to 10 days	Inaccurate. High-risk results should be reconfirmed by other tests	Widely available
Triple/Quadruple/Leeds/ Bart's Test Combination of AFP and other blood tests. Can detect abnormalities such as Down's syndrome, spina bifida or anencephaly (absence of the brain)	7–10 days	Painless, no risk of miscarriage	No definite answer. Only 60–70% accurate for Down's and spina bifida. Dilemma is then whether you go further and have an amnio	Only widely available in the south-east but can be arranged privately
Amniocentesis Amniotic fluid is removed with a fine needle under general anaesthetic. Cells are then cultured to a stage when they can be tested for certain disorders including Down's syndrome	Mostly after 16 weeks but in some places available at c.11 weeks	Highly accurate at detecting disorders. Particularly useful for women over 35 who are more at risk of having a Down's baby	There is a risk of miscarriage (less than 1%). Results take about 3 weeks which can be stressful as a positive result may lead to a termination at a late stage of your pregnancy	More readily available to older mothers. Often an option following a bad result from the Bart's test
Ultrasound Scan of womb which enables soundwaves to be transmitted to a screen to give a picture of the foetus's bones and tissues. The trained eye can check all sorts from this, but to the majority it's just a lot of moving blobs! Can pinpoint due date and detect multiple births	Mostly at 18–20 weeks. Can be earlier for dating purposes or if there are other problems	No risk of miscarriage. Non-invasive. You get to see your baby (very reassuring to know you're not just getting fat!)	No one knows if repeated scanning can have an effect on the foetus so the fewer the better. The jelly they put on your tummy first is always cold	Widely available

BIRTH

TOP TIPS

- Know what's going to happen, and when, in advance.
- Attend antenatal classes and read as much as you can on the subject. See directory for reading list.
- Request epidural pain relief early if required: get it written into your hospital notes beforehand.
- Prepare your other children for the new arrival.
- Make sure there will be a friend or family member to take care of other children when you go into labour.
- Get as much sleep/rest as you can in the weeks preceding the birth.
- Pack the freezer with easy meals to cut out the hassle of cooking in the first few weeks.
- Spring clean before the birth and organize someone to help tidy up daily after the birth.
- Make a list of videos to rent: there will be a lot of sitting around especially if breast-feeding.
- Shop in advance.

PRE-BIRTH SHOPPING LIST

- Clothes: about six Babygros with feet, six baby vests that fasten under the nappy, two cardigans, one jacket, hat, mittens, socks or bootees.
- Sleeping: cot or Moses basket, sheets, warm blankets, baby monitor.
- Cleaning: baby bath, baby soap, newborn-size nappies, zinc and castor oil cream, cotton wool, babywipes (these can cause an allergic reaction), Sudocreme in case of nappy rash, small towels, plastic changing mat.
- Travel: a pram or lie-down buggy, a car seat and sling.
- If breast feeding: breast pump and storage bags.
- If bottle-feeding: six bottles, teats and caps, sterilizing equipment, bottle brush and powdered baby milk (the use-by date should be at least one month after your due date).
- Approximate cost for this list: £400. Some items can be bought secondhand but check for wear and tear and that all parts are safe.

WHO'S WHO?

- **Midwife:** specially trained to care for mothers and babies through pregnancy, labour and birth. They will care for you at home, in the community and at the hospital where they will deliver your baby assuming there are no complications.
- **GP:** your local doctor will monitor your pregnancy and help you plan your antenatal care.
- **Obstetrician:** a doctor specialized in looking after women during pregnancy, labour and birth.
- **Paediatrician:** a doctor specialized in the care of babies and children.
- **Obstetric physiotherapist:** one trained to help with the physical changes of pregnancy and birth. Can give advice on breathing, posture, exercise and toning up after the birth. Often attached to antenatal clinics.
- **Health visitors:** nurses with extra training who work in the community and look after the health of your whole family either in local health centres or at home after the birth of a new baby.

WHERE AND HOW?

- **Home delivery**

For many, a home birth is the most fulfilling way to bring a new baby into the world and a good way of involving the whole family. Monitored by a trained midwife, the birth takes place in familiar and informal surroundings. Should any difficulty arise, you will be taken straight to hospital.

It is now recognized that GPs and midwives could be better trained to support home births. As it is, only 1.9% of births are at home and 40% of these end up transferring to hospital during labour. There is no clear statistical evidence that home birth is unsafe in uncomplicated pregnancies but many doctors are reluctant to encourage it. If you are carrying twins or have had any problems in pregnancy or labour you will be advised to have your baby in hospital. Home delivery is not allowed for a first pregnancy in some districts but you can discuss this with your GP who may be able to transfer you to another borough.

- **Hospital delivery**

Most babies are born in hospital. You go into hospital when labour begins and leave approximately 48 hours later if there are no complications. 40% of births require some form of medical intervention, however small, so if you are looking for absolute security choose a hospital birth.

- **Delivery rooms** are relaxed environments with beanbags and armchairs which can help you get more comfortable during labour.
- **Domino Scheme:** this is an NHS scheme that encourages you to stay with your personal midwife at home until you are close to giving birth. They then take you to the hospital for your baby's delivery.
- **Water-birth rooms:** some hospitals have birthing pools where you can sit in warm water during labour and actually give birth in water. If your hospital does not have one you may be able to hire one. Many women rent birthing pools for home births and say that the warm water is relaxing, soothing and alleviates pressure. There can be drawbacks however, and these should be investigated fully before making a decision. The Active Birth Centre can give you more information.

PACKING FOR HOSPITAL

- **Make it fun:** pack some surprises that will take your mind off your painful contractions on the day.
- **Clothes:** front-opening nighties/big pyjamas, nursing/front-opening bras, breast pads, large-size pants, extra absorbent sanitary towels, baby clothes.
- **Washbag:** aromatherapy oils, deep treatment conditioners, face packs, nail varnish, shower/bath gels, body creams, make-up, small mirror: anything to physically pamper yourself.
- **Communications:** change for the payphone, phonecard, mobile phone, phone numbers and address book, pen, paper, stamps.
- **Entertainments:** magazines/books, cards, games, portable TV.
- **Recording the event:** camera, film, video-recorder, Polaroid camera, diary, baby book.

PAIN RELIEF

Deciding in advance on what kind of pain relief you will need is very important. It's now possible to have your baby with relatively little pain and discomfort while awake and alert. However, for some women experiencing the full pain of birth is something that they really want.

- **Self-help/alternative methods:** using relaxation techniques, keeping mobile, taking a warm bath, massage and aromatherapy can all help.
- **Transcutaneous Electrical Nerve Stimulation (TENS):** some hospitals provide these machines or you can rent your own. Electrodes are taped to your back and connected by wires to a battery-powered pulsar. Small electric currents are supplied which are believed to increase the body's natural painkillers (endorphins) by reducing the pain signals that are sent to the brain by the spinal cord. There are no known side-effects for you or baby.
- **Epidural:** a local anaesthetic which can give complete pain relief to most women. It is given by an anaesthetist and takes a minimum of 40 minutes to insert and begin working. It is possible for the midwife to let the anaesthetic to wear off slightly towards the end, which will allow you to feel the contractions as you actually push the baby out. If for some reason you need a Caesarean section, the doctors can operate using the same epidural so that you are awake and alert to see your baby as soon as it is born. An epidural may not be a good idea if you suffer from back problems and you should discuss this with your health visitor or doctor before making a decision.
- **Mobile epidural:** a different combination of drugs which allows you to move your legs while still providing effective pain relief.
- **Pethidine:** given by injection it takes about 20 minutes to work and lasts between two and three hours. It can make you feel light-headed, nauseous and not in control.
- **Gas and air:** a mixture of oxygen and nitrous oxide is self-administered through a mask which you can hold yourself. It is not a total pain block but can make it easier to bear. It takes about twenty seconds to work so you breathe in just as a contraction begins. There are no harmful side-effects but it can make you feel both dizzy and sick.
- **General anaesthetic:** in some more complicated cases it is necessary for you to be put to sleep before your baby can be delivered by Caesarean section. Administered by injection, it works instantly and when you wake up, it's all over.

STAGES OF LABOUR

There are four different stages to giving birth.

• **Early signs of labour:** regular contractions (a painful tightening and gradual relaxation of your abdomen) begin to get stronger and more frequent. If your waters break you will notice either a slow trickle or a sudden gush of water from your vagina. When this happens use a sanitary towel and if you are going to have your baby in hospital, go straight there. You may also experience backache, nausea, vomiting or diarrhoea – nice! If you can manage to, eat a light meal: you will need all the energy you can get later in labour as you cannot eat or drink until the baby's born.

• **Dilation:** the contractions help to soften the cervix (the neck of the womb) which will gradually open up to about ten centimetres 'fully dilated' to allow baby out. Sometimes if labour is progressing too slowly the doctor can speed things up by giving a hormone to encourage contractions or breaking the waters for you. The softening of the cervix can take many hours and if you are in hospital you will be left alone with your partner and checked intermittently. Having a portable TV can help while away the time and take your mind off things.

• As you fully dilate you will feel the urge to push but the midwife will tell you not to until she can see the baby's head. Your baby's heart will be monitored for any signs of distress throughout your labour and sometimes if the pads on your stomach don't pick up a strong enough heartbeat a clip will be attached to the baby's head while it is still inside you.

BIRTH

• **Delivery:** as the baby moves down into the vaginal opening the head and hair will be visible. You will have been pushing hard, and when half the head can be seen the midwife will ask you to either stop or push gently so that the baby's head can be born slowly, giving the perineum (the area between your vagina and back passage) time to stretch without tearing.

Sometimes the skin won't stretch and may tear or need to be cut (**Episiotomy**, see below). This allows the doctors to get the baby out quickly if s/he needs oxygen. Once the head is out, one push brings the baby into the world and s/he can be given straight to you even before the cord is cut. Midwives recommend a maximum of one hour for pushing. Any longer and they will consider how best to speed up the birth.

• **Placenta:** after the birth your womb expels the placenta. This can happen naturally within about half an hour or you can receive an injection which both speeds up the elimination of the placenta and contracts the womb to prevent heavy bleeding after the birth.

BIRTHING PARTNERS

It is a good idea to have someone with you when you are giving birth. Your partner can be anyone from the baby's father, your mother, or your best friend. Whoever is with you can help by simply keeping you company, making you comfortable, telling doctors and nurses if something is upsetting you or requesting extra pain relief. They can help with breathing techniques and tell you what is happening that you can't see for yourself as the baby is being born.

Some men can feel isolated by the birth experience and it is important to try and involve them: this is something you are going through together. It's difficult for your partner to see you in pain and it can be even more upsetting if there are complications. Some men faint and others can't watch if you need an episiotomy or forceps. Try to be understanding!

WHAT YOU SHOULD KNOW

• **Episiotomy:** performed when the perineum tears or needs to be cut to allow the baby an easier, quicker birth. You will be stitched up under local anaesthetic once the baby has been born and the wound should heal completely within about six weeks. Sitting down can be painful afterwards – an inflatable rubber ring beneath your bottom will allow you to take pressure off your healing wound. To avoid infection keep the stitched area clean and dry and change your sanitary towel (postnatal bleeding) frequently. Put 20 drops of tea tree oil, a natural antiseptic, into your bath to help you heal. Drink lots of water to dilute your urine.

- **Induction:** an artificially started labour perhaps because you are overdue or your waters have broken but nothing else has happened. Methods include a pessary inserted into the vagina or a hormone drip given in the arm or hand which starts contractions and brings on labour.
- **Forceps:** if your baby needs to be helped out of the vagina the doctor can place forceps around the baby's head and gently pull her/him out. A local anaesthetic is normally given if you have not already had an epidural. Sometimes the baby will have red marks on its head from the forceps. An episiotomy is nearly always needed for a forceps delivery.
- **Ventouse (vacuum extraction):** a shallow rubber or metal cup is fitted to the baby's head by suction. You can help by pushing when the obstetrician asks as s/he pulls the baby out. Ventouse is often combined with forceps to deliver the baby. An episiotomy is not always needed but is unfortunately quite likely.
- **Caesarean:** is sometimes performed in an emergency or because of prior knowledge of complications with the birth. The baby is delivered by cutting through the abdomen and then into the womb. The cut is done below the bikini line and is hidden when your pubic hair grows back again. You will be given an epidural anaesthetic and a screen will hide the operation from you. In more complicated cases or emergencies a general anaesthetic will be used. It takes longer to recover from a Caesarean birth – you have to stay in hospital for a week (your stitches are taken out within five days) and it is six weeks before you can drive or exercise. If you have a Caesarean section it doesn't mean that you can't have a normal delivery next time you have a baby. Most doctors wouldn't recommend that you have more than three or four Caesarean sections. The Caesarean Support Network offers help and support to women who have had or may need a Caesarean.
- **Breech:** when a baby is born feet or bottom first. Many doctors consider it necessary to deliver by Caesarean section. Breech babies can be born quite normally but it is much more complicated and requires an epidural and forceps.

AFTER THE BIRTH

- You may feel period-like pains as your womb begins to shrink. These can be worse for breast-feeding mothers.
- You will bleed and have a discharge for anything up to six weeks though it will become lighter.
- Use sanitary towels rather than tampons and take an iron and zinc supplement especially if you are losing a lot of blood.
- Expect to feel a bit strange when you come home from hospital.
- Do your postnatal exercises and rest as much as you can.

POST-NATAL DEPRESSION

- Up to 80% of women who have just given birth experience the baby blues – a mild depression that lasts a few hours or days after the birth and then disappears. Mums feel tired, anxious and upset and all the more so when there are some slight difficulties with either the birth or baby's general health.
- Postnatal depression occurs in about 10% of mothers who find that the baby blues don't go away and they become progressively more anxious and depressed.
- Women who feel consistently anxious, tense, are having panic attacks, sleeping difficulties, low libido and obsessive thoughts, may need to be treated medically.
- Developing depression should not be dismissed as 'just hormones'. A depressed mother is suffering from a chemical imbalance, is genuinely ill and needs lots of help and support from friends and family if she is to fully recover.
- Isolation can be a contributory factor and depressed mothers should always have a close, trustworthy friend, relative or partner with them until they are well enough to cope alone.
- The Pill can aggravate depression in women so if

you are suffering from depression you should stop taking it. However, the last thing a depressed mother needs is another baby so she should get an alternative method of contraception sorted out before stopping the Pill.

- The Association for Postnatal Illness has the latest information and can offer advice and support, and you will find many other support groups in the **Directory**.

TREATMENT
If depression continues

- You may be prescribed tranquillizers, anti-depressants or a tricyclic drug. These drugs may make you feel drowsy and leave your mouth dry. These feelings wear off gradually but if your drugs make you feel worse rather than better let your doctor know immediately so that s/he can change them.
- If you are prescribed medication for postnatal depression, finish the course of medicine even if you feel better very quickly.
- Good diet and lots of rest can help; and vitamin and mineral supplements especially vitamin B6 and zinc are important.
- It is very beneficial for depressed mothers to be able to talk about how they feel: try a local support group or counselling.
- Some women find that the depression becomes worse at around the time of their period and doctors may recommend progesterone therapy to help at these times.
- Women who have experienced postnatal depression after the birth of a child may find that it recurs with subsequent births.

BABY CARE

KEY POINTS

- Breast-feed if you can: contact the Association of Breast-feeding Mothers.
- Keep your new baby near to you so that s/he can hear your voice when not in your arms.
- Nap while your baby sleeps in the day.

- Involve your partner and other children in taking care of the new baby.
- Limit visitors until you feel ready to cope.
- Do your postnatal exercises.
- Eat healthily: avoid junk food and fad diets.
- Keep all your hospital and health visitor appointments.
- Register and immunize your baby.
- Learn to recognize signs of illness in a new baby.

FEEDING A NEW BABY

Talk to midwives, health visitors and other mothers. Health professionals will recommend breast-feeding unequivocally. Other mothers will balance the advice and help you to make the right choice for you and your baby.

There are only two options and each has its advantages and disadvantages.

BREAST-FEEDING FACTS

- Exclusive breast-feeding for the first 13 weeks of life boosts natural immunity and protects your baby from illness and allergy.
- The more your baby sucks at your breasts, the more milk your breasts create.
- It's economical.
- Breast milk supplies all your baby's nutritional needs and adapts to changing needs as s/he grows.
- It's hygienic: there's no chance of infection.
- It's easy: there's no need to sterilize bottles.
- It's portable: you can bring your baby with you and feed anywhere.
- You can express and store milk in the freezer for up to three months.
- Your local National Childbirth Trust (NCT) rents electric breast pumps and has breast-feeding counsellors who give practical advice.
- You can mix breast and bottle after three months to help wean your baby.
- La Leche League (Great Britain), the Association of Breast-feeding Mothers and the NCT run local support groups and provide information for those who are having problems breast-feeding.

BOTTLE-FEEDING FACTS

- All equipment must be sterilized.
- A sterilized teat stored inside a sterilized top will remain safe for 12 hours.

- Always use a recommended infant formula.
- Feeds need to be made up freshly each day.
- Feeds must be made to the exact recommendation on the tin.
- The remains of the feed must be thrown away once the sterilized bottle has been used.
- You will need about six 8-ounce bottles per day for a three-month-old baby.
- Allows you to leave your baby with another carer at any time.
- Your partner can be more involved in feeding.
- With twins it means others can help with feeding.
- Requires equipment which means expenditure.
- If you are HIV positive you should bottle-feed.
- Never give a small baby cow's milk or any other type of milk, except breast or formula.
- A decision to bottle-feed can be made at any time.
- The NCT provides counsellors to help with feeding if necessary.

WEANING
- The longer you leave weaning, the more difficult it becomes.
- Whenever you decide that enough is enough, be prepared to take things slowly.
- Gradually cut out daytime breast-feeding and only feed at night or in the morning.
- To introduce the bottle, fill it with breast-milk initially and gradualy add formula.
- If your baby refuses to take a bottle and is old enough to hold things by her/himself see if you can go straight to a trainer cup.

HYGIENE AND BATHING
- If your baby is born in winter make sure that the room you bathe her/him in is uncomfortably hot for you.
- Test the temperature of the bath water with your elbow as baby's skin is very delicate and can scald easily (or use a bath thermometer).
- Most babies don't need a bath every day and can simply be wiped with a cloth while they keep most of their clothes on.
- Never leave a baby or small child unattended in a bath.
- Try having a bath with your baby.
- When changing nappies always wipe from front to back so that the the vagina or foreskin is cleaned first.
- Use water and cotton wool or dip the baby's bottom into a warm basin of water and then dry it before smoothing on zinc and castor oil cream.
- If you are using disposable nappies be careful not to get any cream on the nappy as it takes away the stickiness from the fastening tapes. Keep a roll of masking tape by your changing mat for the ones that do go wrong.
- Always wash your hands after changing a nappy.

WARMTH
- Babies chill easily and it is very difficult for them to regain their normal body temperature if it suddenly drops. If your baby gets very cold, snuggle him/her against your body, under your clothes and gently rub the skin to gradually warm it up.
- If your baby still feels cold and the room has been warm for some time, consult your doctor immediately.
- It is generally better for your baby to have several light layers of clothing rather than one very heavy one. Keep a hat on a newborn baby in a cold environment: we lose most of our body heat through the head.
- Don't put a newborn baby to sleep wearing a hat as s/he may overheat or it could slide over the mouth and nose preventing breathing. The ideal night-time room temperature is 18˚C. If the weather is very warm, dress your baby in light clothing as they can easily overheat.

BEDTIME TIPS
- Follow the cot death prevention guide-lines, see overleaf.
- If you are putting your baby to sleep out of hearing distance, use a baby monitor.
- The older your baby gets, the more difficult it is to alter sleeping arrangements without upsetting him/her.
- Having your baby in your bed can impringe on your relationship with your partner who may not feel the same desire to share you with the baby all night as well as all day.

COT DEATH

- Cot death is the sudden and unexpected death of a baby for no obvious reason. 80% of cot deaths occur in the first six months of life with a peak at two to three months. There is no known cause and 520 babies die this way each year.
- Boys, premature/low birth-weight babies and twins or multiple births are more at risk. If one twin dies of cot death the other twin may be admitted to hospital for observation to make sure that the pattern does not repeat itself.
- 57% of cot deaths occur in the winter months and it seems to happen more frequently to families living in difficult circumstances and to the babies of young mothers.
- Cot death is not hereditary and there is no evidence that it is linked to baby vaccinations.
- To minimize any risk of cot death follow these sleeping guide-lines for your new baby.

Cot death prevention guide-lines

Note: since the introduction of these guide-lines cot deaths in the UK have dropped by over 50%.

- Put your baby to sleep lying on his/her back.
- Check that your baby is not over-wrapped and not wearing a hat in bed.
- Don't smoke or allow others to smoke near your baby.
- Place your baby to sleep at the foot of the cot so that s/he can't slide down under the covers.
- Choose a fully tested and approved mattress that is firm rather than soft.
- Make sure there is no gap between the cot mattress and the sides of the cot which could trap your baby or into which s/he could slide.
- Don't give a small baby a pillow, duvet, hot water bottle or electric blanket.
- Don't bring your baby to sleep in your bed if you have been drinking alcohol or taking drugs.
- Don't have cot padding, ribbons, strings, mobiles, loose plastic sheets near your baby.
- Contact the Foundation for the Study of Infant Deaths for more information and support.

CRYING/SLEEPING

All babies cry. It is the only way that they can communicate with you and it is often difficult to know why. If your baby is having trouble settling:

- S/he could be hungry, wet, uncomfortable, too hot or cold, or have wind or colic.
- S/he may not be tired: try more activity and stimulation in the day and a relaxing evening bath combined with a consistent bedtime in the same place each night.
- If your baby sleeps a lot during the day you need to gradually change his/her routine so that the pattern is for sleeping at night.
- S/he may need some comfort and reassurance: try cuddling, gentle rocking, quiet talking or singing.
- At bedtime stay with him/her to reinforce that you're there, speak reassuringly and gently rub his/her back until s/he falls asleep. Gradually remove physical contact and try to make your baby feel secure by pottering around, going in and out of the room without talking to him/her until s/he can go off to sleep alone.
- Try playing a tape of your voice reading a story, but be there to respond if s/he gets upset so that s/he doesn't think you're ignoring him/her.
- If your baby cries more than normal and you cannot settle or comfort him/her, consult your doctor: s/he may be coming down with something.
- If you're alone with a crying baby and feeling at the end of your tether put him/her in a safe place (the cot, for example) and leave the room closing the door behind you. Wait a full five minutes before re-entering. Make a cup of tea, listen to some music, call a friend. Your baby will come to no harm and a few minutes away will help you to calm down and rethink.
- CRY-SIS is a self-help and support group for parents with children who cry excessively or don't sleep.

TEETHING

- Cutting teeth rarely causes any problems in babies younger than three months so if your two-month-old baby is upset and crying a lot, it is unlikely to be caused by teething.
- Teeth initially appear as a small bump under the gum which breaks through after a few days.
- Babies start chewing with their gums and should be given hard foods to suck by about four months when they begin mouthing on toys and exploring their environment. The more babies

chew at this stage the stronger their gums will become.

- At around six months a baby gets the front two teeth on the bottom gum, closely followed by the top two.
- By about one year a baby will have their back chewing teeth.
- If your baby is really miserable, a tiny amount of baby paracetamol can help: read the label to see how much s/he should have based on age.
- If your baby is miserable over an extended period always look out for other signs of illness. A few babies each year reach hospital in a serious condition because parents mistook real signs of illness for teething.
- As soon as your baby has a few teeth you should begin gentle brushing with baby toothpaste.

COLIC

- If your baby cries constantly in the evenings at around the same time and draws his/her legs up to the chest as if s/he has a tummy ache, s/he may be suffering from colic – a digestion difficulty common among small babies.
- There are some remedies available from the chemist which may help but holding your baby over your shoulder or face down across your lap whilst you gently rub the back can help give him/her some relief. Try sitting your baby on your knee and holding their back straight with your hand supporting under their chin. This stretches out the stomach and allows wind to escape more easily.
- If you are bottle-feeding try changing milks and if breast-feeding, think about things in your diet that might be causing it (e.g. spicy foods or citrus fruit?). Ask your doctor if it could be your Pill. Often a drive around the block or a ride in the pram will help settle a baby but s/he may cry again whenever you stop.
- If you feel it's becoming unbearable, reassure yourself that it should only last a maximum of 12 weeks. Try and get someone else to help you when things get very difficult. Call CRY-SIS.

USEFUL REMEDIES FOR NEWBORNS

Newborn babies should not be given any medicine except those prescribed or recommended by a GP, but some minor ailments can be helped naturally.

- **Constipation:** a little boiled water with a tiny amount of dissolved brown sugar on a sterilized spoon or in a bottle can help loosen the stool. This may help a colicky baby too.
- **Teething:** your clean little finger that has been cooled with ice can be soothing for gums.
- **Cradlecap:** olive oil rubbed into the scalp can help shift flaky skin.
- **Nappy rash:** for mild nappy rash, airing the skin will always help. Avoid shop-bought baby wipes which can irritate; use cotton wool and water instead. Avoid bubble baths and other detergents. Keep the skin as dry as possible: after a bath try blow-drying baby with the hairdryer keeping your own hand in front of the blast of warm air to disperse it. Give baby some sterilized water to drink if s/he will take it and if the rash doesn't improve, or gets worse, see a doctor.
- **Sticky eye:** use sterile cotton wool and a mild saline solution (sterile salt water) and clean the stickiness off the eyelashes by wiping in towards the nose. Alternatively use breast milk to moisten the cotton wool. See your doctor if it does not clear up.
- **Blocked nose:** you would only do this for your own baby, but if they are really stuffed up and uncomfortable you can place your mouth over their nostrils and gently suck the greenies out.

ILL BABIES

GENERAL ILLNESS

- If your baby becomes feverish, stops drinking and vomits up feeds, it is advisable to see your GP immediately.
- Even if you have already spoken to your doctor, if you feel that your baby is not improving or is getting worse, call your doctor again that day.
- As a rule, major changes in established behaviour patterns are important clues to baby illness and parents are the first to recognize them.

OFTEN SERIOUS
- croup or a hoarse cough with noisy breathing
- cannot breathe freely through his nose
- unusually hot, cold or floppy
- repeatedly refuses feeds especially if unusually quiet
- continuous vomiting and diarrhoea – babies dehydrate very quickly so get help fast
- continuous dry nappies
- stiff neck
- blotchy skin, rash spots that don't immediately go pale when pressed
- vomiting or sleepiness after a head injury
- unusual or high-pitched cry that suggests your baby might be in severe pain

EMERGENCY
- if your baby has a fit or convulsion, turns blue or very pale
- if your baby has difficulty breathing or makes grunting noises when breathing
- if your baby is exceptionally hard to wake, unusually drowsy or does not seem to know you
- first of all – don't panic
- call an ambulance (999) or go straight to your nearest casualty department
- while you wait for an ambulance try any of the following:

Resuscitation
- Try and stimulate a response by picking your baby up or flicking the soles of the feet.
- If this gets no response place your baby on a firm surface and suck the nose clear.
- Support the back and the neck, tilt head backwards and hold chin upwards.
- Open your baby's mouth wide and take a breath.
- Seal your lips around the baby's nose and mouth.
- Breathe GENTLY into baby's lungs until the chest rises.
- Remove your mouth to allow the air to come out and let baby's chest fall.
- Repeat gentle inflations a little faster than your normal breathing rate removing your mouth after each breath.
- Your baby should begin to breathe within a minute or so.

Fit or convulsion
- Lay your baby on its tummy with the head low and turned to one side.
- Clear your baby's mouth and nose of sick or froth.
- If your baby is hot, cool him/her by sponging the head with tepid water.

Burn or scald
- Put the burnt or scalded part immediately in cold water.
- Lightly cover the part with a clean cloth or sterile dressing.
- Do not apply ointments or prick blisters.
- Paracetamol may provide pain relief: check the dosage, and see a doctor.

Accidents
- Give first aid if you know how.
- If your baby has swallowed pills, medicines or household detergents take the bottle with you to the hospital.

SIGNS OF MENINGITIS
The illness begins like flu but develops into a very high temperature with symptoms such as vomiting, difficulty waking, pale blotchy skin, high-pitched cry, dislike of bright lights, headache and stiff neck or painful joints.

If your baby or child gets a rash of small reddish purple spots which don't go white when they are pressed get your baby to casualty immediately. Early action and treatment is vital with this illness so trust your instincts and act quickly.

THE LAW

- Parents have up to six weeks to supply all the details for registration of the birth at the District Registrar for Births, Marriages and Deaths, or at a local register office.
- There is no legislation governing the naming of children. The name can be changed after it has been registered, and if the change is made within a year it can be done without question.
- A child is considered to be legitimate if the

parents are married when it was born, irrespective of whether they were married at the time of its conception, or if either parent was married to someone else. If a couple were married at the time of the baby's conception, but divorced at the time of its birth, or if the father has died between conception and birth, the child is still considered to be legitimate. If the father marries the mother of their illegitimate child, the child becomes retrospectively legitimate, can be re-registered and obtain a new birth certificate.

Rights of the mother
- Unmarried mothers have the same rights as wives to claim financial support for their children from the father through the Child Support Agency.
- The mother need not be single to claim; she can be married to someone else. See **Money** chapter.
- There is no limit to the lump sum on top of the agreed regular payments.
- The unmarried mother starts off with sole legal control, but the father has the right to acquire joint parental responsibility. This can either be agreed between the parents, or settled in court.

Rights of children
The law treats legitimate and illegitimate children in exactly the same way, except that an illegitimate child cannot succeed to a hereditary title, nor is s/he automatically entitled to British citizenship.

PARENTAL RESPONSIBILITY FORMS
- Unmarried parents may take joint legal responsibility for the child by completing a special court form called the Parental Responsibility Agreement, without having to appear before a judge. This is a serious commitment. The mother will give up her sole rights over the child's upbringing; the father will have an equal and independent say. The shared responsibility entered into through this agreement lasts until the child comes of age at 18.

- The Parental Responsibility Agreement form is easily obtained from local county court offices, is clearly set out and easy to understand. It must be filled in, signed, then two copies posted to the

Family Division, Somerset House, Strand, London WC2R 1LP. There is no fee for this.

DNA TESTING
- Not all fathers of illegitimate children are prepared to admit it. DNA testing methods are now used which are virtually 100% accurate.
- Bodily samples required from parents and child.
- If the father refuses to take the test, the court will act in the child's best interests and will usually assume that the refusal signals guilt. On this basis the father can be made to contribute financially.
- A man may also request a test to prove either that he is or isn't a child's father.

IMMUN- IZATION

- Vaccinations are given to babies after two months to protect them from a range of serious and fatal diseases. They are a safe and effective protection for your child and are available free to all children from your local GP or health centre.
- There have been some arguments about the safety of vaccinating children and the possibility of brain damage being caused by the DTP injection. Major research programmes in the United States and Britain have failed to find any evidence to support this theory and all bodies emphasize that the risk of harmful effects from the actual diseases are far more serious than the remote possibility of complications from the vaccine.
- Homoeopaths strongly support the immunization programme and it is recognized that homoeopathy is not an adequate protection for children against these serious diseases.
- Parents may argue that these diseases are very rare and the chance of your child getting them is very slim. If parents stop vaccinating their children these diseases will become much more common again.
- Vaccines contain small amounts of the bacterium, chemical or virus that causes a disease. Putting

tiny quantities of vaccine into your baby stimulates its immune system to make its own antibodies which defend it against the illness if the baby ever comes into contact with it in the future.

- There can be side-effects to immunization but these are not a reason to avoid vaccinating your child. Babies can develop a fever or site swelling and can be given a correct dose of baby paracetamol. Call a doctor if you are worried, and if there is a serious problem contact the Association of Parents of Vaccine Damaged Children.

THE VACCINES

- The Hib vaccine protects against some strains of meningitis, epiglottitis, pneumonia, septicaemia, infections of the bones and joints.
- The DTP vaccine protects against diphtheria, tetanus and whooping cough.
- Polio.
- The MMR vaccine protects against measles, mumps and rubella.
- The BCG jab protects against tuberculosis and hepatitis B.

The full course of vaccinations for babies and children spans the first 15 years of their life.

- At two, three and four months your baby is given one injection for Hib and DTP, and one polio vaccine by mouth.
- At 12 months your baby will get one MMR injection. At three to five years (before school) they will get an MMR injection, diphtheria and tetanus booster injection and a polio booster by mouth.
- At 10–14 children receive one BCG injection. At 15–18 they should get one injection for tetanus and diphtheria and one polio vaccine by mouth.

MULTIPLE BIRTHS

Who is most likely to have twins (or more!)?

- The twinning gene only appears in females. If a man is a twin or carries the gene he can pass it on to his daughter who may have twins, but he cannot cause his wife to bear twins as a result of his genetic make up.
- Identical twins happen by chance: any woman can have them.
- One in every hundred births is twins. One in every thousand births is identical twins.
- If there are any twins in your direct family (you are a twin or one of your parents is a twin) you are more likely to have twins yourself.
- Older women and women who have already had lots of children have an increased chance of bearing twins (peak risk at the age of 35).
- Black people have more twins than whites, who in turn, have more twins than orientals.
- IVF or other forms of aided conception dramatically increase the chances of a multiple birth.
- There is a 1% chance of you having twins if you have conceived naturally, with the chances rising to 7% if you have taken fertility drugs.
- Twins, triplets, quads, etc. are likely to arrive earlier than the full 40-week term and home births are not likely to be an option.
- Some local authorities can offer home help for a short period after a multiple birth though this is subject to circumstances (call TAMBA for your local support group).

SPECIAL CARE

NEONATAL UNIT

Neo-natal units are designed specifically to give medical help to newborn premature, small or sick babies. There are different levels of care depending on how serious your baby's condition is. Neo-natal staff are all specially trained to take care of tiny babies and 'premmies' can be very, very tiny – babies, weighing only one pound have been successfully cared for. If your baby is small, but has no complications or congenital defects, the chances of your taking home a normal baby when its weight reaches five pounds or more are very good. If your baby has a congenital defect you need to discuss the implications of the specific problem with the staff in the unit.

THE FACTS

- Ten per cent of births are admitted to special care units on arrival.
- Most of these babies are born before 32 weeks or weigh less than four pounds.
- Not all hospitals can provide neonatal intensive care, so unless you live near a major hospital you may find that your baby is transferred quite a distance from your home.
- Multiple births are much more likely to end up in intensive or special care units.
- Problems with small babies are often respiratory.
- If your baby's delivery can be delayed by 12 or 24 hours, the doctors can inject you with a drug which helps your baby's lungs to mature more rapidly prior to birth.
- BLISS offers a network of support for those who have babies in intensive care.

WHAT CAN YOU DO?

- Spend as much time as you can holding your baby on your chest: babies who get this kind of care are known to cry less and spend longer periods sleeping which is good for their progress. Their breathing is also improved and they have fewer episodes of apnoea (stopping breathing). This approach is called 'Kangaroo Care'.
- Find out your hospital's policy on lung surfactant. This is an early treatment that helps prevent respiratory distress syndrome which may not be available for financial reasons. Would it help your baby?
- As soon as your baby is born begin to express and freeze breast milk for your baby until s/he is ready to receive it by tube.
- Manage as much of your baby's care routine as possible: extra small babies still need to be cleaned, dressed and have their nappies changed.
- Know as much about your baby's condition as the doctors and nurses.
- Maintain existing routines for children at home.
- Explain to them what is happening with the new baby.
- Recognize and accommodate your own anxiety and the possibility of postnatal depression.
- Call BLISS and see if the neo-unit can recommend a counsellor if you feel you can't cope.
- Read *Your Premature Baby* and *Born too Soon, Born too Small*.

DISABILITY– KEY POINTS

- If your baby has special needs ask your doctor whether there is a specific name for the problem.
- Are more tests needed to give a clear diagnosis or to confirm what's been found?
- Is it likely to get better or worse, or will it stay roughly the same?
- Where is the best place to get medical help?
- How much medical help will be required and how often?
- Get in touch with other parents who have children with a similar problem.
- Find out how best to help and care for your child.
- Find a support group – if there isn't one, see if you could set one up yourself with help from your local authority.
- Call the Citizens' Advice Bureau to get help in claiming disability living allowance, invalid care allowance and mobility allowance.
- There is a diverse range of groups nationwide offering support and advice for those who have a child with a special need or disability.

ADOPTION/ FOSTERING

The adoption of children can be a gruelling process. In 1994 in Britain fewer than 7,000 orders for adoption were granted and nearly half of these were to step-parents. Because there are more potential adopters than adoptees, the selection agencies can be extremely 'picky'. Be prepared for lots of frustration and disappointment. It's worth inquiring about the basic qualifications set out by the agency as these will differ.

There are 200 authorized adoption agencies, which, by law, are not allowed to charge a fee for their services. Private adoption is illegal in Britain, and even adoptions within families require an adoption order by a court, dependent on a report supplied by the social services. Contact the British Agency for Adoption and Fostering (BAAF) who can give you more information on the subject. You may also want to contact Parent-to-Parent Information on Adoption Services (PPIAS) for advice based on first-hand experience.

REQUIREMENTS

- Adopters must be at least 21 and although it's not 'law', most agencies set an upper age limit of 35 for a woman, and 40 for a man.
- They do not have to be especially well off, but must be able to afford a child.
- If a joint adoption is applied for, the couple must be married. However, single people, unmarried, widowed, separated or divorced can apply.
- Joint applications are not accepted from heterosexual unmarried couples, or homosexual couples.
- A sole application by one partner in these cases is acceptable but the other partner remains legally 'unrecognized'. There have been successful sole applications from lesbian couples (although very few), but virtually none from homosexual men.
- A medical examination.
- Registration with your local social services department.
- Regular 'assessment' visits by social workers.
- Completion of a home study course: these can be free or cost up to £2,500 depending on your local authority.
- A clean police record.
- Contact BAAF (British Agency for Adoption and Fostering).

INTER-COUNTRY ADOPTION

There is still no formal legislation in this country for adoption abroad and many couples have found themselves in deep water by going behind authorities' backs. Contact your social services, the Department of Health, the Home Office and the British Embassy of the country concerned, for information on the correct procedure and an estimate of how long it will take. Contact STORK which specializes in inter-country adoptions.

TRACING A PARENT

- The Adopted Children's Register is kept at the Office of Population Census and Surveys' main office in Hampshire and certified copies are available by applying in person at the London office.

The entry states the child's sex, date of birth and new name, and gives the adopters' names, occupations and the date and place of the adoption order. It does not give the natural mother's or father's name and address.

- This is the child's new 'birth certificate', and it can be replaced by a Short Form Certificate which makes no reference to the fact that the child has been adopted.
- The Adoption Contact Register was set up in 1989 and keeps up-to-date records of parents, and anyone else related to the child by blood or marriage, who wish to supply their details. Adopted children who apply to be registered are also listed. The Registrar General stresses that this is strictly voluntary, and information will be passed on only if both parties want it. You have to be over the age of 18 to trace your genetic parents. The Attachment Parents' Network at PPIAS may also be able to give you more information and help.

FOSTERING

Essentially, any responsible adult can apply to foster children, but as with adoption, the vetting process can vary with different local authorities.

- Fostering is a temporary arrangement for children in need where you care for the child in your home on the basis that if the child's family sorts itself out the child can return to them at any stage.
- The fostering agency will monitor the placement and give you an allowance to cover the child's costs related to their age and the nature of their difficulties.
- To become a foster parent you have to study and become involved in the local foster care structure.
- When you have a child placed in your care you will be required to attend case conferences and maintain contact with the child's family.
- For more information, contact your local authority. The National Foster Care Association (NFCA) can send you an information pack.

GETTING HELP

WHERE TO LOOK FOR CHILDCARE
- local authority for registered child-minders, play groups, crèches, nurseries
- local libraries, noticeboards/general information
- local paper for nurseries, au pairs, nannies
- agencies for au pairs and nannies
- *Yellow Pages* for crèches and nurseries
- The National Childminding Association
- health visitors, available via your local GP or health clinic
- contact the Daycare Trust or Choices in Childcare
- *The Lady* magazine
- *Nursery World*: as above
- Parents at Work give advice on childcare provisions.

CHILDCARE OPTIONS
Playgroups
There are two million playgroup places in the UK. Playgroups usually require parental involvement and operate from about 9.30 am until 12 noon, Monday to Friday, for a small fee of about 50p per child. Children over the age of two and a half can be left with qualified carers and this can help prepare them for a nursery place at age three. They vary in standard from borough to borough. You could also find out about the Pre-school Playgroups Association (PPA).

Childminders
- 25% of under-fives in Britain are looked after by childminders.
- They are defined under the 1989 Children Act, as anyone (except parents or foster parents) who is paid to look after a child under the age of eight for two hours a day or more.
- They must be approved by the local council. After having been vetted by the council, they are included on a register, and their premises should be regularly checked for basic health and safety standards. If they do not register, they are acting illegally and could be fined.
- The council is obliged to tell the parent everything in its knowledge about the prospective childminder which could affect the care of the child.
- The number and age of children that a childminder can look after is strictly controlled and she should be able to give other mothers as referees.
- Childminders usually have children of their own and your child will have the benefit of their company while you are away.
- A childminder is accustomed to looking after children on her own terms so if you have strong feelings about smacking, nutrition, watching videos, religion (or anything else) you should raise them at the outset to avoid potential conflict.
- Childminders will charge anything from £2.50 to £5.00 per hour and when choosing one make sure that they are flexible about doing extra hours in case you are ever delayed.
- Since 1994, childminders have the legal right to smack a child, although not excessively, and only with prior parental consent. If the childminder or the Council can be proven to have acted negligently towards your child, the parent (or the child) can sue for damages.
- Contact the National Childminding Association or for information on all aspects of childcare, the National Childcare Campaign.

Crèches/workplace nursery
- Only 2% of under-fives are lucky enough to have a place at a workplace nursery.
- Crèches or nurseries are usually attached to large institutions or training facilities. They will be run to a timetable, and your child will not get the undivided attention of one carer. Many have long waiting lists, so it is a good idea to put your child's name down for a place as early as you can.
- Working for Childcare offer expert advice.

Live-in nanny
- For parents with more than one pre-school child this is likely be the most secure option for your children. If you have space in your home and enough income to afford it, a live-in nanny offers you freedom and flexibility.
- A nanny should either be a qualified nursery nurse or have experience with babies or small

children. She will usually demand certain conditions such as her own bedroom, TV, two free days a week (usually consecutive), and paid holidays. Live-in nannies should be able to give you previous references, or you can call their college directly.

- Nannies will be looking for a salary of about £200 per week gross (before tax) and can be found through agencies (who charge a fee if they successfully place someone) or specialized magazines.

- You can ring the training colleges which sometimes do probationary schemes where nursery nurses complete their course by working with a family for a year. At the end of their year you write a report on their abilities and, assuming they pass, they are then qualified and free to carry on working for you, if you/they wish, on a renegotiated salary.

Live-out nanny

- In terms of qualifications and references a live-out nanny is much the same as a live-in. They come to your home in the morning and leave when you get home at night.

- You will have to find alternatives for babysitting unless your nanny lives near by and you can negotiate some into your deal.

- Live-out nannies will have the same problems getting to work on time as you do.

- You could also arrange to share a nanny with another family. The cost will depend on whose house s/he is based at, whose car is used, etc. and how many other children are involved. You will need to negotiate a salary with the nanny and the other family.

Au pairs

- Au pairs are usually young people who come to the UK to learn English. They live with a family and help look after children for a certain number of hours per day in return for their board and a small wage. They usually attend a local school or college to learn the written language.

- An au pair is unlikely to have had much experience with children and therefore it might not be a good idea to expect her/him to look after very young babies. You can expect them to babysit

and maybe do some housework but you should clearly set out your expectations and the ground rules at the outset.

- They must enter the country as an au pair (not as a visitor) and can work for two years maximum.

- If you are not planning to leave your kids constantly in their sole charge, au pairs are a great way of getting extra help, but some au pairs can bring all the problems of being a self-absorbed homesick teenager into your home; it may feel like having an extra child to look after.

Things to consider

- The level of English can vary considerably.

- They stay for approximately seven to nine months, so your children will regularly lose someone they may have grown attached to.

- The best way to get an au pair is through an agency. They will normally charge a fee if they place one, and should allow you to interview them in advance. See **Interview questions.**

- If your au pair does not work out within the first month the agency should change or replace her/him at no extra charge.

- The agency will also be able to help your au pair get to know of colleges and other au pairs who are placed locally. It should also help with visa problems, etc.

- Don't take on an au pair without meeting them first and don't be persuaded to take a foreign friend/business colleague's daughter as your au pair.

- You don't have to pay tax and National Insurance for au pairs, and they are entitled to NHS medical and dental care.

Jargon

- Nursery duties only: will only take care of the kids and anything kid-related, i.e. won't bung your undies in with the kids' washing.

- Sole charge: they have complete responsibility for the children during their waking hours.

- NNEB: fully qualified with the Nursery Nurse Educational Board.

- Net pay: after-tax salary usually calculated by deducting 25% of the gross pay.

- Gross pay: pre-tax salary.

Questions to ask on the telephone

- What qualifications do you have?
- How much experience have you got, and with what age children?
- How old are you? (Maturity is a bonus.)
- Can you drive?
- Do you smoke?(if that's important).
- What are your rates?
  If the answers to these questions are satisfactory, arrange an interview in person.

Questions to ask in an interview

- What age children do you prefer looking after?
- What do you like about children and how do you feel you can encourage them to develop in your care?
- What are your views on nutrition, can you cook, will you stick to my policies on sweets/junk food?
- Do your ideas on discipline sit easily with mine?
- What are your long-term ambitions?
- Keep copies of his/her references and make use of them! Read them very carefully and make notes of any points that need clarifying to raise with the referee.

If your child/children have any special needs, you should discuss this in the interview.

Observations during the interview

- If you have a new baby, ask if s/he is confident about caring for one. If the baby is there, try getting him/her to hold it during the interview and see how s/he handles it.
- If you have older kids introduce them briefly and see how they interact.
- How punctual was s/he when s/he arrived for the interview? Does s/he wear a watch?

- Is s/he neat, tidy and presentable looking?
- If his/her history has any gaps, or the dates don't make sense, ask what s/he was doing during the time that is not on record.
- Is s/he relaxed? How would s/he cope in an emergency? Does s/he have any first-aid experience?
- Does s/he sound too good to be true, over-confident or pushy? Remember, most people being interviewed for a job would be a little nervous.
- Do you feel comfortable, and do your instincts tell you that this person is trustworthy?
- Is s/he the kind of person that you wouldn't mind spending some time with yourself?
- This person will be a major influence on your child: does that thought make you feel at all nervous?

If it isn't working

- If your child is constantly upset in the first month, try and give the carer more pointers on distracting and calming. Give advice on ways that you think s/he could improve the relationship, and perhaps make lunchtime visits to check out the situation.
- Get a breakdown of the day's activities and the times when your child gets most upset. See if you can find ways for the emotional triggers that set him/her off to be avoided.
- If you monitor the situation and your child still seems to be upset, clingy and withdrawn, you may need to change the carer. It may be no reflection on the carer but most children should get used to an arrangement within a couple of months and it is better to trust your instincts and try again, no matter how inconvenient.

FAMILY

These days the traditional family seems to be the exception rather than the rule. Families can be a tremendous source of joy and support, but they can also include people you would never normally speak to if you weren't related by blood. The conservative image of the 'nuclear family' generally consists of a mother and father (married to each other) and 2.4 children. In fact, the term 'family' covers any two (or more) people related to each other by blood, adoption, marriage or mutual agreement. Although the legal definition of 'families' often excludes cohabiting heterosexual or gay couples, in this book we are defining families as any structure which contains children, includes the growing number of single parents.

Theories on how to raise children have changed dramatically over the last few decades. Beyond providing love, care and attention, there is no 'correct' way to bring up children, although they do now have very specific legal rights which must be respected. This chapter concentrates on the practicalities of raising children: their education, their emotional and physical changes and the laws that govern them between the ages of nought and 18.

FROM
THE
CRADLE
TO THE
CLUB

Age	Physical development	Intellectual development	Interests	Legalities
	Children develop physically at different rates and the times given below are only approximate. Children will do things only when they themselves are ready.	Each child is unique and so is their intellectual development. Parents know their children better than anyone and are the best and most attentive teachers they will ever have.		
Birth	No physical control over their muscles. Can see contrasting images and will look at simple black and white patterns which can be hung over their cot. May not like having clothes removed, being naked or having a bath: top and tail your baby with a sponge or have a bath with her/him until s/he feels more secure.	Most relaxed and happy when being held close to you. Sleeps nearly all the time – except of course when you want to. S/he may be startled by sudden loud noises or upset by too many people handling them. Expose your baby to general household noises so that s/he gets used to sleeping through them.	Getting used to a strange new environment. The only thing your baby recognizes is you, your voice, your touch, the familiarity of your heartbeat. At two weeks a baby can see enough to recognize its mother's face.	You must name and register the birth of your child within the first 6 weeks.
6 weeks	The neck muscles are stronger. Begins to try to lift head while lying on tummy.	Smiles now make everything worthwhile. Can follow a brightly coloured moving toy held about 8in away. May recognize other voices.	Touching you, playing with you, examining your face, enjoying your soft breathing on her/his face, interesting sounds, close physical contact.	6 weeks is the deadline for registration.
3 mths	Can support own head. Makes cooing noises. Begins to reach out for objects. At two, three and four months s/he should be immunized with HIB, DTP and polio vaccines.	Begins to respond to all sorts of stimulation. Cause and effect: a baby of this age soon works out that hitting the toys on the baby gym makes them move, this keeps baby busy and develops early hand/eye co-ordination.	Likes to sit where s/he can see everything that is going on. Enjoys kicking or swiping at a baby gym.	

Age	Physical development	Intellectual development	Interests	Legalities
6 mths	Starts to make more sounds. Can see across a room. Can hold an object and get it into her/his mouth to suck. May cut the first teeth: two bottom front ones are quickly followed by top front two. (Stock up on baby paracetamol.) Begins to eat pureed veg, mashed banana and loves to chew on raw carrot, apple or hard crusts of bread which help build up healthy gums.	Will repeat something over and over again, trying to get it right. Babies learn by their mistakes so they must be allowed to make them, even though they may become very frustrated by their inability to do things.	Exploring the world around them. Puts everything in the mouth: safety and hygiene are priorities, toys should be cleaned regularly. For miraculous results rub grimy old plastic with baby wipes and rinse. Loves physical play, jumping in a baby bouncer, being bounced on the bed. Is entertained by noisy toys, toys that move or are made of different materials or consistencies, and of course the contents of your handbag.	
8 mths	Sitting up unsupported brings a degree of independence. May try to stand by pulling her/himself up on the furniture. Can pass things from one hand to the other. May be crawling or getting ready to, though some babies shuffle along on their bum or go straight to walking.	Her/his main concern is mobility. Your baby begins to realize that s/he is a separate individual.	Likes to push cars and crawl along with them. Pictures of other babies fascinate. Mirrors let babies explore their own identity and the fact that they are separate individuals. Once a baby can sit up, having a bath is much more fun. Never leave a child unattended in the bath even for a second.	
12 mths	Walking or getting ready to. Needs an MMR vaccination. Back teeth may be painful as they break through the gum.	Will imitate all your behaviour – good and bad. Will begin to remember things. Points to things. Makes sounds like 'dada' which don't mean what you want them to but are the start of speech.	Climbing stairs: if s/he is fully supervised let her/him have a go but otherwise block stairs with a gate. Block sockets, keep cleaning fluids/medicines/shampoo, etc. out of reach. Safety is now a major issue all of the time.	Within 12 months of registering a birth you can change the name and any errors on the birth certificate.

Age	Physical development	Intellectual development	Interests	Legalities
2 yrs	Begins to develop bladder control which eventually means the end of nappies in the daytime. Encourage her/him to use the potty but don't push it. May still need a nap in the daytime but should have a set routine and a fixed bedtime. This is a good time for the first dental check-up.	Language has begun to develop with simple one-word identification which rapidly progresses over the next 6 months. Becomes more self-confident. Mum is no longer the absolute centre of attention but s/he may have mood swings, 'terrible twos', as s/he tries to find a balance between being a baby and an independent toddler. Teach her/him to stay on the footpath and always to hold your hand when crossing the road.	Mimics you in play with plastic food, telephones, dolls, buggies, etc. Enjoys books and stories and repetitive word and song games. Looks after dolls and teddys and forms very strong attachments to certain toys. Let her/him make choices, choosing clothes, toys, books, etc. Will enjoy Parent and toddler groups and one-o'clock clubs.	
3 yrs	Should begin to get through the night without wetting the bed – lift her/him to the loo before you go to bed. More co-ordinated, able to kick a ball, hop, skip and pour water from one vessel to another without spilling. MMR and diphtheria injections, tetanus and polio boosters	May be getting bored at home by now and ready to go to a playgroup and form her/his own friendships. Your local authority under 8's group will have details of local playgroups, nurseries and primary schools.	Enjoys playing with other children and begins to learn to share and take turns (a bit). Drawing, painting, model making, collage and printing all aid hand and eye co-ordination and give a sense of personal achievement. Lego and building blocks aid spatial development.	Can begin attending a nursery school.
4 yrs	Should be able to build with bricks, thread beads and do relatively intricate work with hands. Should be able to catch and throw.	Can draw a simple face with eyes, nose, mouth, hair and body, though not very well. Plays imaginatively with friends or alone. Can say or sing most of the alphabet and recognize the shapes and letters of their own name. Knows product brands, shops – the start of reading.	Nature/animals are fascinating and educational. Enjoys gardening and watching pot plants grow from seed. Enjoys simple puzzles/jigsaws.	Children are legally entitled to a nursery place.

Age	Physical development	Intellectual development	Interests	Legalities
5yrs	Physically able to do pretty much anything. The school day may be tiring for her/him and s/he may need a rest or a quiet time in the afternoon. A new school exposes children to new bugs so s/he may come down with more coughs and colds than usual until s/he builds up her/his resistance. In the next year starts to lose milk teeth and gets her/his final set.	Begins primary school (see **Education** section). Starts to read, write and do basic maths. Begins to grasp morality and the concept of right and wrong. Begins to grasp monetary values. Listen to them read every day.	Friends (very important) to play with, dressing up, making up games with small figures, cars, dolls' houses, farm animals. Card or board games that can be played with friends develop concentration and patience. Will be very interested in her/his own personal history, looking at photos, hearing stories about her/his development, etc.	Must receive full-time education. Can attend a U or PG film. Can drink alcohol at home. Must pay a reduced 'child fare' on public transport. (Only two children under the age of five are allowed to travel free per adult.)
7yrs	Should be getting lots of exercise at school and at home. Participating in sports together as a family keeps everyone fit. Should be swimming unaided.	Should be reading, writing and doing simple arithmetic. If ability in these areas does not match her/his general ability in other aspects you may want to speak to an educational adviser. May not believe in Santa Claus any more.	7 year olds tend to keep themselves very busy with extra curricular activities, friends, playing, reading, school, etc.	Can draw money from a TSB or PO savings account. If s/he appears to understand basic banking transactions some banks will allow them to open an ordinary account.
10yrs	The onset of puberty is happening or is just around the corner. BCG injection required.	You should be mentally preparing her/him for the emotional, physical and social changes that s/he is about to experience. Choosing a secondary school that is right for her/him both socially and academically needs research.	Interests for boys and girls may have diversified and become more gender specific.	Criminal responsibility starts. If it can be shown that they knew they were doing something 'seriously wrong' they can be convicted of a crime and fined up to £250. Boys can be convicted of indecent assault or rape and sent to a young offenders' institution.

Age	Puberty	Teen angst	The diplomatic parent	Legalities
	The onset of puberty gradually happens between the ages of 10 and 16. Girls generally mature earlier than boys though everyone develops at different rates. Some kids will be fully mature at 12 and others not till they are 16. All these time frames are based on averages, so if your child matures earlier or later don't worry.	Surviving the trauma of being a teenager requires tactical skill and intense preparation. First of all make sure s/he knows what is going to happen physically and emotionally. Then try and let your child know that you can be relied on to be diplomatic, sensitive and accommodating for the next 6 years.	S/he may or may not want to include her/his parents in her/his development. The best you may be able to do is keep the lines of communication between you and your child open and objective. Let them know that they can turn to you when they want advice but only raise personal issues when they are ready.	
12yrs	Girls will develop small breasts at some time between the ages of 10 and 12. About a third of boys develop small lumps of tissue under nipples. Don't worry. The lumps are caused by newly working hormones and will disappear in a few months.	S/he may feel embarrassed by their obvious physical development especially if their friends are less mature.	Be diplomatic and discreet. Pre-empt your child's needs. Anticipate your child needing tampons, bras, spot creams, etc. in advance to save them the embarrassment of having to ask.	Can buy a pet. Persistent offenders can be put under 2-year secure training orders.
13yrs	Hair, usually curly, grows under the armpits, over the pubic bone and may become more dense on the legs and arms. Perhaps slightly later, boys also develop hair, their voice deepens, their testicles become larger, drop lower, and they begin to produce sperm which may cause wet dreams. Boys of this age need some privacy.	Finally a teenager. Most of your child's friends will be developing physically at about the same rate and they will want to spend lots of time with them. Your phone bill may suddenly escalate. Your child will want some freedom.	Leave books on sex, love, family relationships and women's health on the lower level bookshelves so they can be reached. Your child's room should be a private place for her/him.	Can open a bank account at the manager's discretion. Can work part time outside school for 20 hours per week but not for more than two hours on school days and Sundays.

Age	Puberty	Teen angst	The diplomatic parent	Legalities
14yrs	Girls may already have their periods though some girls get them a bit later. Extra hormones mean that s/he may be suffering from acne, blackheads, greasy hair, genital or foot odour. If a girl is thinking about contraception anyway you may find that a low-dosage progesterone pill also helps clear up her acne.	The average age for a girl to have her first sexual experience is 14. May already be finding herself in situations where it is becoming increasingly difficult to say no. When she does eventually find herself in a relationship where she might actually consider going all the way, help them think about the consequences beforehand.	This could be the time to discuss a better allowance in return for more help around the house. Get her/him a BT chargecard so that s/he can phone home (only) – the cost of the call goes on to your home telephone bill. If you worry about her/him going out at night a pager or a mobile phone might be a good Christmas present. You may have to work out together how to pay the bills though.	Can be convicted of a criminal offence or sent to a young offenders' institution. Boys can be convicted of rape and unlawful intercourse with a girl under the age of 16. Can be fined up to £1,000 if s/he commits a criminal offence. Can own an airgun. Can go into a bar with an adult but cannot buy or consume any alcohol. Can have her/his finger and palm prints taken by the police if they have obtained a magistrates' court order. Can take the responsibility for fastening her/his own seat belt in a car.
15yrs	S/he is probably nearing maturity and is much more conscious of her/his physical appearance. Though her/his body will change a great deal in the next 10 years her/his basic physique will stay the same. Will need tetanus and diphtheria and polio booster injections. 1 in 5 young people has had full sexual intercourse by the age of 16.	At 15 s/he is waiting for her/his brain to catch up with her/his body. S/he is probably trying to deal with exams, boyfriend/girlfriend troubles and wondering what the hell to do with her/his life. S/he is nervous about the future, bored with the past and generally impatient for things to happen. Try and help her/him take the long view. S/he is practising for the main event.	Your child suspects you think they are a pain in the ass. You know they are a pain. It really is a phase. S/he wants freedom, needs to dye her/his hair blonde. Could s/he get a job? They may be willing to strike a deal on hairdos, nights out, etc. in return for chores, babysitting, etc. Stay informed. Make a point of letting her/him know that if s/he is in control, well prepared and fully informed it's OK.	Can own a shotgun and ammunition with a licence. Can be sent to a youth custody centre. Can gain admittance to a '15-rated' film.

Age	Puberty	Teen angst	The diplomatic parent	Legalities
16yrs	Most of them don't use contraception or protection because the event isn't planned. Important to be fully aware of contraception available. They have a mutual responsibility to organize themselves. Going on the pill does not prevent her/him contracting Aids, so condoms are the best bet.	Should s/he drink or take drugs just to be a part of the crowd? The chances are s/he will try everything once but encourage her/him to make her/his own decisions. Peer groups can be a positive support but the pressure to conform should not include doing things that they are not comfortable with.	You might want to catch up on the social scene, what goes on and who does what. Let them know that you will be more accommodating if reassured you can trust them to be responsible.	Have the right to say no to medical treatment. Can consent to heterosexual sex. There is no legal age for homosexual sex between women. Must pay full prescription charges unless s/he is a student, pregnant or the mother of a child under one. Can marry with her/his parents' consent. Can leave school and work full time. Can buy lottery tickets. Can drink beer in a pub with a meal and can buy cigarettes. Must pay full fare on the Underground, buses and railway.
17yrs	Physically s/he is probably exploring her/his sexuality (see **Sex** chapter). Feeling comfortable about sex so that s/he can be as confident as possible, means reading as much as s/he can and experimenting alone. Over one third of the population are unfit, so before s/he rushes to learn to drive, think. Remind her/him of the physical and environmental benefits of sticking with her/his bicycle.	Most girls have their first sexual experience with someone who is a bit older than them but it is usually a fairly unsophisticated event with little regard for her satisfaction. Once he comes it's over. It's important to place early sexual experiences in context. Like everything else it gets better with practice. Boys may also have their first sexual experience with someone older.	Money determines where s/he can go, what s/he can do and how good s/he looks when s/he is doing it. Working in the holidays or at weekends will get kids out of the house, earn them some cash and help them meet new people. They need to start finding ways of being more self-sufficient.	Can drive a car or motorcycle. Can go into a betting shop (but not bet). Can be tried on any charge in an adult court and sent to prison. Can be fined up to £2,000. Can vote. Can marry without parental consent. Can apply for a passport. Can change her/his name.

Age	The diplomatic parent	Legalities
18yrs	S/he is now an adult even if s/he doesn't behave that way. If you are still on speaking terms after years of adolescence, things are looking good. To maintain cordial relations the best advice is to let them get out and get on with their life. To really grow s/he needs to escape and it's amazing, once s/he is out on her/his own, s/he will want to come home and spend time with her/his family – even if it is only to use the washing machine!	Is eligible for jury service. Can donate blood and organs. Can own land and own a house. Can sue in her/his own name. Can enter into binding contracts and obtain credit cards and cheque books. Can make a will. Can buy drinks at the bar of a pub. Can be tattooed. Can bet. Can be admitted to an '18-rated' film. Her/his identity can be disclosed to the media if s/he is a witness or defendant in any court case.

HEALTH

MEDICAL EMERGENCY

You are in an emergency first-aid situation, the ambulance has been called: what do you do? It may seem daunting but there are a few procedures to follow. Most importantly, a casualty needs unobstructed breathing and blood circulation.

- Check vital signs.
- Check whether the air passage is blocked by food or vomit, with the casualty on his/her back.
- Check breathing: this can be difficult, but put your ear over mouth and nose and listen.
- Check pulse: the most reliable pulse is around the neck and should be the easiest to find. Turn face to one side and slide fingers from voice box into depression alongside and press gently.
- Check for bleeding: major external bleeding will be obvious, but internal is not. Look for pale, grey skin, cold skin, shallow rapid breathing, weak or rapid pulse.

BREATHING

If the casualty has stopped breathing they will die in minutes. If the airway is clear, but there is no breathing, begin artificial 'mouth to mouth' respiration. This gets air into the lungs.

- Lay casualty on back.
- Tilt head and chin and open mouth, loosen clothing around throat and chest.
- Seal your mouth over casualty's mouth and hold their nose.
- Blow two quick breaths into the mouth, watch the chest which should rise. If it doesn't the airway may be still blocked and you may need to treat them for choking.
- Continue at a rate of 12–16 blows a minute until breathing is restored.

CHOKING: UNCONSCIOUS

Breathing has stopped and artificial respiration has failed to raise the chest. The airway is blocked; you must remove the obstruction.

- From the lying on back position turn the head to one side and sweep the inside of the mouth with two fingers, taking care not to push anything

further down throat. If this fails:
- Back slaps: roll the body onto one side and support the chest with your thigh, put head well back to open airway.
- Slap between the shoulder-blades with the heel of your hand, repeating four times if necessary.
- Check the mouth.
- If this fails, try an abdominal thrust or 'Heinrich manoeuvre'. The idea is to use the air in the chest to dislodge the blockage by a series of thrusts to the upper abdomen. *Use only as a last resort as you could damage internal organs.*
- Place body lying on back with head tilted back.
- Kneel astride casualty's thighs.
- Place your hands one on top of the other with the heels of your hands resting above the navel and fingers upwards.
- With your arms straight make quick thrusts upwards and inwards as if up into the centre of the ribcage. Repeat if necessary up to four times.

CHOKING: CONSCIOUS

- The person may be panicking and clasping throat; unable to speak, with noisy breathing and obvious difficulty.
- Encourage casualty to cough out the blockage. If they cannot, help them to a chair and bend head between their knees so that it is lower than their lungs.
- Slap sharply between shoulder-blades using the heel of your hand. Slap up to four times if necessary.
- Check mouth to see if it has dislodged. If not, stand them up and stand behind them.
- Put your arms around them and make a fist of one hand and press it thumb inwards above the navel but below the breastbone and clasp the other hand on it.
- Pull upwards and inwards quickly in succession up to four times. If there is no response, return to back slaps.

SEVERE BLEEDING

The loss of 0.5 litres of blood causes faintness, 1.5 leads to collapse, 2.25 can be fatal. Immediate action must be taken to stop blood loss. Bleeding may not be apparent but internal bleeding may be occurring.

- For small wounds, apply pressure for 5–15

minutes to let clotting take effect.

- If a limb is bleeding; lay the casualty down, raise limb and prop it up above the heart level.

SIGNS OF MENINGITIS

- Meningitis is a bacterial infection which begins as a flu-like illness but develops rapidly into a very high temperature with symptoms such as vomiting, difficulty waking, pale blotchy skin, high-pitched cry, dislike of bright lights, headache and stiff neck, painful joints or generally floppy and unresponsive. Early action and treatment is vital with this illness so trust your instincts and act quickly if you think your child is very sick.

- If your child gets a rash of small reddish-purple spots which don't go white or skin-coloured when they are pressed, take your child to casualty immediately. Don't wait for your GP to come to you first.

VIRAL/BACTERIAL INFECTION?

- A virus may give you the same symptoms as a bacterial infection but it behaves in a very different way. A virus must invade your own cells in order to multiply, which makes it very difficult to treat because if you want to destroy the virus you also destroy the cells that you are trying to cure. Antibiotics do *not* cure a viral infection.

- A virus is usually contracted by 'droplet infection': you inhale the spray from someone else's sneeze or cough. Viruses can also be eaten in food that has been contaminated with faeces, or may be transmitted through the surface of the skin through a flesh wound, e.g. rabies if bitten by a rabid dog.

- Viral infections can turn into bacterial infections if left untreated. A viral 'cold' can turn the natural bacteria that live in your throat into bacteria which invade the respiratory system and cause bronchitis.

- Viral infections include colds, flu, measles, chickenpox, malaria and smallpox.

- There are millions of different types of bacterium in, on and outside our bodies which do no harm and a great deal of good (helping our bodies digest our food, for example).

- Occasionally these bacteria become dangerous and can multiply and divide causing infection to spread. Because they do not invade our cells they can usually be isolated and treated. Bacterial infections can be treated effectively with antibiotics.

- Bacterial infection can be spread in the same ways as viral infections. If someone is ill with a serious or life-threatening bacterial infection such as meningitis, all members of their family will be treated with antibiotics to prevent it spreading.

- Epidemics of bacterial infection can be spread by a 'carrier' – someone who carries harmful bacteria without actually suffering any symptoms themselves.

- Some examples of bacterial infections are meningitis, typhoid, gastro-enteritis, streptococcal throat or bronchitis.

SCHOOL

PRE-SCHOOL CHILDREN

- Details of local playgroups, one-o'clock clubs, state and private nurseries are available in a free booklet from your local authority department dealing with children's services.
- Phone the ones you are interested in and make an appointment to visit.
- Talk to the staff, get a feel for the school/nursery and its approach. At this stage of development the emphasis is on energy and creativity not academic achievement.
- What are the class numbers and the staff-to-children ratio?
- Has the school/nursery been inspected? If it has, you are entitled to read the report.
- Will you be allowed to stay with your child until s/he settles in?
- Is there a waiting list?
- Are there after-school or holiday-playschemes?

NURSERIES

Day nurseries are set up to look after and educate children while their parents are otherwise occupied. Children can attend for full or half days depending on the policy of the nursery and sometimes the age of the child. Some nurseries will take children from the age of six weeks but many are for older pre-school children in the age range from 2–5. Nurseries must be registered with the local authority and will be inspected on a regular basis. Make sure you visit the nursery and read the reports before you commit to send your child there. They are run by professional staff with training and experience and a certain minimum staff to child ratio must be maintained at all times with younger children clearly demanding more staff. These figures will be set by the local authority and can include students and volunteers in the number of carers. Costs range from free for children in need to very expensive (£170 per week in inner cities).

There are basically four types of nursery:

1 Workplace
Where your employer provides nursery facilities.

2 Community nurseries
You are likely to have to live in a certain catchment area and may have to fulfil special criteria for your child to qualify, e.g. low income or single parent. Some of these nurseries also sell some of the available places at full cost to working parents who can afford the full fees.

3 Council nurseries
These are usually for children of families with difficulties and the places are often filled by referrals from social workers or health visitors. Like community nurseries some full price places may also be sold to those who can afford them.

4 Private nurseries
Often run as small businesses or part of a chain of nurseries. These may well be more flexible and take children from an earlier age.

Contact your local authority or the National Childcare Campaign for further information.

PRIMARY/SECONDARY SCHOOL

One of the most important and increasingly difficult decisions a parent makes is how to educate their child at primary and secondary level.

- Standards of education vary dramatically from school to school and paying for a private education does not necessarily guarantee that your child will be academic.
- If you can afford to educate your child privately you will not be limited by the boundaries of your borough but state education is almost entirely determined by where you live.
- Many families actually move house to be in the catchment area of a good school.
- Your local authority will provide you with details of all the schools that your child might be accepted by. Some of these schools will be open to all locals, others may give priority to practising members of a specific religious group.
- All children are entitled to free education until they are 18 years old and education is compulsory from 5 until the age of 16.
- Contact the National Association for Primary Education for advice or your local authority for more information about availability.

FINDING THE RIGHT SCHOOL

- Visit as many as you can.
- What is the headmaster/mistress like: progressive, conservative, confident, boring? Their personality will have a major influence on the atmosphere and attitudes throughout the school.
- What is their admissions policy and does your child fit the criteria?
- How many children will be admitted and if they have a siblings policy does that reduce the chance of a place for your child?
- Examine their OFSTED reports and look at the pattern of their academic results. Are they getting better or worse?
- Ask more than two parents who have children at the school what they think of it.
- What are the facilities like?
- Is it their policy to encourage individual development and what number of children reach further education?
- What are the class sizes and the ratio of teachers to children?
- What is the turnover of staff? If they change very frequently it might indicate that teachers are finding the school difficult.
- All schools will say that they actively encourage parent involvement but ask how.
- What extra-curricular activities are available and are they free: e.g. each school has a policy on charges for music lessons, expeditions, etc.
- What are the travel arrangements to and from the school; is financial help available?
- Check the involvement and consistency of teachers.
  If you need help finding your child a school/help with payments contact the Family Welfare Association or the National Association for Maternal and Child Welfare.

THE RIGHT TO APPEAL

If your child is refused entrance to the school of your choice (a local authority decision), an appeal can be made. The appeals procedure is available from the authority, but in general all appeals must be made in writing to the school as soon as possible. It is difficult to win an appeal if you live outside the school's catchment area. Having appealed you will go to an interview at the school to present your case. If you are unsuccessful at this stage, you can complain of 'unreasonable admission arrangements' to the Secretary of State for Education, but this is rarely effective.

Schools allocate places on the following criteria

- the child lives very near the school or in the catchment area
- the child's siblings go to the school
- medical or social reasons (support this with a doctor's certificate)

Schools refuse places for the following:

- the class is already full with children who live nearer to the school than your child does
- it would be incompatible with normal admissions policy (i.e. you are the wrong religion)
- the child has inadequate 'ability or aptitude' (has failed the 11+, for example)

THE NATIONAL CURRICULUM

- This applies only to children in state schools (private schools are exempt, e.g. Montessori) between the ages of 5 and 16.
- All schools have to teach the following foundation subjects: English, mathematics, science, technology (and design), history, geography, a modern foreign language, information technology, music, art and PE. Each subject has standard assessment tasks to ascertain pupils' understanding of knowledge and skills.
- Leaflets on national assessment (SATs: Standard Assessment Tests) are available to parents, and the controversial 'league tables' of SAT results are published in national newspapers. More information is available by applying directly to the National Curriculum Council.

TYPES OF SCHOOL

Most primary and secondary schools are county schools and are funded by the local education authority (LEA). Some state schools have a special agreement that allows them to take children of a certain religion. There are a variety of religiously orientated schools: Catholic, Church of England, Muslim, Jewish and Quaker.
If the LEA decides a child has 'special educa-

tional needs' they must consult the parents before making their formal assessment. They produce a written statement of the child's needs, which the parents can appeal against. They can also ask for a reassessment. Wherever possible, children with special needs are kept in ordinary schools and extra funding can be made available for specialist teaching. Advice is available from Citizens' Advice Bureaux, or specialist educational advice bodies.

- **Direct grant schools** were usually former grammar schools which opted for independence from the state-run system. They manage their LEA budgets and appoint their own governors and teachers.
- **Grant-maintained** is a relatively new type of school, transferring control from local authority to central government. Their financing comes direct from the Department of Education.
- **Public schools:** there are about 2,200 public schools in Britain, educating 7% of the school population. A list of these is available from ISIS, the Independent Schools Information Service, based in London. Public schools are not obliged to provide information about themselves as state schools are. If you decide to send your child to a public school, you will be entering into a legal contract with the school, and you should be fully aware of what this entails before making a decision. Most relevant information is found in the school prospectus, which should be examined in the same way any contract is examined. You should clarify up front anything that concerns you (e.g. corporal punishment) and have this information confirmed in writing.

SCHOOL RULES

Sex education: schools are not obliged by law to provide sex education classes, but it is considered appropriate.

School uniforms: uniforms don't have to be a special brand. If a similar item of clothing (a blazer/sweater) is available elsewhere cheaper, you are entitled to buy that one instead. However if your child doesn't wear a uniform and they are meant to, the head can suspend them. The LEA produces an *Information for Parents* booklet which gives details of school uniform rules. Shoes for schools don't have to be a specific type though you may have to stick to a recommended colour and trainers may not be allowed. Don't feel obliged to buy expensive brand-name shoes because they are 'better for your child's feet'. If the shoe you choose is the right size with plenty of room and good support your child's feet will be fine.

Religion: schools are required by law to provide lessons, and to start each day with an 'assembly' or collective worship; in county schools, this 'worship' must be non-denominational. However, many schools ignore this obligation. Children do not have to attend either assembly or lessons if the parents object.

Discipline: corporal punishment is illegal in state schools and although this does not extend to public schools it is becoming increasingly rare. Teachers who hit pupils can be charged with assault.

Exclusion: this may be on medical grounds (e.g. the child has nits). Pregnant girls are often excluded, although the LEA is duty bound to continue educating them.

Suspension: this is generally resorted to when children break the school rules more than once. The headteacher has the power to suspend a pupil for 'any cause which s/he considers adequate'. The head has to inform the governors (and may need their consent), who will then consult the LEA. The child remains on the school register so the LEA is not obliged to find another school for them. Parents of a suspended child should write to the head asking why the child was suspended, how long the suspension will last and whether they have the right to appeal. Copies of this correspondence should be sent to the governors and the LEA.

Expulsion: this is the most dramatic action a school can take and reflects serious, or persistent, breaking of the school rules (or the law). The consequences are quite different depending on whether or not the child is in a public or state school. In either case, the head does not have the power to expel a pupil: expulsion is at the discretion of the LEA, or the governors, or both. If a pupil is expelled from a state school the child is removed from the register. As it is the duty of the

LEA to provide the means for a child to be educated, they are then responsible for finding an alternative school. For this reason, suspension is often favoured over expulsion. Expelled state school pupils have a right of appeal, which means that many expelled pupils may be readmitted.

- **School attendance and truancy:** if you have not opted for an alternative method of education, and your child fails to attend school regularly, it is you, the parent, who is committing the offence, even if you were not aware that your child was not going to school.

LEARNING AT HOME

Teaching our children at home is not really an option for most of us. Unless we have something very special to offer or there are extraordinary circumstances or a precocious talent to nurture, most of us feel that school benefits children both intellectually and socially, helping them to form their own relationships outside the home. If you live in an area where there are no schools or the quality of available schooling is inadequate you may decide you have no other option, but it is not a decision to be made lightly. You don't have

to notify the authorities. However, if they contact you, you must be able to prove that your child is receiving a 'suitable education' – full-time and appropriate to your child's age and ability. The local authority can't tell you what, or how, to teach your child. It helps if you are a qualified teacher, but it is not essential. If they are not satisfied they can take out a supervision order, and, in extreme cases, take the child into care if it appears that there will be no other access to an education. The LEA also offers a home tuition service.

CHILD ABUSE

All children have basic needs: anything that interferes with these needs – whether by act or omission – constitutes abuse. The emotional repercussions for a child subject to abuse are endless. They can develop a warped sense of their worth, feel unloved, powerless and cynical. In 1996 more than 10,947 children called ChildLine about physical and sexual abuse: 95% of them knew the abuser. Abusers might be parents, uncles, aunts, grandparents, teachers, family friends, siblings, other children. In 1994 there were 50 convictions for incest, 274 for gross indecency and 110 for unlawful intercourse with girls aged under 13.

BEHAVIOURAL INDICATIONS
Children who suffer any kind of persistent mistreatment over a period of time can develop some or all of the following traits:
• difficult/challenging behaviour
• fear of doing or saying the wrong thing
• excessive attention-seeking behaviour
• incapacity or unwillingness to play
• excessive pseudo-mature behaviour
• need to take responsibility for parent/s
• a 'frozen watchfulness'
If you think you can detect signs of abuse, contact Child Watch, The National Children's

Bureau, the NSPCC, Barnardos, the Child Protection Helpline or BASPCAN (British Association for the Study and Prevention of Child Abuse). ChildLine is a charity set up for children (and adults who were abused as children). It offers 24-hour telephone advice and issues bulletins to promote public understanding. Publications and videos are available for children, advising them how to deal with threatened or actual abuse. If you feel you cannot cope or that there is a possibility you may abuse your children contact Parents Anonymous.

SEXUAL ABUSE
This is when children are forced into sexual acts or situations by others.
Some physical indications of sexual abuse are
• itching, irritation, discomfort in genital/abdominal areas
• difficulty in walking or sitting
• stained clothing or bedding; evidence of clothing being tampered with
• recurrent urinary-tract infections

Concern should be shown for the child who
• shows excessive preoccupation with, or precocious knowledge of adult sexual behaviour
• shows a marked fear of adults, usually men, but occasionally both men and women
• has depressive symptoms, uses narcotics or alcohol, makes suicide attempts, or runs away
• suddenly begins to 'wet' her/himself frequently
• has a sudden drop in school performance and in general concentration
• avoids PE or swimming or will not undress for medical examinations
• has a poor relationship with the father figure in the household
• shows little warmth towards her/his mother
• has few friends
• manifests very low self-esteem
• indicates sexual activity through play or drawings

PLAYGROUND/PEER GROUP ABUSE
Bullying from peers is one of the most prevalent forms of abuse. Having a combination of emotional and physical (and this may include sexual) elements, bullying will have similar effects

on the child as those listed under the abuse headings above. If you suspect that your child is being bullied, remember:

- Don't underestimate the child's need to protect aggressors out of a mixture of terror and empathy.
- Avoid confrontation with the abuser, or his/her parents.
- Do not wait for absolute confirmation of your fears. At the first possible opportunity, seek professional help from your GP, health visitor, social services or school.
- Try to create an especially nurturing environment, without being over-protective. The child's sense of independence and ability to look after her/himself has been shattered; build it back up.
- Contact the Anti-Bullying Campaign for more information.

WHO TO CONTACT

If you are concerned for the well-being of a child and have even the smallest indication that they are subject to abuse, contact one of the following:

- **Local authority:** your town hall or local government offices will have a social services department with an office set up for child welfare and with a brief relating to abuse. They may have an out-of-hours emergency number.
- **School:** if you have any contact with the child's school and feel you could speak with them, make an arrangement to see the child's teacher and/or headteacher.
- **Social workers:** if you have any direct contact with a social worker, or know that the child has been allocated one, approach them.
- **Local hospital:** some hospitals have a social work department or children and families specialists. If the child has approached you in a distressed state and you feel they need medical attention, go straight to accident and emergency.
- **NSPCC**.
- **The police**.

WHAT WILL HAPPEN

Any of the above authorities or welfare institutions can organize an investigation into the child's well-being.

A Child Assessment Order (CAO) allows social workers to make an assessment of a child's needs over a period of seven days. A Supervision Order allows social workers full access to monitor or supervise the welfare of a child. An Emergency Protection Order (EPO) is issued when local authorities or the NSPCC are denied access to a child or believe the child to be in danger. A Recovery Order is issued if parents have disappeared to avoid the local authority, and taken the child with them.

However, local authorities have a statutory duty to take reasonable steps to reduce the need for supervision orders. They may provide counselling, day care and key social workers for both child and parents. They may also set up collaborations between housing, education and health sectors so that any needs affecting the well-being of the family are met.

CHILDREN IN CARE

Before a child is taken into care the local authority must consult the child, the parents or anyone with parental responsibility. The local authority must actively promote contact between the child and its family, unless it has been decided that this would be to the detriment of the child's well-being. A child leaving care between the ages of 16 and 21 is eligible by law for aftercare services. This may just take the form of help and advice in easing back into a life independent of institutionalized care. The local social services department will supply details: depending on the authority's resources, aftercare can include financial help.

BEING SUSPECTED OF ABUSE

As a parent, relative, carer, step-parent or partner of a parent, you may be a victim of intimidation on the part of a child (or young adult). If you feel that there are issues that could be helped by social services, your GP, independent welfare groups or helplines, then use whatever resources you can. PAIN (Parents Against Injustice) is an organization set up to deal with the intense stigma of accusation and to help with care proceedings.

ALTERNATIVE FAMILY STRUCTURES

SINGLE-PARENT STATISTICS

- 1.4 million lone parents care for 2 million children in this country.
- 57% are women who are divorced, widowed or separated, 34% are women who have never been married.
- 9% are men.
- Single parents cost the country £9 billion a year, one tenth of the entire benefits budget.
- 1,040,000 lone parents are on income sup-port and living on, or below the poverty line.
- 43% of single parents have a maintenance agreement with their former partner but only 30% receive it. The average payment is £20 per week which is deducted from income support.
- 90% of lone parents would like to work but can't afford adequate childcare.
- 45% of single-parent families have a total income of less than £100 per week.
- A single six-year-old child is estimated to cost a middle income family about £104 per week.
- The National Council for One Parent Families (NCOPF) and Gingerbread offer help and advice for parents and children in one-parent families.

LIVING TOGETHER

Unmarried couples have fewer rights than married couples. If you have been living with your partner for some time and are thinking about having children you might want to consider the following.

- If you live with your partner but don't pay rent you can be evicted at any time if things go sour. Even if he is violent, the fact that he owns/rents the property means you are the one that will end up going.
- If the relationship finishes you are not entitled to maintenance.
- If your partner dies you are not entitled to a widow's pension.
- If you are not married and your partner dies without making a will, you will not be entitled to inherit anything and it will go to your partner's nearest family. However if you have children together you can appeal on their behalf through the courts and the court has the power to alter the will in favour of you and the children.
- Although unmarried partners cannot insure against the other's death, they can insure their own lives and make their partner the beneficiary.
- There is no legal formality in ending an unmarried partnership.
- On a more positive note if you need legal aid but are unmarried, the fact that you are living with a billionaire won't disqualify you.

STEP-FAMILIES

- 36% of all marriages are re-marriages. 50% of these fail, so the step-family may not survive as a new interpretation of the extended family.
- One in 12 families are step-families and if current trends continue that number will rise to one in eight.
- The National Stepfamily Association has a confidential telephone counselling service and recommended reading for step-families who are finding things difficult to cope with.

GAY PARENTING

- Lesbian and gay parenting is increasing.
- It may not be an issue for parents but it probably will be for their children particularly as they get older.
- Lesbian and gay parents are not 'legally' defined as families and campaign to have the same legal rights as their married counterparts.
- Read the Guide to Lesbian and Gay Parenting.

DEATH

Death is generally a taboo subject. Although it is inevitable, most of us feel uncomfortable even contemplating, let alone discussing, the possibilities. But embracing it and planning a special ceremony can help to turn mourning into a celebration of the life of the person who has died. Taking an active part in burial can begin to help heal the sense of loss. Alternatively, you may have very strong feelings about the way you want to be remembered which you want to plan in advance.

Traditionally religious ceremonies and wakes provided a formal structure for mourning, remembrance and reuniting friends and family. As traditions fade, we have to find new ways of accepting death. While they may be less formal, their personal nature can be extremely comforting – there are many different ways to honour someone you love privately. With around 600,000 funerals a year in Britain, 'death' has become a business. This means, at least, that you should be able to find arrangements to suit your taste and finances. There is no legal requirement to use a church or cremation ceremony, you can choose whatever most helps you cope with the situation.

The emotional shock of a sudden death can be compounded by the additional stress of legal and practical details. This chapter takes you through the practicalities, has suggestions for alternative funerals and outlines some of the ways of coping with grief.

BASICS

IF SOMEONE DIES AT HOME

- Call the doctor and nearest relatives.
- The doctor will bring a medical certificate which will be signed certifying the cause of death. If the doctor wishes to know more about the exact cause of death, even if an illness was known, s/he may ask permission to carry out a post-mortem examination at a mortuary, after which the death can then be registered.
- If you don't want funeral directors involved, or for the body to be taken away immediately, a nurse can help you lay out the body and plug all the orifices.
- If you keep the body at home until the burial you must make sure it is kept cold, either with dry ice or in a cool area of the house, e.g. the cellar. For more information read *The Natural Death Handbook*.
- If the death followed illness from HIV or Aids there may be special rules about handling the body. Contact the London Lighthouse, or the Terrence Higgins Trust.
- Find the will: there might be a pre-paid burial site or special wishes which you will have to recognize.
- You must register the death within five days. All the relevant details about the deceased have to be filled in at the Registry of Births, Marriages and Death (for your local office look in the phone book) and both the death certificate and NHS card handed over.
- Inform any banks, brokers, insurers, credit card agencies and the Department of Social Security.
- Apply for any pensions that are applicable, such as widow's pension.
- Return the deceased's passport to the issuing office and their driving licence to the DVLA.

UNEXPECTED DEATH

- Call an ambulance.
- Contact the family doctor, the nearest relative and the police.
  The coroner will carry out a post-mortem to determine cause of death if:
- a doctor hasn't seen the deceased in the last 14 days

- the death was violent, unnatural or occurred under suspicious circumstances
- the cause of death is not known
- death occurred while patient was undergoing an operation
- death was caused by an industrial disease
- death occurred in prison or in police custody
  Before registration of the death you need the coroner to forward the necessary papers direct to the Registrar of Deaths.

IF DEATH OCCURS ABROAD

- You have to register the death according to local regulations and get a death certificate.
- Register the death with the British authorities, You will be able to get a copy of the death certificate from the consulate later.

DONATING TO SCIENCE

- If organs are to be donated, a medical certificate must be issued before anything can happen. If the death has to be further investigated by a coroner consent must be obtained. The body might not be accepted if there has been a post-mortem.
- Call the nearest hospital immediately.
- Most organs have to be removed within six hours of death, kidneys must be removed within 30 minutes.
- Eyes are the only body parts which you are allowed to donate after the age of 55.
- If the whole body has been left to medical research, contact your nearest medical school who will arrange an undertaker to collect the body. They are obliged to organize a funeral within two years.

INQUESTS

An inquest is an inquiry into the medical cause and circumstances of a death. It is held in public, sometimes with a jury. The coroner will organize this. There will be an inquest if the death was: violent or unnatural, caused by an industrial disease, occurred in prison, or if the cause of death remains uncertain after a post-mortem.

- It may be important to have a lawyer present if circumstances could lead to a claim for compensation.
- If inquiries take some time, you can ask for the

coroner to give you a letter confirming the death which can be used for Social Security and National Insurance purposes.

- The coroner may give you an Order for Burial or a Certificate for Cremation so that a funeral can take place before the inquest is completed.
- The coroner will also send a Certificate after inquest stating the cause of death for the registrar, allowing the death to be registered.

REGISTERING A DEATH

- The death must be registered by the Registrar of Births, Marriages and Deaths within five days, unless there are special circumstances.
- When you go along to register the death, take:
- medical certificate
- pension books
- pink form (Form 100) from a coroner if you had one
- birth and marriage certificate
- life insurance policies

TELL THE REGISTRAR

- the date and place of death
- the deceased's last address
- last occupation
- whether the deceased was getting a pension or allowance from public funds

THE REGISTRAR WILL GIVE YOU

- A Certificate for Burial or Cremation (green form), unless the coroner has given you an Order for Burial form or a Certificate for Cremation.
- A Certificate of Registration of Death. This is for Social Security purposes only.
- A death certificate if you want one for the will, pension claims, insurance policies, savings certificates, etc.
- If you are registering the death of a stillborn baby, the registrar will give you a Certificate for Burial or Cremation and a Certificate of Registration of Stillbirth.

RESPONSIBILITY

- If someone dies and you are the closest living relative the burial is your responsibility even if you have never met.
- If you cannot afford the cost of the funeral, ask

for form SF200 from the Department of Social Security and apply for their £500 grant/loan scheme to pay for it.

- If you are unwilling to dispose of your relative's body for whatever reason, the local authority are obliged to, but they will send you the bill.
- If they deny their responsibilities for the burial, quote the Public Health Act 1984, Control of Disease part 111, disposal of dead bodies, Section 46.

GRIEF

Everyone has their own way of dealing with bereavement. There are no hard and fast rules about how best to get over death. For many people, shared remembrance and special funerals go a long way towards helping initially, but when the ceremony is over, it's the day-to-day loneliness that can lead to depression. As a rule, talking about what has happened, physically expressing your emotion and keeping yourself busy will all help. Older people who lose someone they have spent most of their life with may feel there is little worth living for and they will need continued support from their family. Depression and loneliness can lead to ill health so they need to be treated. If you (or someone you know) is not coping with bereavement, talk to your GP who can refer you for some counselling. Time does heal but that is not much consolation when you are in the depths of despair.

- Contact the Bereavement Line, Compassionate Friends or CRUSE.

LOSING A CHILD

When a child dies, parents go through many different emotions and sometimes they feel physical side-effects. Some parents imagine that they hear their child crying or feel aching in their arms as they long to hold their baby. Some have nightmares and become over-protective of their other children. Mothers who have lost a baby may find their breasts ache or leak milk at the thought of their infant. Fear of being alone is common, and this may apply to siblings of the dead child who may need extra comfort and want to sleep with the light on for a while. Coping with the outside world may take time, and well-meaning people will find ways to say all the wrong things. But gradually memories become less painful, especially if you have examined what went wrong and understand the events surrounding your child's death. If you blame others or yourself it is important to get those emotions out and talk about them. Hospital staff will answer your questions as best they can, but in many situations the reason for a baby's death are never established even after a post-mortem.

- Though family and friends will be a great support to bereaved parents, professional counselling may also be needed. Contacts include Child Death Helpline and the Stillbirth and Neonatal Death Society (SANDS).

FUNERALS

There is no legal requirement to use a church or crematorium.
- You can arrange the funeral once you have registered the death, or been given the go-ahead by the coroner.
- A good funeral director can make burial very easy but doing it yourself may be more cathartic. Most funeral directors belong to the National Association of Funeral Directors which has a code of practice.
- If you have no religion and don't know where to start, contact the British Humanist Society. It is a subject worth thinking about well in advance of having to arrange a burial.
- The average funeral costs £1,300 but doing it yourself can cost as little as £120.

CREMATION
- An application is signed by the next of kin at the crematorium.
- Two cremation certificates are signed by different doctors.
- A certificate is signed by the crematorium's medical referee.
- The average price of cremation is £173.
- 70% of people in this country choose cremation.
- You can scatter ashes in a favourite place or keep them at home on the mantelpiece.

- Special objects may be placed in the coffin but some materials are not allowed, e.g. plastic.
- You can design and make your own coffin.
- A few crematoria will cremate bodies wrapped in a sheet in the Hindu way.
- The Cremation Society of Great Britain publishes a guide to crematoria in this country.

CEMETERIES/CHURCHYARDS
- Look up Cemeteries in the *Yellow Pages* and ring up to see if there is space available: most suburban churchyards are now full so you may have to search for a space unless you have a family plot.
- Obtain the registrar's green Certificate for Burial.
- The Church of England has set fees: £43 for a service, £70 for burial.
- Gravediggers cost between £60 and £100.
- Headstones, bell ringers, choirs and organists are extra: funerals, like weddings, can cost whatever you want to spend on them.
- The price of plots is variable, just as house prices in more exclusive areas are more expensive: a plot in Highgate Cemetery, London (home to a host of dead celebrities from Karl Marx to Bram Stoker) costs around £2,200 but the average price per plot around the country is £291.
- Eco-friendly funerals are increasingly popular, which means burial can be in cardboard coffins, simple woollen shrouds or woven willow pods. Contact the Natural Death Centre.

AT HOME
Consider whether you'll want to move house. It does give you the opportunities to build a mausoleum but you will have to apply to your local planning authority for permission and different councils have definite policies on this issue. Burying someone in your back garden will knock 10% off the value of your property.

DEEP FREEZE
The Alcor Life Extension Foundation offers cryonics: freezing your body in a steel flask full of liquid nitrogen so that you can come back to life in your original body just in case they ever do discover the secret of resurrection. Costs from £40–£100,000.

W☺MEN UNLIMITED DIRECTORY

This is a list of all the reading material and organizations mentioned in the text and details of many others which will help you get further information.

THE DIRECTORY consists mainly of telephone helplines although addresses have been included where appropriate.

The Telephone Helplines Association (0171 242 0555) can provide further information about regional helpline numbers.

In addition to the information you can obtain by calling helplines or organizations, the Internet provides a growing source of information that you can browse. It is not necessary to have a specific website address to access a subject. Internet search engines such as Yahoo!UK and Ireland on (www.yahoo.co.uk). Lycos(www.uk-lycos.com/) and Infoseek (www.infoseek.com/) allow you to enter a search reference or browse directory listings to access thousands of public websites both in the UK and abroad.

All major organizations are likely to have their own websites providing information about their products and services as do all UK newspapers, financial organizations and broadcasters. A few examples of these will be scattered throughout the Directory.

If you would like your organization, publication or website address included in **THE DIRECTORY**, simply write to us at the following address

Women Unlimited
c/o Penguin Books
27 Wrights Lane, London
W8 5TZ.

WORK

STARTING OUT
Reading
Diane Burston,
The A–Z of Careers and Jobs
CEPEC Recruitment Guide:
a directory of recruitment agencies and search consultants in the UK
Kogan Page careers series
Overseas Jobs Express

CAREERS COUNSELLING
Useful numbers
Careers Development Centre for Women 0181 892 3806
Institute of Career Guidance 0181 883 1878
Careers, Occupation and Info. Centre (COIC) 0114 275 3275
Careers Research and Advisory Centre (CRAC) 01223 460277
Department of Education and Employment 0171 925 5000
Education Help Desk 0171 580 4741
Further Education Development Agency 0171 962 1280
Industrial Society 0171 262 2401
London Chamber of Commerce and Industry 0181 302 0261
National Alliance of Women's Organizations 0171 242 0878
TEC National Council 0171 735 0010

Useful Websites
http://www.bbc.co.uk/
http://www.telegraph.co.uk (Telegraph newspapers)
http://www.guardian.co.uk
http://www.marketinguk.co.u/

A–Z OF CAREERS
Useful numbers
Accountant
Chartered Association of Certified Accountants 0171 396 5800
Institute of Chartered Accountants 0171 920 8100
Association of Cost and Management Accountants 0171 272 3925

Actor
British Actors Equity Association 0171 379 6000
National Council for Drama Training 0171 387 3650
Acupuncturist
British College of Acupuncture 0171 833 8164
British Acupuncture Council 0181 964 0222
Advertising
Advertising Association 0171 828 2771
Institute of Practitioners in Advertising 0171 235 7020
Anthropologist
Royal Anthropological Institute of Britain and Ireland 0171 387 0455
Archaeologist
Council for British Archaeology 01904 671417
Institute of Archaeology 0171 387 7050
Architect
Architects Registration Council of the United Kingdom 0171 580 5861
Royal Institute of British Architects 0171 580 5533
Artist
ADAR (Art and Design Admissions Registry) 01432 266653
Barrister
Council of Legal Education 0171 404 5787
Faculty of Advocates 0131 226 5071
General Council of the Bar 0171 242 0082
Broadcasting
BBC Corporate Recruitment Service
PO Box 7000
London W5 2PA
ITV Network Centre Personnel Department 0171 843 8000
Skillset at Channel 4 0171 306 8585
Building
Construction Industry Training Board 01553 776677

Women's London Manual Trades 0171 251 9192
Catering and accommodation management
Hospitality Training Foundation 0181 579 2400
Hotel and Catering International Management Association 0181 672 4251
Chemist
Royal Society of Chemistry 0171 437 8656
Chiropractor
British Chiropractic Association 01734 757557
Civil Service
Graduates and Schools Liaison Branch 0171 270 5697
Commerce
Commerce and Industry Management Information Centre/Institute of Industrial Managers 01536 204222
Company secretary
Institute of Chartered Secretaries and Administrators (ICSA) 0171 580 4741
Computing
British Computer Society 01793 417417
Association of Computer Professionals 01372 273442
Women's Computer Centre 0171 430 0112
Conservation
English Nature 01733 340345
National Trust 0171 222 9251
Natural Environmental Research Council 01793 411500
UK Institute for Conservation and Historic and Artistic Works 0171 620 3371
Dancing
Royal Academy of Dancing 0171 223 0091
Council for Dance Education and Training (UK) 0181 741 5084
Dentist
General Dental Council 0171 486 2171
Designer
Design Council 0171 208 2121

Detective
Association of British Investigators
ABI House
10 Bonner Hill Rd
Kingston upon Thames
Surrey KT1 3EP
Dietitian
British Dietetic Association
0121 643 5483
Economist
Institute of Economic Affairs
0171 799 3745
Electrician
Institute of Electrical Engineers
0171 240 1871
Engineer
Civil Engineering Careers Service 0171 222 7722
Engineering Council
0171 240 7891
Estate agent
National Association of Estate Agents
01926 496800
Fashion
CAPITB Trust 0113 239 3355
Film production
Broadcasting, Entertainment, Cinematography and Theatre Union (BECTU)
0171 437 8506
British Film Institute
0171 255 1444
Skillset 0171 306 8585
(The industry training organization for broadcasting, film and video)
Florist
Florist Training Council
01635 200465
Food science and technology
Food and Drink Industry Training Organization
0171 836 2460
Forensics
Forensic Science Society
01423 506068
Garage work
Retail Motor Industry Federation
0171 580 9122
Gardener
Royal Horticultural Society
0171 834 4333
Hairdresser
Hairdressing Training Board
01302 342837
National Hairdressers Federation 01234 360332
Health Service
Institute of Health Services Management 0171 388 2626

Homoeopathy
British School of Homoeopathy 01225 790051
Society of Homoeopaths
01604 21400
Hotel work
Hotel and Catering International Management Association 0181 672 4251
Information technology
British Computer Society
01793 417 417
Institute for the Management of Information Systems
0181 308 0747
Insurance
Chartered Insurance Institute
0171 606 3835
Insurance Industry Training Council 01732 741231
Interior designer
IDDA 0171 349 0800
Jeweller
National Association of Goldsmiths
0171 613 4445
Journalist
Chartered Institute of Journalists 0171 252 1187
National Council for the Training of Journalists
01279 430009
Landscape architect
Landscape Institute
0171 738 9166
Local government
Local Government Management Board
01582 451166
Management consultant
Institute of Management
01536 204222 ext 212
Women in Management
0171 382 9978
Institute of Management Consultants 0171 242 2140
Marine biologist
Institute of Biology
0171 581 8333
Plymouth Marine Laboratory
01752 222772
Marketing
Chartered Institute of Marketing 01628 524922
Medicine
British Medical Association
0171 387 4499
Royal College of Nursing
0171 409 3333
Musician
Incorporated Society of Musicians 0171 629 4413
Musicians Union
0171 582 5566

Optician
British College of Optometrists
0171 373 7765
Pharmacist
National Pharmaceutical Association 01727 832161
Photographer
British Institute of Professional Photography
01920 464011
Association of Fashion, Advertising and Editorial Photographers 0171 608 1441
Physiotherapy
Chartered Society of Physiotherapy 0171 242 1941
Plumber
Institute of Plumbing
01708 472791
Construction Industry Training Board 01553 776677
Police
Police Recruiting Department
Room 516
Home Office
Queen Anne's Gate
London SW1H 9AT
(contact your local station)
Psychologist
British Psychological Society
0116 254 9568
PR
Institute of Public Relations
0171 253 5151
Publishing
Publishers Association
0171 580 6321
Women in Publishing
0171 278 4411
Secretary
Institute of Qualified Private Secretaries 0115 973 3235
Social work
CCETSW
0171 278 2455
Solicitor
The Law Society
0171 242 1222
Sports
Institute of Professional Sport
0171 630 7486
Sports Council
0181 778 8600
Stockbroker
Securities Institute
0171 626 3191
Surveyor
Royal Institution of Chartered Surveyors 0171 222 7000
Teacher
Teacher Training Agency
0171 925 5880/5882
Translator

Centre for Information on Language Teaching and Research
0171 379 5110
Institute of Linguists
0171 359 7445
Translators Association
0171 373 6642
Travel agent
ABTA 01483 727321
Institute of Travel and Tourism
01727 854395
Vet
British Veterinary Association
0171 636 6541
Writer
Society of Authors
0171 373 6642
Institute of Scientific and Technical Communicators
0171 436 4425
Youth and community work
National Youth Agency
0116 285 6789
Zoologist
The Institute of Biology
20–22 Queensberry Place
London SW7 2DZ

WORKING IN THE EU
Useful numbers
CEPEC 0121 200 5903
Central Bureau for Educational Visits/Exchanges, British Council
0171 389 4880
Commission for the European Communities
0171 973 1992
Department of Education and Employment
0171 925 5555
Federation of Recruitment and Employment Services (FRES)
0171 323 4300
Overseas Jobs Express
01273 440220
Vacation Work
01865 241978

TRAINING AND RESKILLING
Reading
Biblios, *Sponsorship for Students*
Charities Aid Foundation, *Directory of Grant Making Trusts*
DoE, *Student Grants and Loans*
DoE, *European Choice: A Guide to Opportunities for Higher Education in Europe*

Directory of Social Change, *Educational Grants Directory*
Dan Finn, *Unemployment and Training Rights Handbook*
Local DSS office, *Grants to Students*
Local tax office, *Tax Relief for Vocational Training* (IR119)
Second Chance: A National Guide to Adult Education and Training Opportunities and Occupations, from local library
Universities and Colleges Admissions Service, *UCAS 97 Handbook*
Women's Returners' Network, *Directory of Training*

Useful numbers
Biblios 01403 710971
BTEC 0171 413 8400
Career Development Loans 0800 121 127
Charities Aid Foundation 01732 520000
City and Guilds 0171 294 2468
Department for Education and Employment 0171 925 5000
Educational Grants Advisory Service 0171 249 6636
Lucy Cavendish College 01223 332190
National Council for Vocational Qualifications 0171 387 9898
National Extension College 01223 316644
nec@dial.pipex.com
National Union of Students Grants Department 0171 272 8900
Open College of the Arts 01226 730495
Open University 01908 274066
Royal Society of Arts 01203 470033
RSA Examination Board Scottish Qualifications Authority 0141 242 2214
UCAS (Universities and College Admissions Service) General 01242 222444, **Applicant enquiries** 01242 227788
Women's Returners' Network 0171 468 2290

HOW TO WRITE A CV
Reading
Max Eggert, *The Perfect*

Interview
Joan Fletcher, *How to get that Job*

NEW WAYS TO WORK
Reading
Christine Ingham, *New Work Options*
Ingham, *101 Ways to Start your own Business*
Sharon Maxwell Magnus, *Making Serious Money from Home*
Pam Walton, *Job Sharing: a Practical Guide*

Useful numbers
Business Links 0345 567765 (gives details of your local centre)
Home Run 01291 641222
100117.27@compuserve.co (magazine offering advice to people working from home)
New Ways to Work 0171 226 4026
Parents at Work 0171 628 3578

PROBLEMS AT WORK
Reading
Commission for Racial Equality, *Advice and Assistance from the CRE*

Useful numbers
Arbitration and Conciliation Service (ACAS) 0171 396 5100
National Association of Citizens' Advice Bureaux 0171 833 2181
Central Office of Industrial Tribunals 0171 730 6105
Commission for Racial Equality 0171 828 7022
Commissioner for the Rights of Trade Union Members 01925 415771
Employment Appeal Tribunal 0171 273 1041
Employment Rights Advice Service 0171 713 7616
Equal Opportunities Commission 0161 833 9244
Health and Safety Executive Public Enquiry Point 01142 892345

Public Concern at Work 0171 404 6609
Women Against Sexual Harassment 0171 721 7592

STARTING A BUSINESS
Reading
Patricia Clayton, *Law for Small Businesses*
Peter Hingston, *The Great Little Business Book*
Graham Jones, *How to Start a Business from Home*
Dennis Millar, *Starting and Running your own Business*
Robson Rhodes, *Getting Started*
Booklets from major high street banks

Useful numbers
Business in the Community 0171 629 1600
Companies House 01222 380 801
Department of Trade and Industry 0171 215 7877
Training and Enterprise Council see phone book for local number
National Federation of Self Employment and Small Businesses 01253 720911
Trademark Registry 0171 438 4722

TECHNO-LOGY

Reading
Bill Gates, *The Road Ahead*
Ed Krol, *The Whole Internet*
Shelley O'Hara, *10-Minute Guide to Buying a Computer*
Douglas Rushkoff, *Cyberia*
Richard Wentk, *Which? Guide to computers*

Useful numbers
Women's Computer Centre 0171 430 0112

Internet Cafés
(look up in your phone book for nearest branch or local Internet café)
Café Surf – Birmingham 0121 622 4010
Café Internet – Liverpool 0151 255 1112

CBI – Cambridge 01223 576306
Culture Café – Northampton 01604 232388
Cyberia Café 0171 681 4200
cyberia@ cyberiacafe.net
Cyberia – Edinburgh 0131 220 4403
Cyberpub – Nottingham 01159 475394
Hub Intercafé – Bath 01225 427441
Web – Manchester 0161 236 5960
Zap cybercafé – Brighton 01273 888244

Useful websites
http://www.techweb.com/ (news and technical advice)
http://www.limitless.co.uk/inetuk/ (UK internet service providers)

Major suppliers
AppleCentre 01444 870044
IBM 0800 181182

Internet Service Providers
See national press advertising

Magazines
Computer shopper
Mute
Net, the Internet Magazine
The Net Directory
Wired

GADGETS
Mobile phones
BT 0800 222 639
Carphone Warehouse 0800 424 800
Cellnet 01753 504000
Ericsson 01483 303 666
Mercury One2One 0500 500 121
Motorola 01734 582 031
NEC 0171 734 4455
Nokia 0500 500 121
Nortel 0171 439 1300
Orange 01454 618500
Sony 0990 111 999
Vodaphone 01635 33251

Pagers
BT 0800 222 638
Mercury 0500 505 505
Motorola 01256 842220
Psion UK 0990 134 224
Sharp 0161 205 2333
Vodapage 0171 490 0101

MONEY

BANK/BUILDING SOCIETY
Building Societies Ombudsman
0171 931 0044
Building Society Commission
0171 663 5000
Banking Ombudsman
0171 404 9944

Useful websites
Check out the websites of all banks, building societies and financial institutions.

PLASTIC
Useful numbers
American Express
0171 930 4411
Barclaycard
01604 234234
Diners Club
01252 516261
Mastercard
01702 352255
TSB Trustcard
01273 724666

CREDIT REFERENCE AGENCIES
CCN Group Ltd
0115 941 0888
Equifax Europe UK Ltd
0171 298 3000
Office of the Data Protection Registrar 01625 545745
Office of Fair Trading
0171 242 2858

ADVICE ON FINANCE
Money Management Register of Fee-Based Advisers
0171 976 9444
Personal Investment Authority Ombudsman
0171 538 8860
Securities and Investments Board (SIB)
0171 638 1240

SAVINGS AND INVESTMENTS
Reading
Danny Oshay, *Financial Times Investing for Beginners*
Investors Chronicle, Beginners Guide to the Stockmarket
Which?, Be your own Financial Adviser
Anthony Price, *Accounts Demystified: How to Understand and Use Company Accounts*

Useful numbers
Association of Investment Trust Companies (AIT)
0171 588 5347
Association of Private Client Investment Managers and Stockbrokers (APCIMS)
0171 247 7080
Investment and Management Regulatory Organization (IMRO) 0171 390 5000
Investment Ombudsman Office
0171 796 3065
National Savings
0191 386 4900/374 5023
Personal Investment Authority Ombudsman Head Office
0171 538 8860
Securities and Futures Authority
0171 378 9000
Securities and Unit Trust Associaty
0171 831 0898

LOANS – PERSONAL BORROWING
Seek help from your local Citizens' Advice Bureau or call the
National Debtline
0121 359 8501

MORTGAGE
Reading
Which? Way to Buy, Sell and Move House
Which? Way to Buy, Own and Sell a Flat
The Which? Guide to Renting and Letting
Office of Fair Trading, *Using an Estate Agent to Buy or Sell your Home*

Useful numbers
Building Society Commission
0171 437 6628
Building Societies Ombudsman
0171 931 0044
National Debtline
0121 359 8501

PENSIONS
Useful numbers
Freephone Pension Helpline
0800 666 555
Occupational Pensions Advisory Service
0171 233 8080
Pensions Ombudsman
0171 834 9144

(deals with public complaints about companies and pension schemes)
Pension Schemes Registry
0191 225 6393
(traces pension entitlements you may have built up from previous employment)
Personal Investment Authority
0171 538 8860
Society of Pension Consultants
0171 353 1688

TAX
Reading
Various *Which?* guides to taxation
Many of the major financial institutions and the quality national press publish their own tax guides, particularly after the budget; some are free; available in the financial sections of good bookshops.

Useful numbers
Capital Taxes Office
0115 974 2222
(for official list of exemptions)
Inland Revenue 0345 161514
(see phone book for local tax office)
Inland Revenue Adjudicator
0171 930 2292
Institute of Taxation
0171 235 9381

INSURANCE
Useful numbers
Association of British Insurers
0171 600 3333
British Insurance and Investment Brokers Association
0171 623 9043
http://www.biiba.org.uk
Chartered Institute of Arbitrators
0171 837 4483
(runs Personal Insurance Arbitration scheme)
Incorporated Society of Valuers and Auctioneers
0171 235 2282
Institute of Insurance Brokers
01933 410003
Insurance Ombudsman Bureau
0171 928 7600
National Independent Schools Information Service (ISIS)
0171 630 8793

Royal Institution of Chartered Surveyors
0171 222 7000
School Fees Insurance Agency
01628 34291
Subsidence Claims Advisory Bureau 01424 733727

HEALTH INSURANCE
Health Care Matters
0500 136 442
Medical Fees Insurance Agency
0116 2362420
Insurance Ombudsman Bureau
0171 928 4488
Personal Insurance Arbitration Scheme (PIAS)
0171 837 4483
Pet plan
0800 282 009
Private Health Care Partnership
01943 851133

MATERNITY AND FINANCE
Reading
Maternity Rights booklet available from the Citizens' Advice Bureau, libraries or job centres

Useful numbers
Employment Rights Advice Service 0171 713 7616
Maternity Alliance
0171 588 8582
(campaigns for childcare/family-friendly policies at work)
Working for Childcare
0171 700 0281
(advice for parents, employers and trade unions on developing childcare facilities at work)

BENEFITS
Benefit Enquiry Line
0800 882 200
Child Support Agency National Enquiry Line
0345 133 133
Freeline Social Security
0800 666555

WILLS
Reading
The Which? Guide to Wills and Probate

Useful numbers
Institute of Professional Will Writers
01905 611165

MENCAP 0171 454 0454
Society of Will Writers
0800 838270
Principal Family Registry
0171 936 7000
(holds copies of all wills)
Terrence Higgins Trust
0171 242 1010
Voluntary Euthanasia Society
0171 937 7770

CARS

LEARNING TO DRIVE
Reading
AA, *Your Driving Test: Pass First Time*
Driving Standards Agency, *Complete Theory Test for Cars and Motorcycles*
Highway Code

Useful numbers
AA Driving Schools
0800 607080
BSM 0181 540 8262
Driving Instructors Association
0181 665 5151
Driving Standards Agency
0115 955 7600
(See phone book for local no.)
DVLA 01792 772151
Licensing Centre
Swansea SA6 7JL
Institute of Advanced Motorists
0181 994 4403
Skid School
01327 857177
Brands Hatch 0990 125250

Useful Websites
http://www.autotrader.co.uk/index-ie3.html
http://www.topgear.com
(BBC magazine)

CAR CARE AND GARAGES
Reading
Auto Marketing, *Motorist's Guide to Car Repair*
Thatcham Motor Repair Research Centre, *Parts Price Guide*
Peter Burgess, *The Which? Car Owner's Manual*

Useful numbers
Chartered Institute of Arbitrators 0171 837 4483
DVLA Customer Enquiry Unit
01792 772134 vehicles

01792 772151 drivers
Office of Fair Trading
0171 242 2858
Retail Motor Industry Federation
0171 580 9122
Society of Motor Manufacturers and Traders
0171 235 7000
Transport 2000
0171 388 8386
The Vehicle Builders and Repairers Association
01132 538333
Motor Repair Research Centre
01635 868855

BREAKDOWN
Useful numbers
AA 0800 887766
Europ Assist
01444 442211
Green Flag
01132 393666
(national breakdown recovery club)
Mondial Assistance
0181 681 2525
RAC 0800 828282

CAR SAFETY AND THE LAW
Reading
AA guide to Child Seats, from AA shops
Britax Child Car Safety Guide, Britax Helpline 01264 33343
RAC, *Child Safety Video*, 0800 550055
RAC, *Childseat safety, a parent's guide*
Which? Car 1997

Useful numbers
AA technical advice line
0161 488 7295
Accident Line run by the Law Society
0500 192 939
(free initial consultation after an accident)
Britax customer services helpline
01264 386034
RAC, Legal Service
0345 300400
Royal Society for the Prevention of Accidents
0121 248 2000

CAR SECURITY
Useful numbers
Association of British Insurers
0171 600 3333

Motor Insurance Research Centre
01635 868855

BUYING A USED CAR
Useful reading
Loot
Exchange & Mart

Useful numbers
AA Vehicle Inspection Department
0345 500610
CCN (car finance check)
0800 234999
Department of Transport
0171 276 0800
DVLA Customer Enquiry Unit
01792 772134 vehicles
01792 772151 drivers
HM Customs and Excise
0171 620 1313
HPI Autodat 01722 422422
(for mileage checks)
Office of Fair Trading
0171 242 2858
RAC Car Examinations
0800 333660
Retail Motor Industry Federation
0171 580 9122
Society of Motor Auctions
01788 576465
British Motor Auctions
01428 607440
Central Motor Auctions
0181 944 2000
National Car Auctions
0191 419000

BUYING A NEW CAR
Reading
AA overseas Motoring Package on importing and exporting a car (for members only)
Permanent Import of Motor Vehicles into GB, Dept of Transport booklet P11
BBC publications, *Top Gear's The Good Car Guide*
What Car? magazine
Which? Car 1997

Useful numbers
AA Head Office
0990 500600
Association for Consumer Research
0171 486 5544
Department of Transport
0171 276 0800
DVLA Customer Enquiry Unit
01792 772134 vehicles
01792 772151 drivers

Retail Motor Industry Federation
0171 580 9122
HM Customs and Excise Helpline
0171 202 4227
Office of Fair Trading
0171 242 2858
RAC
0800 550550

CAR FINANCE
Useful numbers
Financing and Leasing Association
0171 491 2783
Retail Motor Industry Federation
0171 580 9122
Society of Motor Manufacturers and Traders
0171 235 7000

SELLING A CAR
Reading
Loot
Parker's Guide
Exchange & Mart

Useful numbers
Cardata
0181 882 8888

CAR INSURANCE
Reading
Department of Transport, *The Mavis Pamphlet*

Useful numbers
AA Insurance
0800 444 777
Chartered Institute of Arbitrators
0171 837 4483
British Insurance and Investment Brokers Association
0171 623 9043
http://www.biiba.org.uk
Institute of Insurance Brokers
01933 410003
Insurance Ombudsman
0171 928 7600
Motor Insurance Research Centre 01635 868855
Motor Insurers Bureau (MIB)
01908 240000
RAC Insurance Service
0345 121 345

BIKES
Reading
Motorcycle News
What Bike?

Useful numbers
Autocycle Union
01788 540519
British Motorcyclists
Federation
0181 942 7914
Consumers' Association
(*Which?*) 0171 830 6000
Royal Society for the
Prevention of Accidents
0121 248 2071
(advanced motorcycle training
scheme)

LAW

THE LEGAL SYSTEM
Reading
Fenton Bresler, *Law Without a Lawyer*
Chambers and Partners' *Directory of the Legal Profession*
John Pritchard, *New Penguin Guide to the Law*
Pritchard, *The Legal 500*
Reader's Digest, *You and Your Rights*
Smith and Keenan, *English Law*
Solicitors' Regional Directory (from library)
Daily Telegraph Guide to Everyday Law

Useful numbers
Allied Legal Auditors
0171 430 2223
Commission for Racial
Equality 0171 828 7022
Equal Opportunities
Commission 0161 833 9244
Law Society 0171 242 1222
Legal Services Ombudsman
0161 236 9532
Supreme Court Taxing Office
0171 936 6093
(leaflet explains the taxing process)

Useful websites
http://www.law-enforcement.com/

GETTING LEGAL ADVICE/ FINDING A LAWYER
Useful numbers
Accident Line
0500 192939
General Council of the Bar
0171 242 0082
Law Centres Federation
0171 380 0133
(has offices nationwide)

The Law Society
0171 242 1222
http://www.lawsoc.org.uk
Legal Aid Board
0171 813 1000
Legal Services Ombudsman
0161 236 9532
Magistrates Association
0171 387 2353
National Association of
Citizens' Advice Bureaux
(NACAB) 0171 833 2181
Office for the Supervision of
Solicitors (OSS)
01926 822007/8
Solicitors Complaints Bureau
01926 820 082
Solicitors Indemnity Fund
0171 566 6000
(advice and info having lost
money due to solicitor's
dishonesty)

CONSUMER LAW
Reading
Which? Book of Consumer Law

Useful numbers
Chartered Institute of
Arbitrators 0171 837 4483
Consumers Association
0171 486 5544
Data Protection Registrar
01625 545700
Direct Selling Association
0171 497 1234
Market Research Society
0171 490 4911
Office of Fair Trading
0171 242 2858
Which? Personal Service
0800 252100
(advice and help on consumer
issues services)
Consumer programmes
BBC Television
0181 743 8000
Watchdog (BBC1)
White City
201 Wood Lane
London W12 7TS
BBC Radio 4
0171 580 4468
Face the Facts, You and Yours,
In Touch
Broadcasting House
London W1A 1AA

THE SMALL CLAIMS COURT ARBITRATION
Useful numbers
Advisory Conciliation and
Arbitration Service (ACAS)
0171 388 5100

Chartered Institute of
Arbitrators
0171 837 4483

CRIMINAL LAW
Useful numbers
Criminal Injuries
Compensation board
0171 636 9501
Liberty
0171 403 3888
(information on civil liberties)
Justice
0171 405 6018
(law reform pressure group)
National Association of
Victims Support Schemes
0171 735 9166
Police Complaints Authority
0171 273 6450
(for complaints against the
police)
RELEASE
0171 729 9904
(advice on legal emergencies
related to criminal/drug
law)

POLITICS

GOVERNMENT
Useful numbers
Crown Prosecution Service
0171 273 3000
European Parliament
Office
0171 227 4300
The Hansard Society
0171 955 7478
House of Commons
Information Office
0171 219 4272
House of Lords Information
Office
0171 219 3107
Local Government
Ombudsman
0171 915 3210
National Council for Civil
Liberties
0171 403 3888
National Consumer
Council
0171 730 3469
Office of Fair Trading
0171 242 2858
Parliamentary Ombudsman
0171 276 2130
Useful websites
http://www.parliament.uk/
http://www.foe.co.uk/
(Friends of the Earth)
http://www.parliament.the-

stationeryoffice.
co.uk/pa/cm/cmhansard.htm
(Hansard)
http://www.greenpeace.org/uk

WOMEN AND WESTMINSTER
Reading
Any A-level book on politics
Hansard Society report, *Women at the Top*
J. Lovenduski and V. Randall, *Contemporary Feminist Politics: Women and Power in Britain*
David Robertson, *The Penguin Dictionary of Politics*
Women's Communications Centre, *Values and Visions: The What Women Want Social Survey*

Useful numbers
The 300 Group
01895 812229
Commission for Racial
Equality
0171 828 7022
Conservative Central Office
0171 222 9000
Emily's List
0171 352 7759
Equal Opportunities
Commission
0161 833 9244
European Parliament
Information Office
0171 227 4300
Fawcett Society
0171 628 4441
Green Party
0171 227 4300
Hansard Society
16 Gower Street
London WC1E 6DP
House of Commons
Information Office
0171 219 4272
Labour Party
0171 701 1234
Liberal Democrats
0171 222 7999
Women's Communications
Centre
0181 563 8601

HOW TO CAMPAIGN
Reading
Mark Latimer, *The Campaigning Handbook*
Directory of Social Change, various publications on fundraising
Des Wilson, *Campaigning: A–Z of Public Advocacy*

Useful numbers

Amnesty International
0171 413 5500
Audit Commission Enquiry Line 0117 900 15588
National Audit Office
0171 798 7000
British Library at Colindale
0171 636 1544
British Libraries Business Research Service
0171 323 7457
Charity Commission
0171 210 3000
National Association of Citizens' Advice Bureaux
0171 833 2181
Civic Trust
0171 930 0914
Clerk of Public Petitions
0171 219 3317
Community Matters
0171 226 0189
Association of Community Technical Aid Centres
0151 708 7607
Development Trust Association
0171 706 4951
New Economics Foundation
0171 377 5696
Environmental Information Service
01603 871048
European Commission
0171 973 1992
European Environment
0171 722 0090
Friends of the Earth
0171 490 1555
Greenpeace
0171 865 8100
HMSO
0171 873 0011
MINTEL International
0171 606 4533
Policy Studies Institute
0171 387 2171
Centre for Policy Studies
0171 828 1176
Institute for Public Policy Research 0171 379 9400
Sergeant at Arms
0171 219 3060
Directory of Social Change
0171 209 0902/4422
Department of Social Security 0171 210 5983
Central Statistical Office
0171 217 4905
The Treasury 0171 270 3000
Worldwide Fund for Nature
01483 426444

SEX etc.

SEX
Reading
Margo Anand, *The Art of Sexual Fantasy*
K. and D. Botting, *Sex Appeal: The Art and Science of Sexual Attraction*
Dr Alex Comfort, *The Joy of Sex*
Betty Dodson, *Sex for One*
Nik Douglas, Penny Slinger, *Sexual Secrets*
Erich Fromm, *The Art of Loving*
Sheila Kitzinger, *Women's Experience of Sex*
Brenda Love, *The Encyclopedia of Unusual Sex Practices*

Useful numbers
Association of Sexual and Marital Therapists
c/o Dr C. M. Duddle
Student Health Centre
University of Manchester
Manchester M13 9QS
(send SAE for details of your nearest therapist/clinic)
British Association of Counselling
01788 578 328
Skydancing Institute – UK (Tantric Sex Institute)
01736 788 304
(seminars, training)

Useful websites
http://eng.hss.cmu.edu/gender/(gender and sexuality)
http://www.newfrontier.com/nepal/(tantric sex)
http://www.well.com/user/woa/index.html(web of addictions)

ALTERNATIVE SEXUALITY
Reading
E. de Savitch, *Homosexuality and Transsexuality*
B. Fairchild and N. Howard, *Now that you Know: Everything Parents should know about Homosexuality*
Dr Richard Green, *Sexual Identity Conflict*
Lynn Sutcliffe, *There must be Fifty ways to Tell your Mother*
April Martin, *Guide to Lesbian and Gay Parenting*
Magazines/papers
DIVA
Gay Times
Pink Papers

Gay Scotland
Bi community news
Time Out
Cassels *Pink Directory* lists all lesbian/gay organizations in the UK

Silver Moon (women's bookshop)
64–68 Charing Cross Road
London WC2 0BB
Gay's the Word Bookshop
66 Marchmont St
London WC1

Useful numbers
Beaumont Society
0171 730 7453
(transvestites helpline)
Bi-sexual Helpline
0181 569 7500
Charing Cross Hospital Clinic
0181 846 1516
Gay and Lesbian Legal Services 0171 253 2043
Gender Identity Consultancy Services
BM Box 7624
London WC1 N3XX
(help for transsexuals)
Gender Trust
01305 269222
http://www3.mistral.co.uk/gentrust/index.html
FTM Network
0161 432 1915
Identity
0181 742 2381
(support group for under 26s)
Jewish Lesbian and Gay Helpline
0171 706 3123
Lesbian and Gay Switchboard
0171 837 7324 (24hrs)
Lesbian and Gay Bereavement Project
0181 455 8894
Lesbian Line
0171 251 6911
Mermaids
01305 269222
http://ourworld.compuserve.com/homepages/Christine
Burns/mermaids.html
(support for teenagers coping with gender identity issues)
National Union of Students Lesbian, Gay, Bisexual Campaign
0171 561 6517

CONTRACEPTION
Reading
Family Planning Association,

Your Guide to Contraception
Flynn and Brooks, *A Manual of Natural Family Planning*
Swarewski and Guilleband, *Contraception: a User's Handbook*
Health Education Authority booklist

Useful numbers
Brook Advisory Service
0171 713 9000
(free, confidential advice and help with contraception, pregnancy testing, unplanned pregnancies, sexual counselling)
Emergency Contraception Helpline 0800 494847
Family Planning Association
0171 837 5432
(sexual health and contraceptive info service)
Health Education Authority Customer Services
01235 465565
(extensive book list on full range of topics)
Health Promotion Information Centre
0171 413 1995
Marie Stopes Clinic
0171 388 0662
(charity providing family planning and women's health advice, see phone book for local centres)

HIV AND AIDS
Useful numbers
Body Positive
0171 373 9124
(counselling service and support for women, their family, partners and friends affected by HIV and Aids)
MASTA (Medical Advisory Service for Travellers Abroad)
0171 631 4408
National AIDS Helpline
0800 567123 (24hrs)
(calls are free and confidential)
Minicom on 0800 521361 for people who are deaf or hard of hearing; info in other languages also available
Positively Women
0171 713 0222
(info, practical and emotional support for women with Aids or an HIV-positive diagnosis)
Terrence Higgins Trust helpline
0171 242 1010

SEXUALLY TRANSMITTED DISEASES

Useful numbers

Brook Advisory Service
0171 713 9000
Hepatitis Helpline
0990 100360
Herpes Association
0171 609 9061
Mortimer Market Centre
0171 530 5000
(NHS STD clinic)

ALCOHOL

Useful numbers

ACOA (Adult Children of Alcoholics)
0171 229 4587
Alcoholics Anonymous
0345 697555
(will give you local number)
Alcohol Concern
0171 928 7377
ALATEEN
0171 403 0888
(teenagers whose lives are/have been affected by others' drinking)
AL-ANON
0171 403 0888
(for families of alcoholics)
Drinkline 0345 320202
Women's Alcohol Centre
0171 226 4581

ADDICTIONS

Reading

Melody Beattie, *Co-dependants' Guide to the Twelve Steps*
Dr Robert Lefever, *How to Identify Addictive Behaviour*
Mooney, Eisenberg and Eisenberg, *The Recovery Book*
Department of Health leaflets

Useful numbers

CITA (Council for Involuntary Tranquilizer Addiction)
0151 949 0102
CODA (Co-dependants Anonymous for Dysfunctional Families) 0171 376 8191
DAWN (Drugs and Alcohol Women's Network)
0171 253 6221
Department of Health Leaflet Unit 0171 972 2000
(leaflets on drug use and treatment)
Depressives Anonymous
01482 860619
Depression Alliance
0171 721 7672

Eating Disorders Association
01603 621414
Families Anonymous
0171 498 4680
(for relatives and friends of people with drug problems)
Gamblers Anonymous
0171 384 3040
Narcotics Anonymous
0171 251 4007
National Drugs Helpline
0800 776600.
(free 24hr advice)
Overeaters Anonymous
0161 762 9348
(for those with bulimia, anorexia and food disorders)
see also **Eating disorders** in **Health** chapter
RELEASE
0171 603 8654
(24hr helpline; info and help, including legal, about drugs)
Samaritans
0345 909090
Sex Addicts Anonymous
0181 442 0026
Workaholics Anonymous
01993 878220/
0171 834 5736

HOW TO STOP SMOKING

Useful numbers

Action on Smoking and Health (ASH)
0171 935 3519
Nicotine Anonymous
01932 893173
Quit
0171 388 5775
Quitline
0800 002 200

SELF-DEFENCE AND RAPE

Useful numbers

Rape and Sexual Abuse Support Centre
0181 239 1122
Rape Crisis Centre
0171 837 1600
Suzy Lamplugh Trust
0181 392 1389
(info and advice on avoiding/dealing with attacks)

RELATION-SHIPS

Reading

Dr Henry Goldburg, *Directory of Dating Agencies*
Sara Litvinoff, *The RELATE*

Guide to a Better Relationship
Robin Norwood, *Women Who Love Too Much*
Dagmar O'Connor, *How to Make Love to the Same Person for the Rest of Your Life*
Linda Sonntag, *Finding the Love of Your Life*

Useful numbers

Association of British Introduction Agencies
0171 937 2800
Advertising Standards Authority
0171 580 5555
RELATE 01788 573241
Society of Marriage Bureaux
0171 935 6408
Single Again 0181 749 3745

Useful websites

http://www.planetout.com/ (gat and lesbian)
http://www.samaritans.org.uk/
http://www.timeout.co.uk/ (*TimeOut* magazine)

MARRIAGE

Reading

Garlicle and Shepherd, *The Good Marriage Guide*
Noble's *Wedding Venues Guide*
Louise Roddon, *Have Bride Will Travel* (wedding/honeymoon adventures)

Useful numbers

Directory of wedding venues
01704 550002

ABUSIVE RELATIONSHIPS

Useful reading

Dee Dee Grant, *All my fault: Why women don't leave Abusive Men*

Useful numbers

Domestic Violence Women's Support Service
0181 748 6512
Celestial Fund for battered women and children Lifeline 01262 674505
(24hr helpline for victims of sexual abuse, incest and violence)
Pain and Strength
c/o London Women's Centre
4 Wild Court, London WC1
(self-help and campaign group for lesbians who have survived abusive relationships)

RELATE

01788 573241
(confidential counselling on relationship problems, see phone book for local branch)
Samaritans 0345 909090
(24hr helpline)
Victim support: contact police domestic violence unit local number in phone book
Women's Aid Federation Helpline
 0117 944 4411
(advice on refuges, publications and services)

DIVORCE

Reading

BBC, *Survivor's Directory*
Helen Garlick, *Which? Guide to Divorce*
Dr John Gray, *Men are from Mars, Women are from Venus*
Louise M. Hay, *How to Heal your Life*
Pia Melody, *Co-dependent No More*
Jeremy Rosenblatt, *How to do your own Divorce*
Legal Aid Board, *Legal Aid: A Practical Guide*
W. H. Smith, *The Legal Eagle Divorce Pack*

Useful numbers

Both Parents Forever
01689 854343
(counselling service for staying in touch with the kids after separation)
Child Support Agency
0345 133133
Family Mediators Service
0171 720 3336
(professional mediators in divorce situations)
Families Need Fathers
0171 613 5060
National Council for the Divorced and Separated
01162 708880
National Family Mediation
0171 383 5993
(has the list of 68 local mediation services)
National Council for One Parent Families
0171 267 1361
Parent Line ~~05055~~
01702 559900 002222
(helpline for all parents on how to handle the emotional complexities of kids)
RELATE 01788 573241

(mediators and counsellors for all marital/relationship situations)
Solicitors Family Law Association 01689 850227 (database of solicitors dedicated to keeping conflict to a minimum)

HEALTH

FOOD
Reading
Brostoff and Gamlin, *The Complete Guide to Food Allergy and Intolerance*
Clark and Hill, *Food Facts*
Sharon Faelton, *The Allergy Self-Help Book*
Elson M. Haas, *Staying Healthy with Nutrition*
Anita Hill, *Food and Nutrition*
van Straten and Griggs, *Superfoods*
Ruth Winter, *The People's Handbook of Allergies and Allergens*

Useful numbers
AAA (Action Against Allergy) PO Box 270, Twickenham TW1 4QQ (send SAE for info)
British Allergy Foundation 0181 303 8525 (free advice and booklets)
British Society for Allergy, Environmental and Nutritional Medicine 01703 812124
Medic Alert Foundation 0800 581420 (internationally recognized organization providing emergency help to those with specific allergies and medical conditions)
National Asthma Campaign 01345 010203
National Eczema Society 0171 388 4097
Organic Growers Association 01570 423280
Sainsburys Wellbeing for Pregnancy Helpline 0114 242 4084
Society for the Promotion of Nutritional Therapy Alternatives 01825 872921
Soil Association 0117 929 0661 (association of organic food producers, where to buy it)

Women's Nutritional Advisory Service 01273 487366 (nutritional advice for women suffering from PMS/menopause)
Vegan Society 01424 427393
Vegetarian Society 0161 928 0793 (free pack on nutrient balance in diets)

Useful websites
http://acupuncture.com/
http://204.181.198.34:80/ Homeopathy Online
http://ificinfo.health.org/ (International Food Information Council)
http://yogaclass.com/central. html

EATING DISORDERS
Reading
M. Duker and R. Slade, *Anorexia Nervosa and Bulimia: how to help*
Eating Disorders Association, *A to Z of Anorexia Nervosa* (and other publications)
R. L. Palmer, *Anorexia Nervosa*

Useful numbers
Eating Disorders Association 01603 621414
Overeaters Anonymous 0161 762 9348

EXERCISE
Reading
Anne Goodsell, *Your Personal Trainer*

Useful numbers
General
Crystal Palace National Sports Centre 0181 778 0131
Disability Sport England 0171 490 4919
Exercise Association of England 0171 278 0811
Keep Fit Association 0171 233 8898.
Sports Council (what, where and how?) 0181 778 8600.
Sportsline (what and where?) 0171 222 8000
YMCA 0171 637 8131

Personal Fitness

Association of Personal Trainers 0171 836 1102
National Register of Personal Trainers 0181 944 6688

A–Z OF EXERCISE
British Aikido Board 01753 819086
Amateur Athletics Association 0121 440 5000
Badminton Association of England 01908 568822
Boxernasium 0171 281 5223
Equestrian
British Horse Society 01203 414118
Amateur Fencing Association 0181 742 3032
Football Association (women's football) 01707 651840
British Ultimate Frisbee Federation 0116 284 1785
Golf Foundation 01920 484044
National Ice Skating Association 0171 253 3824
British Judo Association 0116 255 9669
British Jujitsu Association 0114 226 6733
British Mountaineering Council 0161 445 4747
All England Netball Association 01462 442344
British Orienteering Federation 01629 734042
Pilates 0171 431 6223
Quindo Centre 0181 455 8698
British Federation of Roller Skating 01952 825253
Amateur Rowing Association 0181 748 3632
English Ski Council 0121 501 2314
Squash Rackets Association 0181 746 1616
British Sub-Aqua Club 0151 357 1951
British Surfing Association 01736 60250
Amateur Swimming Association 01509 230431

National Organization for Water Fitness (NOWFIT) 0181 287 2466
British Trampoline Federation 0181 863 7278
British Wheel of Yoga 01529 306851

WOMEN'S HEALTH
Reading
Boston Women's Health Collective, *The New Our Bodies, Ourselves*
Nikki Bradford, *The Well Woman's Self-Help Directory*
Susan Curtis and Romy Fraser, *Natural Healing for Women*
Joanna Goldsworthy, *A Certain Age: Reflections on the Menopause*
Shirley Jebb, *Living with PMT*
Dr Ann Nazzaro, *The PMT Solution*
Dr Anne Robinson, *The Which? Guide to Women's Health*
Dr Miriam Stoppard, *Woman to Woman*
Robert M. Youngson, *Women's Health*

Useful numbers
General
HealthLine 0800 665544 (free NHS helpline on health problems and treatments)
Women's Health Concern 0181 780 3916 (help and research)
Women's Health Information and Support Centre 01604 39723
Women's Nutritional Advisory Service 01273 487366
Women's Therapy Centre 0171 263 6200
Women's Health Helpline 0171 251 6580
Cancer
BCC (Breast Care Campaign) 0171 371 1510 (benign cancers)
Breast Cancer Care 0500 245345 (info, help and support)
BACUP (British Association of Cancer United Patients) 0800 181199
Cancer Help Centre 0171 980 9500 (teaching cancer patients to help themselves)
CancerLink 0800 132 905

New Approaches to Cancer
01784 433610
(self-help encouragement and centres)
Women's Nationwide Cancer Control Campaign
0171 729 2229
PMS/Menopause
National Association for Premenstrual Syndrome
01732 741709
National Endometriosis Society
0171 222 2776
National Osteoporosis Society
01761 471771
(addresses of your nearest bone scanner)
PMS Help
0171 243 1313
Other
National AIDS Helpline
0800 567123
National Institute of Medical Herbalists
01392 426022
National Federation of Spiritual Healers
0891 616080

NHS
Useful numbers
Health Service Ombudsman
0171 276 2035
(complaints about the NHS)
British Medical Association
0171 387 4499
BMA House
Tavistock Square
London WC1H 9JP
General Medical Council
0171 580 7642
178 Great Portland Street
London W1N 6JE
Action for Victims of Medical Accidents
0181 291 2793
Bank Chambers
1 London Rd
Forest Hill
London SE23 3TW
(medical negligence help)
Patients Association
0171 242 3460
8 Guildford Street
London WC1
(for victims of medical negligence)

STRESS, ANXIETY AND DEPRESSION
Reading
Louise L. Hay, *You Can Heal*

Your Life
Alice Miller, *The Drama of Being a Child*
M. Scott Peck, *The Road Less Travelled*
Robynn Skynner and John Cleese, *Families and How to Survive Them*
Royal College of Psychiatrists fact sheets on depression

Useful numbers
Anxia
0181 559 2459
(free advice on all types of anxiety disorder)
Anxiety Disorders Association
0181 270 0999
Depression Alliance
0171 721 7672
Depressives Anonymous
01482 860619
British Holistic Medical Association
01743 261155
(stress reduction techniques)
HOPE
0171 923 1396/4444
(help overcome panic effects with self-help groups)
International Stress Management Association
Southbank University, LPSS
103 Borough Rd
London SE1 0AA
(write for nearest practitioner)
Manic Depression Fellowship
0181 974 6550
MIND (National Association for Mental Health)
01345 660163
Phobic Action helpline
0181 559 2459
Phobic Society
0161 881 1937
RELATE (marriage guidance)
01788 573241
Relaxation for Living Trust
01608 646 100
Royal College of Psychiatrists
0171 235 2351
Samaritans 0345 909090
(phone book for local number)
SANE line
0171 724 8000 (London)
01345 678000 (elsewhere)

OPTIONS FOR TREATMENT
Useful numbers
Afro-Caribbean Mental Health Association
0171 737 3603
British Association of Art Therapists 0181 469 0195

Institute for Arts in Therapy and Education
0171 704 2534
British Association of Counsellors
01788 578328
Institute for Family Therapy
0171 391 9150
UK Association for Family Therapy 01222 753162
Gestalt Centre
01727 864 806
Institute of Group Analysis
0171 431 2693
Royal College of Psychiatrists
0171 235 2351
National Register of Hypnotherapists and Psychotherapists
01282 699378
British Association of Analytical Psychotherapy
01273 303382
British Psychological Society
0116 254 9568
British Association of Psychotherapists
0181 452 9823
British Association of Behavioural and Cognitive Psychotherapies
0181 869 2325
Centre for Psychoanalytical Psychotherapy
0181 800 8329
Group Psychotherapy Advisory Service
0171 435 6455
National Register of Hypnotherapists and Psychotherapists
01282 699378
UK Council for Psychotherapy
0171 436 3002
Institute of Psychoanalysis
0171 580 4952
Society for Analytical Psychology
0171 435 7696
Society of Stress Managers
14 Haddon Close
Grange Park
Swindon SN5 6ER
(send a SAE for list of registered experts)
Institute for Transactional Analysis
0171 404 5011
Women's Therapy Centre
0171 263 6200
(counselling and psychotherapy for women by women)
Women and Mental Health
0171 281 2673

ALTERNATIVE TREATMENTS
Reading
Dianne M. Connelly, *Traditional Acupuncture: the Law of the Five Elements*
Susan Curtis and Romy Fraser, *Natural Healing for Women*
Louise Hay, *How to Heal Your Life*
Liz Hodgkinson, *Alexander Technique*
Dr A. Lockie and Dr N. Geddes, *Women's Guide to Homoeopathy*
Penelope Ody, *Home Herbal: Natural Cures to Common Complaints*
Julian Scott, *Natural Medicine for Children*
Thorsons Health publishing has an interesting and useful selection of titles
Weeks and Bullen, *The Bach Flower Remedies*
Jaqueline Young, *Acupressure for Health: A Complete Self-care Manual*

Useful numbers
British Acupuncture Council
0181 964 0222
Alexander Technique International 0171 281 7639
Aromatherapy Organizations Council
01858 434242
Dr Bach Centre
01491 834678
Institute of Bioenergetic Medicine
01202 733762
Association of Chinese Medicine
0171 284 2898
Register of Chinese Herbal Medicine
0181 904 1357
British Chiropractic Association
01734 757557
Colonic Irrigation Association
0171 483 1595
Community Health Foundation 0171 251 4076
Council for Complementary Alternative Medicine
0171 724 9103
Institute of Complementary Medicine 0171 237 5165
Affiliation of Crystal Healing Organizations
0181 398 7252
Feng-Shui International

Network 0171 935 8935
Floatation Tank Association
0171 627 4962
**Confederation of Healing
Organizations**
01442 870667
**National Federation of
Spiritual Healers**
0891 616080
**British Herbal Medicine
Association**
01453 751389
**British Homoeopathic
Association**
0171 935 2163
Faculty of Homoeopaths
01604 21400
Society of Homoeopathy
01604 21400
**Central Register of Advanced
Hypnotherapists**
0171 359 6991
**Association of Applied
Kinesiology**
0181 399 3215
**Guild of Naturopathic
Iridologists**
0171 834 3579
**The Magnetic Healing
Foundation**
0116 259 2048
Natural Medicine Society
01773 710002
**Osteopathic Information
Service** 01734 512051
British Rebirthing Society
01278 722536
**British Reflexology
Association** 018868 21207
SAD Association
(light therapy) 01903 814942
Shiatsu Society
0171 483 3776
Transcendental Meditation
0800 269303
British Wheel of Yoga
01529 306851

BEAUTY

Reading
Sarah Stacey and Josephine
Fairley, *The Beauty Bible*
British Union for the Abolition
of Vivisection, *The Approved
Guide to Cosmetics and
Household Products*

Useful numbers
**British Association of
Dermatologists**
0171 383 0266
British Association of

Electrolysists
01582 487743
**British Association of Skin
Camouflage**
01226 790744
Doreen Savage Trust
0898 881905
British Dental Association
0171 935 3963
**Disfigurement Guidance
Centre**
0898 881905
**Wigs and Hairpieces
Angels and Bermans**
0171 836 5678

Useful websites
There are nearly 2,000 entries
under skin care alone.
Recomend highly
http://www.cosmeticscop.com
(low-down on brand-name
cosmetics)
http:www.boots.co.uk/(advice
form Boots the Chemist: from
beauty to pregnancy)
http://www.facialsurgery.com/
(plastic surgery: before and
after, plus other details)

COSMETIC SURGERY
Reading
Leslie and Susannah Kenton,
Raw Energy
Leslie Kenton, *Ageless Ageing:
the Natural Way to Stay Young*
Cindy Jackson, *Guide to
Cosmetic Surgery*

Useful numbers
**British Society for the
Abolition of Vivisection**
0171 700 4888
**Non-Surgical Face Lifts
Bio Therapeutics**
01926 633020 (for nearest
salon)
**Cosmetic Surgery
British Association of
Cosmetic Surgeons (BACS)**
0171 323 5728
**Cosmetic Surgery Counselling
Service Ltd**
0171 224 4448
**British Association of
Dermatologists**
0171 383 0266
**General Medical Council
(GMC)**
0171 580 7642
(lists specialist surgeons
including plastic surgeons, with
work record of at least 6 years
with NHS)

Good Salon Guide
01705 812233
(over 600 salons, with a star-
rating system)
**British Association of
Aesthetic Plastic Surgeons**
0171 405 2234
**British Association of Plastic
Surgeons** 0171 831 5161
Royal College of Surgeons
0171 405 2234

HOME

RENTING AND LETTING
Useful websites
http://www.readersdigest.co.uk
http://www.gfg.ic/net.co.uk
(going green)

Reading
Consumers' Association, *The
Which? Guide to Renting and
Letting*
Housing Corporation's leaflet,
*Renting a Housing Association
Home*
The Housing Corporation,
*Guide to Buying a Housing
Association Home in Stages*

Useful numbers
**Your local Citizen's Advice
Bureau**
**CARLA (Campaign Against
Residential Leaseholder
Abuse)**
01787 462787
Housing Corporation
0171 393 2000
National Housing Federation
0171 278 6571
NFT@BTinternet.com
Institute of Rent Officers
01392 72321
Lands Tribunal for Arbitration
0171 936 7200
**Association of Residential
Letting Agents** 01494 431680
Small Landlords Association
0181 780 9954
**Shelter, London Housing Aid
Centre (SHAC)**
0171 404 7447/6929
National Housing Federation
0171 278 6571
**National Tenants
Organization
Voluntary Action Centre**
0181 690 8920
**National Federation of
Women's Aid Helpline**
0345 023468

BUYING A HOME
Reading
Consumers' Association,
*Which? Way to Buy, Sell and
Move House*
Office of Fair Trading, *Guide for
Buyers and Sellers*

Useful numbers
**Architects and Surveyors
Institute**
0171 584 2346
Banking Ombudsman
0171 404 9944
British Property Federation
0171 828 0111
Building Society Ombudsman
0171 931 0044
**Royal Institution of Chartered
Surveyors (RICS)**
0171 222 7000
**Society of Licensed
Conveyancers**
01245 349599
**Leaseholders Enfranchisement
Advisory Service (LEASE)**
0171 493 3116
**National Association of Estate
Agents, Homelink Service**
01926 496 800
Housing Corporation
0171 393 2000
National Housing Federation
0171 278 6571
Law Society 0171 242 1222
Link Up Properties
01444 457 999
Property Sales Register
01242 227188
**Incorporated Society of
Valuers and Auctioneers**
0171 235 2282

SELLING YOUR HOME
& MOVING
Reading
Consumers' Association,
*Which? Way to Buy, Sell and
Move House*
Office of Fair Trading, *Guide for
Buyers and Sellers*

Useful numbers
**Royal Institution of Chartered
Surveyors**
0171 222 700
**National Association of Estate
Agents** 01926 496 800
**British Association of
Removers**
0181 861 3331
**Guild of Removers and
Storers**
01494 792279

**Incorporated Society of
Valuers and Auctioneers**
0171 235 2282

DESIGN YOUR HOME
Reading
Cadogan Market Guides, *British
Markets*
Nonnie Nieswande,
Contemporary Details
Phaidon series on style and
design
SALVO directory of salvage
suppliers

Useful numbers
Architectural Salvage Register
01483 203221
British Cement Association
01344 762670
Glass and Glazing Federation
0171 403 7177
**Loft Conversion Advisory
Centre**
0181 346 8491
Paint Research Association
0181 977 4427
Auro Organic Paint Supplies
01799 584886
BioFa Natural Paints
01952 883288
SALVO
01688 216494
Stone Federation
0171 580 5588
**Women's Environmental
Network Directory of
Information**
0171 704 6800

BUILDING WORK
Reading
RIBA bookshop
*Standard Form of Agreement
for the Appointment of an
Architect* (SFA 92)
Conditions of Engagement
(SE95)
*Engaging an architect:
Guidelines for Clients*
Department of the Environment
publications
Home Renovations Grants
(90HOU08)
*Planning Permission: A Guide
for Householders* (94LGP474)
Association of British Insurers,
*Guide to House Rebuilding
Costs*
Association for Environment
Conscious Building, *Greener
Buildings: Products and
Services Directory*
Edward Harland, *Eco*

*Renovation: the Ecological
Home Improvement Guide*
English Heritage, *A Guide to
Grants*
RICS practice note, *Mortgage
Valuation or Survey*

Useful numbers
**Royal Institute of British
Architects (RIBA)**
0171 580 5533
public info service
0891 234 400
**Architects Registration
Council of the United
Kingdom** 0171 580 5861
Avongard 01275 849782
(equipment for monitoring
building cracks)
Federation of Master Builders
0171 242 7583
**Building Employers
Federation**
0171 580 5588
**Institute of Structural
Engineers**
0171 235 4535
**Royal Institution of Chartered
Surveyors (RICS)**
0171 222 7000
**Department of the
Environment (DOE) publica-
tions division**
0181 691 9191
**Institution of Electrical
Engineers**
0171 240 1871
**National Inspection Council
for Electrical Installation
Contracting**
0171 582 7746
**Association for Environment
Conscious Building**
01559 370 908
Institute of Plumbing
01708 472 791
**National Association of
Plumbing**
01203 470626
(heating and mechanical
services)
English Heritage
0171 973 3000
Association of British Insurers
0171 600 3333
**Insurance Ombudsman
Bureau** 0171 928 7600

ELECTRICS
Reading
Jackson and Day, *Collins DIY
Guide to Wiring and Lighting*
Reader's Digest, *Complete DIY
Manual*

Useful numbers
Electrical Association
0171 963 5700
(coordinating body for elec-
trical suppliers)
**Electrical Contractors
Association**
0171 229 1266
**Institution of Electrical
Engineers**
0171 240 1871
MVM Starpoint
0117 9744477
**Office of Electricity
Regulation (OFFER)** 0121
456 6209

PLUMBING
Reading
Jackson and Day, *Collins DIY
Guide to Plumbing and Central
Heating*

Useful numbers
Institute of Plumbing
01708 472791
**National Association of
Plumbing, Heating and
Mechanical Services
Contractors**
01203 470626
**Office of Water Services
(OFWAT)**
0121 625 1300
Water Research Centre
01491 571531
Water Services Association
0171 957 4567

HEATING
Useful numbers
**Centre for Alternative
Technology**
01654 702400
**Confederation for the
Registration of Gas Installers
(CORGI)**
01256 372200
**Department of the
Environment's Home Energy
Efficiency Scheme (HEES)**
0800 181667
**Draught Proofing Advisory
Association Ltd**
01428 654011
National Energy Service
01908 672787
**Energy and Environment
Office (DOE)**
0171 276 6477
Local Energy Advice Centres
0800 512012
Gas Consumers Council
0171 931 0977

**Heating and Ventilating
Contractors Association**
0171 229 2488
Home Heating Linkline
01345 581158
OFGAS
0171 828 0898
OFTEC
01737 373311
(oil-firing technical association
for the petroleum industry)
**National Association of
Plumbing, Heating and
Mechanical Services
Contractors**
01203 470626
Solar Trade Association
01208 873518
UK Solar Energy Society
01654 702992
Solid Fuel Advisory Service
0800 600000

MAINTENANCE
Useful numbers
National Asthma Campaign
0345 010203
British Allergy Foundation
0171 600 6166
Consumers' Association
0171 830 6000
Dylon International Ltd
0181 663 4801
**Fabric Care Research
Association Ltd**
01423 885977
**Home Laundry Consultative
Council**
0171 636 7788
Mailing Preference Service
0345 034599
**British Pest Control
Association**
01332 294288
National Recycling Forum
0171 248 1412
**Royal Society for the
Prevention of Accidents**
0121 248 2000
WasteLine run by Waste Watch
0171 248 0242
**Women's Environmental
Network Directory of
Information** (eco household
tips)
0171 704 6800
**British Wood Preservation
and Damp Association**
0181 519 2588

APPLIANCES
Reading
Which? magazines from your
local library

Useful numbers
Association of Manufacturers of Domestic and Electrical Appliances 0171 405 0666
Consumers' Association 0171 830 6000
Women's Environmental Network Directory of Information 0171 704 6800

TRADESPEOPLE
Useful numbers
AA Home Assistance 0990 994499
RIBA (Royal Institute of British Architects) 0171 580 5533
Barclaycard Home Assist 0800 670800
Federation of Master Builders 0171 242 55881
National Register of Warranted Builders 0171 404 4155
National Association of Citizens' Advice Bureaux 0171 251 2000
Building Employers Confederation 0171 580 5588
National Inspection Council for Electrical Installation Contracting 0171 582 7746
Electrical Contractors Association 01689 870538
Institution of Electrical Engineers 0171 240 1871
Confederation of Gas Installers (CORGI) 01256 372400
Green Flag Assistance 0800 800678
Institute of Plumbing 01708 472791
National Federation of Roofing Contractors 0171 436 0387
British Wood Preservation and Damp Proofing Association 0181 519 2588

HOME SECURITY
Reading
Home Office, *Your Practical Guide to Crime Prevention*
Reader's Digest, *Complete DIY Manual*

Useful numbers
Association of British Insurers 0171 603 3333

Master Locksmiths Association 01327 262255

BABIES

Reading
Pamela Armstrong, *Beating the Biological Clock*
Bergman, Thorpe and Windridge, *Older Mothers, Conception, Pregnancy and Birth after Thirty-five*
Eisenberg, Murkoff, Hathaway, *What to expect, the first year*
Flynn and Brooks, *The Manual of Natural Family Planning*
John Guillebau, *Contraception*
Annette Karmelloff Smith, *Baby it's you,*
Penelope Leach, *Baby and Child*
Penelope Leach, *Babyhood*
Juliet Leigh, *The Baby Bible*
Doctors Penny and Andrew Stanway, *Breast is Best*

Useful websites
http://www.hti.nrt/whd/allergy/ (asthma and allergies)
http://kidshealth.org/

ASSISTED CONCEPTION
Reading
Joseph Bellina and Josleen Wilson, *The Fertility Handbook*
Prof Robert Winston, *Making Babies, A Personal View of IVF Treatment*

Useful numbers
CHILD 0181 893 7110 (infertility charity)
Child Charter House 01424 732361 (self-help organization offering info/support for problems of infertility/childlessness)
Human Fertilization and Embryology Authority 0171 377 5077
ISSUE, National Fertility Association 0121 359 4887

MISCARRIAGE

Useful numbers
LIFE 01926 421587 (charity offering info and advice on pregnancy, abortion, miscarriage, stillbirth)
Miscarriage Association 01924 200799

PREGNANCY
Reading
Wendy Doyle, *Teach Yourself Healthy Eating for Pregnancy*
Eisenberg, Murkoff and Hathaway, *What to Expect when you're Expecting*
Health Education Authority, *New Pregnancy Book*
Sheila Kitzinger, *The New Pregnancy and Childbirth* (Penguin)
Margie Polden and Barbara Whiteford, *The Postnatal Exercise Book*
Peter Saunders, *Your Pregnancy Month by Month*
Dr J. Scher and Carol Dix, *Pregnancy: Everything you need to know*

Useful numbers
ACAS (Advisory, Conciliation and Arbitration Service) 0171 396 5100 (advice on time off for antenatal care and matters like unfair dismissal)
Active Birth Centre 0171 561 9006
Citizens' Advice Bureaux (CABs) 0171 833 2181
Child Poverty Action Group 0171 253 3406 (campaigns on behalf of low-income families, provides info on available benefits)
Institute for Complementary Medicine 0171 237 5165
Maternity Alliance 0171 588 8582 (info on all aspects of maternity services, rights at work and benefits for families)
Association for Improvements in the Maternity Services (AIMS) 0181 960 5585 (voluntary pressure group aims for improvements in maternity services; support and advice on parents' rights, complaints procedures and choices within maternity care, including home birth)
Independent Midwives Association (free advice on home birth; offers full care to women who book with them for home births)
National Association of Homoeopaths 01604 21400

National Childbirth Trust (NCT) 0181 992 8637 (charity with branches throughout the UK; antenatal classes, info on labour, practice of relaxation, breathing, massage and birth)
Toxoplasmosis Trust helpline 0171 713 0599

BIRTH
Reading
Sheila Kitzinger, *The New Pregnancy and Childbirth*
Sheila Kitzinger, *Home Birth and other alternatives*
Herbert Brant, *Childbirth for Men*
Doctors Penny and Andrew Stanway, *Breast is Best*

Useful numbers
Active Birth Centre 0171 561 9006 (classes and workshops in childbirth and parenting)
Caesarean Support Network c/o Sheila Tunstall 2 Hurst Park Drive Hyton Liverpool L36 1TF (emotional support/practical advice for mothers who have had/may need a Caesarean delivery)
National Childbirth Trust (NCT) 0181 992 8637

POSTNATAL DEPRESSION
Reading
Katharina Dalton with Wendy M. Holton, *Depression after Childbirth*

Useful numbers
Association for Postnatal Illness 0171 386 0868
MAMA (Meet a Mum Association) 0181 665 0357 (support/help for women suffering from postnatal depression, feeling isolated and tired after having a baby, or just in need of a friend to share problems; local groups)
Parents Advice Centre 01232 238800
Parents Anonymous 0171 263 8918 (for parents who can't cope)

PARENTLINE
01702 559900
(support for troubled parents
in times of stress or crisis,
chiefly through a confidential
and anonymous telephone
helpline)

BABYCARE
Reading
Elizabeth Fenwick, *The
complete book of mother and
baby care*
Sheila Kitzinger, *The Crying
Baby*
Lansdown and Walker, *Your
Child's Development: Birth to
Adolescence*
Penelope Leach, *Children First*
Leach, *The Parents' A–Z, for
Children's Health, Growth,
Happiness*
Ochaeffer and Petronko, *Teach
your baby to sleep through the
night*
Robb and Letts, *Creating Kids
Who Can*
Roddwell and Tidyman, *Working
Parents' Survival Handbook*
Michael Rosen, *Just Kids:
Surviving the 2–12s*
Nanny Smith, *Coping with
Temper Tantrums*
Dr Miriam Stoppard, *The Baby
and Child Health Care
Handbook*
Hetty van de Rijt and Frans
Plooij, *Why they Cry*

Useful numbers
British Acupuncture Council
0181 964 0222
**Association of Breastfeeding
Mothers** 0181 778 4769
**La Leche League (Great
Britain)**
0171 242 1278 (24hr answerphone)
(help and info for women
breastfeeding their
babies/personal counselling for
mothers with problems in
breast-feeding)
**National Childbirth Trust
(NCT)**
0181 992 8637
(charity with branches
throughout UK; runs antenatal
classes giving info on labour,
practice of relaxation,
breathing, massage and birth)
**Centre for Pregnancy
Nutrition Helpline**
01742 424084

Eating For Pregnancy Helpline
0114 242 4084

ILL BABIES
Elizabeth Fenwick, *The
complete book of mother and
baby care*
Penelope Leach, *The Parents'
A–Z*
Dr Miriam Stoppard, *The Baby
and Child Health Care
Handbook*

Useful numbers
National Asthma Campaign
0345 010203
**BLISS (Baby Life Support
Systems)**
0171 831 9393
(support network providing
practical/emotional help for
parents/families who have
babies who need intensive and
special care)
Cot Death Helpline
0171 235 1721
CRY-SIS
0171 404 5011
Society for Homoeopaths
01604 21400
**Foundation for the Study of
Infant Deaths**
0171 235 1721
**National Institute for Medical
Herbalists**
01392 426022
Action for Sick Children
0171 833 2041
**Action for the Welfare of
Children in Hospital**
0165 56512
(advice and support for families
with sick children; gives advice
over the phone)

IMMUNIZATION
Useful numbers
**Association of Parents of
Vaccine Damaged
Children**
01608 661595

MULTIPLE BIRTHS
Reading
Dr Carol Cooper, *Twins and
Multiple Births*
Cherry Rowland, Elizabeth
Friedrich, *The Twins Handbook*
Useful numbers
**Twins and Multiple Births
Association (TAMBA)**
0151 348 0020
TAMBA (Twinline)
01732 868000

SPECIAL CARE
Reading
Helen Harrison,
The Premature Baby Book
Frank Manginello, *Your
Premature Baby*
Pete Moor, *Born Too Early*
Kolvin Neligan, *Born Too Soon,
Born Too Small*

DISABILITY
Useful numbers
National Autistic Society
0181 451 1114
**Royal National Institute for
the Blind (RNIB)**
0171 388 1266
(info, advice and services for
blind people)
Changing Faces
0171 706 4232
(offers advice, info and support
to carers of young children with
facial disfigurements)
**CLAPA (Cleft Lip and Palate
Association)**
0171 824 8110
(info and counselling for
parents of newborn babies,
contacts for local groups)
Coeliac Society of the UK
01494 437278
Contact a Family
0171 383 3555
(charity offering info, advice
and support to parents of children with special needs/disabil-
ities)
Cystic Fibrosis Trust
0181 464 7211
**National Deaf Children's
Society** 0800 252 3800 9
**SENSE (National Deaf-Blind
and Rubella Association)**
0171 272 7774
(advice/support for families of
deaf-blind/rubella handicapped
children)
British Diabetic Association
0171 323 1531
Council for Disabled Children
0171 843 6061
(info for parents and details of
organizations)
National Disability Advice
0800 882200
**Royal Association for
Disability and Rehabilitation
(RADAR)**
0171 250 3222
Disabled Living Foundation
0171 289 6111
Disability Information Trust
01865 227592

**Down's Syndrome Association
(DSA)**
0181 682 4001
(practical support, advice and
info)
**National Eczema Society
(NES)**
0171 388 4097
**Advisory Centre for
Education (ACE) Ltd**
0171 354 8321
(independent education advice
service for parents and children
with special needs)
Enable
0141 226 4541
(Scottish society for the
mentally handicapped and a
comprehensive info and
support service for people with
learning difficulties)
Genetic Interest Group
0171 430 0090
(umbrella body for support
groups working with those
affected by specific genetic
disorders; provides info about
services available within the
NHS and elsewhere)
GROWTH
0116 247 8913
(support for parents who have
a child with a growth problem)
Child Growth Foundation
2 Mayfield Avenue
Chiswick, London W14 1PW
(info and advice for parents
concerned about their child's
growth, send large SAE)
Haemophilia Society
0171 928 2020
**Meningitis Research
Foundation**
01454 413344 (24hrs)
National Meningitis Trust
0345 538118
MENCAP
0171 454 0454
**Research Trust for Metabolic
Diseases in Children
(RTMDC)**
01270 250221
(grants and allowances for
medical treatment and care of
children with metabolic
diseases; puts parents in touch
with each other)
Muscular Dystrophy Group
0171 720 8055
**REACH (Association for
Children with Hand or Arm
Deficiency)**
01604 811041
(info and support)

SCOPE
0800 626216
(advice and support to parents
of children with cerebral palsy)
Sickle Cell Society
0181 961 7795/4006
Sickle Cell and Thalassaemia
Centre 01222 471055
UK Thalassaemia Society
0181 348 0437
Spina Bifida Association
0131 332 0743
Speech disorders
Association for all Speech
Impaired children (AFASIC)
0171 236 3632/6487
Invalid Children's Aid
Nationwide (I CAN)
0171 374 4422
(advice and info for parents of
handicapped children, especially those with severe speech
and language disorders)

ADOPTION AND
FOSTERING
Useful numbers
British Agency for Adopting
and Fostering (BAAF)
0171 407 8800
National Foster Care
Association
0171 828 6266
National Organization for
Counselling of Adoptees and
Parents
01865 87500
Parent to Parent Info on
Adoption Services
013272 60295
Post Adoption Centre
0171 284 0555
Overseas Adoption Helpline
0990 168742
STORK 01306 880189
(self-help inter-country adop-
tion organization)

GETTING HELP
Reading
Charlotte Breese and Hilaire
Gomer, *The Good Nanny Guide*
Dorling Kindersley in
association with the British Red
Cross, *The Babysitters*
Handbook
Useful numbers
Helpline on Childcare
0171 837 5513
(help and advice on setting
up/running parent and toddler
groups/playgroups)
Choices in Childcare
0114 276681

National Childcare
Campaign/Daycare Trust
0171 405 5617/8
(campaigns for the provision of
good childcare facilities, publications are also avaialble)
National Childminding
Association
0181 464 6164
(organization for childminders,
childcare workers, parents)
Kids Club Network
0171 512 2100
(out-of-school care and holiday
schemes)
National Association for
Maternal and Child Welfare
0171 383 4117
National Association of Toy
and Leisure Libraries
0171 387 9592
Parents at Work
0171 628 3578
(info and advice on childcare
provision for working parents)
Pre-school Playgroups
Association (PPA)
0171 837 5513
Working for Childcare
0171 628 3578
(advice and info for employers,
trade unions and others on
workplace childcare)

FAMILY

Reading
J. Defraine, *The Single Parent's*
Survival Guide
Christina Hardyment, *Perfect*
Parents
Lansdown and Walker, *Your*
Child's Development: Birth to
Adolescence
Penelope Leach, *Children First*
Leach, *The Parents' A–Z for*
Children's Health, Growth,
Happiness
Rosalind Miles, *The Children we*
Deserve
Robb and Letts, *Creating Kids*
Who Can
Michael Rosen, *Just Kids:*
Surviving the 2–12s

Useful numbers
Asian Family Counselling
Service
0181 997 5749
National Childcare Campaign
0171 405 5617
Institute of Child Health
(advice and info to children,

young adults, parents, and
professionals on bed-wetting)
ChildLine
0800 1111
(free national helpline for children in trouble or danger)
Child Support Agency
01345 133133
CRY-SIS
0171 404 5011
(self-help/support for families
with excessively crying, sleep-
less and demanding children)
Family Health Services
Authorities (FHSAs)
(see phone book; will give list
of local doctors including those
with special interest in pregnancy and childbirth)
Family Welfare Association
0171 254 6251
(charity providing free social-
work services)
Hyperactive Children's
Support Group 01903 725182
(info on problems related to
hyperactivity and allergy)
Missing Persons Helpline
0500 700700
National Association for
Maternal and Child Welfare
0171 383 4117
(advice line on childcare/family
life)
NSPCC
0171 825 2500
ParentLine
01702 559900
Parent Network
0171 485 8535
Exploring Parenthood
Helpline
0171 221 6681
Rainbow Trust Children's
Charity
01372 453309
(care and support for children
with terminal illness)
Young Minds Helpline
0345 626376
(info/advice on mental health
of children)
Useful websites
http://www.yell.co.uk/ (directory
of family-based websites by
Yellow Pages)

SCHOOL
Reading
Catherine Itzin, *How to Choose*
a School
Mason and Ramsay, *A–Z of*
Education
The Parents' Charter

Useful numbers
Advisory Centre for
Education (ACE)
0171 354 8321
Department of Education
0171 925 5000
British Dyslexia Association
helpline
01189 668271
Helen Arkell Dyslexic Centre
01252 792400
Independent School
Information Service (ISIS)
0171 630 8793
KIDS
0181 969 2817
(services for families of children
with special needs)
National Childcare Campaign
0171 405 5617
National Curriculum Council
0171 229 1234
National Confederation of
Parent-Teacher Associations
01474 560618
National Association for
Primary Education
01604 36326
National Association for
Special Education Needs
01827 311500

CHILD ABUSE
Reading
NSPCC pamphlets and books
National Children's Bureau
books
M. Elliott, *Why My Child?*
C. Lyon and P. de Cruz, *Child*
Abuse

Useful numbers
NSPCC
0171 825 2500
Child Protection Helpline
0800 800500
Child's Legal Centre
0171 359 6251
Child Poverty Action Group
(CPAG)
0171 253 3406
Advice, Advocacy &
Representation for Children
0800 616101
Anti-Bullying Campaign
0171 378 1446–9
10 Borough High St
London SE1 9QQ
(send A4 SAE and £2.50 for
parents' pack)
British Association for the
Study and Prevention of Child
Abuse
01904 613605

ChildLine
0800 1111
Mothers of Abused Children
016973 31432
ParentLine
01702 559900
CRY-SIS
0171 404 5011
(support with crying babies)
Child Abuse Survivor Network
0171 278 8484
ChildWatch
014823 25552
KidScape
0171 730 3300
Mental Health Media Council
0171 700 0100
National Children's Bureau
0171 843 6008
PAIN
01279 656564
Parents Anonymous
0171 263 8918
(helpline run by volunteers for parents under stress who feel they can't cope or might abuse their children)
Parents Under Stress
0181 645 0469
Streetwise Youth
0171 370 0406

ALTERNATIVE FAMILY STRUCTURES
Reading
Evelyn S. Bassoff, *Between Mothers and Sons*
Joy Dickens, *Family Outing for Parents with Gay Offspring*
Anne Coates, *Your Only Child*
Carol Dix, *Working Mothers: You, Your Career, Your Child*
Suzie Hayman, *Other People's Children, Surviving Stepfamilies*
Hughes and Cod, *Step Parents, Step Children*
Adrienne Katz, *The Juggling Act: Working Mothers*
B. Kaye Olsen, *Energy Secrets for Tired Mothers on the Run*
Sheila Kitzinger, *The Crying Baby*
Mike Lilley, *Successful Single Parents*
April Martin, *The Guide to Lesbian and Gay Parenting*
Roddwell and Tidyman, *Working Parents' Survival Handbook*

Useful numbers
Gingerbread
0171 336 8183
National Council for One-

Parent Families
0171 267 1361
(info on benefits and employment rights in pregnancy, social security, taxation, housing problems, maintenance)
Parents Advice Centre
01232 238800
(24hr confidential service offering support and guidance for parents under stress)
Parents Anonymous
0171 263 8918
(helpline run by volunteers for parents under stress who feel they can't cope or might abuse their children)
Parents Under Stress
0181 645 0469
National Stepfamily Association
0171 209 2464

DEATH

Reading
Paul Harris, *What to do when Someone Dies*
Penny Mares, *Caring for Someone who is Dying*
Jane Spottiswood, *Undertaken with Love*
Cemetery Journal (newsletter from 46 Broadmead, Hitchin, Herts SG4 9LX)

Useful numbers
Alcor Life Extension Foundation Bereavement Line
0181 332 7227
Asian Family Counselling Services
0181 997 5749
British Humanist Society
0171 430 0908
(advice on non-religious funerals)
Carer's National Association
0171 490 8818
Child Death Helpline
0800 282986
Compassionate Friends
0117 953 9639
(advice/support for bereaved parents)
Cot Death helpline
0171 235 1721
Cremation Society of Great Britain
01622 686292
CRUSE
0181 940 4818
(bereavement care)

Green Undertakings
01984 632285
(ecologically correct suppliers of coffins etc.)
Heaven on Earth
0117 924 0972
(made-to-measure funerals)
London Anatomy Office
0181 846 1216
(leaving your body to science)
London Lighthouse
0171 792 1200
Ministry of Agriculture Fisheries and Food (MAFF)
0171 238 5872
(for sea burial advice)
Miscarriage Association
01924 200799
National Association of Bereavement Services
0171 247 1080
National Association of Funeral Directors
0121 711 1343
Natural Death Centre
0181 208 2853
Stillbirth and Neonatal Death Society (SANDS)
0171 436 5881
Support After Murder and Manslaughter (SAMM)
0171 735 9166
Survivors of Bereavement by Suicide (SOBS)
01482 565387
Terrence Higgins Trust
0171 242 1010